LONGMAN LINGUISTICS LIBRARY

AN INTRODUCTION TO BILINGUALISM

General editors
R. H. Robins, University of London
Martin Harris, University of Essex

Pidgin and Creole Languages
SUZANNE ROMAINE

General Linguistics
An Introductory Survey
Fourth Edition
R. H. ROBINS

Structural Aspects of Language Change
JAMES M. ANDERSON

A History of English Phonology
CHARLES JONES

Text and Context
Explorations in the Semantics and Pragmatics of the Discourse
TEUN A. VAN DIJK

Generative and Non-linear Phonology
JAQUES DURAND

Introduction to Text Linguistics
ROBERT-ALAIN DE BEAUGRANDE AND WOLFGANG ULRICH DRESSLER

Modality and the English Modals
Second Edition
F. R. PALMER

Semiotics and Linguistics
YISHAI TOBIN

Spoken Discourse
A Model for Analysis
WILLIS EDMONDSON

Multilingualism in the British Isles I: the Older Mother Tongues and Europe
EDITED BY SAFDER ALLADINA AND VIV EDWARDS

Psycholinguistics
Language, Mind, and World
DANNY D. STEINBERG

Dialectology
W. N. FRANCIS

Multilingualism in the British Isles II: Africa, Asia and the Middle East
EDITED BY SAFDER ALLADINA AND VIV EDWARDS

Principles of Pragmatics
GEOFFREY N. LEECH

Dialects of English
Studies in Grammatical Variation
EDITED BY PETER TRUDGILL AND J. K. CHAMBERS

Generative Grammar
GEOFFREY HORROCKS

Norms of Language
Theoretical and Practical Aspects
RENATE BARTSCH

A Short History of Linguistics
Third Edition
R. H. ROBINS

The English Verb
Second Edition
F. R. PALMER

An Introduction to Bilingualism
CHARLOTTE HOFFMANN

Contents

List of maps

Preface

During the last decade or so researchers into bilingualism have been extraordinarily prolific, and considerable advances have been made in our understanding of the subject. To those who have either a professional or a personal interest (or both) in this area, it has indeed been exciting to observe the progress made. At the same time, the task of presenting an introductory study has been made more difficult, in that it has become necessary to make more decisions about what aspects to include in the discussion of each topic dealt with and which contributions by scholars to exclude.

As an introduction to bilingualism, my aim in writing this book has been to discuss the most important aspects and pertinent concepts of individual and societal bilingualism, endeavouring to give some idea of the complexity of some of the issues involved, as well as of the present state of the relevant research. The need to be selective has led to the decision to focus on the patterns of bilingual acquisition and use among bilingual children in Part I and to the adoption of a European bias in Part II, where examples are taken primarily from European multilingual settings – the discussion of which necessarily reflects the author's own aquaintance with certain aspects of European culture. Similarly, illustrations of linguistic points (e.g. of language use among bilinguals) often involve the European languages of which the author has either specialist knowledge or a degree of familiarity. This European orientation may have the advantage of enabling the reader to see how truly normal and widespread the phenomenon of bilingualism is, even on a continent where most component countries still like to perceive themselves as monolingual nation states.

The structure of the book was originally conceived on the basis of courses on Bilingualism taught to final-year Modern Language students and to postgraduates who had undergone training in European languages. While no previous knowledge of the subject of bilingualism is assumed here, I have presupposed familiarity with basic linguistic concepts (e.g. 'semantics', 'loan words', 'phonological development'). Technical terms are given in inverted commas (e.g. 'blend', 'code-switching') or italics (*language shift*) where they may be first introduced, but thereafter they may be used without inverted commas or emphasis. In both Parts, the individual chapters have been organized so that the general discussion precedes the examination of specific aspects. It is possible, however, to read sections of the book on their own or out of sequence; in this case, the cross-references can serve as pointers to related issues.

In preparing the pages that follow, I have drawn widely on my own experience of bilingualism, which therefore needs to be explained briefly. I grew up speaking two languages (Danish and German) and was trained as a linguist; as a young adult, I moved from Germany to Britain, where I settled and married a Spaniard. I use different languages depending on whom I am speaking to or what I am talking about, and I feel a different kind of cultural and emotional attachment to the languages involved. In other words, I use and relate to language in the same way as many bi- or multilinguals, immigrants, migrants and children of linguistically mixed parentage. The initial impetus for pursuing the study of bilingualism was provided by my children, as the experience of seeing bi- and trilingual language development at first-hand brought the whole subject alive. The same has happened to many other linguist-parents, who have raised their children to use more than one language and have recorded their observations, thus providing data for the analysis of bilingual language acquisition. The study of child language requires a good deal of close observation, for which parents may be in a privileged position – one of which they are entitled to take advantage of. This, I feel, explains the frequent mention of the language use of linguists' own children (the present author's included).

My experience of bilingual speakers of both sexes and all ages has led me to adopt a usage of personal pronouns which may seem odd. I employ 'he' or 'she', and also the less personal '(s)he', in reference to noun phrases such as 'the bilingual', 'the individual speaker' and 'the child', because I often, though not always, had particular people in mind.

A CAMPUS Scholarship awarded by my University enabled me to

undertake research in the context of linguistic minority settings. Many colleagues helped in the task of completing the book. My former Chairman of Department, Martin Harris, provided both the initial stimulus and subsequent patient support. Several members of staff in the Department of Modern Languages at Salford gave me cheerful encouragement, furnished me with examples, observations and anecdotes about their own bilingual experiences, and generally commented on parts of earlier drafts. I am particularly grateful to Andy Hollis for his meticulous and good-humoured scrutiny of several chapters and for his remarks on matters of content as well as style; without his suggestions this book would contain many more Teutonisms and bilingual speech markers than it does already (incidentally, I hope that he, too, now sees himself as one of Europe's bilinguals). Andrew Dobson, of Keele University, kindly advised me on several points in Chapter 10, which draws heavily on other disciplines. Alan Yates, of Sheffield University, and my colleague Enlàlia Torras, read Chapter 13 and made some useful comments. Suzanne Romaine read the final draft and made many detailed and valuable points, thus generously sharing with me her knowledge and understanding of bilingualism. To all these colleagues my sincere thanks. Needless to say, I alone am responsible for any shortcomings of content or infelicities of English style that remain.

Many friends and relatives in a number of European countries and beyond demonstrated their support for my project in different ways which I now gratefully acknowledge. My greatest debt is to my children and my husband. Cristina and Pascual unwittingly provided numerous instances of bilingual speech behaviour and, rather more consciously, endured a good deal of discussion on the subject at the family table. They rarely complained when my writing took preference over family life. I thank them for their help and tolerance. My husband was my ever-willing critic and sounding board; without his unfailing support and his enthusiasm for bilingualism this book could not have been written. I can only hope that it justifies the *ilusión* he imbued in me.

The Publishers are grateful to the following for permission to reproduce copyright material: The Society for the Psychological Study of Social Issues, and the author, for a figure from Joshua A. Fishman, 'Bilingualism with and without Diglossia: Diglossia with and without Bilingualism', *Journal of Social Issues* XXIII, No 2; Department of

Sociology and Social Psychology, University of Tampere for a figure
from Skutnabb-Kangas, T. and Toukomaa, P.

(1977) *Teaching migrant
children's mother tongue and learning the language of the host
country in the context of the socio-cultural situation of the migrant
family* (Research Report 15); Multilingual Matters Ltd. for a figure
from Baker, C.

(1988) *Key Issues in Bilingualism and Bilingual Education*, a table from Baetons Beardsmore (1982) *Bilingualism: Basic
Principles* and a table from Skutnabb-Kangas (1984) *Bilingualism or
Not;* A figure by Joan Rubin from *Readings in the Sociology of Language* (1968: 526), edited by J. Fishman. Copyright 1968 Mouton &
Co. Reprinted by permission of Mouton de Gruyter, a division of Wal-
ter de Gruyter & Co.

NOTE: All references to the Federal Republic of Germany in this
book are to West Germany prior to German reunification in 1990.

This book is for

Paco, mi bilingüe favorito;

für meine Kinder Cristina und Pascual;

og til min mor, som startede det hele.

Introduction

Bilingualism – a natural phenomenon

To what extent can we ever speak, within a European context, of communities or languages which have developed in isolation, without contact with other peoples, cultures and languages? One would have to look to the outer fringes of the continent. Iceland and perhaps Portugal are probably the only European states which are genuinely monoethnic – but their inhabitants are not necessarily monolingual. The usual state of affairs elsewhere in Europe, and in most of the rest of the world, is that over the years and the centuries, communities establish links with one another, whether friendly, commercial or belligerent. The experience gained from such associations can be either positive or negative for those concerned. One constant factor in such contacts, however, is that they always influence in some way the speech behaviour of the people involved – and therefore, eventually, their languages. Sometimes the result is bilingualism, sometimes the languages are affected by borrowing or change. With the passage of time, one community may undergo gradual language shift, replacing bilingualism with monolingualism, as is the case, for instance, in Brittany, where Breton is giving way to French. Or a sudden change in the conditions of life in a community may cause it to adopt a hitherto unused language on a widespread basis, as became common during colonial times in many parts of Africa and Asia.

Linguistic frontiers rarely coincide with political ones. The former, however, if they are marked by geographical features, such as wide waterways or high mountains, sometimes prove to be remarkably stable, whatever happens to the latter. In general, both political and linguistic demarcations are subject to change. Virtually everywhere countries have, in the course of their history, seen their borders expand or retract according to political fortune. Yet historians seldom record the linguistic impact on people made by occupation, annexation or enforced change of allegiance as a result of war, political marriage or some other cause. I find such scant reflection on linguistic matters quite surprising considering the role language plays in our lives.

Centuries of political, economic and cultural interaction have made Europe a continent with widespread bilingualism. At a political level, most of the world's sovereign states consider themselves to be monolingual, an attitude held by dominant élites and no doubt influenced by the pervasiveness of political philosophies that promote the one-nation-one-language ideal. But this ideal does not reflect reality as, at the societal level, multilingualism exists, almost everywhere, as a result, on the one hand, of historical events bringing about major shifts in power and numerous border changes, and, on the other, of immigration and migration.

As far as western Europe is concerned, it is necessary to add that, whereas multilingualism at the level of society is common, bilingualism among individual speakers in some of the larger countries is less frequent. There are a dozen or so languages spoken by sizeable communities in France and Germany, and well over a hundred in Britain, but, in spite of this, the majority of Britons, Germans and French people are monolingual in the sense that they use only one language for their normal day-to-day communication.

Of the five languages spoken by 45 per cent of the world's population (English, Spanish, Russian, Hindi and Chinese), the first three are used in many countries as second or official languages, and Hindi serves as a religious language for many, as well as being the national language of India. There are an estimated 5000 tongues in the world (Wardhaugh 1987; Crystal 1987), but only some 190 states, so it follows that many countries must contain many different languages, i.e. be multilingual. Approximately 95 per cent of the world's population are speakers of the 100 most frequently used languages.

In Europe only six countries are *officially* bilingual or multilingual: Belgium, Finland, Greenland, Switzerland, the USSR and Yugoslavia, and a handful of others accord official status of some kind to one or more of the languages of their linguistic minorities, e.g. the Netherlands to Frisian, Italy to German and the Federal Republic of Germany to Danish. In western Europe people tend to live in monolingual environments where there are relatively few natural contact situations requiring the use of more than one language, unless the speakers are members of linguistic minorities. Being born into a minority community or into a bilingual family are the most common ways for Europeans to become bilingual. There are, of course, other reasons – personal, social or cultural – why individuals become bilingual. At one time, for example, French was spoken by all members of the European aristocracy as the use of this language signalled membership of the élite. Prussia's Frederick the Great once expressed the belief that German was suitable only 'for horses and soldiers' and professed that he spoke German 'like a coachman'. Incidentally, he also left proof that he did not write it very well. Today, when Scandinavian, German and Dutch technologists, academics or business people meet, they are likely to discuss their work in English, because this is the language most widely used by such specialists for international communication. And Flemish-speaking Belgians embarking upon an administrative career in Brussels need to be fluent in French. For many Europeans adding another language to their repertoire has become desirable and often necessary. In other continents natural linguistic diversity is more prevalent, and for many communities bilingualism is a normal requirement for daily communication and not a sign of any particular achievement.

The role of attitudes
Bilingualism arises as a result of contact. Whether it spreads throughout the community and is maintained depends on whether the conditions for its development are right. These, in turn, are determined by individual and group attitudes towards (1) the two languages involved, and (2) bilingualism itself. In Europe there is considerable linguistic diversity, yet this fact is rarely reflected in the official policies adopted by most European countries. Few states encourage the learning of minority languages, for instance, as part of the school curriculum for both minority and majority children. Attitudes towards bilingualism range from officially promoting or accepting it, as is the case in the officially bilingual countries mentioned earlier, to granting some regions within a state the right to use the regional language in administration and education, as happens in Spain with regard to Catalan, Basque and Galician. Government acceptance of bilingualism, rather than active promotion, seems to be the attitude that underlies bilingual arrangements in Wales, where some schools offer Welsh-me-

dium instruction and others use both English and Welsh, while some public institutions (but not all) offer services in both languages. Whereas West Germans and Danes may regard individual bilingualism positively, especially if it involves languages which are considered 'useful' (e.g. English or French), they may express less admiration about bilingualism of their Turkish migrant communities. In Britain, the suggestion that the children of the majority might profit from learning the languages of some of the immigrant groups (such as Cantonese or Urdu) has been greeted by many people with indifference and by some with outright hostility.

As a result both of political developments and social pressure, attitudes towards bilingualism are changing for the better in many parts of the world. One of the landmarks in this process is what happened in the United States during the 1960s. At the same time as the position of minorities was being revised in the wake of the Civil Rights movement, the United States experienced large-scale immigration from Spanish-speaking people who neither assimilated by Anglo-Saxon culture and values nor shed their mother tongue as readily as previous generations of immigrants had done. The debate that took place both in intellectual and political circles eventually led to legislation supporting bilingual education programmes.[1] At about the same time Canada declared itself a bilingual state and officially enshrined the language rights of its French-speaking minority in law, by means of a number of legislative measures. This came about after a series of political crises prompted by the social and economic grievances of French Canadians and the threat of secession by the province of Québec. However, little was done to promote the language needs of Canada's many other minorities, such as the indigenous Inuit and the immigrants from Poland, Ukraine and Hong Kong, to name but a few.

Bilingualism as a problem and as a resource
Individual bilingualism has, in the past, often been blamed for a bilingual child's underachievement at school and in intelligence tests; and it has been considered to lie at the root of minority members' lack of assimilation to mainstream society. Some of these claims are analysed in Chapters 6 and 7, where it is suggested that social causes, rather than bilingualism, are usually responsible for problems of this kind.

Societal multilingualism can also be seen as a problem, if one believes that language itself (not just people) can cause conflict. For example, Fasold (1984: 4) suggests that 'multilingualism works against nationalism' in countries which are still undergoing a process of nation building and where there is no universally agreed language to unify a state's diverse ethnic groups. Wardhaugh's (1987) study of language spread and decline focuses on issues raised by the competition of languages within countries which have been linguistically invaded from outside the national borders. He argues that some kind of conflict between languages will ensue once the boundaries between them (territorial, ethnic, political or functional) come under pressure, and that this may result in a major change in a group's language patterns:

> When such boundaries are weak, the languages will not only be in contact, they will also be in competition. As one gains territory, speakers, or functions, all others lose. Bilingualism may not be a real choice in such circumstances; it may be no more than a temporary expedient, a somewhat marginal phenomenon, because when one language encroaches on another, bilingualism may prove to be only a temporary waystage to unilingualism in the encroaching language as the latter assumes more and more functions and is acquired as the sole language by greater numbers of speakers.
>
> (Wardhaugh 1987: 17)

Any such process is likely to lead to tension and resentment on the part of the group(s) involved. Speakers of the 'losing language(s)' may find themselves pushed to the political, social or cultural margin, and they may feel that their national or ethnic identity is under threat, along with the survival of their language.

Language contact usually results in an uneven distribution of language patterns among the groups involved. If distribution were identical, i.e. if the languages concerned were perceived as having equal prestige and they were each used to the same degree and in equivalent situations, then there would probably be no problem. But this is not often the case.

A preoccupation with the problems associated with bilingualism should not, however, obscure awareness of its likely benefits. In the first place, individual bilingualism is often experienced as an enriching attribute that facilitates a better understanding of the nature of language and provides an opportunity for gaining a deeper insight into two cultures. However, this favourable perception appears to depend on the socio-cultural context of bilingualism, as it is unlikely to be shared by those members of linguistic minorities who find themselves discriminated against by the dominant majority (which itself may have

negative attitudes towards bilingualism). A second possible advantage
for members of multilingual groups is that they have at their disposal a
wider range of linguistic resources than those who belong to monolingual communities. This may enable them to communicate with others
in a more flexible and diverse way – a benefit which, in a world of
increasing international communication, should be obvious. The study
of bilingualism can provide greater awareness of the versatility of
social organizations and the resourcefulness of human behaviour. In
general, an appreciation of the issues involved in bilingualism may
help to eliminate prejudice or fear.

The remit of the study of bilingualism
An examination of bilingualism involves looking at the many factors
that contribute to its development, maintenance and loss, and at the
different ways in which individuals or communities respond to the linguistic challenges they encounter. Bilingualism and multilingualism are
not static conditions. In many immigrant groups the shift from the
'old' home language to that of the host country takes place over three
generations; but the process is sometimes more rapid, leaving only the
immigrant generation as bilingual. At other times, however, the shift
takes much longer, or does not occur at all, leading to well-established
bilingualism over many years. For the immigrant, learning to live in a
new culture or to accommodate to a new language is a dynamic process. Individuals go through phases in their lives when one of their
languages becomes weaker, or stronger, as the case may be; or they
add new languages to their daily communicative repertoire, developing
clearly defined situations in which each code will be used.

The field of study is multidisciplinary. We approach the study of
bilingualism from at least three different perspectives, i.e. those of:

(1)   the individual;
(2)   the group;
(3)   the language systems.

A wide range of social sciences contribute towards our understanding of bilingualism: sociology, ethnology, anthropology,
education, psychology and most branches of linguistics, including
pragmatics. Each participating discipline brings with it its own methods and terminologies, and studies in bilingualism reflect the academic
background of the researcher. Language behaviour is highly complex,

and no one academic subject alone can hope to explain it completely. Linguistic performance is influenced by emotional factors, by the speaker's linguistic knowledge, and by perceived social values and norms. The interplay of these (and other) determinants becomes even more intricate if the speech patterns of whole groups of people are under examination. Research into bilingualism must be multi- and interdisciplinary so that all the relevant phenomena can be described and accounted for. The ultimate aim, as in other social sciences, is to establish a valid theoretical construct.

One of the problems encountered by researchers into societal bilingualism relates to the reliability of data. When considering patterns of language use, one needs to handle such statistical information as is made available by official (or national) agencies. But many countries do not include questions on language use on their census questionnaires, or they may ask only one question, without specifying function or degree of competence, e.g. 'What language(s) do you speak?', which can be interpreted in a variety of ways. Nelde (1984) warns that language census data should always be approached critically, adding that in areas where there is conflict and minorities are disadvantaged results may not be at all meaningful. In such cases, he argues, the replies of minority members tend to be influenced by a number of extra-linguistic considerations which, in sociolinguistic analysis, it may be difficult to come to terms with. For instance, census returns may indicate a minority group's aspired rather than actual linguistic affiliations, and this may favour the dominant rather than the minority language. Socio-economic factors, too, may cause bias in answers to questionnaires, usually in the direction of the majority language.

The systematic description of bilingualism, particularly using a sociolinguistic approach, is of relatively recent origin. Einar Haugen's work on the Norwegian language in America (1953) and on bilingualism in the Americas (1965) constituted the first large-scale sociolinguistic analyses of bilingualism. Uriel Weinreich's book *Languages in Contact* (first published in 1953) quickly became a classic and was seminal in developing research methods combining both social, psychological and linguistic dimensions. Robert Lado's *Linguistics across Cultures* (1957) did much to arouse linguists' interest in cross-cultural and bilingual communication, and to open their eyes to the sociolinguistic reality of language use, thus weaning them away from an exclusive preoccupation with linguistic forms and norms.

Education plays a crucial role both in the personal and social development of the bilingual individual and for the success of societal multi-lingualism. It has been attested (e.g. by Skutnabb-Kangas 1984a), for instance, that unless the educational system takes proper account of minority children's special language needs (in both languages), they will not become fully functional in the minority and the majority codes. On the other hand, a minority language that finds its way into the school curriculum will enjoy enhanced prestige and this can, in turn, positively affect public attitudes towards the language concerned and its speakers, who may then find it easier to maintain it. The issue of how best to educate minority children has become particularly urgent in many countries which have been affected by large-scale migration and emigration. Research in the area of bilingual education has often come as a response to such pressing needs.

Coverage and organization of this book

The organization of this book broadly reflects the two main strands in the study of bilingualism: in Part I individual bilinguals and their language use constitute the central focus, while in Part II a broader sociological and sociolinguistic approach is adopted for the discussion of multilingualism in society. Educational matters are raised in both parts, as they affect the development and maintenance of bilingualism in both the individual and society.

Part I seeks, from a microlinguistic point of view, to embrace both the psycholinguistic and the purely linguistic dimensions of bilingualism. Starting with the discussion of some definitions of bilingualism, Chapter 1 looks at individual bilingualism in a general way. Chapter 2 narrows the discussion to bilingual children, while Chapter 3 focuses specifically on the bilingual acquisition process. Chapters 4 and 5 examine the linguistic perspective, concentrating on bilingual competence and speech on their own terms, i.e. from the bilingual (rather than the monolingual) angle. In the last two chapters (6 and 7) of this part the discussion is broadened again to take in some of the major factors of a social, cultural, psychological and cognitive nature that are considered to be important in the acquisition and maintenance of bilingualism in the individual. In line with the general bias of this book, in Chapters 3, 4 and 5 certain aspects of bilingualism in children are given prominence; on the other hand, Chapters 5 and 7 deal with issues which apply to both bilingual children and adult users of two or more languages.

In the macrolinguistic approach adopted in Part II, the discussion ranges from the general to the more specific. Chapter 8 looks at the different patterns of multilingualism which can result from language contact and at some of the factors which are influential in the emergence of societal multilingualism. Questions such as 'By what criteria do bilingual communities organize their language behaviour?' and 'Why do some of them seem to be so much more successful than others in maintaining their language(s)?' are dealt with in Chapter 9. Decisions by the state on whether to promote or suppress particular languages can have a powerful effect on people's language behaviour, and the aims of Chapter 10 are to assess the possible role of language for social and national identification, and to look at how decisions on language matters are made by the state. Chapter 11 touches on a wide area, as the discussion of linguistic minorities must take into account many of the major issues in sociolinguistics: contact between dominant group and minority; the linguistic behaviour of both communities; attitudes towards the groups and languages involved; questions of identity, conflict and integration; and topics relating to language provision, maintenance and shift. In order to illustrate the complex issues raised in Chapter 11, three linguistic minorities that have little in common with each other, and that have perhaps been less accessible to English-language readers, have been chosen for more detailed consideration. The aim here is to show that language contact in Alsace, Catalonia and West Germany manifests various degrees of intensity and distinct dynamics, and that this results in different patterns of bilingualism.

The European dimension of this book has made it possible, on the one hand, to be selective in the choice of examples. On the other hand, choosing Europe as a general frame of reference has entailed the exclusion of certain important aspects of the study of bilingualism, pidgins and creoles, for instance. Neurolinguistic aspects of bilingualism, issues of language contact and language change and the question of attitudes towards bilingualism can be seen, perhaps, as less central for an initial introduction to the subject and have therefore not been included. The interested reader should turn to other introductory works (e.g. Appel and Muysken 1987, Hamers and Blanc 1989, and Romaine 1989).

In many books and articles the words *multilingualism* and, occasionally, *plurilingualism* are used almost interchangeably with *bilingualism*, the difference being quantitative rather than qualitative. The former two are favoured in some of the European linguistic traditions (e.g. in Belgium, and also in Germany and Switzerland, where the subject is more frequently referred to as *Mehrsprachigkeit* ('multilingualism'), than *Zweisprachigkeit* ('bilingualism'). The use of the term *multilingualism* allows one to take a broader view of language and dialect varieties. There are even scholars (e.g. Wandruszka 1979) who speak of 'intralingual multilingualism', referring to an ability to operate on a number of different levels of style, register and dialect in the mother tongue.

Hamers and Blanc (1989) use the terms 'bilinguality' and 'bilingualism' as reflecting a different level of analysis. The former, for them, refers to the 'psychological state of the individual who has access to more than one linguistic code as a means of social communication' (p. 265). Bilingualism, on the other hand, is defined in a more general way as 'the state of the individual or a community characterized by the simultaneous presence of two languages' (ibid.). This distinction may have its advantages for certain types of analysis, but it has not yet found wide acceptance and it is not adopted here. Normally, *bilingualism* is used in the literature for individuals and communities in which two languages are present; the term *multilingualism* can refer to societies where more than two languages are found. They are essentially the same phenomenon. Both terms are employed in this book in the description of language contact at the societal level, but only the former is made use of in the discussion of individual bilingualism. When speaking of a bilingual or multilingual community we are referring to the presence of two or more languages in that particular setting, without implying that all (or most) of the members of the group in question have competence in those languages. On the other hand, when adopting a linguistic or psycholinguistic approach in the study of the bilingual individual, the use of 'bilingualism' does imply the ability to use both codes.

Notes

1.   It should be noted, however, that in the 1980s the commitment to bilingual education shifted notably. The issue was no longer felt to be one of national federal concern, and public funds were withdrawn from many schemes; it was left to individual states to decide the extent of official support for bilingualism.

PSYCHOLINGUISTIC ASPECTS OF BILINGUALISM

Chapter 1

Individual bilingualism

1.1   Societal and individual bilingualism

When looking through introductions to the study of bilingualism one sees that it is often mentioned that over half the population of the world is bilingual. Such general statements are open to different interpretations, in view of the fact that patterns of language use found in bilingual communities can be quite varied and that many are changing even as we observe them.

Statistics can mislead, particularly when they do not distinguish between societies and individuals, as there is a fundamental difference between societal and individual bilingualism. We may say that India, Switzerland and Belgium are multilingual countries, that Canada is officially bilingual, as is Finland, or that Paraguay is an example of bilingualism and diglossia, and Luxembourg one of triglossia. In such contexts the labels 'bilingual' and 'multilingual' reflect official policies towards some, or all, of the countries' minorities. On the whole, however, they say nothing about the degree or the extent of bilingualism among the inhabitants of these areas. It is only when language planning policies find their way into a nation's education system with the explicit aim of fostering bilingualism (rather than promoting the majority or the minority language) that bilingualism may be the norm in such parts of the world. Of the countries mentioned above, individual bilingualism may be widespread only in Luxembourg and Paraguay. Mackey (1970) claims that there are actually fewer bilingual people in bilingual countries than there are in so-called unilingual ones, and he points out that the main concern of multilingual states has often been the guaranteed maintenance and use of two or more languages in the same nation, rather than the promotion of bilingualism among its citizens. This observation is particularly relevant in the non-European context, since in western Europe we find only three states which are officially multilingual, Belgium, Switzerland and Finland, and the first two pursue policies of territorial monolingualism (see Chapter 8).

In this part of the book attention focuses on the bilingual speaker as the 'locus of language contact' (Weinreich 1968: 1). Naturally, language interaction involves communication in a wider sociocultural setting. We therefore need to bear in mind certain aspects of the context in which the bilingual finds herself or himself, as this provides us with information about the ways in which the two or more languages form part of the person's everyday life. Equally, it may be relevant to take note of psychological factors that may influence, or affect in some way, the linguistic behaviour of the bilingual, just as one must also be aware that neurological, pathological and general cognitive factors can come into play.

1.2 Describing bilingualism

The most salient feature of bilingualism is that it is a multi-faceted phenomenon. Whether one is considering it at a societal or an individual level, one has to accept that there can be no clear cut-off points. As bilingualism defies delimitation, it is open to a variety of descriptions, interpretations and definitions. We can consider some examples. In Britain people do not usually think of Wales as a bilingual part of the state, yet one does happily use the label 'bilingual' when referring to certain types of schools found in the principality. Many people would readily call 'bilingual' the two-year-old child of a French–English couple, and the fact that the toddler's vocabulary may consist of some 200 French and English items in all does not seem to be of importance. Similarly, size of vocabulary may not carry much weight in the case of a graduate in French, who may have spent a considerable amount of time in France and studying the language, and whose total lexicon will be several hundred times larger than the child's. This person is not, however, often thought of as a 'bilingual', and would not normally claim the label for himself or herself. 'Multi-cultural' and 'multi-ethnic' are adjectives freely used by many people in the English-speaking world, and the children who start school in the UK with little knowledge of English may be referred to as 'minority children' or 'ESL

(English as a second language) pupils', but not as 'bilinguals'. Why should all this be so?

1.2.1 Some definitions of bilingualism

The notion of bilingualism is firmly established in the mind of the lay person. It may be tinged with bias, and it frequently carries either positive or negative connotations. In the specialist's mind the concept is also well established. However, the latter is expected to apply objective criteria and to aim for precise delineations. Yet some of the definitions of bilingualism that have been put forward are surprisingly vague, and even contradictory.

Uriel Weinreich, one of the founding fathers of bilingual studies and a bilingual himself, offers one of the shortest definitions in his well-known book *Languages in Contact*: 'The practice of alternately using two languages will be called bilingualism, and the person involved, bilingual.' (Weinreich 1968: 1).

An oft-quoted definition is found in one of the early books on modern linguistics, Leonard Bloomfield's *Language*, first published in the USA in 1933. When mentioning that foreign language learning among immigrants may result in language shift, Bloomfield pays special attention to users who become so proficient in the new language that they are indistinguishable from the native speakers around them. He says:

> In the cases where this perfect foreign-language learning is not accompanied by loss of the native language, it results in 'bilingualism', native-like control of two languages. After early childhood few people have enough muscular and nervous freedom or enough opportunity and leisure to reach perfection in a foreign language; yet bilingualism of this kind is commoner than one might suppose, both in cases like those of our immigrants and as a result of travel, foreign study, or similar association. Of course, one cannot define a degree of perfection at which a good foreign speaker becomes a bilingual: the distinction is relative.
>
> (Bloomfield 1933: 55–6)

No doubt Bloomfield had a clear notion of bilingualism, but his definition and subsequent qualifying remarks are not without some degree of contradiction: if one cannot define 'a degree of perfection' in bilingualism, how can we talk of 'perfect foreign-language learning'?

In his article 'The description of bilingualism', William Mackey offers a definition that incorporates Weinreich's alternate use of two languages and is preceded by Bloomfield's reservation with respect to the degree of proficiency:

It seems obvious that if we are to study the phenomenon of bilingualism
we are forced to consider it as something entirely relative. We must more-
over include the use not only of two languages, but of any number of
languages. We shall therefore consider bilingualism as the alternate use of
two or more languages by the same individual.

(Mackey 1970: 555)

1.2.2 Some types of bilinguals

The three definitions mentioned so far say nothing about how well the
languages need to be known, whether both have to be mastered in all
sorts of skills, whether they must be used in similar or different situations, or about any particular requirements regarding the uses to
which the languages are put. Yet such considerations would probably
be relevant in deciding whether any, or all, of the following should be
considered as bilinguals:

(1) the two-year-old who is beginning to talk, speaking English to
     one parent and Welsh to the other;

(2) the four-year-old whose home language is Bengali and who has
     been attending an English playgroup for some time;

(3) the schoolchild from an Italian immigrant family living in the
     United States who increasingly uses English both at home and
     outside but whose older relatives address him in Italian only;

(4) the Canadian child from Montréal who comes from an English-
     speaking background and attends an immersion programme
     which consists of virtually all school subjects being taught
     through the medium of French;

(5) the young graduate who has studied French for eleven years;

(6) the sixty-year-old scholar who has spent a considerable part of
     her life working with manuscripts and documents written in
     Latin;

(7) the technical translator;

(8) the personal interpreter of an important public figure;

(9) the Portuguese chemist who can read specialist literature in his
     subject written in English;

(10) the Japanese airline pilot who uses English for most of his professional communication;

(11) the Turkish immigrant worker in the Federal Republic of Germany who speaks Turkish at home and with his friends and work colleagues, but who can communicate in German, in both the written and the oral forms, with his superiors and the authorities;

(12) the wife of the latter, who is able to get by in spoken German but cannot read or write it;

(13) the Danish immigrant in New Zealand who has had no contact with Danish for the last forty years;

(14) the Belgian government employee who lives in bilingual Brussels, whose friends and relatives are mainly Flemish speakers but who works in an entirely French-speaking environment and whose colleagues in the office (whether they are Flemish or not) use French as well;

(15) the fervent Catalanist who at home and at work uses Catalan only, but who is exposed to Castilian Spanish from the media and in the street and has no linguistic difficulty in the latter language.

So what *is* bilingualism? Many specialists would say that all the above individuals could be classed as bilinguals; but public opinion, and at least some of these people themselves, would probably disagree. It is possible to think of a number of explanations for the difficulties involved in arriving at a precise definition. The elusiveness of the phenomenon has already been referred to. Another factor is the nature of the subject itself. Language use is part of human behaviour, and as such not readily accessible to scientific investigation and experimental research. The study of bilingualism is hampered by a host of methodological problems and theoretical shortcomings. These difficulties stem from the complex interplay and variability of social, psychological and chance factors which determine individual conduct – and therefore often render generalizations invalid. Research into bilingualism is, consequently, interdisciplinary in character, as scholars from different academic fields, such as sociology, psychology, linguistics, anthropology and education (and others) bring different methods, criteria and assumptions to bear upon studies of bilingual situations.

'Bilingualism as a concept has open-ended semantics', Hugo Baetens Beardsmore (1982: 1) points out at the beginning of his comprehensive discussion of a number of different definitions of bilingualism. Ultimately, all definitions are arbitrary to a greater or lesser extent. It is not necessarily a problem, therefore, that there are so many of them, since in this way the researcher is able to choose the one that best suits her or his purpose.

1.2.3 Factors taken into account when describing bilingualism

One of Baetens Beardsmore's contributions to the subject under discussion is his exposition of a series of descriptive labels, which have been chosen by various specialists so as to provide a frame of reference. There are many and different areas around which the study of bilingualism can be centred; some of them are fairly clear-cut, whereas others are not. The following list contains some selected examples (a fuller discussion of the issues involved can be found, for instance, in Baetens Beardsmore 1982 or in Skutnabb-Kangas 1984a).

(1) The *age* of the bilingual at the time of the acquisition may result in considerable differences, as suggested by the terms 'early bilingualism' and 'late bilingualism'. An early bilingual may be a case of 'infant bilingualism' (Haugen 1956: 72) or of 'child bilingualism'. The cut-off point is not firmly established, but it can be set arbitrarily (see, for example, McLaughlin 1984: 73) at the age of three – and between the child bilingual and the case of 'adult bilingualism' at the age of puberty. Tove Skutnabb-Kangas's (1984a: 80 ff.) analysis of definitions of bilingualism recognizes four main types. Her first type comes under the heading of 'origin', which at this stage can be taken to correspond with 'age'. This factor, however, is more useful for the description than for a definition of bilingualism.

(2) We can widen the ambit of the discussion to include considerations of *context*. The infant/child who acquires two languages from the speakers around him/her in an unstructured way can be called a 'natural bilingual' or a 'primary bilingual' (Houston 1972). Adler (1977) refers to this specification with the expression 'ascribed bilingualism'. The two languages may have been presented to the infant/child bilingual either in a 'fused' context (both parents using both languages to the child; it can also mean that the context of acquisition is such that the two languages are spoken in the same locality where the young learner

is beginning to use them – as for example in a multilingual society) or in 'separate' contexts (the parents follow the one-parent-one-language principle, or one language is learnt in one country and the other in a different one). The person who becomes bilingual through systematic or structured instruction (that is, undergoing some kind of training) is also known as a 'secondary bilingual', and the result can be called 'achieved bilingualism' (Adler 1977). Skutnabb-Kangas (1984a: 95 ff.) establishes the dichotomy of 'natural bilingualism' and 'school bilingualism/cultural bilingualism'. The distinction between these two is interesting. School bilingualism is, as its name implies, involved with formal language teaching at school, during which the learner (as the author points out) does not normally have much opportunity to practise the language outside the classroom environment. Cultural bilingualism coincides in many respects with school bilingualism, but it is more often the result of language learning by adults who wish to use a foreign language for purposes of travel, leisure or work; the assumed cultural value (that an educated person is one who knows one or more foreign languages) is reflected in the term.

(3) The *relationship between sign and meaning*, i.e. the mental organization of the speech of bilinguals, was first mentioned by Weinreich (1968), whose pioneering work was very much concerned with the phenomenon of interference, that is, the influence of the bilingual's language systems upon each other. He distinguishes different types of bilinguals according to the relationship that exists between the linguistic sign and the semantic content. In Type A the individual combines a sign ('signifier' is the term used by Weinreich) from each language with a separate unit of content (or 'signified', or 'semanteme'). In Type B the subject identifies the two signs ('signifiers') but regards them as a single compound, or composite, unit of meaning ('signified'). His examples, using English and Russian, are:

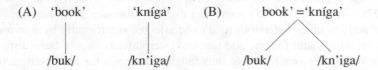

   (A) 'book'   'kníga'   (B)   book' ='kníga'

      /buk/   /kn'iga/   /buk/   /kn'iga/

Weinreich also considers a third possible interpretation of the sign. Type C relates to people who learn a new language with the help of another (Weinreich calls this process the 'indirect method'), i.e. by finding equivalent signs (signifiers, or words). For example, 'to an English learner of Russian, the signified [or referent, i.e. the object that the word refers to] of the form /kn'iga/ may at first be not the object [the thing itself, the book], but the English word *book*, with which he is already familiar':

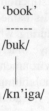

'book'

/buk/

/kn'iga/

(Weinreich 1968: 9–10)

Weinreich calls his Type C 'subordinative' bilingualism, as it describes the kind of bilingual whose second language or L2 is seen to be very much influenced by his/her first language or L1 (see also Paradis 1977b), whereas the expression he uses for Type A is 'coordinative'. In later research by Ervin and Osgood (1954) Type A is called 'coordinate' bilingualism and Types B and C considered together as 'compound bilingualism'. This latter notion, in particular, has been interpreted differently by a number of linguists, and a variety of hypotheses have been formulated, in relation with contexts, linguistic ability and age at the time of acquisition (see, for instance, Lambert et al. 1959; Macnamara 1967b; Jakobovits 1968; Lambert 1972; Baetens Beardsmore 1974 and Paradis 1977a; for a detailed discussion of the question, see Skutnabb-Kangas 1984a: 98 ff.). Others have cast some doubt on the validity of such an attempt at classification (Diller 1972) or claimed that there can be little significance in the distinction, even if all the types could be convincingly established (Albert and Obler 1978). Wölk (1984: 125) points out that the processes of mental transfer and linguistic behaviour tend to be affected significantly by a series of sociolinguistic factors, and that this interplay has largely been disregarded in previous research, thus fudging the basis for the description of bilingualism. He claims that distinguishing carefully among the various factors and processes at play will make it easier to describe bilingualism on the basis of clear criteria: 'Vor allem die Unterscheidung zwischen soziolinguistischen Bestimmungfaktoren und kognitiven Vermittlungs – oder sprachlichen Verhaltensprozessen kann bessere Ansätze und Kriterien für die Beschreibung und das Verständnis der Zweisprachigkeit liefern.'

(4) The *order and consequence* of bilingual language acquisition is reflected in such labels as 'incipient bilingualism' (Diebold 1961) and 'ascendant bilingualism' (Baetens Beardsmore 1982), which indicate an increase in the person's ability to use two languages, whereas 'recessive bilingualism' (Baetens Beardsmore 1982) points to a decrease. Qualitative, as well as quantitative, judgement is expressed by the terms 'additive bilingualism' and 'subtractive bilingualism' (Lambert 1974). The former implies that the addition of a second language to a person's first can result in enriched, or at least complementary, social, cognitive and linguistic abilities, whereas the latter suggests that the L2 is learnt at the expense of the L1. As a consequence of various social pressures, many minority groups in Europe find themselves undergoing a process of language shift, away from their ethnic tongue and towards the national language of the country they now live in. This means that, although they are becoming more proficient in the L2, they are losing skills in the L1; therefore, as the latter is not being maintained, it is actually being 'subtracted' from their bilingual proficiency.

(5) One of the most challenging aspects to address concerns the question of how proficient a person needs to be in both languages. There are a number of definitions based on this criterion of *competence*. Some authors, as was seen earlier, define bilingualism as 'near-native control of two or more languages' (Bloomfield 1933: 56), or 'complete mastery of two different languages without interference' (Oestreicher 1974: 9), or see the bilingual as 'a person who knows two languages with approximately the same degree of perfection as unilingual speakers of those languages' (Christopherson 1948: 4). Such definitions express a perfectionist or *maximalist* view. The labels used are, for example, 'perfect bilingualism', 'true bilingualism' and 'ambilingualism'. Halliday, McIntosh and Strevens (1970: 141) describe an 'ambilingual' as a speaker who has complete control of two languages and makes use of both in all uses to which he puts either. True ambilingual speakers are very rare creatures. Who ever has identical linguistic input and output in both languages? And who would habitually use both languages for the same purposes, in the same contexts?

At the other end of the pole we can place those definitions which express a *minimalist* stance. Haugen (1953: 7) sees 'the point where a speaker can first produce complete meaningful utterances in the other language' as the beginning of bilingualism. Others, such as John Macnamara, see a minimal degree of competence, in one of the four language skills (speaking, writing, reading and understanding speech) as sufficient: 'I shall consider as bilingual a person who, for example, is an educated native speaker of English and who can also read a little French. This means that bilingualism is being treated as a continuum, or rather a series of continua, which vary among individuals along a variety of dimensions' (Macnamara 1969: 82).

Where one view is obviously too narrow, the other is too broad to be of much help. However, somewhere in the middle of our continuum we can accommodate the notion of 'equilingualism' or 'balanced bilingualism'. We would expect a balanced bilingual to possess roughly equal proficiency of the two languages, but with no implication that the knowledge this bilingual has in either language is compared to monolingual standards. The term 'balanced bilingual', as used by Lambert, Havelka and Gardner (1959), is intended to refer to individuals who are fully competent in both codes. As in the case of the 'ambilingual', the 'balanced bilingual' is likely to be something of an ideal, since most bilinguals tend to be more fluent or generally proficient in one language, or at any rate in some uses of it, i.e. they will have a stronger or 'dominant' language and a weaker one. (There is, incidentally, a convention among scholars to list the dominant language first, so that a Spanish–German bilingual should not be confused with a German–Spanish one.)

The language a bilingual feels more at home in, the 'preferred language', may coincide with the dominant one, but this will not necessarily happen in every case. The experienced immigrant technician who has made good progress in her profession in her country of adoption, but who still has strong emotional ties with the people and the culture of her country of origin, could constitute a valid example. It is also possible for the dominant and the preferred language to change roles in the course of the bilingual's life.

The notion of relativism, as first expressed by Bloomfield (see his definition earlier), is a central one in the discussion of any type of bilingualism. Most bilingualism can be identified only in relative terms. If we accept that there are degrees of bilingual competence, this implies that bilingualism is measurable. The question of measurabilty has received a good deal of attention (see Kelly 1969; Baetens Beardsmore 1982; Skutnabb-Kangas 1984a; Saunders 1982a), and useful insights can be obtained from the descriptions of tests, as well as the discussion of relevant criteria, for appraising bilingualism. The fundamental problem lies in the question of norms. What (or who) should be the basis for the assessment? Monoglot terms of reference are often used, but they should not be, as they can be relevant only in the (exceptional) case of an ambilingual whose control of the two language systems may be almost 'complete' (assuming we know what this means) and who displays no traces of interference. For the vast majority of bilinguals, 'bilingual competence' is not measurable in terms of monolingual standards. It is, of course, possible to provide a description of a bilingual person's proficiency in Language A and in Language B using accepted methods of language testing. But over and above these two competences there is the bilingual's specific competence, which may manifest itself in such features as switching from one code to another (code-switching) or making use of items or linguistic knowledge from one language when speaking the other (mixing), which may enhance his/her communicative ability (see Chapter 13).

(6) Statements about most cases of bilingualism centring on the description of the relative proficiency in each language usually fall short of including references to the *use* or *function* that the bilingual's languages fulfil. Function-based definitions reflect the view that language is not an abstract entity, but a tool employed for taking part in acts of communication. Thus, for example, the definitions by Mackey and Weinreich (see above) point to the bilingual's habit of alternating between the two languages. Els Oksaar (1966 and 1983: 19) suggests a combination of the criteria of competence and function when she defines bilingualism as: 'the ability of a person to use here and now two or more languages as a means of communication in most situations and to switch from one language to the other if necessary.' To this she adds that such a broad definition needs to be made more specific 'according to the languages and the situation. Reality does not demand of a multilingual that he use his languages in all kinds of situations.'

Skutnabb-Kangas (1984a) explains the emergence of function-related definitions in the context of the development of linguistic thought in general and ideas about bilingualism in particular. The very narrow delimitation of language competence put forward by some theoretical linguists of the transformational-generative school, and especially the notion of the 'ideal speaker/hearer' (i.e. 'someone living in a completely homogeneous speech community', according to Chomsky) could not satisfy those whose interests moved away from the descriptions of grammars and towards the variability of language uses and language users. Mackey introduces an article on bilingualism with the categorical statement that 'Bilingualism is not a phenomenon of language; it is a characteristic of its use. It is not a feature of the code but of the message. It does not belong to the domain of *langue* but of *parole*' (Mackey 1970: 554).

Just as we have to accept linguistic proficiency as something variable and unstable, we must acknowledge the existence of varying degrees of functional bilingualism. Different bilinguals have distinct uses, as well as various levels of competence, for each code. Where precisely the threshold of bilingualism is set will depend on whether one takes a maximalist or a minimalist viewpoint, and also on the factors that one considers relevant for the description. For instance, we may talk about 'receptive bilingualism' in relation to a person who is able to understand a second language, either in its spoken or written form, such as the Turkish wife in Germany mentioned before or the Portuguese chemist. The term 'passive' bilingualism covers more or less the same ground, although it has certain negative connotations and does not do justice to the active decoding processes involved in understanding language.

At the other end of the scale, functional bilingualism can be described in terms of 'productive (= active) bilingualism', which implies the ability to speak as well as understand the languages, to write as well as read them. There are many intermediate stages which can be illustrated with examples from language learners who follow different types of programmes designed to improve their language skills, both oral and written, or cases like that of the immigrant who enters his new country of residence with only a limited knowledge of either the spoken or, perhaps, the written language, and who over the years adds to his active and passive ability in the new code while at the same time maintaining his mother tongue. There are, clearly, many conceivable patterns of individual bilingualism, as can be seen by looking at the table in which Baetens Beardsmore represents some of the possible combinations for bilingual ability across the four language skills (although no information is given on the extent of skill for each language):

TABLE 1.1 Patterns of individual bilingualism

Language skills   *Productive bilingualism*

Language skills						
Listening comprehension:	L1 L2	L1 L2	L1 L2	L1 L2	L1	
Reading comprehension:	L1 L2	L1 L2	L1 L2			L2
Oral production:	L1 L2	L1 L2	L1 L2	L1 L2	L1	
Written production:	L1 L2	L1				L2

Language skills   *Receptive bilingualism*

Language skills					
Listening comprehension:	L1 L2	L1 L2	L1	L1 L2	L1
Reading comprehension:	L1 L2	L1	L1 L2		L2
Oral production:	L1	L1	L1		
Written production:	L1	L1	L1		

Source: Baetens Beardsmore 1982: 17

It is not difficult to find examples of the various combinations suggested above, particularly if one bears in mind that in many parts of the world biliteracy is not to be assumed as an attribute of active bilingualism – just as bilingualism among young children usually excludes any form of literacy. The last case, i.e. that of the receptive bilingual who is illiterate in his L1 but is able to read in the L2 (as it emerges from the end of the last column in this table) is perhaps uncommon in western Europe today. However, one can come across people (e.g. Muslim immigrants) who cannot read in the language they speak habitually but have learnt to read the Holy Scriptures of their religion, i.e. the Koran, in Arabic. Another example would be the adult immigrant who came to Britain from the sub-Asian continent and attended adult literacy programmes; he may have learnt to read English to some extent yet have difficulties in following many types of conversation in this language; and he may be unable to write English at all.

(7) Skutnabb-Kangas (1984a) includes the issue of *attitude* in her discussion, a point taken up by Kielhöfer and Jonekeit (1983: 11), who stress also that it is crucial that the individual should be conscious of

his bilingualism. What is meant by 'attitude' is self-identification or identification by others, i.e. whether a bilingual feels herself or himself totally 'at home' in, or identified with, his or her languages, and whether the individual is accepted by others as belonging to both the one and the other linguistic community. Attitudes are more accessible to observation in the context of societal multilingualism, as for example in the case of bilinguals among minority groups, where it is easier to notice that cultural, social and motivational factors can influence a group's maintenance or loss of bilingualism. The child whose parents speak different languages, or whose home language is different from that of the society around him or her, may well be bilingual but not have developed strong links with other speakers of the parents' original speech community, or with the culture associated with the language. In the case of many families, it can prove very difficult to achieve such sociocultural embedding in both languages/ cultures, as this requires a conscious effort on the part of the parents and also a fair amount of access to the other country and its culture.

Some of the definitions presented can only be applied to specific purposes – which may, of course, be exactly what was intended. Other authors try to combine two or more criteria. Skutnabb-Kangas goes further when she says:

> A bilingual speaker is someone who is able to function in two (or more) languages, either in monolingual or bilingual communities, in accordance with the sociocultural demands made of an individual's communicative and cognitive competence by these communities or by the individual herself, at the same level as native speakers, and who is able positively to identify with both (or all) language groups (and cultures) or parts of them.
>
> *Source*: Skutnabb-Kangas 1984a: 90

This definition is almost the expression of an ideal. It may be attributed to the fact that (as she herself states) Skutnabb-Kangas had a specific group in mind, namely immigrants and minority children, 'who I hope will be given the opportunity to *become* so completely bilingual that they satisfy the demands of my definition, something I think of as entirely possible' (my italics). Her table sets out clearly the criteria and other details involved in the definition (see Table 1.2):

TABLE 1.2 Defining bilingualism

Criterion	The mother tongue is the language		A speaker is bilingual who
Origin	first learned (the speaker has established her first lasting linguistic contacts in)	(a)	has learnt two languages in the family from native speakers from the beginning
		(b)	has used two languages in parallel as means of communication from the beginning
Competence level of proficiency	best known	(a)	complete mastery of two languages
		(b)	native-like control of two languages
		(c)	equal mastery of two languages
		(d)	can produce complete meaningful utterances in the other language
		(e)	has at least some knowledge and control of the grammatical structure of the other language.
		(f)	has come into contact with another language
Function use	most used		uses (or can use) two languages (in most situations) (in accordance with her own wishes and the demands of the community)
Attitudes identity and identification	(a) identified with by self (internal identification)	(a)	identifies herself as bilingual/ with two languages and/or two cultures (or parts of them)
	(b) identified by others as a native speaker of (external identification)	(b)	is identified by others as bilingual/ as a native speaker of two languages

Source: Skutnabb-Kangas 1984a: 91

1.3 Semilingualism

A brief mention must be made of the notion of so-called 'semilingualism', which has been at the centre of considerable argument. Like 'subtractive bilingualism', it appears to suggest a negative view, to the effect that, if a person has to use two languages, this can have detrimental results on general linguistic ability, i.e. that the person is liable to suffer from some kind of linguistic deficiency in both languages. The expression was first used by Scandinavian linguists who were considering the language of Finnish minority children in Sweden (Hansegård 1968; Skutnabb-Kangas and Toukomaa 1976, 1979). The Swedish term *halvspråkighed* was rendered into English as 'semilingualism' or 'double semilingualism'. It was particularly in connection with matters related to bilingual and vernacular education that the notion became controversial. According to the observations of these linguists, the children of Finnish immigrants in Sweden showed retardation in their linguistic ability when compared to their Swedish and Finnish peers. They claimed that this backwardness could become a permanent feature among these immigrants. It was argued that, if this happened it would probably contribute to the continued stigmatization and, as a consequence, isolation of the immigrant groups in question, as they would be cut off from sufficiently varied linguistic input from Finland Finns and, equally, from that of Swedish native speakers (see also section 6.3).

The phenomenon is not a new one. When she introduced the concept in America, Christina Bratt Paulston (1974) pointed out that it had been quite vividly described by Bloomfield in 1927 when dealing with an Indian speaker of Menomini who had learnt English, of whom he said that he spoke 'no language tolerably', and he added: 'perhaps this is due, in some indirect way, to the impact of the conquering language'. It seems that Bloomfield had some sort of purely linguistic explanation in mind. Today one would probably prefer to try to seek out the particular social and psychological circumstances of the case under study, as they are often seen to affect linguistic competence.

1.4 Biculturalism

The reference to attitudes to bilingualism itself can open the discussion to wider aspects, not strictly linguistic in nature. Language is always used within a cultural environment, and this context tends to vary from one speech community to another. We may take it that a native Italian speaker is more or less conscious of Italian culture, familiar with a whole set of shared experiences and assumptions. However, it does not follow automatically that those who know two languages are bicultural. The English-Italian bilingual from the Bronx, in New York, may perhaps be aware of aspects of Italian culture relating to the home, family, food, etc., but she is likely to be unaware of the popular culture of, say, present-day Naples; on the other hand, she will be conversant with the culture (or subculture) that is peculiar to Italian immigrants in the Bronx. The British student of French life and letters, in contrast, may be highly knowledgeable about French cultural affairs past and present, yet feel insecure and be non-fluent when it comes to dynamic oral interaction. Just as a bilingual may possess varying degrees of competence in the two (or more) languages, (s)he may also exhibit different degrees of biculturalism. Normally, we can expect less fluent bilinguals to be less bicultural as well, in the same way as one would predict that a fluent bilingual will be more familiar with both cultures; but it will depend on the way they have acquired their languages. Making use again of the idea of a continuum, it is possible to imagine the probable patterns emerging from various likely combinations of bilingualism and biculturalism. The chances are that one will find a greater concentration of people towards the monolingual/ monocultural end of the scale, and then a decreasing number of individuals with a high degree of bilingualism and biculturalism, in line with the statement previously made that ambilingualism (and equi-lingualism) are rare occurrences. But other situations are also feasible.

Oksaar (1983) defines biculturalism (she uses the term 'multiculturalism') on the basis of a broad view put forward by Soffieti (1955) which sees culture as 'the ways of a people', i.e. the defining characteristics of a person or a group, including behaviour patterns: 'Multiculturalism of a person is realized in his ability to act here and now according to the requirements and rules of the cultures' (Oksaar 1983: 20).

She states that, in the case of immigrants, the two languages usually fulfil different roles and functions, their distribution being decided by a number of social and psychological factors. More often than not, the mother tongue belongs to the individual sphere and the language of the host country to the official and sociocultural one. But, she argues, these relations can change, and the distribution of L1 and L2 in relation to the cultural spheres may be an important criterion for the immigrant's degree of assimilation or isolation in the host country. One could perhaps add that the distribution of the two languages and cultural spheres will not necessarily be the same for all the members of the same family. Parents may be witnesses of how the culture of the country of residence begins to dominate their children's individual sphere and how they increasingly regard the culture(s) of the parents as something that belongs to a different sociocultural environment. This can lead to conflicts which are, potentially, much more frustrating than they would probably be if they were caused by language use only.

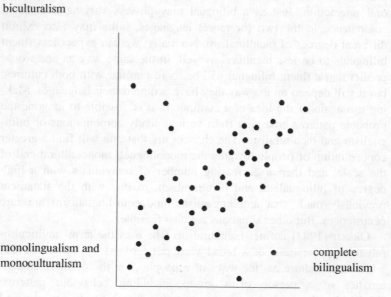

FIGURE 1.1 The relationship between bilingualism and biculturalism

Many foreign language programmes of study attempt to strike a balance between imparting 'language' knowledge and teaching 'culture', not only because of the intrinsic value that cultural matters are assumed to have, but also because of the realization that effective communication can proceed without hindrance only when the speakers are aware of the cultural implications (see, for example, Byram 1986c; 1988). To apply the same set of cultural values as are used for Language A when addressing native users of Language B is likely to lead to misunderstanding; the speaker may, quite unintentionally, appear to be rude, arrogant, strange or ignorant, simply because the concordance of linguistic items and cultural conventions is not observed. In addition, the more fluent the bilingual becomes, the fewer allowances will be made and the less tolerant the native speakers of the other language will be of violations of cultural assumptions. As Baetens Beardsmore (1982: 20) puts it: 'the further one progresses in bilingual ability, the more important the bicultural element becomes, since higher proficiency increases the expectancy rate of sensitivity towards the cultural implications of language use.'

1.5   A bilingual profile

From whatever angle we look at it, bilingualism is a relative concept. All definitions presented here go some way towards characterizing the various forms it may take, but there is not one that is equally acceptable, or useful, for everybody approaching the subject. Instead of trying to make people fit into previously established definitions, it may be more fruitful and practical to aim at setting up a bilingual profile for each individual (or group) which takes account of such variable aspects as:

(1) language development (i.e. acquisition), maintenance and/or loss of L1 and L2;
(2) sequential relationship of L1 and L2, i.e. whether they are acquired simultaneously of subsequently;
(3) language competence, that is, degree of proficiency in L1 and L2, and language dominance;
(4) functional aspects of language use: what, when and to whom L1 and L2 are used;
(5) linguistic features, such as code-switching, borrowing and interference;
(6) attitudes towards L1 and L2, speakers of L1 and L2, and bilingualism itself;
(7) internal and external pressures (motivational, social, psychological, perhaps others);
(8) environmental circumstances surrounding the bilingual;
(9) biculturalism, that is, degree of familiarity with the cultures of L1 and L2.

In line with the objectives pursued in other social sciences, the ultimate goal would be to set up a comprehensive theory of bilingualism. This is not to say that attempts at partial theoretical explanations have not been undertaken (see, for instance, the account in Baetens Beardsmore 1981). The more detailed bilingual profiles become, the more insights we shall gather and the nearer we shall get to valid generalizations on which to base such a theory.

Chapter 2

The study of bilingual children

2.1 Early and late bilingualism

The distinction between early and late bilingualism was introduced in Chapter 1. In the following discussion the terms 'early bilingualism' and 'child bilingualism' are both used to refer to the child who has been in contact with two languages from birth, and also to the one who acquired a second language in early childhood, after the first language had been established.

'Early' and 'late' bilingualism were sometimes used, in former publications on the subject, to refer to natural or primary bilingualism and to the artificial, secondary kind. Adler (1977) introduced the expressions 'ascribed bilingualism', used (mainly, but not exclusively) with reference to children, and 'achieved bilingualism' to denote older individuals. There was, however, some inconsistency in the use of all these terms. As far as the anglophone countries are concerned, for a long time studies of bilingualism took second place to linguists' preoccupation with other aspects of applied linguistics and psycholinguistics. In fact, a fair amount of research in bilingualism was concerned with second-language learning and teaching in American or Canadian school/college settings. This may help explain why the adult bilingual was, more often than not, thought of as someone who had *learnt* a second language (as different from having *acquired* it under natural conditions). This assumption finds expression in the definitions of bilingualism which convey a minimalist view of language competence (see Chapter 1).

From the end of the 1960s there was a widening of the scope of attention to include different groups of adults and children, and members of linguistic minorities (especially non-indigenous migrants and immigrants such as the Hispanos in the United States, the 'guestworkers' in the Federal Republic of Germany and other European countries, and the immigrants from the ex-colonies of the British Empire, the Netherlands, Belgium and France). From that time on the meaning of the term 'bilingual' has been extended to include members of immigrant or migrant communities who rarely became users of a second language through formal teaching and learning methods. A new and vigorous area of research into second language acquisition sprang up, looking into ways in which both the older and younger members of these groups *acquire* the language of their host country in a 'natural' way, rather than learning it by formal means.[1] Their learning, or acquisition, of the second language (i.e. that of the host country) depends on the interplay of a number of different factors, some of which are examined in section 14.3 in connection with the discussion of the linguistic situation of migrant workers in West Germany.

So the original dichotomy 'early'–'late' bilingualism should be taken only as a reflection of the *age* of the bilingual, i.e. whether the invididual becomes bilingual during childhood or as an adult. Late bilingualism may be the result either of L2 acquisition in a natural environment (e.g. the migrant worker from Turkey who takes up a job in Germany without any previous knowledge of German), or of second language learning, as with the person who has studied the L2 for years, using graded language-teaching materials, attending courses, etc. Thus, late bilingualism may be of the natural or the artificial kind, the primary or the secondary, the ascribed or the achieved type. On the other hand, early bilingualism will, in most cases, be the natural, ascribed sort, especially in the case of the pre-school child.

There are a number of differences between early and late bilingualism; some of them will be referred to in this section. The most basic difference lies in the nature of child language acquisition. When the child learns to speak, (s)he learns to use language as a means of expression, communication and social contact. The child acquires the formal aspects of a language, its sounds, words, meaning relationships, i.e. its grammar. But at the same time (s)he is also learning to use language as a tool for understanding and manipulating the world around her/him, i.e. (s)he is learning that (s)he needs language to form relationships with the people who surround her or him. In other words, language is an essential ingredient of the child's socialization process. First language acquisition thus differs from all subsequent language acquisition or learning in that the young child experiences language use, for the first time, in a social context, with the social consequences that this fact may entail; this is the case whether one or more languages are being acquired from birth. The learning processes involved in late bilingualism can draw on the social and communicative experiences gained in childhood. This represents a considerable, yet often underestimated, advantage enjoyed by the older learner. Language patterns and assumptions about linguistic usage which have been acquired in the mother tongue are likely to help the learner when coming into contact with a new code, as he/she will extend them by analogy – although the other side of the coin is that this habit may result in interference when the two systems diverge.

2.1.1 Is early bilingualism 'better' than late bilingualism?

There is a widespread belief that equates child bilingualism with 'true' bilingualism, and some specialists seem to adhere to this view. For example, Adler (1977: 13) says: 'One fact is clear: whether a person in his future life really masters two languages completely is decided in early childhood. When he does not learn the languages then he will never be completely perfect in both.' Two points need to be addressed here: one, the idea that the person 'will never be completely perfect in both'; the other is the assumption that children per se have better language learning abilities than adults.

With regard to the first point, it is unrealistic to suggest that the bilingual speaker achieves complete, 100 per cent mastery of two languages (ambilingualism). The total linguistic repertoire of a fluent bilingual consists of items from both languages which complement each other and may overlap to varying degrees (see Chapter 4). As far as the second point is concerned, it is not possible to find solid proof that children are better than adults at acquiring a second language. It is possible to get the impression that small children achieve fluency in a second language more quickly than older people, but this idea is not supported by hard evidence, simply because one is not comparing like with like. The apparent ease with which a child acquires a second language and the greater analytical abilities of the older learner are important factors which are simply not comparable.

Although we can establish that there is a fundamental difference between the processes involved in first language acquisition and subsequent language learning, this does not mean that the difference is of either a qualitative or a quantitative kind. The only exception may be pronunciation. Children are believed to have greater phonetic-auditory ability, which enables them to distinguish and reproduce new sounds quite easily, whereas adults may experience some degree of interference from their L1 (more about this later in the chapter).

2.1.2 The Language Acquisition Device (LAD) and the Critical Period Hypothesis

Two ideas taken from first language acquisition are relevant in this context. Both have had considerable influence on linguistic thinking and on the belief that children have better language learning abilities than adults. In 1959, in a famous review of the book *Verbal Behaviour*, by the psychologist B. F. Skinner, Chomsky expressed his conviction that children acquire language with amazing speed and efficiency, and that this cannot be accounted for ultimately in terms of stimulus and response, as suggested by Skinner, an exponent of the Behaviourist (or 'mechanistic') theory. Chomsky cites the example of the immigrant child who has no problems with the acquisition of his new country's language, whereas his parents struggle with it, learn less successfully and show strong signs of phonological and syntactic interference from their native tongue in their use of the second language. In the 1960s it became a main pillar of 'mentalist' theories of language acquisition to postulate that children are somehow specially pre-programmed, or predisposed from birth, to acquire language. The 'Language Acquisition Device' (LAD) was the expression used to refer to a hypothesized innate gearing towards language, which needed only to be activated to start functioning, i.e. the child just had to come into natural contact with a human language for the LAD to be set off.

Some research into psychological and neurological aspects of language appeared to back up the idea that there is a 'critical period' during which children are particularly adept at acquiring language (Penfield and Roberts 1959; Lenneberg 1967), which came to be known as the Critical Period Hypothesis. This period was supposed to last from about the second year to the age of puberty. There was said to be a biological link to the development of the brain's dominance of language function through lateralization, i.e. the specializing of one side of the brain (usually the left) in dealing with language. Before the age of two language acquisition is not possible, it was thought, because of maturational factors, and after puberty the brain loses its plasticity, i.e. is no longer particularly receptive for the task.

The suggestion of the critical period has been reviewed by a number of psycholinguists (see McLaughlin 1984 for a thorough account), and both the upper and lower age limits have been questioned. In the early 1970s it was suggested that lateralization might be complete long before adolescence (Harshman and Krashen 1972; Berlin et al. 1972), and possibly essentially complete at birth (Krashen 1975). Seliger (1978) proposed the idea of different critical periods for distinct abilities as a way of explaining why a number of aspects of language can be acquired at varying ages. The relationship between a presumed critical period and lateralization has not been satisfactority dealt with so far. The notion therefore remains very much a hypothesis (see also section 11.2).

It is possible, however, that there is a period during which a child has a special facility for neuro-muscular patterns, i.e. during which (s)he finds it particularly easy to acquire any pronunciation features.[2] There is some evidence (many of the authors of the case studies mentioned in section 2.4 later, for example, make this point) that supports the popular impression that children are good at acquiring a native-like accent in a second or foreign language, but the issue has by no means been established beyond doubt. What is generally accepted, though, is that children have certain qualities that favour second language acquisition: they make good mimics, they lack some of the inhibitions that get in the way of many adult language learners, and they have a greater capacity for learning by playing. All this can positively affect their fluency and pronunciation.

2.1.3 Children are not necessarily better bilinguals

Chomsky, as we have seen, was impressed by the apparent speed and efficiency with which children acquire language. But closer investigation of the issue, it has been noticed more recently, can produce a different impression, even the opposite one. If we suppose that the acquisition process starts at birth, as the infant is exposed to language from that moment, we can claim that children actually spend a long time hearing language, before they start using it actively at around the age of two. Furthermore, to say that language development is complete by the age of five or six is something of an exaggeration. On the other hand, the linguistic standards expected from a child are generally much lower and less sophisticated than what it is hoped any adult will produce. In fact, it can be maintained quite reasonably that it is the adult who appears to learn fast and to master quite a wide range of language uses in relatively little time, when one considers the time taken in first language acquisition. Observation of young language learners can also indicate that children are rather unsophisticated in their learning process, as they lack a number of skills which the older learner usually has, and which can facilitate (for the latter) transfer from one language to another: children do not normally perceive the similarities between languages, and they are unable to abstract, classify and generalize to the extent that adults can.

For some time there was support from certain academic fields for the idea that children's language aptitude is, in general, superior to that of older people. Perhaps as a consequence of this, and in analogy to such belief, there was a widely held view that children make better bilinguals than adults. But as no scientifically based evidence suggesting that there is a biological basis for a critical period has been put forward, we cannot say that children have an intrinsic language ability of a superior order, with the possible exception of a phonetic-auditory ability. The child may well be linguistically more adept with respect to the acquisition of the phonological system; and certain psychological factors (relating to favourable disposition towards mimicry, playfulness and lack of inhibiting barriers) may facilitate early fluency. But that is all that we are entitled to claim.

Apart from this possible advantage, then, children cannot be said to be better bilingual learners. What is more, adults possess a number of analytical skills that can stand them in good stead when learning a second language. In view of all this, the successful establishment of bilingualism may well depend on psychological factors (such as attitudes, motivation and willingness to identify with the speakers of the L2), rather than physiological or biological ones. If this is so, it will apply to children as well as adults.

2.2 How does the child become bilingual?

2.2.1 Some examples

The obvious answer to the question of how the child becomes bilingual is: by growing up in a bilingual environment. But what constitutes a bilingual environment? Why do some children appear to become bilingual almost spontaneously, while others seem to need extra help and encouragement? Grosjean (1982: 167ff) mentions the example of two children of the same age, who live in the same American city, both bilingual, but who have become so by very different routes. Ingrid, the daughter of an English-speaking American father and an Swedish mother, was brought up to speak the two languages from birth; both parents were professional people, they spoke their respective native languages to their daughter consistently and made conscious efforts to provide her with rich and varied linguistic stimuli. In the case of Swedish (i.e. the language which was not the one in everyday use around Ingrid outside the home) this meant books, cassettes and other material in Swedish and as much input as possible from Swedish-speaking friends and relatives. When Ingrid entered school she was a happy and bright child who was a fully functional bilingual.

The case of Dieudonné was quite different. When he was five he moved with his parents to the United States. He spoke Haitian Creole, and after their arrival his family continued to speak this language to him. Since both parents went out to work, Dieudonné spent a good deal of time with his brothers and sisters, or playing with other children, many of them Puerto Rican, Black American and Haitian, and he picked up some English from them (and other English-speaking friends) and from television programmes, but not enough to be placed in a mainstream class when he started to attend school. He joined, together with other minority children, a programme in which English was taught as a second language, and he experienced many problems there, as he was unhappy and withdrawn and was said to be making little progress. After a frustrating period he was transferred to a school where he was taught in Creole, and where the other children also used this language. English was introduced slowly, and then progressively used as the medium of instruction. Eventually he went on to mainstream American education, his bilingualism having been firmly established.

Graciela is a recent acquaintance of mine. She is Spanish, lives in Madrid and is about to start at university. Her mother speaks Spanish only. Her father was born and grew up in Catalonia, speaking both Catalan and Spanish. Although he does not use Catalan with his children, the family spend most of their holidays in a Catalan-speaking environment in which some of the relatives insist on addressing everyone in Catalan only; so Graciela has, over the years, gained enough understanding of spoken Catalan to be able to converse fluently, understand TV programmes and generally cover her needs in this language, although she does not write it and prefers reading books, newspapers and magazines written in Spanish. For her entire schooling Graciela has attended an English school in Madrid. Almost all the staff are native speakers of English, and for most of her time there, particularly in the lower school, English was used as the medium of instruction, although the children would use Spanish among themselves and either English or (some of the time, when in the upper school) Spanish with the teachers. Graciela has no problem understanding spoken or written English, she can write it quite well and is able to speak it with confidence, although she does not sound like a native speaker as she lacks this kind of fluency and her pronunciation is not faultless.

There are many children in the world who, like Ingrid, Dieudonné and Graciela, have become bilingual, or even trilingual, at some earlier or later stage of their childhood, some under more favourable circumstances than others. Clearly, there can be a multitude of different ways in which children may achieve bilingualism. A number of them have been studied in some detail, as we shall see later, others have been described in books written by parents or linguists (sometimes both coinciding in the same person) and published as 'guides' or 'handbooks' for interested lay persons, parents, teachers and others involved in the care of bilingual children (e.g. Saunders 1982; Kielhöfer and Jonekeit 1983; de Jong 1986; Harding and Riley 1986; Arnberg 1987.[3]

2.2.2 Bilingual patterns

The ways in which children can become bilingual, and their bilingualism be maintained, vary a great deal from one family or individual case to another. In this section some commonly found patterns are outlined.

(1) *Immigration* Immigration involves leaving the country of origin in order to settle, once and for all, in a 'host' country. Nations like the United States and Canada have, over the centuries, seen large numbers of immigrants entering their territories. Britain, France, Belgium and the Netherlands have also seen considerable quantities of immigrants settling in their lands, after the emancipation of their colonies. The children of immigrants usually acquired their first language at home,

from their parents and family, and their second, that of their new country of residence, from people outside the home. In the majority of cases there was no special provision made for them when they entered school, so they had to 'sink or swim' as best they could. In most countries immigrants were expected by public opinion to 'assimilate' (i.e. adapt to the norms and customs of the host country) as quickly as possible, and this of course included linguistic assimilation. The result usually was that, for many generations of immigrants, bilingualism was a transitory stage, lasting only a limited number of years:

First generation	Second generation	Third generation	Fourth generation
LA + LB	LA and LB	+LA, LB	LB

(+ = 'some'; LA = Language A; LB = Language B)

(2) *Migration* Many western European countries experienced large-scale migration in the three decades after the Second World War, as people moved across frontiers in search of work and better living conditions. In some cases they took their families with them from the outset or sent for them later, in others they found partners from the host country or from other ethnic groups. The children of migrants may grow up hearing the language of their parents only, if they live in a community composed mainly of migrants of homogeneous origin, and their contact with the second language may not begin in earnest until they are of school age. Their experiences may be similar to those of the child mentioned above, Dieudonné. On the other hand, they may mix to a larger extent with the children of the host country, go to a kindergarten or playgroup where the local language is used – or they may learn it from one of their parents. In other words, whether second-generation migrant children become bilingual or not depends very much on family circumstances and the surrounding social conditions that affect them. Migration is seen as involving temporary movement only, i.e. an eventual return to the country of origin is contemplated. For migrants it is therefore important to maintain their language, but by the same token the host country may feel relieved of any obligation to make special educational provision for their children, with respect to both distinct second language programmes and mother-tongue teaching.[4] The ways in which these children become bilingual, if at all, are

more unpredictable than in the case of immigrants.

Lewis (1972), in his interesting account of multilingualism in the Soviet Union, includes a discussion of the development of what the author calls 'mass' or 'popular' bilingualism. Movement of people from one Republic to another and consequent inter-ethnic marriage are apparently quite common in the USSR, and many children become bilingual as a result. Another way of becoming bilingual in the USSR is through the school system, as educational planning includes a provision for the teaching of, and in, Russian at school in non-Russian-speaking areas. Many Soviet children may, therefore, acquire either one or two languages at home (from their parents), and another language during their schooling.[5]

(3) *Close contact with other linguistic groups* In some multinational states or countries with rich linguistic diversity, contact between members of different language groups is quite common. It may be brought about by urbanization or by internal migration, and bilingualism is likely to be found among children as well as adults. The children may have parents or other family members who speak different languages, or they may hear one language at home and another one outside it. In Europe this kind of scenario is usually found among minorities (e.g. in Wales, the Basque Country, South Tyrol or Friesland). This element of dominant majority and subordinate minority, however, is absent in Mkilifi's (1978) analysis of the language situation in Tanzania. Many of the children he studied had, before entering school, acquired Swahili, in addition to the local language, in part from the father (usually from him, as the men tend to have more outside contacts through their work, and therefore usually know Swahili better than the women) and partly from other members of their community who would frequently use it as the means for wider communication. Mkilifi reports that bilingualism is a widespread and natural outcome in these circumstances, and that the children he observed were often not even aware that they spoke two different languages.

(4) *Schooling* Nowadays education can play a very important role in making children bilingual. The educational system may deliberately be geared towards fostering bilingualism, as is the case, for instance, with the French immersion courses in Canadian schools, designed for children from the English-speaking majority, and also, increasingly, with Catalan courses for Spanish-speaking children in Catalonia. Another

example is the compulsory use of a second language as a medium of instruction at the level of secondary education (or earlier, in some parts) in the USSR, where, as Lewis (1972) points out, three important linguistic changes have been brought about since the introduction of universal education: first, the development of mass bilingualism, whereas previously there was only a limited amount; second, the fact that this so-called 'popular' bilingualism is now of a literate nature, while formerly it was mainly oral; and third, that becoming bilingual is now an option open to the vast majority of Soviet children and no longer the prerogative of an élite.

The various International Schools, the European School (as discussed, for example, in Baetens Beardsmore 1979; 1980), and the American, English, French, German and Spanish schools in a number of European and other countries, also contribute towards establishing bilingualism, as does the practice of having one's children educated in a different country, e.g. German or Spanish parents sending their children to a British boarding school, in the western European context. The numbers involved under this last heading are not very significant, as these schools are accessible only to the children of highly mobile and well-off families. It is clear, therefore, that in such cases we are, in fact, talking about élite bilingualism (see section 2.3).

Only a few European minorities have obtained the right and the necessary financial provision to have their children educated through the medium of the minority language, even though it is quite clear that without such support a large number of minority languages are likely soon to be lost. The Welsh had to wait until the late 1960s to see the establishment of the first Welsh-medium schools. Some would argue that too little has happened too late for the decline of the Welsh language to be halted. Schooling in the non-mainstream language can assume paramount importance for the survival of a linguistic monority. In a perceptive study of the German minority in Denmark, Michael Byram (1986b) shows that the role of the German school goes far beyond the provision of a German education for its pupils and a focal point for the community: 'Although at first sight the minority is 'German' because of the language and culture it possesses, more careful observation suggests that the existence of the minority depends on its schools.' (Byram 1986b: xii).

More often than not, at any rate in western Europe, the education system reflects the one-state-one-language principle followed for a long time by many countries. Children from linguistic minorities are treated in the same way as those belonging to the majority group, which means that no provision is made with regard to their special linguistic needs. In the past many schools in Europe have pursued strict anti-minority policies, even to the extent of punishing or ridiculing children who used the minority language at school. The repressive methods employed in places such as Gaelic-speaking Scotland, Wales, Brittany, Catalonia and Galicia (in north-west Spain) were remarkably similar and, sadly, usually just as effective. Because there was no support for the minority language, children had to acquire the language of the majority as well as they could under difficult circumstances. What bilingualism existed was often of a transitory nature, and the shift towards the majority language took only one or two generations. Today we see less overt oppression of linguistic minorities. In the most favourable cases the schools offer some kind of programmes in the child's mother tongue (as happened with Dieudonné), or there are special classes to help children learn the second language before they join the main body of the education system, e.g. ESL (English as a Second Language) provision in the UK or 'Deutsch als Zweitsprache' classes for migrants' children offered in some states of the German Federal Republic. There are also certain private schemes which aim at teaching minority languages to children already in mainstream education, for instance in the Scandinavian countries, Germany, France and Britain. But, as participation is voluntary, their success must depend on such factors as motivation, resources and length of attendance.

(5) *Growing up in a bilingual family* At the family level there are many different strategies to choose from for bringing children up bilingually. Many of the children observed in the case studies listed below (see 2.4) came from families where one parent spoke the language of the wider community and the other parent a 'foreign' language. This was the case of Danny, a Swedish–English bilingual, the father being Swedish, the mother American, living in Sweden; or of Lisa and Giulia, Italian–German bilinguals, whose father is Italian and mother German-speaking, who live in Italy. In such families the one-parent-one-language principle was adopted and bilingualism established. The degree of success will depend mainly on such factors as whether the parents are consistent in their language use, whether the child has enough exposure to the 'home-only' language, whether (s)he perceives the need to use both languages, and whether (s)he receives the right kind and amount of social support. Providing the first two

conditions, consistency and exposure, are met, the establishment of bilingualism is not usually problematic. However, the *maintenance* of the 'home-only' language, at an early age as well as later, is much less certain. Some children may not see much point in using the language of one parent, once they realize that he or she also speaks the language of the other. This happens quite often, particularly when the latter is also the language of the society where the family lives. When the child is older the input from the weaker language may be too one-sided, too limited in register and style (when compared with the rich stimulus in the outside language, which is of course also used at school) for the two languages to develop on the same level. In fact, judging from parents' accounts (and my own experience), bringing children up bilingually requires considerable effort, expense and ingenuity. There are many families who cannot afford such luxuries as frequent visits abroad or the purchase of books, cassettes, videos and films, quite apart from the time needed to use these with the children.

In those families where a minority language is spoken by one or both of the parents, the aim may be either to introduce the two languages to the child from birth, or to begin with the majority language after the minority one has been established at home but before the child starts school (where the latter will be used). The successful development of bilingualism will depend on the same considerations as before: exposure, consistency, perceived need and social support from both majority and minority communities. But social support is likely to assume increased importance. Whether the attitudes of the majority towards the minority (and vice versa) are positive or negative, and whether the knowledge of the minority language is considered an asset or not will be very influential factors.

Not all families opt for a consistent pattern of language use; nor do they always adhere to the one-parent-one-language principle. The parents, and other family members, may use both languages; they may apply, perhaps inconsistently, practices such as one parent using one language when alone with the child and the other when other family members are present; or they may follow no specific pattern at any time. For the establishment of bilingualism this kind of strategy tends to be less successful, as then the choice of using a particular language at any given time will depend on arbitrary factors, and the child may find this confusing. If this happens, the majority language may soon become the dominant one, and the incidence of mixed language output is likely to be high.

There are many possible answers to the question of how children become bilingual; only a small proportion of them have been mentioned here. Individual family circumstances, as well as those prevailing in the wider community, may decide whether, and to what extent, a child becomes and stays bilingual, and a number of psychological, social and educational determinants will come into play also (see further discussion of this in Chapters 6 and 7).

2.3   Types of bilinguals

Skutnabb-Kangas (1984a) suggests a classification of the world's bilinguals into four groups. In drawing distinctions between these four categories she takes the following factors into account:

(a)   pressure to become bilingual;
(b)   the prerequisites for bilingualism;
(c)   route by which the individual has become bilingual;
(d)   the consequences entailed in failing to become bilingual.

She identifies the groups as follows:

(1) *Élite bilinguals* These are people who have freely chosen to become so (e.g. because they want to work or study abroad), and children who belong to families who change their country of residence relatively often and/or who are sent to be educated abroad. In these cases, the normal situation is that the acquisition of both languages proceeds unhindered, with the two languages receiving wide social support and the mother tongue, in particular, enjoying a firm and stable position. The second language may have been either learnt or acquired but, as the attempt to establish it firmly will have been quite voluntary, failure to gain sufficient command of it (if failure there is) will carry no serious consequences for the subject. Children who live temporarily in a different linguistic environment may feel a greater need to learn the language of the host country in order to make social contacts or be able to follow the school curriculum. Their attempt to make progress in the L2 will usually be met at the very least with friendly approval, and they will confidently expect that one day they will return to the country of their mother tongue.

(2) *Children from linguistic majorities* These are children who learn another language (e.g. that of a minority group) at school, such as in

immersion programmes or in foreign language classes. The learning of the second language may, for example, be considered advantageous either because it is seen as a way of enhancing the prestige of the minority language (as with French in Canada) or because it is believed to be of wider educational or vocational benefit (for instance, English as a foreign language in the Netherlands or in many other countries). Usually majority children experience little or no pressure (from family or society) to become bilingual; a variety of well-prepared materials, designed especially for them, will facilitate the learning; and the risk involved in failing to achieve the learning objectives tends to be relatively small.

The children from these two groups tend to come from monolingual backgrounds, in contrast with the following two.

(3) *Children from bilingual families* These are children whose parents have different mother tongues. The child will experience considerable societal pressure to become fluent in the official language, but there will be no external compulsion to become bilingual. Bilingualism will be desirable because (and to the extent that) there are internal family pressures requiring the child to communicate in the language of the parent(s). The emotional relationship between the child(ren) and the parent(s) may suffer somewhat if bilingualism does not develop. But for the child's educational success and complete social integration the only important thing, ultimately, is that (s)he acquires the language of the country. So the consequences of failure to become bilingual may possibly be problematic within the family, but not too serious at the societal level.

(4) *Children from linguistic minorities* These children have parents who belong to a linguistic minority; they are under intense external pressure to learn the language of the majority, particularly if the language of the minority is not officially recognized. Yet there may be little support offered to them in terms of bilingual education programmes or primary/secondary school teaching. They often find themselves also under the influence of strong internal forces that encourage them to learn the language of their parents and to form social relationships with the members of the wider (minority) group. The risk of failing in the attempt to become bilingual is greater than for any of the above groups. As Skutnabb-Kangas says, the effects of lack of success in attaining bilingualism may be catastrophic, ranging from loss of

educational and future opportunities to problems of rootlessness and alienation.

2.4 Case studies of bilingual children

Much of what is known today about bilingual language development is based on the findings presented in case studies; some of them are listed below. Of these, a few are quite well known, above all perhaps the work of the German-born linguist Leopold, who lived in the United States and studied in detail the English–German bilingual development of his daughters Hildegard and (later) Karla over a period of some ten years. His diary entries and analyses have become a standard work of reference for any student of child language development, not just bilingual development. A number of these case studies are reviewed by McLaughlin (1984: 88) and Skutnabb-Kangas (1984a: 146–9).

In many cases the children studied are the linguists' own. In terms of the prevailing socio-economic background, one imagines that these children could be classed as élite bilinguals, as they all received a good deal of support from inside, and more often than not also from outside, the family. Thus becoming bilingual was not absolutely essential for them. Tabouret-Keller is an exception: he studied a French/Alsatian-speaking child with working-class parents. Some of the purely linguistic observations made in these case studies can be taken to be applicable to children from a wider range of backgrounds. But generalizations about the psychological, social and educational factors concerning the establishment of bilingualism should be made with a great deal of caution.

Quite often these studies make fascinating reading, as they provide a wealth of linguistic and other detail, and also many insights about the cognitive development and family life of the bilingual child. They are usually based on carefully planned and well-conducted surveys or collections of diary entries and recorded data, sometimes supplemented by anecdotal evidence. There is even the case of the linguist who reports on his own bilingualism (Elwert 1973). However, all such studies should be approached as critically as possible, because they may suffer from certain shortcomings.

Before cassette and video recorders were available, data had to be transcribed or taken down in longhand. Problems of reliability have not been totally solved by technology. We can now record children's speech, but unless the material is transcribed (itself an extremely time-consuming exercise) very soon afterwards, it may be quite unintelligible for the researcher at some later stage. Adults may be very good at understanding what children mean when they experience it in a communicative situation, but if it is taken out of its context vital clues can easily be lost. A less obvious drawback is that data might be restricted to one or two children, often the eldest child in the family, so the findings may have less bearing on bilingual development among the younger siblings or on the question of differences across several children within the same group. A further issue, in particular with respect to some of the earlier case studies, is that they tried to cover a large number of developmental aspects in a relatively short period. The more recent studies include a greater amount of detail, and they provide information not only on the acquisition of the linguistic systems but also on such aspects as general communication ability, biliteracy and attitudes (e.g. Saunders 1982a; Taeschner 1983; Fantini 1985). We are just beginning to see the emergence of longer-term studies, extending over the whole of infancy and childhood (for instance, Saunders 1988, which was a study of developing bilingualism up to adolescence). This is an important step forward, as little is yet known about such issues as how older children maintain their bilingualism, what effect school has on it, whether biliteracy is attempted, and with what result, etc.

Another welcome development is the initiation of research projects involving the bilingual development of several children (e.g. Redlinger and Park 1980; Oksaar 1980; Meisel 1984; Kutsch and Desgranges 1985).[6] This kind of research allows comparisons between children, and also across languages, under more controlled conditions, which makes it likely that the results will be more reliable. It is, of course, possible to draw comparisons between the various case studies. Some attempt at this is included in the discussion of patterns of bilingual language acquisition (Chapter 3). But one must not lose sight of the (perhaps severe) limitations on validity imposed by the facts that a large number of uncontrollable variables are involved in individual longitudinal case studies and that many of these variables (e.g. those relating to language input) have not been acknowledged or considered. In addition, no two studies have applied the same types of tests to measure the degree of bilingualism or of relative competence in each language involved. Perhaps these disadvantages can be avoided to some extent in the newer kind of studies. Another advantage of the latter is that they allow the team of researchers to look at specific aspects of bilingual acquisition, such as language differentiation, code-switching or the acquisition of particular syntactic elements such as negation or word order. Perhaps these studies, and others, possibly of a less longitudinal nature, involving groups of children, will eventually throw some light on questions about which at the moment we know little for certain: e.g. why some children are more successful than others in the same family in becoming bilingual, or whether there are crucial moments or stages in their linguistic and cognitive development at which certain things should, or should not, happen.

TABLE 2.1 Some long-term studies of simultaneous language acquisition in bilingual children

Author and date	Languages	Age at time of study	Concerns of study	Number of children
Ronjat (1913)	French/German	first 5 yrs	P, Se, I	1
Pavlovitch (1920)	French/Serbian	first 2 yrs	P, Se, E, I, Mix	1
Hoyer and Hoyer (1924)	Russian/German	first 12 months	B	1
Smith (1935)	English/Chinese	first 4 yrs	Se, I, Mix	8
Emrich (1938)	German/Bulgarian	first 3 yrs	I	1
Leopold* (1939, 1947, 1949a, 1949b)	English/German	first 2 yrs (and 2 to 12)	B, F, Se, DS, Si, M, OP, E, I	2
Burling (1959)	English/Garo	1:4 to 2:10	P, Se, S, M, I, Mix	1

Author and date	Languages	Age at time of study	Concerns of study	Number of children
Tabouret-Keller (1962)	French/Alsatian	1:8 to 2:11	Se, I	1
Raffler-Engel (1965)	English/ Italian	first 4 yrs	P, Se, M, I	1
Murrell (1966)	Swedish/Finnish/ English	2:0 to 2:8	F, Se, DS, S M, I, WO, I, Mix	1
Imedadze (1960, 1967)	Russian/Georgian	0:11 to 3:0	Se, E, S, M DS, I	1
Rūķe-Draviņa (1967)	Swedish/Latvian	first 6 yrs	P, Se, DS, I, Mix	2
Mikeš (1967)	Hungarian/Serbo-Croat	first 6 yrs	S, M, DS, I, Mix	3
Oksaar (1970)	Swedish/Estonian	0:2 to 3:0	F, Se, E, S M, I, Mix	1
Swain[$] (1972)	French/English	2:4 to 4:0	S, M, DS, I	1
Volterra and Taeschner (1978)	Italian/German	1:0 to 3:0	Se, E, S, M, I	2
Itoh and Hatch[+] (1978)	Japanese/English	2:6 to 3:1	Pe, Se, S, M, I, Mix	1
Celce-Murcia (1978)	French/English	2:4	P, Se, S, M, I, Mix	1
Redlinger & Park[+] (1980)	German/Spanish German/English German/French	2-3 yrs (for 5-8 months)	Se, M, I, Mix	4
Arnberg (1981)	Swedish/English	first 5 yrs	M. LL	4

Author and date	Languages	Age at time of study	Concerns of study	Number of children
Cunze (1980)	German/Italian	first 5 and a half yrs	M, S, DS	1
Vihman (1982)	English/Estonian	1:1 to 2:10	P, Se, S, M, I. Mix	1
Saunders* (1982a, 1988)	English/German	first 13 yrs	M, S, WO, I	2
Taeschner* (1983)	German/Italian	first 8 yrs	P, Se, S, M, WO, DS, I	2
Fantini* (1985)	English/Spanish	first 11 yrs	P, S, M, WO, Mix	1
Vila (1984)	Catalan/Spanish	1:2 to 3:2	Se, E, DS	3
Hoffmann (1985)	English/German/ Spanish	first 8 yrs	P, S, M, DS, I, Mix	2
Meisel + (1984, 1987)	German/French	1:0 to 4:0	M, S, WO, I	2
De Houwer* (1990)	English/Dutch	2:7 to 3:4	M, S	1
Stavans§ (1990)	English/Spanish/ Hebrew	5.5 to 6.11 and 2.6 to 4.0	C	2

Notes

$ unpublished PhD thesis (entitled 'Bilingualism as a First Language')
+ these studies are cross-sectional rather than longitudinal
* studies that have been published in book form
§ unpublished PhD thesis

Key

B = babbling	P = phonology	M = morphology
S = syntax	Se = semantics	I = interference
DS = developmental sequence		WO = word order
LL = language loss	E = extension of meaning	C = code-switching

Ayse Öktem and Jochen Rehbein, of the Centre for Research into Multilingualism at Hamburg University, West Germany, have compiled a useful annotated bibliography of child bilingualism. They list over seventy longitudinal and cross-sectional studies of bilingual children and include a bibliography consisting of some 550 entries. It was published in 1987.

Notes

1. Incidentally, the term often used by German scholars, 'ungesteuerter Zweitsprachenerwerb', is more explicit than 'second language acquisition', as it includes reference to the unstructured, untutored nature of the language acquisition process in these cases. The English convention is to use 'acquisition' in the context of first language development and 'learning' for the addition of a second, or third, etc., language in adolescence or adulthood as a result of a conscious learning effort.

2. On the other hand, language teachers can quote many examples of adults who have had complete success in mastering a new language fully, inclusive of its pronunciation system, just as there are many immigrants about whom the same can be said. It might be relevant to ask by whose standards the pronunciation is considered to be 'perfect' – the phoneticians', the language teachers' (or some of them), the native speakers'? And what criteria would one apply in judging a 'native' accent – impressionistic comparability with the (very well) educated person's accent, the possibility of taking the person for an ordinary native speaker purely on the basis of the accent (in these cases, who would be a reliable judge?), or some other basis?

3. From 1983 onwards a *Bilingual Family Newsletter*, for bilingual families throughout the world, has been published by Multilingual

Matters, a British publishing firm, edited by the Australian, George
Saunders, with the aim of supporting bilingualism within the family
and enlightening the non-specialist on matters bilingual.

4. As a result of EC legislation, as well as individual and national
   initiatives, the situation in western Europe is undergoing certain
   changes. Many countries now offer mother-tongue programmes
   and/or special instruction in the school language, so as to enable
   non-native children to be integrated into state mainstream education.
   However, there are vast discrepancies in the resources allocated for
   these children's education among EC members, and hardly any
   commonly agreed policies so far.

5. Enforced mass bilingualism has great administrative advantages for
   a multinational state such as the USSR. However, it is also a potential liability. When the people involved see their national identity
   and language threatened as a result of one-sided policies they may
   withdraw their support for the system, or even rebel against it, as
   events in the late 1980s in the Baltic states, Armenia, the Ukraine
   and Belorussia, have shown.

6. The studies by Redlinger and Park concern children who were bilingual in different languages, although they all shared German.
   Those by Meisel relate to French-German bilinguals (this is an on-
   going project which so far has reported findings on language
   differentiation and the acquisition of case markers and word order).
   The children described by Oksaar were bi-, tri- and quadrilingual in
   German, Swedish, English and Estonian, and they lived in Germany, Sweden and Australia; twenty-one children from different
   social backgrounds were involved. Kutsch and Desgranges report on
   a longitudinal study of some thirty Turkish children acquiring German.

Chapter 3

Patterns of bilingual language acquisition

3.1 The description of bilingual language acquisition

This chapter aims at presenting a general overview of the ways in which children can acquire two (or more) languages. The data mentioned here are taken from some of the studies listed in Chapter 2. In virtually all cases the children studied acquired their languages simultaneously from birth. But those children who acquired more than two languages (e.g. Oksaar 1970; Murrell 1966; Hoffmann 1985) were not necessarily infant bilinguals in all their languages. For instance, my daughter Cristina had already started to speak Spanish and German when she came into contact with English at the age of two and a half. Her brother, three years younger, did hear English spoken around him (e.g. from TV, radio, his sister's friends) from birth, although English was not spoken in the home by any of the family members. So Cristina could be classed 'infant bilingual' in Spanish and German and 'child bilingual' with respect to English, whereas in Pascual's case the distinction is less clear-cut; one might call him an 'infant trilingual', although the development of his three languages did not proceed in a parallel fashion. It is quite clear that the individual circumstances of bilingual language acquisition must be at least slightly different in the case of almost every infant/child bilingual/trilingual, and that many of them will not fit perfectly into any descriptive category.

The description of bilingual acquisition outlined here follows the sequence of child language development only loosely. In the one-word (or holophrastic) stage one can already observe features of the developing phonological and lexico-semantic systems. As the child's utterances increase in length and complexity, it becomes possible to observe the emerging syntax and the ways in which (s)he differentiates the two codes and keeps them separate. Phonological and lexical development will be discussed here before dealing with the acquisition of morphology and grammar. However, this should not give the impression that language development necessarily follows a linear progression. Language operates on two levels, so that meaningless units of sound combine together to form units of grammar (morphology and syntax) which have meaning. Learning to speak thus involves the simultaneous activation, and evolution, of a number of different processes.

3.2 Phonological development

From the more recent research into first language acquisition we know that a child's receptive language skills begin to develop in very early infancy – hence the recommendation that bilingual upbringing should start from birth. The newborn baby reacts differently to human and non-human sounds, and it soon begins to distinguish pitch and stress features. The recognition of features such as vowel length and quality, or friction, plosion and nasality, require an analytical ability which operates regardless of the specific language input. Similarly, the process involved in producing the first speech sounds in the child's holophrastic stage largely follows the same route in bilinguals as in monolinguals. Fantini (1985) reports numerous entries in the diary he kept on his son Mario's Spanish development, which illustrate early recognition and differentiation of sounds. At the age of 0:4 (four months) the boy is said to have been able to recognize his parents' voices, and by age one he was producing sounds which followed familiar intonational patterns, even if the sounds themselves were meaningless. When he was 1:10, at a party surrounded by people all unknown to him, he apparently responded enthusiastically to those who addressed him in Spanish, while consistently ignoring those who spoke English to him (at that time he had had virtually no contact with the latter language).

Jakobson's theory (1941) of the child's sound system developing phonemically by a series of binary splits was readily accepted by a number of psycholinguists. Leopold (1947), in the second of his four volumes on bilingual language acquisition, discusses the emergence of his daughter Hildegard's sound system during her first two years. He looked at his data from the point of view of Jakobson's theory of contrasts, and he found that it worked relatively well, although it did not match in all details. One of the most interesting points of this early piece of research is perhaps Leopold's claim that the sound system develops phonemically rather than phonetically (i.e. by building up meaningful units of sound, or phonemes, rather than a succession of sounds as they come), and that sound substitutions, far from being random, follow a systematic pattern.

Whereas the bilingual's processing of the sound system follows the same pattern as that of the monolingual speaker, the task involved is obviously made more complex because two sound systems are involved. A larger number of features have to be recognized and produced, and this bigger cognitive load may well lead to a later onset of speech production or even an initial period of some confusion. Thus, for instance, Burling (1959) observed that his son Stephen's English sound system developed later than his Garo phonological system (he had more exposure to the Garo language than to English); at the age of 2:9 separation of the English and Garo vowel systems seemed to occur, but the consonant systems never became really differentiated, Garo consonants replacing English ones; the latter emerged properly only when, at age 3:6, contact with Garo ceased (as the family returned from the Garo Hills, in Assam, India, to the United States).

However, the absence of sound confusion has been remarked upon more often than its presence. Already Ronjat (1913), one of the earliest observers of bilingual language development this century, stated that his son Louis realized the phonemes of German and French correctly when he was 3:5, and that he would give the appropriate phonetic shape to the loan words he used. More recently, Oksaar (1970), whose son Sven acquired Swedish and Estonian (and later German as third language), noted that there was no confusion of the sound systems. As an example she describes her son's mastery of the prosodic feature of length, which is a prominent characteristic of Estonian (but not Swedish) vowels and consonants. The child had acquired the three different degrees of length before internalizing all the segments of Estonian, and he never used Estonian length features when speaking Swedish. Similarly, Raffler-Engel (1965) reported no confusion with respect to sound in her son's English and Italian, although there was a certain amount of mixing in the morphology of both; she interpreted this dichotomy between phonology and morphology/syntax in the child's speech as a clear reflection of the duality of structure, a well-known basic characteristic of language: it is maintained that language is not organized monolithically, but on two different levels – the phonetic/phonological and the morphosyntactic.

In connection with this last point McLaughlin (1984) refers to the theories implicit in the so-called 'Critical Period' hypothesis (see section 2.1.2). As is generally known, linguists of the Transformational Generative school proposed the view that the child has a special capacity for language that the adult has lost. After reviewing the literature on the hypothesis, McLaughlin concludes that there is no clear evidence as to how long the critical period lasts or how it relates to lateralization of language function: in other words, we cannot prove anything about the nature of the relationship that may exist between the specialization of the human brain, on one hand, and the ending of its special capacity for acquiring language, on the other. With regard to language functions, many scholars would say nowadays that there is more flexibility than was previously supposed, and that the functions relating to the neuromuscular patterns involved in speech (i.e. the production of speech sounds and prosodic features) may operate quite independently from other language skills. Authors on child language acquisition also emphasize the relative importance of social and cultural factors over the purely biological ones.

The Critical Period hypothesis seems more convincing when applied only to motor aspects of language acquisition. There is a quite considerable body of conclusions based on research on second language acquisition and second/foreign language learning which shows that younger learners are better at acquiring a native-like accent than older ones. But there are also those who argue that, given proper instruction, a favourable learning environment and the right psychological attitude, older learners, too, are able to achieve native-like control of the pronunciation of a second language.

With regard to the phonological development of bilingual children, it seems that the two systems are largely acquired separately. During this process the child may adopt certain strategies, such as substitution or avoidance of certain features, just as monolinguals do. Rūķe-Dravi-ņa (1965; 1967) observed her two children learning languages with different r-sounds: Latvian, which has an apical roll /r/, and Swedish (or, rather, a southern Sweden variety with an uvular roll /R/, similar to the German). She found that the uvular roll was acquired before the apical one had been properly mastered, and that the former tended to be used in both languages. The same phenomenon occurred in my daughter's speech for a while (Hoffmann 1985). She initially acquired

Spanish and German, languages in which there is an apical and an uvular roll respectively. By the age of three she had internalized both phonological systems with the exception of the Spanish /r/ and some German and Spanish consonant clusters, notably those involving the uvular and apical roll. At the beginning the /R/ replaced the Spanish /r/ in initial position, e.g. in *rojo*, which she pronounced, for a time, as [Róxo]; I was able to observe only one instance of substitution of /r/ – by an unaspirated /t/ (in the name 'Mary', which she pronounced [méti]. In syllable-final position /r/ was avoided, e.g. *mi hermano* was realized as [mi eɐmáno], so that the /r/ appeared to have been displaced by a dark schwa, which does occur in German in this position. In consonant clusters /r/ was omitted for some time, e.g. *padre* [paðe] *fruta* [fúta], etc., just as some monolingual Spanish children do; but in Cristina this period of non-production was probably longer. Certainly, it was much shorter in the case of her younger brother, so that perhaps it may have been an individual difference, without linguistic significance. Cristina did not add the phoneme /r/ to her repertoire until after the equivalent clusters had been acquired in German, i.e. *drei* had changed from [dai] to [dRai], *Frosch* from [fɔʃ] to [fRɔʃ], etc. Another example of simplification strategy was provided by my son, who for some time (starting at 1:9) referred to both a frog and a duck by the onomatopoeic 'quack-quack', which he pronounced [βa'βak]. He replaced this difficult sequence (Spanish *cuác* [kwák] or German *quack* [kvák], i.e. a voiceless velar plosive followed by either a semivowel [kw], or a voiced labiodental fricative [kv]) by a voiced bilabial fricative [β], a sound that occurs neither in German (anywhere) nor in Spanish (in initial position). Compared with his sister's general phonetic development, his progression was rather slow, since his acquisition of sounds lasted well into his fourth year (a third language, English, having been added to his regular exposure by then). The features of simplification, particularly of replacing consonant clusters by single consonants, was very noticeable in Pascual, and also the fact that he used sequences of sounds which did not appear (either at all or in the positions in which he used them) in any of the languages he was acquiring. (Both children, at the time of writing aged thirteen and ten, pronounce their three languages without traces of the phonetic peculiarities that characterized their earlier acquisition stages.)

Apart from some initial mixing and some 'blends' (forms made up of two languages, with one phonetic shape used in either language – see Vihman and McLaughlin 1982; Grosjean 1982: 184 gives the example 'shot' as a blend of French 'chaud' and English 'hot', from a two-year-old English–French bilingual), bilingual children acquire the language system of each language side by side and seem to develop a feeling for their distinctiveness. This is borne out by observations that bilingual children will borrow words from one language and use them in the other after giving them the appropriate phonetic shape. But the extent to which children keep the two systems apart depends, possibly, on linguistic factors, and certainly on environmental ones. It has been argued, e.g. by Rūķe-Draviņa (1965; 1967) and Hoffmann (1985) that interference will be the more likely the closer the languages involved are in their phonological and morphological characteristics, intonation features being the first to be affected. Métraux, in her 1965 study of English–French bilingual children, comments on the importance of playmates and friends in counteracting the influence of accent inter-ference. My own observations would appear to confirm this. In children, to a greater extent than in adults, prolonged absences from a particular speech community result in loss of fluency of intonation. But once contact with the spoken language, especially that of other child-ren, has been renewed, an enriched repertoire of stress, rhythm and intonation features can be noticed, as well as the ability to apply subtle variations (e.g. in role-play and story telling). It stands to reason that one must recognize the need for varied and continued language input. If one of the languages the child is exposed to dominates considerably over the other, then the subordinate language is likely to be affected by it at the phonological level as well as all others. And if exposure to one language ceases, it will not be long before that language disappears from the child – in the case of Burling's son (1959) it was a matter of only some six months; Murrell's daughter (1966), who was born in Helsinki, began with three languages around her, but exposure to Fin-nish was irregular and it ceased at 2:1, so the little of this language that she had acquired vanished in some four months.

3.3　Semantic and lexical development

3.3.1　General acquisition processes

The cognitive processes which underlie the development of the meaning system are essentially dependent on the intellectual maturity of the individual child, and they are basically the same for all children, irrespective of whether they are acquiring one language or growing up as bilingual speakers. The task involved is to attach phonetic forms to referents (objects, events, activities, sensations, etc.) and to abstract concepts so that, for instance, not only all creatures with ears, a tail, four legs, covered in fur and making certain kinds of noises are 'dogs', whatever the length of the ears or tails or their vociferousness, but also representations of them in plastic, soft material or books, just as the family pet who is generally referred to as 'Fido' is a dog, too. The young child's first utterances resembling adult speech consist of words, or 'holophrases', and they may have several meanings and functions. 'Teddy' may be used to refer to all kinds of cuddly toys, just as it may be uttered with the meanings 'Here's a/my teddy', 'I want my teddy', 'Where's Teddy?' or even 'I want to sleep' (the teddy being associated with sleeping because it is taken to bed).

Overextension of meaning is very common in young children. By referring to all moving machines (lorries, cars and airplanes) as [i:júm] Pascual at 1:9 concentrated on the characteristics of movement and noise, disregarding features such as shape or size. The above-mentioned example of [βa'βak] is another instance. De Villiers and De Villiers (1979) recount a charming example of overextension: when their son Nicholas was about one year old he learnt to call the family dog by its name, Nunu; he then used the word for all dogs, and went on to use it for other animals as well, and even for slippers and coats. When he was 1:1 he had his first encounter with a black olive (in a salad), which he referred to as Nunu, too. After some puzzlement, the parents recognized the similarities of the features 'round, black, shiny, wet, cold' with Nunu's nose!

As the child's vocabulary increases, (s)he learns to differentiate meanings and acquires the necessary linguistic forms to express these (finer and finer) distinctions. Certain items used during the one-word stage are abandoned, notably those that are dissimilar to the adult forms and are not kept alive as 'family words'. Thus Pascual's [i:júm] developed, eventually, into 'Auto/coche/car', 'Flugzeug/avión/aeroplane', etc. There have been reports on individual differences, and on general trends, in the way in which children's vocabulary develops – for instance, by Hernández Pina (1984), who observed various aspects of her son Rafael's acquisition of Spanish, paying particular attention to semantic and syntactic development. Peters (1977) distinguished different approaches to learning, which she called 'analytical' (i.e. beginning with the parts and building up the whole) and 'Gestalt' (that is, trying to produce complete phrases and then taking them down, therefore going from the whole to its parts). Others have emphasized individual differences among children, e.g. Nelson (1973), who divides them into 'referential learners' and 'expressive learners'. Allowing for certain individual differences, then, all children use overextension and differentiation of meaning, and all abandon some earlier forms as their lexis increases.

3.3.2 Lexical development in bilingual children

Leopold's first volume (1939) contains a careful analysis of his daughter's vocabulary development. Apart from describing the emergence of her German and English words, he also offers a semantic classification, and some comments on her phonetic accuracy. He pays special attention to those words that gradually faded from active use, attemping to give reasons for their transience (Leopold uses 'mortality'), such as avoidance of difficult forms, rejection of non-standard usages, acquisition of more specific terms, and shifts from words used in one language to items in the other, usually the more dominant one at the time. Leopold's detailed studies have become reference works for those interested in first language acquisition as well as researchers of bilingualism.

There is considerable agreement among those who have reported on bilingual language acquisition that, at the beginning, particularly the one-word stage, the child uses words from both languages indiscriminately. Sometimes this has been termed 'confusion' or 'initial mixing' (see further discussion of mixing in Chapter 5.4). Grosjean (1982) also points to the occurrence of certain forms, such as compounds and blends, used at this stage, like 'bitte-please' (also reported by Leopold and Saunders) and 'pinichon' (a blend from English 'pickle' and French 'cornichon'). Mixed elements in early language production have been interpreted as evidence of an undifferentiated language system. Volterra and Taeschner (1978) propose a three-stage model which reflects their interpretation of mixing: in stage (1) the child operates only one lexical and syntactic system which comprises items from both languages; in (2) the lexicon becomes differentiated but there is continued unification of syntax; and in (3) differentiation of the syntactic system appears. This model, and particularly the idea of an early unified system, found at the time considerable support (see later in this chapter).

In fact, whether children who are acquiring two languages simultaneously during infancy initially operate one system or two incipient ones is currently a controversial issue. Evidence has been gathered from all aspects of language acquisition as support for one view or the other, but no firm conclusions have yet been reached. We shall return to this question later (see section 4.2).

3.3.3 Acquisition of equivalents

In analysing the lexical development of two Italian–German bilingual children, Volterra and Taeschner (1978) distinguish two stages. During the first, the child has one lexical system only that includes words from both languages. The second stage starts when (s)he is beginning to use equivalents. In her 1983 book, which represents a longitudinal study of the acquisition of Italian and German by her two daughters, Taeschner maintains the claim for the validity of this distinction. In relation to stage one she gives word lists which contain German, Italian and neutral words; the latter include onomatopoeic items, baby words and proper names that have the same meaning in German and Italian. She attaches much significance to the fact that very few equivalents were present – and where they did occur, e.g. 'da' and 'là' (both meaning 'there'), they were not recognized as such. Taeschner (1983: 27) describes the relationship of these pairs of words in terms of hyponymy (or partial inclusion of meaning), not of synonymy (or similarity of meaning). With reference to the few other equivalents in the lists, she explains that their occurrence was much more frequent in one language than in the other. The first stage lasted for about five to six months, and the vocabulary contained some 65–85 items.

Taeschner paid special attention to the acquisition of equivalents during the second stage. She presents her data in the form of lists and graphs, organizing her lexical analysis under traditional categories like articles, nouns, adjectives, verbs, etc. In all cases there was a time interval between the acquisition of a new item and that of the equivalent, ranging from three to eight months. For the older child this period tended to be longer than for the younger one. The data show different patterns in the acquisition of equivalents. Articles were acquired almost simultaneously, but categories such as adverbs and conjunctions overlapped in the temporal sequence or with little difference in time between the acquisition in German and in Italian, whereas for nouns and verbs the new acquisitions always preceded by several months that of their equivalents in the other language. This is quite logical, in view of the large number of content words (nouns, verbs and adjectives) in any language. Taeschner suggests: 'It would seem that the child learns first to use a word well in one language to refer to specific events or objects, and only after having used it for a certain period of time begins to use its equivalent also' (Taeschner 1983: 30).

Vila (1984) looked into the language development of three children, bilingual in Catalan and Spanish, which he compared with that of a reference group of three monolingual children (one in Spanish, two in Catalan), focusing in particular on the increase in vocabulary in both groups. His conclusion was that the language development was similar in the two cases. As regards equivalents, according to his count they amounted to only about 10 or 12 per cent of the total forms, and he suggests that this can be explained by the linguistic proximity of the two codes. However, if one counts the words he calls 'neutral', i.e. very similar or identical in Catalan and Spanish, then the total comes to some 29 per cent, which is much closer to Taeschner's results.

The analysis of her daughters' lexis at 2:4 and 2:10 respectively led Taeschner to the conclusion that approximately one-third of their entire vocabulary was made up of equivalents, while the remaining two-thirds were new acquisitions: 'It is in this relation that the bilingual child is able to acquire two lexical systems simultaneously' (1983: 33). To generalize and attach actual figures to the acquisition process may strike observers as a somewhat bold undertaking. Taeschner's study suffers from a certain methodological weakness, since it is based on data transcribed in orthographical rather than phonetic form and it contains scarcely any indication of contextual features. Children's early vocalizations can be very difficult to interpret with certainty, and when transcribing bilingual children's output the transcriber may, quite involuntarily, take important decisions about the particular form or language the child under observation has used. We may have to wait for the results of other longitudinal studies to see how much support these figures receive. Equally, more comprehensive lists taken from the first stage (lexical mixing) are needed to ascertain whether the absence of equivalents is observable in all children or whether it is largely determined by the linguistic input. We know that, in the case of very young children, the roles of those who look after them (parents, childminders, etc.) are usually quite clearly defined and, for this reason, the daily routines involved in looking after the child are not often shared in an equal way, which means that the subject is presented with varying language input and models, in contexts at least partially separated, and this can have some influence on the acquisition of equivalents. In any

case, the *absence* of an equivalent can be interpreted in two ways: it
may be an item genuinely not known yet or, simply, a form not produced; limitations in the sampling procedures are such that in many
cases one cannot be sure. The acquisition of equivalents seems to be of
relative importance only in the early development of bilingualism.

As a last point, it may be added that equivalents are rarely learnt by
analogy. Bilingual children seldom recognize cognates (e.g. 'Papier,
papel, paper'), nor do they attempt to refer to cognate forms in one
language consciously in order to deduce the probable shape of equivalent words in another. It seems that the same happens when bilingual
children begin a foreign language at school. Children, at that stage,
lack the maturity for such analytical linguistic operations.

3.3.4 The semantic load

The importance of the child being able to keep the two systems apart
has been mentioned earlier. Different contexts, environmental or
human, enable the child to distinguish the codes and to develop
strategies for language choice. This process requires a considerable
cognitive effort. In assigning words to meanings the bilingual child has
to carry out the two-fold task of allocating two labels, rather than one,
for each semantic unit. Apart from this, relating words to meanings
always includes making generalizations and abstractions, but for the
bilingual it requires, in addition, the recognition that not only do objects, events, actions, etc. have two names, but the semantic relations
between them can be different in one language and the other. The capacity for acquiring new words and equivalents in bilinguals is
therefore subject to individual variation: it depends on such variables
as cognitive maturity and memory, and also on interactional factors
related to the sociocultural environment of the child. The bilingual's
linguistic capacity has to encompass the two languages. But this does
not mean that his lexicon is twice as big as that of the monolingual.
The bilingual is able to denote the same number of objects, events, etc.
as the monolingual, although he does so by dividing his linguistic
repertoire between items from both codes, with varying degrees of
overlap.

The driving forces behind language development are the communicative needs. In order to express what (s)he wants to say the child does
not have to possess a particularly rich vocabulary – an adequate one
will do. Doyle, Champagne and Segalowitz (1978) compared twenty-

two bilingual children with twenty-two monolingual ones, all aged between 3:6 and 5:7, and they found that the monolinguals had a larger
vocabulary than the bilinguals in their dominant language. But the bilinguals showed superior verbal fluency in their story-telling, and also
in the number of concepts per story expressed by each child. So,
whereas the semantic load involved in the lexical development is clearly bigger for the bilingual than for the monolingual child, the overall
resulting lexicon need not be (in fact rarely is) twice as big. Successful
communication depends less on the number of lexical items a child
possesses than the way the available ones are used. There are those
who believe that, because of their familiarity with more than one linguistic system, bilingual children are more flexible and creative in
handling language (a point that will be taken up in Chapter 7).

3.4 Development of grammar

3.4.1 Morphological development

Morphology has received less attention than syntax in the various
studies on bilingual language acquisition. Languages vary quite considerably as to the complexity of their morphology, and whereas in some
(e.g. English) the absence of morphological markers is not likely to
lead to a frequent breakdown in communication, in others (for
example, the Romance languages in their verb systems) the accurate
use of inflections is very important. Many of the case studies listed in
section 2.4 involve languages of the former kind; this may explain, in
part at least, the relative scarcity of data on morphological development. In this section reference is made to some of the observations on
morphology made by various authors, before proceeding to discuss
syntactic development.

Leopold (1949a) noted that by the end of her second year his
daughter's morphology was still largely undeveloped. Apart from the
possessive marker (which is the same in English and German), she
used some plural forms (mainly regular, only some irregular ones) in
English, but hardly any in German. She had no noun or verb endings
in German, and only a few adjectival endings in English derivations.
Burling's case study (1959) is interesting because it involved a non-
European and highly inflected language. He reported that his son's
morphological and syntactic development was already well under way
by the time the boy was two. He could use Garo suffixes indicating

future, past, imperative, present and habitual aspects, and other categories, on all verbs he used, and he was beginning to use negatives, possessives and some noun suffixes. For English Burling had recorded only the possessive marker. But Garo was the dominant language for the child at the time, and this must have contributed to his faster acquisition of the Garo morphology than the English one (in the latter there are, in any case, fewer inflections). Murrell (1966) summarily says that his daughter did not use any morpheme affixes at all before she was 2:8. My own data show that the first markers both my children began to use systematically, in their second year, were: the possessive -s for German and also, incorrectly, for Spanish, although not for very long; the morphemes for plural in nouns, adjectives and verbs in Spanish; and some plural forms, mainly with nouns, in German. Incidentally, later, when he was just three and had started to use some English as well, Pascual went through a period during which he added an -s (the English, or the Spanish, plural marker?) to many German forms which were already plural, as in:

Pascual (3:1):   'Mami, nimm die Blumens aus die Suppe'
                  ('Mummy, take the flowers out of the soup'
                  – he called parsley 'flowers')

Pascual (3:2):   'Unter die Decke, ihr Kinders!'
                  ('Get under the blanket, children!', as he was putting
                  his toy animals to bed)

It has been observed (see, for instance, McLaughlin 1984) that, generally speaking, syntax develops before morphology except in those languages in which a very close relationship holds between the two. Morphology is an aspect of language acquisition that may make demands on quite complex cognitive processes. Apart from the general structural relationships with other morphemes (one and the same marker may signal several grammatical functions, e.g. case, gender and number, in many German endings), there are also perceptual aspects: as suffixes, they receive less salience in the pronunciation and may thus not be noticed by the child. Also, languages contain a variety of clues about grammatical categories and functions (object, agent, etc.), so that communication can be quite successful without the use of markers on nouns, adjectives and verbs in many instances; and if they are not perceived as vital in every case, it is not surprising that it takes the bilingual child a little longer to achieve this difficult learning task with total accuracy.

Vihman (1985) states that inflectional markers in Estonian presented considerable difficulties to her son, and that this could account for his use of the easy English equivalents in certain cases. She concluded that the use of English (e.g. 'me' and 'mine' for a range of Estonian equivalents) could be seen in part as a strategy for putting off production of the Estonian system until he had more time to assimilate it. Vihman's examples were taken from the time when Raivo was between 1:8 and 1:11. If she is correct in her assumption, it certainly shows that the child had morphological awareness. Another example of such sensitivity towards morphology was provided by my daughter when she was 3:1 – she used the word 'socia' (the feminine form of the noun 'socio', 'member' e.g. of a club) which, although correct, is not commonly used in Spanish; she had certainly not heard it previously.

> Child: '¿Está cerrado el club los sábados?'
> ('Is the club closed on Saturdays?')
> Father: '¿No, está abierto' ('No, it is open')
> Child: '¿Y por qué está abierto?' ('Why it is open?')
> Father: 'Porque va mucha gente, van los socios'
> ('Because many people, the members, go there')
> Child: '¿Y nosotros somos socios?' ('And we are members?')
> Father: 'Sí!'
> Child: '¿Y yo también?' ('Me, too?')
> Father: 'Sí, tú también' ('Yes, you too')
> Child: 'Entonces, yo soy *socia*' ('In that case, I am a [female] member')

(Hoffmann 1985: 483)

In many respects the bilingual child follows the same route as the monolingual. However, the use of particular morphemes is language-specific and may be traced back to separate language input (see De Houwer 1990). Depending on the relative importance of morphology within a given code, the correct forms are acquired sooner or later. The errors that do occur can mostly be explained in terms of overextension or simplification, either developmentally from within the same language or, far less frequently, as a result of the child's knowledge of the other language. The kind of errors monolingual children make (e.g. involving irregular verb forms, plurals or case inflections) are made by bilinguals as well; they may, however, persist much longer in them or even become a feature of their speech. There may be some evidence that suggests that bilinguals have a heightened sense of morphological awareness and that they are able to express it in a way monolinguals cannot. But this awareness does not necessarily extend to earlier mastery of the morphological systems.

3.4.2 Syntactic development

There exists a considerable body of descriptive data on bilingual children's acquisition of grammar. Some of the more recent studies have concerned themselves with the question of whether grammatical categories emerge at the same time and in the same way in monolingual and bilingual children, e.g. Meisel (1984) and De Houwer (1990). By looking at bilingual children and comparing their language development with the results of studies into the corresponding development in monolingual children, Meisel aimed at gaining a better understanding of the processes underlying language acquisition. In particular, he wanted to find out whether the semantic–pragmatic principles that determine much of the child's early language development apply in the same way to monolinguals and bilinguals, and whether pointers that the acquisition of grammar is under way (i.e. the internalization of the morphological and syntactic features of both languages) emerge at the same time. He looked at the language development, between 1:0 and 4:0, of two children who were bilingual in French and German, concentrating on the features of word order and case markers (the latter as evidenced in the use of articles and the pronominal systems). His findings suggest that bilingual children acquire the same items, and in the same sequence of acquisition, as monolinguals. As a general rule, the simpler items are acquired before the more complex ones. He also found that, in contrast to monolingual children, the bilinguals maintained from the start more rigid patterns of word order, that the Subject-Verb-Object order was given preference over other possible structures, and that consistent use of the verb in second position within the sentence constituents (which is a notable feature of German syntax) occurred earlier in bilinguals than in monolinguals. With reference to the use of case morphemes and other markers, he noticed that bilinguals were able to express syntactic functions by morphological means earlier than monolingual German children (Meisel explains that on this point he could not include French examples, as no comparable material was available.)

Other authors (e.g. Leopold 1949a; Imedadze 1967; Raffler-Engel 1965; Carrow 1971; Kessler 1971; 1972) had previously come to the conclusion that the acquisition of syntax in bilingual children follows the same principles as in monolinguals: syntactic and morphological features are acquired earlier or later depending on how salient and how complex they are, relative to each other. An oft-quoted example is provided by Mikeš (1967), who reported on the acquisition of locative markers in a Serbo-Croatian/Hungarian bilingual child. In Hungarian the locative is expressed by noun inflection, whereas in Serbo-Croat both noun inflection and a preposition are needed. The subject learned to express the locative in Hungarian before he could master it in Serbo-Croat. Mikeš points out that this is a feature that is learnt quite late in monolingual Serbo-Croat children as well, and that therefore bilingual presentation did not appear to affect syntactic development.

If the two languages express a semantic relationship by similar grammatical means (e.g. indicating possession by intercalating a preposition between the object and the possessor, as in *die Schuhe von meiner Schwester* and *los zapatos de mi hermana*), then it is likely that they are acquired simultaneously. But it should be remembered here that syntactic forms with a similar degree of complexity in both languages might not appear at the same time in the bilingual. The acquisition will be affected by the way these forms are presented to the child, i.e. whether, and to what extent, the adults around him make frequent use of them. On the other hand, if one language uses a more complex construction than the equivalent one in the other, the acquisition of it may be delayed somewhat.

A substantial part of Taeschner's (1983) book is devoted to the analysis of the syntax of her two daughters. Her approach is based on the linguistic theory of valency grammar, which has received a fair amount of attention among German linguists. In valency grammar the verb is considered to be the centre of sentence structure. The predicate may be defined as the element in an utterance which holds all the other elements together (the predicate can of course be more than just the verb, but in the child's constructions there may not even be a verb form). Taeschner considers that this type of sentence analysis is a suitable instrument to allow her to describe her daughters' progression from single-word utterances to more complex, adult-like structures. She postulates three stages through which children pass, ranging from simple nuclear sentences in the first one to more complex constructions in stage two, and going on to still more sophisticated structures, using connectives to indicate relationships of cause, condition, time, etc., in the third stage. During the first period the girls made no distinction between the two languages, and they used words from both in their utterances. During the more advanced stages various types of constructions developed together in Italian and German; in those cases where differences showed up, reference to the acquisition of such items by monolinguals could provide an explanation. Taeschner, too, like Mikeš and Vila, stresses that bilingual presentation of syntactic structures does not significantly affect the pattern of their acquisition.

Annick De Houwer's study (1990) of the language acquisition of a Dutch–English bilingual child from age 2:7 to 3:4 contains an extensive analysis of Kate's morphological and syntactic development. De Houwer looks at gender, plural formation, diminutive suffixes, verb forms, verb phrases, word order and different types of main and subordinate clauses, and then she analyses her findings by reference to comparable studies of monolingual Dutch and English language acquisition. Her findings show that bilingual language acquisition runs concurrently, each language forming a separate, closed system, and very little influence is noticeable from one on the other. She also makes the interesting observation that 'Kate's third birthday marks a turning point in her linguistic development in general: in both languages, structures start to appear that were absent before. It seems as if the child is suddenly much more intensively occupied with the formal aspects of language and their possibilities than before' (De Houwer 1987: 424).

In contrast to Taeschner, she does not believe in an initial unitary language system for any stage of language development (this point is taken up again in section 4.2). The fact that both languages are affected simultaneously by this heightened linguistic awareness leads De Houwer to consider the possibility of including changes in linguistic behaviour under the general changes for which advances in cognitive development are responsible:

> Although the actual 'contents' of Kate's speech production is quite language-specific, there appears to be a mechanism at work here that concerns both languages at once. Now obviously, as Kate is getting older, she is also maturing on the cognitive level. Might it not be that general cognitive development here leads to changes in behaviour in general, thus including the quite drastic changes in linguistic behaviour?
>
> (De Houwer 1990: 308)

Taeschner's and De Houwer's studies differ not only in their conclusions but, more fundamentally, with respect to their theoretical and methodological approaches. Whereas De Houwer adopted a holistic view of the child's social, cognitive and linguistic development, Taeschner's description is presented in terms of separate stages.

Clearly, if one describes language acquisition one has to proceed one step at a time. This does not mean, however, that the acquisition of a first or a second language itself follows a linear sequence. The use of the term 'stages'[1] may be misleading as it suggests chronologically successive steps that can be counted, which in turn implies that one phase has to be completed before the next one starts. Language develops gradually, sometimes by leaps and bounds, often appearing to stagnate or even regress. Several features may develop simultaneously and overlap, others may show a clear progression from one point to the next. Some may regress in one language while progressing in another. At all times the acquisition is dependent on social, psychological and environmental factors, and these can be particularly noticeable in bilingual language development. It is generally accepted today that unfavourable changes in the environment, withdrawal of psychological or social support, or decrease in exposure to one of the languages (or a combination of them) can have negative effects on the bilingual's language acquisition. He or she may, in the end, develop full competence in only one language.

Notes

1. Roger Brown (1973) uses the term 'stages' in a clearly defined way. He proposes the use of a child's mean length of utterance (MLU) as a useful index of language development. On the basis of a sample of 100 utterances, the MLU is calculated in terms of the number of morphemes used. Taking MLU as the basis, Brown suggests that there are five stages of language development, ranging from MLU values of up to 1.75 in Stage I (which covers the one- and two-word stages), 2.25 in Stage II and going up to 4.00 in Stage V. These proposals have found wide acceptance in language acquisition research, and they have been used in the comparison of monolingual as well as bilingual speech production. However, the concepts of MLU and stages should be used charily, for at least two reasons: differences in data collection methods and in the background of the children studied may affect MLU and thus the comparability of

stages; also, MLU as defined by Brown refers to English and cannot automatically be transferred to other languages. Other researchers have suggested more than five stages, e.g. Wells 1985.

Chapter 4

Aspects of bilingual competence

4.1 The bilingual's linguistic competence

The study of child language acquisition is concerned with linguistic aspects, such as the emergence of the phonological, morphological and syntactic systems, the processing of linguistic items and developmental features such as progression, e.g. in terms of semantic or grammatical complexity. A number of other facets are also taken into account, like the general cognitive development of the child, his/her social environment, the language input (s)he receives and her/his interaction with adults and other children, as these are thought to shape the resulting linguistic competence to a significant extent (Oksaar 1983; Romaine 1984).

Some of these areas may prove to be more complex in bilingual language development than in monolingual language acquisition, but in principle they have the same relative value for both types of children, and similar patterns of progression can be discerned. What will, however, be quite different is the child's linguistic competence. Bilingual competence should not be seen as the sum of two separate parts, one code and the other, but as a composite ability which may manifest itself in the expression of competence in one language and the other and, in addition, also in a system that combines elements of the two and enables the speaker to use speech strategies not normally at the disposal of the monolingual.

Grosjean makes the pertinent point that research into bilingual competence should not be conducted in terms of the bilingual's individual and separate languages, but it ought to take a holistic or, as he writes, bilingual view of bilingualism. The speaker should not be considered to be the aggregate of two complete (or perhaps incomplete) monolinguals: 'Rather, he or she has a unique and specific linguistic configuration. The coexistence and constant interaction of the two languages has produced a different but complete language system.' (Grosjean 1985a: 470–1).

The linguistic competence that the bilingual speaker develops in either of her/his two languages hangs upon a number of factors (linguistic, contextual and psychological, among others). Some of them have been discussed in Chapter 2, and others will be dealt with in Chapter 5. The point has already been made that a bilingual speaker is rarely equally fluent in the two languages, because the needs and uses of each are usually quite different. But he is, in Grosjean's (1985a) words, a 'fully competent speaker–hearer' who has developed a communicative competence which may make use of one language, or the other, or the two together in the form of mixed speech.

The main concern of this chapter is to consider, first, a theoretical issue, then some of the factors that appear to be relevant to the formation of bilingual competence, such as language differentiation and language choice, and lastly certain phenomena that manifest themselves in the speech of bilinguals – interference, mixing and code-switching. Some of these (e.g. mixing) have been observed to be more noticeable in young bilinguals, whereas others (for instance, code-switching) appear more frequently in the case of older speakers. While the former seems to be of a more transitory nature, the latter can become a fairly permanent feature of whole speech communities.

4.2   Early bilingualism: one language or two?

The earlier observers of bilingual language development did not address themselves to this question at all, but as advances were made in the description of bilingual acquisition fundamental theoretical issues were approached. With respect to the onset of early bilingualism, two opposing theories emerged, approximately at the same time (the 1970s).

4.2.1   The unitary language system hypothesis

This theory holds that the bilingual child does not, initially, distinguish between the two language systems. Instead, the child starts by using one hybrid system, which only gradually becomes separated. Volterra and Taeschner (1978) proposed a three-stage model of early bilingual development, as has already been mentioned. According to this model, the child at first possesses one lexical system composed of lexical items from both languages. In stage two the child distinguishes two separate lexical codes but has only one syntactical system at her/his disposal. Only when stage three is reached do the two linguistic codes become entirely separate. This model seems attractively neat, and it has found a fair number of supporters, some of whom adopt it explicitly (for example Saunders 1982a and 1988, and Arnberg 1987), while others do so implicitly, by not quoting any opposing view on syntactic development (for instance, McLaughlin 1984) or by referring to the 'slow separation' or 'final separation' (Grosjean 1982) as a common feature of bilingual children's speech.

The evidence used to support this viewpoint is taken from reports of young bilinguals' indiscriminate use of their two languages and children's language mixing. Gradually diminishing mixed utterances were observed by, among others, Imedadze (1967), Oksaar (1971), Swain (1972: the title, significantly, is 'Bilingualism as a first language') and Redlinger and Park (1980), who agreed that they reflected the child's initial inability to differentiate between the two codes.

4.2.2 The separate or independent development hypothesis

According to this view, bilingual children, from a very early age, are able to differentiate their linguistic systems. This conviction was voiced by Padilla and Liebman (1975), and it found support in Bergman (1976), who postulated that in cases of bilingual acquisition each language develops independently of the other. The idea that the bilingual child speaks with a hybrid system was rejected by Lindholm and Padilla (1978; a and b).

In more recent years the unitary language hypothesis has come under intense scrutiny, for instance by Meisel (1986 and 1987), De Houwer (1990) and Genesee (1989). They argue that there is no conclusive evidence to support the existence of an initial undifferentiated language system, and they also point out certain methodological inconsistencies in the three-stage model. The phenomenon of mixing is interpreted as a sign of two as yet imperfect systems existing side by side, rather than as evidence of one fused system.

4.2.3 An assessment of the two hypotheses

Meisel (1987) sees early mixing in bilingual speech as 'a deficiency in the [child's] pragmatic competence'. On the basis of his own empirical research, he says that very young bilingual children seem to use language-specific syntactic constructions even more consistently than monolingual ones, and this leads him to claim that the former are able to differentiate between the two languages as soon as they begin to use syntactic means of expression (as opposed to purely semantic–pragmatic ways, which are common to monolingual and bilingual children). He further proposes the separate term 'fusion' to refer to the 'alleged inability to separate the two systems', a state he does not recognize as existing among the children he studied. Interestingly, there is a footnote in Weinreich (1968: 11), in which he refers to the work of the linguist M. H. Roberts (1939), who also made the distinction between 'fusion' and 'mixture', the former referring to the generative process and the latter to the established result.

Annick De Houwer's original study bore the telling title of 'Two at a time'. Her thorough discussion of the mixed language hypothesis leads her to conclude that finding positive evidence for the single-system stage is virtually impossible, and this is borne out by the findings of her own case-study. She collected two sets of speech data from a young Dutch–English bilingual. One contained utterances only in Dutch and the other only in English. The corpus enabled her to address the question of whether, and to what extent, the girl's two languages were developing separately. The evidence that she found led her to the following conclusion:

> In all aspects of language use investigated that provided unambiguous opportunities for discovering either the presence or the absence of inter-linguistic interaction, we were able to show that Kate's developing morphosyntactic knowledge of Dutch could not function as a basis for her speech production in English, or vice versa. Instead, Kate mostly used Dutch morphosyntactic devices when producing utterances with only Dutch lexical items, and English morphosyntactic devices when producing utterances with only English lexical items. Furthermore, not only were the morphosyntactic devices themselves usually relatable to only one language, they were also used in a language-specific manner. Therefore, I believe, it has been convincingly demonstrated that the Separate Development Hypothesis accurately describes a major part of Kate's bilingual acquisition process.
>
> (De Houwer 1990: 338–9)

As we can see, she based her conclusion on cases that 'provided unambiguous opportunities', i.e. so different in English and Dutch that no possibility existed for the subject to use morphosyntactic devices belonging to one language as the 'basis for her speech production' in the other. But what about the other cases? It has to be borne in mind that Dutch and English are fairly closely related languages, i.e. there are many similarities between them, a fact that could perhaps account for a large part of Kate's linguistic development. One is therefore entitled to doubt whether anything can be proved decisively in this matter.

Genesee's (1989) contribution to the discussion is made in a review article. He re-examines a number of studies of early bilingual development in which mixing had been interpreted as evidence for a unitary system. Again, the unitary language hypothesis is queried for empirical reasons. In order to uphold the theory, Genesee suggests, 'one would need to establish that, all things being equal, bilingual children use items from both languages indiscriminately in all contexts of communication.' (Genesee:1989).

The opposite theory, in contrast, would need to prove that bilingual children 'use items from their two languages differentially as a function of context'. Thus, in a situation where the young child's weaker language was being used (around him and by him) one would expect a higher proportion of items in the weaker language to occur than in contexts where the stronger language was employed. As Genesee points out, most studies supporting the initial hybrid language thesis do not present or analyse their data by context. And he adds: 'Therefore, it is impossible to determine whether the children are using the repertoire of language items they have acquired to that point in a differentiated way.' (Genesee: 1989).

This author refers also to research on the perceptual abilities of very young children, saying that they seem to be capable of fine discriminations, such as noticing phonetic contrasts, and to possess all the necessary prerequisites for speech perception. The assumption is, presumably, that it does not make much sense to suggest that bilingual children are operating only one system when, at the point of their development in which they begin to utter single words, they are already able to perceive two different phonological systems.

It is difficult to see how one can confidently pronounce in favour of one of the two models, although it does appear that the balance is beginning to tip in favour of the separate language development hypothesis. A major obstacle is that we do not as yet have a proper basis for deciding to what extent linguistic knowledge in the very early stages is language-specific, or up to what point we can legitimately postulate a language competence from the child's first utterances. Also, if one sees children's early linguistic competence in terms of several systems rather than just one, it becomes possible to argue that some systems are separate and others fused. In any case, the tools available for description are crude. It can also be misleading to speak of the child's 'lexis' or 'syntax': one would have to define very carefully what precisely constitutes a lexical item, and allow a more general view of syntax when looking at children's one- and two-word utterances, as these can have a variety of meanings and functions.

4.3   Language awareness and differentiation

If one believes that children acquiring two languages in early infancy go through a stage during which they operate one system only, one needs to determine exactly when bilingualism begins. Different answers are possible, depending on one's approach. Volterra and Taeschner (1978) argue that only when the child ceases to classify speakers in terms of their language can (s)he be claimed to be truly bilingual, i.e. only when the systems themselves are acknowledged as possible ways of communicating. A more linguistic, rather than cognitive–behavioural, view is to say that the use of synonyms, or equivalents, is the clearest sign that the child is bilingual. The emergence of bilingualism and language differentiation are seen as closely related issues. Areas of particular interest concern questions such as whether there is any kind of systematicity in early mixed utterances, how the child overextends meanings, and when and how he eventually learns to separate the two language systems he is in contact with. The underlying belief is that only when it is evident that the child is beginning to use two languages and to keep them apart is there proof that he is on his way to becoming truly bilingual. On the other hand, if one subscribes to the view that bilingual children operate two distinct language systems right from the beginning (in terms of perception and, even if imperfectly, production), the question of the onset of bilingualism becomes irrelevant. Similarly, terms such as 'separation' or 'differentiation' of languages make no sense, since they imply that prior to differentiation there was a mixed form.

We can now consider some observations that have been made about the bilingual child's emerging language awareness and the possible manifestations of separate language development. The use of the term 'differentiation' is not meant to indicate a particular theoretical standpoint.

4.3.1 Manifestations of language awareness

A look at some of the case studies will show very considerable variation in the ages at which the children observed are reported to have become aware of operating in two different systems. This is not surprising, as it may well be the case that one child is conscious of the presence of two languages in her environment long before commenting on it or showing any outward signs, while another child may remark on his observations much sooner or manifest his awareness by indirect means. Linguist parents of bilingual children have provided examples of amazingly early, and very perceptive, language awareness (e.g. Ronjat 1913; Saunders 1982a; Fantini 1985; Clyne 1988). However, at least some of the – often highly amusing – remarks by very young children on their own and other people's language use must be taken as a reflection of the emphasis and keen interest in all matters linguistic that they encounter in their environment.

There are many studies, older as well as newer ones, of bilingual children which remark on the apparently indiscriminate use of both languages at the initial stage of the child's speech production and then report that the early mixing subsided once the children involved realized that there were two languages in their environment. This was often, in essence, a reference to the realization by the children that people around them (often the parents) used different languages, which was acknowledged by some kind of comment. Thus Ronjat (1913) describes how his son Louis went through a period of testing the names, phonetic shapes and linguistic allocations of objects (Ronjat refers to this as the 'temps d'essai'). By using words with French or German pronunciation the boy would ask for clarification and assign them to the mother's or the father's repertoire (e.g. 'le casier maman' or 'le casier papa'). This was reported as happening before the child's second birthday. Leopold (1949b) says that his daughters Hildegard and Karla were conscious of using two different systems early in their third year, and that there was active separation of the codes towards the end of that year, i.e. each language clearly developing separately.

My daughter Cristina showed signs of distinguishing the two systems around her second birthday. Addressing each person around her in
the correct language, she would sometimes comment on the fact that
her parents gave objects different names, and she often checked
whether she had got the two labels right by saying, for example:

Cristina: (Looking at her mother, while banging the table)
             'Papá mesa' (= 'Papá sagt "mesa"').

Or, after I had asked her (in German) to pick up a pencil:

Mother: 'Nina, heb den Bleistift auf'

she would ask her father:

Cristina: 'Papá lápiz?'   (= 'Papá, ¿tú dices "lápiz"?')
                                      ('Daddy, you call it "pencil"?')

Kessler mentions the first occasion, at age 3:6, when Lita, a Spanish–English bilingual in Texas, actually named her two languages (the
exchange occurred after her mother asked Lita to give several examples of Spanish and English words):

Mother: '¿Tú sabes hablar mucho o poquito inglés?
             ('Can you speak a lot or a little bit of English?')

Lita: 'Mucho inglés.' ('A lot of English')

Mother: '¿Y tú sabes hablar mucho o poquito español?'
             ('And can you speak a lot or a little bit of Spanish?')

Lita: 'Mucho español'. ('A lot of Spanish')

Mother: 'Y oye, Lita, ¿a ti te gusta hablar el inglés, o el español, o
             los dos?' ('And tell me, Lita, do you like to speak English,
             or to speak Spanish, or both?')

Lita: 'Dos' (holds up two fingers) 'That's inglés' (points to one
             finger) 'And that's español!' (points to another finger)
                                                        (Kessler 1984: 42)

An earlier example from the same child shows clearly that this little
girl was aware of two distinct codes at age 2:3:

Mother: ' ¿Qué quieres, Lita, quieres leche?'
             ('What do you want, Lita, do you want some milk?')

Lita: 'No leche'.

Mother: '¿Quieres agua?' ('Do you want some water?')

Lita: 'No agua'.

Mother: '¿Quieres jugo?' ('Do you want some juice?')

Lita: 'No jugo. Candy, mami'.
Mother: 'No, candy no, Lita'.

Lita: 'Candy!' (with great emphasis, followed by a long pause)
             . . . 'Dame dulce, please' ('Give me candy, please')
                                                        (Kessler 1984: 41).

Carolyn Kessler adds the comment: 'The language switch from English to Spanish in asking for candy took place in a very slow, deliberate manner, evidently with the expectation that the situation to bring about the realization of candy called for Spanish.' (Kessler 1984: 41).

These examples are interesting from two points of view: they show clearly the child's awareness of the two separate systems, and their appropriateness for use with particular people, English- and Spanish-speaking; and they appear to indicate that she is unaware of mixing them when she says: 'dos . . . that's inglés. . . and that's español' and later: 'Dame dulce, please.'

At the age of 2:6 Cristina was able to express her awareness of the two languages by using labels like 'so wie Mami' and 'como dice papá' (Hoffmann 1978; 1985). It is quite normal for small children not to use abstract labels such as 'English', 'German', etc., as the concept of language, and correspondingly 'of the English language' etc. are not present in their minds until a much later stage in their cognitive development. The paraphrases they use often reflect the close association, for them, between language and person(s); for instance, Pascual used 'wie Mami' and 'so wie wir, Mami?' to mean '[in] German', and 'como dice papá' for '[in] Spanish', which he extended to 'wie Ian' and 'como dice Ian' (his friend next door) for the meaning '[in] English'. Another type of paraphrase made use of the different ways of saying 'hello', i.e. as a linguistic label rather than as a form of address:

Pascual (3:7): (telling me off for speaking English to a Spanish-speaking girl)
'Mami, nicht so mit Carmen sprechen!'
('Mami, don't speak to Carmen like that!')
Mother: 'Wie denn?'
('What should I say, then?')

Pascual: 'So, "hola ¿cómo estás?", nicht "hello"!'

Only after his fourth birthday did he start to use the labels 'Spanish', 'German' and 'English'.

Cristina's active language separation became consistent from the two-word stage onwards, but for Pascual separation became evident later; he was generally slower to start developing his languages.

Arnberg gives some examples of a two-and-a-half-year-old who did not yet appear to keep apart his two linguistic systems, English and Swedish:

'Titta, *bunny*' ('Look, bunnie')
'En *block*' ('A block')
'En *piggies* till' ('A piggies more') [i.e. 'one more pig']
'Här är *budda*' (butter) ('Here is butter')
'*Horsie* sova' ('Horsie sleep')
'Ar det *ducks*?' ('Is it ducks?')

(Arnberg 1987: 69)

Arnberg uses these and other sentences as examples of the child's attempt to combine his two languages into a single system. They can, of course, also be cited to support the opposite view, although it has to be recognized that the samples are very limited and there is no indication of the linguistic context in which they were uttered, or of what the input was (linguistic and otherwise). The child was using words from both his languages, but we can observe a certain pattern: the grammatical items ('en', 'det', 'en till') and the verb forms ('är', 'titta') are in Swedish, whereas most of the content words (nouns) are in English. It looks as if the child was signalling his knowledge of two systems but, at this early stage, he still needed to use lexical items (English nouns) in one language to fill in gaps for their equivalents in the other. Perhaps he just did not know them yet, possibly he still associated the animals he was commenting upon with a certain person who spoke English, maybe he knew the item in Swedish but could not recall it at

the moment of speaking. We shall come back (in section 5.4) to the
subject of mixing.

So far we have mentioned the naming of the various languages and
also active separation, i.e. the use of separate languages in appropriate
contexts. There are other signals that the child can give which indicate
that he is aware of using two codes. He can use spontaneous translation to recount to one parent what the other has said, unaware of the
fact that the parents may understand each other's language (see, for
instance, Imedadze 1967; Swain and Wesche 1975; Hoffmann 1985;
Fantini 1985). Ruth Métraux (1965) observed that some of the children
she studied would not react when asked something in one language by
a person they normally associated with the other. This seems to indicate that the child gets himself into one language mode when
communicating with one person or set of people, and into another with
a different (group of) person(s) (see Grosjean 1985a on this point). To
what extent this shifting or switching is a conscious operation we do
not know. It has often been noted that children dislike their parents
addressing them (or even others) in the 'wrong' language (if the one-
parent-one-language rule has been closely adhered to in their
upbringing). The instance of Pascual protesting at me for using English
to the Spanish girl, mentioned above, is one example. Fantini quotes an
instance of both his children's intolerance of his breach of the language
rule when speaking to his wife in English, rather than Spanish:

Carla: '¡No hables en inglés a mamá!' ('Don't speak English to
            Mummy')

Father: '¿Por qué?'

Carla: 'Porque mamá no le gusta hablar en . . . ep. . . ' (Looks
            to Mario for support) ('Because Mummy doesn't like
            speaking in . . . . Sp. . . ')

Mario   (to everyone): '¡Español! A mamá le gusta hablar en es-
            pañol' ('Spanish! Mummy likes to speak in Spanish!')
                                                    (Fantini 1985: 76)

Arnberg has an example of the same two-and-a-half-year-old cited
earlier reacting to the mixed speech of his father:

Child   (to English-speaking mother): 'Jag vill ha en SPOON'

Swedish-speaking father (to child): 'Vill du ha en SPOON?'

Child (upset): 'Nej, sked!'

(Arnberg 1987: 70)

We do not know whether he was upset simply because the Swedish father used a word in English, or whether he thought that the father was mocking him for using the wrong word – whatever the reason, the example illustrates the child's awareness of the two separate systems in his environment.

4.3.2 How does the child keep the languages apart?

We can only speculate about how the child becomes aware of the existence of the two languages. There have been attempts to design tests aimed at bringing out evidence of some kind of mental device regulating the 'on' and 'off' switching of the bilingual's languages. Penfield and Roberts (1959) first proposed a model that came to be called the 'single-switch theory' because it suggested the presence of such a switching mechanism. Its shortcoming was that it could not adequately account for some aspects of the performance of bilinguals, e.g. in Stroop testing.[1]

A more sophisticated theory was formulated by Macnamara (1967), the so-called 'two-switch model', which hypothesized an input and an output switch. The speaker was supposed to be in control of the latter, but not of the former. Various tests were administered to bilinguals to show that switching from one language to another takes time; for example, the subjects had to name numerals in one language and then in another, or to read monolingual passages and bilingual ones, where the sentences contained words from both languages mixed at random. In all cases, the clear conclusion was that bilingual performance takes longer.

The validity of both models has since been questioned, as the problem of explaining the neutral status of a switching device remains unsolved. In any case, research has now shifted towards seeking an explanation for code-switching, a frequent and naturally occurring phenomenon in bilingual speech (see Chapter 5). It seems unlikely that the brain of the individual should have any kind of special mechanism to separate the languages as, after all, the monolingual, too, keeps a number of language registers and styles apart. His language production, like that of the bilingual, involves selecting linguistic items. And both monolinguals and bilinguals make wrong choices.

If one does not try to look for neurolinguistic devices, there are a number of contextual factors that suggest possible explanations for developing language awareness. Among these are the following:

(1)   The child's increased knowledge of the languages could help her to differentiate them.
(2)   More specifically, the bilingual's greater familiarity with the sounds of each language may facilitate recognition of the two codes.
(3)   The accumulation of social experience (i.e. the knowledge of the contexts in which linguistic forms appear) will provide the child with valuable information and thereby increase awareness of the separate systems.
(4)   The improvement of her linguistic sensitivity towards adult standards, as well as her wish to approximate to these models of linguistic behaviour, may also be influential.
(5)   The child wishes to be understood by monolinguals, and this can often force her to seek the correct word, or to explain what she means in a linguistically more refined way than if she were speaking to another bilingual.

4.3.3 The importance of context

The most influential factor in developing bilingual competence is probably the one mentioned under (3) above. Context, particularly human context, is perhaps of paramount importance in deciding the status and role of each language in the child's mind and in helping him to acquire the appropriate linguistic forms. The advantages of following the one-person-one-language rule have been pointed out above. There is evidence that children who have acquired their languages from different persons show less language mixing than those who have acquired them in 'fused' contexts. The assumption is that, in the early stages, and in order to avoid confusion and disorder, the bilingual child needs to use the person as a reference point when organizing his language behaviour, i.e. the bilingual normally chooses the linguistic code according to the language of the person with whom (s)he is interacting.

Naturally, the context does not have to be 'a person', it can be the physical or situational environment as well. In many cases bilingual children grow up to speak two languages by being exposed to one in the home and another one outside, so the contexts of use do not often merge. Another form of separation of context may be a combination of the two possibilities, as for example with the family who decide that they will use the father's language when they are all together but that of the mother in the absence of the former. A separate context for each language is considered to be important for the establishment of bilingualism, as it helps the child to understand that the two codes are possible and distinct means of communication, existing in their own right, rather than being attributes of certain people. This process takes some time to be completed. I have a record of a situation involving Pascual, when he was 1:11, which shows that he had not made that abstraction yet. One evening he discovered a full moon shining through the window. He was fascinated, and when I told him 'Das ist der Mond' he repeated 'Mond, Mond' several times and went, excitedly, to the next room to point out the moon to his father, from whom he learnt to say 'la luna'. The next day a Spanish friend of ours, Pascual and I were sitting at the table when Pascual again discovered the moon outside, and the following dialogue ensued:

> Pascual (1:11): 'Mira, [pijá] (Pilar), Mond'
> Pilar: 'Sí, la luna'
> Pascual (correcting her): 'Mond! Mond!'
> Pilar: 'Sí, la luna'

At this he got visibly upset, insisting on calling the moon 'Mond'; he would not accept my explanation that Pilar used other words like 'sí' and 'niño' where I said 'ja' and 'Kind', for example. Perhaps the two contexts, the human and the physical, were too close for him to separate them as easily as he had done the night before; the acquisition of the two nouns would probably have been easier for the child if the separation of the human context had been accompanied, all the time, by physical separation.

The particular way and the specific context in which the language is presented to the bilingual child are seen to be influential. The advice given to parents who want to bring up their children bilingually is usually that they should follow the one-person-one-language rule or that they ought to keep to one language at home and to the other outside it. It seems reasonable to expect that a separation of context and an input of one language at a time will facilitate the child's learning task. However, there is no empirical evidence to show that other methods have detrimental effects, such as delayed language production. But

studies of early bilingualism do suggest that mixed input is more likely
to cause mixed speech. And there is a popular (but not well-
researched) belief that those who consistently mix languages are not
capable of keeping them apart, i.e. that they somehow have a language
deficiency.

4.4   Language choice in children

As the young bilingual child develops her social and linguistic skills,
she is likely to meet a larger number of people from different linguistic
backgrounds with whom to interact. Which language will she choose
to use? According to what criteria will she select a linguistic code?
The choices available to her can be summarized in the following way.

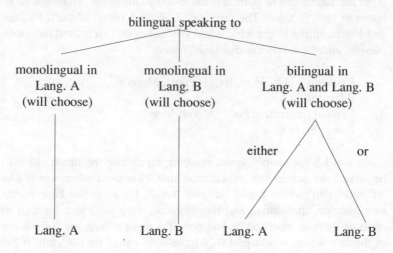

She is likely to make a straightforward choice (between Lang. A
and Lang. B) when selecting the language she is going to use to monolingual speakers. But what makes her decide to go for Lang. A or
Lang. B when talking to a bilingual? And will she stick consistently to
that choice once she has made it?

4.4.1   Language choice in monolinguals and bilinguals

Monolinguals also have to make choices when selecting certain styles
and registers, and when changing from one style to another. Contributions by a number of linguists (e.g. Ervin-Tripp 1964, 1968; Gumperz

1964; Fishman 1965a and 1971 – the latter in an article with the informative title 'Who speaks what language to whom and when?') have elicited a number of factors that can be considered to account for shifting from one variety to another:

(1)   the *setting*, in terms of time and place, and the situation ('domain' is another word used), e.g. whether in the family, at a party or at the work-place;
(2)   the *participants* in the interaction, i.e. features relating to their age, sex, socio-economic status, occupation, etc.;
(3)   the *topic* of conversation;
(4)   the *function* of the interaction, which can be to greet, apologize, exchange information, etc.

The same four categories of variables will decide, at any rate in general terms, the bilingual's language choice. Since two languages are involved, the situation may become more complex, as the switches will involve the selection of different varieties of Lang. A or Lang. B and, in addition, switches from A to B and back from B to A.[2]

4.4.2 Determinants of language choice in bilingual children

Essentially, the factors influencing language choice are the same for adults and children. However, they may not operate in quite the same way for each group. In what follows, a brief account is given of some of the determinants of language selection discussed in the literature on child bilingualism.

(1) *The person(s) engaged in the speech event* This is probably the most important variable for the child's language choice. In studies of bilingual children there are numerous references to children who address one parent in one language and the other parent in the second. As the child grows, he may extend the pattern so that, for a while, all men are spoken to in the father's tongue and all women in that of his mother. Sometimes children may choose a language on the basis of a person's looks: Burling (1959), for instance, reported on his son talking in Garo to an Indian-looking stranger he met on a plane (although he had not used Garo for some time); and in Fantini (1985) there are several examples of Mario associating all persons with dark complexion/hair with the use of Spanish – but assigning English to black people. A person's role with respect to the child may be conceived of

as decisive, e.g. nursemaids, babysitters, teachers who become associated with a particular language.

There is anecdotal reference, as well as empirical evidence, from those who have collected data on young children's language selection, that children tend to follow a consistent pattern. Most of a bilingual's utterances to a monolingual speaker are in the language of that speaker, and incidences of mixing may be remarkably low. There is similar evidence that bilingual children are more inclined to address other bilingual speakers in either language, just as they are prone to produce more mixed utterances in their speech with bilingual interlocutors.

Children may also judge on the basis of the linguistic features apparent in the person, i.e. whether the speaker has a native accent or not. An instance of this is that my children, when answering the telephone, have always switched to Spanish or German when they detected a Spanish/German accent in the caller's English. Fantini (1985: 62) offers an interesting example of Mario's reaction to the language of several Mexican–American classmates who frequently switched between English and Spanish; Mario used English only when speaking to them (the kindergarten was in Texas), and when asked by his father: 'Mario, ¿por qué no hablas en español con esos nenes?' ('Mario, how come you don't speak Spanish with those children?'), the five-year-old boy replied: 'Ah, esos nenes no hablan muy bien' ('Oh, those kids don't speak very well'). Presumably, he was referring to their Spanish as judged by the native-speaker standards he was familiar with.

(2) *The setting/place/situation* This last example shows that another determinant, that of 'kindergarten playground', may also have influenced Mario's choice of English. Pascual, as a two-year-old, would greet any person in the street with 'Hello!' or 'Hello man!' without having been spoken to by them first. But within the home other factors were of greater importance than 'setting' in choosing the language in which to address visiting strangers.

On a visit to her grandmother in Denmark, Cristina (shortly before her third birthday) addressed people who spoke Danish to her in English, which at the time was very much her weakest language, rather than in German, which was spoken to her by her grandmother and her mother. It seems that she made her language choice on the basis of setting, associating English with 'outside the home'. It is also possible that linguistic features played a role, i.e. she may have decided that, since Danish was an unknown system, it somehow called for the choice of her least well-known language.

Harrison and Piette (1980) looked at the factors determining the language choices that bilingual Welsh–English mothers made while raising their children. They were able to show that most of the children were linguistically as their mothers had intended, and that their language choices had often been determined by the mothers. The latter's decisions as to whether to bring up their children monolingually or bilingually had depended on:

(a)   socio-economic considerations: mothers at either end of the social scale were more likely to go for bilingual upbringing than those in the middle;

(b)   the chances of social interaction outside the nuclear family: for example, the availability of Welsh–English bilingual playgroups and schools, and contact with other bilinguals;

(c)   the influence of social interaction inside the family, such as the father's encouragement or lack of support for a bilingual upbringing; and

(d)   socio-psychological factors, as for instance the mother's attitude towards Welsh and child-rearing, or the use of a specific language generally.

The authors conclude that children pick up subtle cues from their environment, and that the mothers' attitudes and language choices will ultimately determine their own.

(3) *The function or purpose of the interaction* Harrison and Piette also mention person and place as possible determinants of young bilinguals' language selection. Their main argument, however, is that bilingual children 'use language as a lever to the world' (1980: 218), just as monolinguals do (see Halliday 1975; Bruner 1975). They give examples from a child who switched from one language to another in the hope that the person she was with would comply with her demand for more playing, and from another subject who, while being in the company of Welsh and English speakers who were discussing whether or not he ought to go to bed, kept switching to Welsh because he felt that there was a better chance that the Welsh speakers would let him stay up. The example from Kessler (1984) given in section 4.3.1. above can be seen in the same light. Lita consciously chose the Spanish word for

'candy', after having used it in English to her Spanish-speaking mother, in the hope of getting some.

A particular language may be chosen in order either to exclude or to include other people present. Some parents report that their offspring do not address them in the usual language when they pick them up from school, for example, or when a monolingual friend is present. Children may also decide to select a particular language, in preference to the other, in order to re-tell a story or a joke, or to cite someone else, or when involved in role play or quoting or making puns, or when providing a 'translation service' for somebody. In all these instances (and many others are possible), the choice is made with the intention that the message should convey a particular meaning or have a certain effect.

(4) *Topic* Only as the child gets older does this variable acquire importance. Once children are of school age and start having a host of new experiences (special school activities, academic subjects, sports, hobbies, TV programmes, etc.), their language selection will become strongly affected by the topic of the conversation or language use.

(5) *Linguistic proficiency* The degree of proficiency which the child (or adult) has in both languages may constitute a mainly linguistic or psycholinguistic reason for language selection. The speaker may prefer to use the language he feels more confident in because of the frustrating experience of not being able to say quickly and with ease what is important at a particular moment. In this kind of situation all the other determinants can be overridden by the one factor of linguistic availability; and the less balanced the bilingual is in the respective competences, the more likely it will be that this factor will come into play. In relation to older bilinguals one would speak of language dominance. With reference to the very young child, whose language development is still an on-going process, Dodson (1981) introduces the concept of the *preferred language*.

Language development is intimately linked with the child's increasing awareness of the language of her/his environment and his/her skill in using it. Bilingual language acquisition involves developing an awareness of two distinct systems, acquiring their features and learning to keep them apart. Becoming bilingual implies making choices between two languages, following rules that are laid down by the environment or that the individual has decided upon by himself. In young children such choices tend to be affected primarily by social and emotional factors (as mentioned under (1) and (2) above), but as they grow older more subtle factors (linguistic, topical and psychological) become more influential. One should point out, though, that the determinants outlined here are all interrelated to varying degrees.

Notes

1. The bilingual version of the Stroop procedure consisted of the elicitation of responses in one language while receiving a visual stimulus in the other. For instance, the English–German bilingual would be shown the word *schwarz* (= 'black') written in yellow ink, and the colour of the word had to be named in English; the correct answer therefore would be 'yellow'. The monolingual version employed words from one language only, i.e. *black* written in yellow ink would be shown. It is known that both monolinguals and bilinguals are slowed down in the naming of the colour, which appears to indicate that both systems are 'on' at the same time – as well as confirming the generally observed ability of bilinguals to listen in one language while speaking in the other, which finds its perfection in simultaneous interpreting.

2. As many bilinguals do not have the same type of competence in both of their languages, their stylistic repertoire in each language may differ. This is often noticeable in children who, for instance, have acquired one code from one side of their family and have not learnt to use the more formal styles requiring specific morphological or lexical forms in that language, whereas in their other language they are able to use 'polite expressions' and certain forms of address for specific purposes.

Chapter 5

Features of bilingual speech

There are people (monolinguals themselves, usually) who advise parents against raising their children bilingually. They argue that the child may become confused, or his intelligence affected in some way, or his speech impaired (by stuttering), and above all they warn of the danger that he may end up not speaking any language 'properly'. And they believe this last possibility can easily be proved by pointing to 'irregularities' present in the bilingual child's speech (or, for that matter, that of bilingual adults).

It is true that, when listening to bilinguals talking to each other, we can notice certain features which are absent from monolingual speech, such as a 'foreign accent', the incorporation (wholesale or in an adapted form) of words or expressions from the other language, and sudden switches from one code to the other, the latter perhaps occurring more than once within the same utterance.

If one holds the view that a bilingual is, linguistically speaking, a composite containing two separate parts (or codes), then the basis for assessing his language competence will be monolingual standards of proficiency in the use of the two systems. In this case, notions of purity of language will be rated more highly than those of communicative competence. But if one looks at the bilingual speaker holistically, as Grosjean (1985a) suggests, i.e. as someone possessing bilingual competence that can manifest itself in various ways, then the picture can be quite different. Phenomena such as interference, mixing and switching become the subject of analysis, helping us to discover patterns and relationships with other features of speech. A non-native accent and the choice of a wrong word (perhaps a loan translation from the other language) are more likely to be detected in bilinguals when they are fatigued or excited. Children tend to mix more if they are frequently exposed to mixed speech. And both bilingual children and adults appear to mix and switch more when they are in each other's company than when talking to monolinguals – indeed, they may well have their reasons for such linguistic behaviour, such as signalling group identity to outsiders or solidarity to other group members, or expressing a shared experience. Certain aspects of bilingual speech will now be dealt with in a little more detail.

5.1   Interference

Most of the authors who have observed bilingual speech have remarked in one way or another on the transfer of elements from one language to the other. The amount of such elements noticed and the importance attached to them differs greatly, however. In the older literature all instances of transfer tended to be subsumed under the heading of 'interference', and the definitions that were put forward did reflect a slightly negative assessment of the phenomenon. In 1953, when he first published his book *Languages in Contact*, Weinreich decided to call interference 'those instances of deviation from the norms of either language which occur in the speech of bilinguals as a result of their familiarity with more than one language, i.e. as a result of language contact.' (1968: 1). In the definition given by Mackey there is, however, no reference to 'norm' or 'deviation': 'Interference is the use of features belonging to one language while speaking or writing another' (Mackey 1970: 569).

Before going on to examine the various types of interference – phonological, lexical, grammatical and cultural – Mackey emphasizes the distinction between interference and borrowing: the former is an instance of 'parole', while the latter is one of 'langue'. Interference, he argues, may vary a good deal according to a number of psychological, situational and discourse factors.

In more recent studies, features of bilingual speech have been dealt with under the separate headings of interference, borrowing, mixing and code-switching, which reflects the various characteristics that have been discerned. But, as so often happens in the fields of linguistics, there are no clear-cut distinctions or commonly agreed approaches to analysis or description, and the definitions one comes across may, at times, seem contradictory. In other cases some of the descriptions may overlap, so that the task of separating, for example, discussions of mixing from those of switching is not as easy as one would like it to be. Each definition offered expresses the researcher's views on and approaches to a particular issue.

Grosjean (1982 and 1985a), like Mackey, prefers a neutral definition of interference: 'The involuntary influence of one language on the other' (1982: 299) – which distinguishes it from borrowing and code-switching, understood to be less involuntary. The latter are quite noticeable features of the speech of bilinguals when addressing each other, whereas interference is also prominent in the speech of bilinguals when addressing monolinguals. According to Grosjean, a bilingual, when speaking to a monolingual, realizes that code-switching and borrowing would impede ease of communication and he therefore avoids them. Three points should, however, be taken into account here: first, that speakers do not always consciously control their speech so as to avoid borrowing and code-switching; second, that situational and emotional factors can affect interference so that, for instance, the Spanish–English bilingual who is normally proficient at producing the English [r], in initial position, and omitting it in postvocalic position, will shout 'Be careful!' with a heavily rolled alveolar [r] after the first vowel when agitated; and lastly, that the distinctions between the four phenomena are less clear-cut in young bilinguals. With respect to the very young bilingual still undergoing the process of language acquisition, it makes little sense to talk about interference at all (particularly if one assumes that at least some early systems are fused, i.e. that separateness does not exist from the very beginning), since neither of the two codes is yet fully or firmly established; the most noticeable feature in the earliest stages is the abundance of instances of mixing. The examples of different types of interference mentioned below are taken from the speech of older children and adults.

5.1.1 Interference at the phonological level

Interference at the phonological level is often called 'a foreign accent'. It is usually more readily noticed by the layman than any other form of interference. Adult bilinguals are more likely than child bilinguals to show features of stress, rhythm, intonation and speech sounds from their first language impinging on their second. It is relatively easy to predict, in general, what kinds of phonological interference are the most probable to occur in given groups of speakers, as the transferred elements are likely to be those that are absent in the other language or dissimilar in the two codes (Lado 1957). For example, speakers of Greek or Italian may tend to use vowel sounds similar to those in their own languages when speaking German or English: Greek and Italian have simple vowel systems, consisting of five and seven phonemes respectively, whereas German and English have complex systems with between sixteen and twenty units (including both pure vowels and diphthongs). Thus native speakers of Greek and Italian may fail to distinguish between long and short vowels, as in *beat* versus *bit* or *Mus* as distinct from *muβ*. Similarly, a native speaker of English may carry over the 'dark' (or velarized) [ɫ] after vowels, as in *halt*, to the same position when using German, which has only a non-velarised or 'clear' [l], thus realizing *behalten* as [bəhaɫtn̩] instead of [bəhaltn̩]; and the German speaker of English may fail to suppress his native final devoicing of plosives and produce only one form, e.g. [kɪt] for the two English forms *kid* and *kit*, or [kʌp] for *cup* and *cub*.

Interference in intonation can be a permanent feature in the adult bilingual, as in the case of a Norwegian speaker who uses his native rising intonation pattern at the end of sentences when speaking English, which has the effect of making every statement sound as if he were asking a question. In children, interference in intonation can often be observed to adapt quickly when they change from one linguistic environment to another.

5.1.2 Interference at the grammatical level

This kind of interference frequently involves such aspects of syntax as word order, the use of pronouns and determiners, prepositions, tense, aspect and mood. For instance, when Pascual, aged 4:2, asked his father: '¿Son ésas las gafas que vas a verlo con?' (instead of the well-formed '¿Son ésas las gafas con que vas a verlo?'), he was using the English word order with the preposition at the end ('Are those the glasses you are going to see it with?'). An example taken from Cristina's speech when she was 11:9 shows, again, the influence of English word order on a second language, in this case German: 'Ich kann das nicht kaufen, weil ich hab' kein Geld mehr' ('I cannot buy it because I have no more money') (instead of '. . . weil ich kein Geld mehr habe').

Saunders, too, remarks on the fact that transference of word-order patterns in his children's speech was predominantly from English into

German, although he also gives some examples of occasional influence in the reverse direction (1982a: 178).

One frequently reported type of interference concerns the word order noun–adjective. Bilinguals who have Spanish or French as one of their languages often use this order (noun followed by adjective), common in Romance languages, when speaking non-Romance ones like English or German. Among English–French bilinguals the reverse has also been observed, that is, a preference for using the adjective–noun sequence in French, which is possible but less idiomatic. (For a more comprehensive treatment of the topic of acquisition and transference of word order, see Romaine 1989: 187 ff.)

The following examples involving the use of the wrong preposition still occur frequently in my children's speech (at ages thirteen and ten):

Cristina: 'Ich fahre *auf* dem Bus nach Hause'
            (instead of the correct '. . . mit dem Bus. . .',
            'I go/am going home on the bus')

Pascual: 'Ich hab' das *auf* dem Fernsehen gesehen
            (instead of the correct '. . . im (= in dem). . .'
            ('I have seen it on TV')

In both cases the phenomenon could be interpreted as interference from English – after all, prepositions appear to be particularly susceptible to interference, as both observers of bilinguals and teachers of foreign languages can testify. However, Suzanne Romaine's discussion of interference and prepositions (1989: 196 ff.) refers to studies of both monolingual and bilingual children acquiring German, and some of the examples given show either the overgeneralization of 'in' (in German and English) or trouble in distinguishing English 'in' from 'to' and German 'in' from 'nach' or 'an'. As monolingual children have problems with prepositions as well, faulty production in bilingual children cannot be explained wholly in terms of interference. According to Romaine, two issues have to be considered: the fact that prepositions are often used with a variety of functions in different languages; and the question of how this varied input affects (in the case of both monolinguals and bilinguals) the order of acquisition (Romaine 1989: 200). The so-called 'interference', then, may well be due (at least partly) to developmental factors.

5.1.3 Interference at the lexical level

Interference at the lexical level is probably the most problematic category for the linguist to account for. In the other types of interference there can be little doubt that the criterion of 'involuntary use' could be applied consistently and convincingly. But at the word level a different situation seems to arise: the bilingual may borrow a word from one language, when speaking in the other to a monolingual, either on an *ad-hoc* basis or in a more permanent sort of way; and he may do the same when addressing another bilingual. The borrowed item may even be 'fitted up' with the appropriate morphology, as if to make the borrowing less obvious. For example, when she was seven years old Cristina asked her father: '¿Te vas a poner. . . te vas a poner el *belto*?' ('Are you going to wear. . . are you going to wear the belt?' But 'belt' in Spanish is 'cinturón', i.e. nothing like *belto*). She had used the proper Spanish word many times before and she quickly realized her mistake; this was a one-off occurrence of involuntary use. On the other hand, the German for 'zip', which is more complex, 'Reißverschluß', and 'to zip up', 'den Reißverschluß zumachen', were less firmly established in her vocabulary, and even at age twelve she still used her own invented forms 'Sippen' (for 'zips') and 'zusippen' (for 'to zip') quite often. A fairly large number of *ad-hoc* formations which clearly showed the influence of the other languages emerged when, at various times, our children were given vocabulary recall tests in Spanish, German and English. They produced such items as, for instance, German 'die Axe' (based on English 'axe') instead of 'die Axt', or 'das Kalf' (based on 'calf', the animal) for the correct 'das Kalb', and Spanish 'las grapas' (based on English 'grapes') instead of 'las uvas', or 'esos ticos' (on the basis of 'those sticks') for 'esos palos'. The incidence of lexical interference increased considerably when the children were aware of being tested, when a time limit was set and when testing in the three languages was done in quick succession.

Another kind of word interference is the overextension of the meaning of a word into the realm of the other language. This may happen, in particular, in the case of idiomatic expressions and items with cognate forms:

Cristina (7:2): 'Tu' mir mehr Creme auf die Erdbeeren!'
                  (meaning 'Give me some more cream for my strawberries'; but whereas 'cream' in English can be of either the edible or the beautifying kind, German 'Creme'

tends to denote the latter only – unless it occurs in a
compound like 'Vanillecreme'.)

Cristina (7:3): 'Und da haben sie sich den Kopf abgelacht' (meaning
'And then they laughed their heads off', for the correct
German 'Und da haben sie sich kaputtgelacht')

Another example was provided by a German boy wishing a student
good luck with his exams, who said: 'I'll press my thumbs for you'
(meaning 'I'll keep my fingers crossed for you', which in German is
'Ich drück' dir die Daumen').

In these instances the interference was clearly from the bilingual's
stronger language into the weaker one. In the case of older bilingual
speakers, e.g. immigrants who have lived for years in their adopted
country, the second language may start to influence the mother tongue,
so that native speakers may come up with cases like the following,
taken from the normal speech of a Spanish lady who has lived in England for most of her adult life: '¡Qué bien miras hoy!' which is quite
impossible in Spanish, being the loan translation of English 'How
good/well you look today!' ('mirar' can only be 'to look at').

5.1.4 Interference in spelling

Interference in spelling is the transfer of writing conventions from one
language to the other. The following example shows that the bilingual
child who wrote this note had, at the time (when aged 11:2), imperfect
knowledge of German orthography and that, for the most part, she was
following the rules of spelling in English (which she knew better) and
her perception of spoken German: 'Canst du bitte die watte
weknehmen? Die hamster machen viel crach wen sie im rat laufen. Ein
hamster ging grade em, aber 2? Ich hoffe daß du viel spaß gehapt
hast.' (In the correct spelling this would be: 'Kannst Du bitte die Watte
wegnehmen? Die Hamster machen viel Krach wenn sie im Rad laufen.
Ein Hamster ging gerade eben, aber 2? Ich hoffe, daß Du viel Spaß
gehabt hast.' Two spelling conventions were therefore ignored: nouns
spelt with initial capitals, and in letters the pronoun 'du' is usually
'Du'. Also, because the pronunciation is followed closely, words which
are subject to final devoicing or assimilation are misspelt, e.g. 'wegnehmen', 'Rad', 'gehabt', 'gerade', 'eben'; and the sound [k] is
represented as 'c' instead of 'k'. (The note explains that when the
mother had gone out and the girl went to bed she stuffed some cotton

wool into her ears so as not to hear her hamsters, and she was asking her mother to remove it.)

5.2 Borrowing

All languages borrow lexical items from other codes, and have always done so. In the European context it can be said that certain languages seem to have been particularly prone to borrowing from others, as for instance German, which has over the centuries incorporated large numbers of words from Latin, Italian, French and, more recently, English. English, too, has over the centuries borrowed extensively from other European languages; today it is the most prolific 'donor', giving words to most languages in Europe and beyond, often replacing indigenous items which, from a linguistic point of view, were perfectly acceptable. Just a few examples:

German	der Computer	[kɔmpju:tɐ]	
	Aids	[ˈe:ts]	
	gestylt	[gəˈʃtaɪlt]	'styled'
French	le weekend	[wikˈend]	
	le parking	[paRkiŋ]	'car park'
	une star	[staR]	'famous actor/actress'
Spanish	un mitin	[mítin]	'meeting'
	el estrés	[estrés]	'stress'
	los líderes	[líderes]	'leaders'

Borrowed items can be adapted either phonetically only (as with French 'star' or Spanish 'estrés') or both phonetically and morphologically (cf. the German formation 'gestylt', the plural 'líderes') – or an effort may be made to copy the native pronunciation (i.e. in the language of origin). It is interesting that 'computer' is pronounced in German more or less in the same way as in English, even though the sequence [pj] does not occur in any German word (one might have expected to hear [kɔmputɐ] or something similar). There is often, in addition, some change in the meaning in the borrowed item, even if it is only in the context in which it is used: thus 'gestylt' applies to anything related to fashion and design, 'un(e) star' is often the leading role in a film, 'estrés' is seen in contexts about the demands or dangers of modern urban life styles, 'un mitin' is mostly of a political kind. Whether a borrowing (also called a 'loan word') becomes adapted or not depends on a number of factors such as frequency of use, how quickly it enters the general lexicon displacing a native word at least partially, and how easy it is to integrate it phonologically and grammatically. The process of adaptation and integration normally takes some time to be completed. The fact that borrowings are very frequent is reflected in the number of lists, sometimes in the shape of dictionaries, that continue to be compiled in many languages, as well as numerous articles on the issue.

Loan words can be assigned to the 'langue' as described my Mackey (1970). Grosjean (1982) uses the term 'language borrowing' to refer to terms that have passed from one language to another and have come to be used even by monolinguals, and he distinguishes them from instances where the bilingual borrows items spontaneously and adapts their morphology, which he calls 'speech borrowing'. The latter clearly fall into the realm of 'parole', and they are unlikely to become a permanent feature of the 'host language' (i.e. the language into which they are borrowed). Grosjean gives (1982: 309) a delightful example uttered by a French–English bilingual: *ça a poppé* ('it popped'). Some of the cases mentioned earlier under 'lexical interference' could be treated as speech borrowings. Many examples are included in Fantini's list of lexical borrowings (1985: 147 ff.) used by his son in both English and Spanish, as for instance:

Mario (3:6):   'Un juguete para el *baby*'
                ('a toy for baby')

Mario (6:3):   'Yo lo voy a *lokar*'
                ('I am going to lock it')
                (the Spanish is 'cerrar con llave')

Fantini proposes a subdivision into 'pure borrowings' ('baby', probably pronounced as in English) and 'adjusted borrowings' ('lokar', from English 'lock' with the Spanish infinitive ending coinciding with that of 'cerrar').

Speech borrowing occurs in adults as well as children. The borrowed item serves a momentary need that may be caused by laziness, fatigue or some form of emotional stress which makes the bilingual forget the correct term. But the reasons for borrowing are not always of a negative kind. A speaker may consciously choose an item from the

other language because (s)he considers it more appropriate or more to
the point. Incidences of borrowing in the speech of bilinguals directed
at other bilinguals do not normally lead to misunderstanding – on the
contrary, they can add interest, humour or intimacy to the conversation
and cause delight to both interlocutors at their shared linguistic knowledge. At the family level there may be a number of items borrowed
from one language into another; these tend to be related closely to a
particular culture and to have no equivalents: German 'Abendbrot' ('a
cold evening meal'), Spanish 'tapas' (what one eats while one drinks
an apéritif) and English 'Wakey, wakey!' are among those used in our
household.

5.3 Individual creations

In the same way as monolingual speakers do, bilingual children can
come up with new, idiosyncratic linguistic creations and novel formations. They may be the source of either confusion or laughter, and
sometimes they are adopted by the family as in-words. Bilingual children can of course draw on the resources of two languages and use their
knowledge to produce forms such as, for example, English 'knackber-
ries' (to mean 'snowberries'; the actual German word is 'Knallerbsen')
or German 'hinterwärts' (to mean 'rückwärts', analogous to English
'backwards'). They can make up new forms in either language and, in
addition, use elements from both and combine them creatively. These
new terms are not the result of either interference or borrowing.

5.4 Mixing

'Language mixing' (or 'code-mixing') has been the object of considerable attention in recent years. In approaching the study of this aspect of
bilingual competence linguists have usually taken one of two possible
broad lines:

(1)   they have described the linguistic phenomenon as observed in
      the speech of adults, focusing in particular on its relationship
      with code-switching;
(2)   alternatively, the discussion of mixing has centred on children's
      bilingual language acquisition and been studied in relation to the
      question of language differentiation.

The large numbers of Hispanic Americans and English-speaking Mexicans living in the USA has provided linguists with excellent opportunities to study the language of speakers whose English contains Spanish items and whose Spanish shows influences of English (e.g. Gumperz and Hernández-Chávez 1971; Hernández-Chávez et al. 1975; Timm 1975; Valdés Fallis 1976; Elías-Olivares et al. 1983; Poplack 1980; Silva-Corvalán 1982, 1983, 1986 and 1989). Mixing has been studied in other parts of the world as well (see, for instance, Gibbons' 1986 comprehensive treatment of code-mixing and code-choice in Hong Kong).

A good example (involving English and Spanish) of one code-mix and two code-switches is given by Valdés Fallis (1982: 220): 'And all of a sudden, I started acting real *curiosa* (strange), you know. I started going like this. *Y luego decía* (And then I said), look at the smoke coming out of my fingers, like that. And then *me dijo* (he said to me), stop acting silly.'

The following two are taken from another study of Chicano Spanish (i.e. the Spanish spoken by some Mexicans living in the United States):

'Pongan los picket signs' (Set up the picket signs)
'A veces, we take too many things for granted' (sometimes, . . .)
(Reyes 1982)

Mixes can be used to clarify the message or make it more precise, a point made by Silva-Corvalán that is illustrated in her example: 'Tenía zapatos blancos, un poco, *they were off white, you know?*' (he/she had white shoes, a little. . .) (1989: 181).

Switches occurring at the lexical level within a sentence (intra-sentential switches) are referred to as 'code-mixes' and 'code-mixing'. On the other hand, changes over phrases or sentences (inter-sentential), including tags and exclamations at either end of the sentence, are called 'code-switches' and 'code-switching' (Poplack 1980; McLaughlin 1984; Appel and Muysken 1987).

It may not always be easy, in fact, to see the difference between speech borrowing and code-mixing in adults. At times there appears to be a good deal of common ground between the two categories, the only differences being of frequency and connotation, as mixing seems to imply a more habitual feature and, possibly, one that is considered somewhat negatively. The study of mixing in bilingual children, on the other hand, touches on theoretical issues. The older bilingual child and the adult bilingual are credited with possessing two different language systems, which they can keep apart; they can switch from one to the other, and they can show code-mixes. But what about the two- or three-year-old infant? Is he displaying one underlying compound system, or merely drawing on the resources of his two incomplete codes when he utters examples like the following?

Thomas (2:2): (English–German bilingual, talking to his English
                grandfather)
                'Lots of *Möven*, Grandad!'

(Saunders 1982a: 46)

Chr. (3:0):   (German–French bilingual, addressing a French-speak-
                ing interviewer)
                'Non, *das ist ein* cadeau'
                'Non, *da* un cheval'

(Schlyter 1988)

And what about the even younger child, whose speech shows mixing at the one-word stage? As we saw in the previous chapter, linguists engaged in research on young children's mixing and language separation have adopted two different theoretical positions, but for neither is there conclusive evidence.

The working definitions used by researchers are often quite straightforward. In the context of her study Schlyter proposes: 'Mixing is defined here quite simply as the child's using words or sentences in the 'wrong' language, in a clearly monolingual situation; language separation is defined as the opposite of mixing'. (Schlyter 1988: 2). Redlinger and Park (1980: 339) write: 'In this study, language mixing refers to the combining of elements from two languages in a single utterance'. Talking about definitions, Genesee (1989) suggests that: 'It is desirable to extend the definition of mixing to include single word utterances from two languages during the same stretch of conversation between a child and caregiver.'

The kind of mixes reported on may involve the insertion of a single element, or of a partial or entire phrase, from one language into an utterance in another, and they can be of a phonological (in the shape of loan blends), morphological, syntactic, lexico-semantic, phrasal or pragmatic kind.

Some instances of morphological mixing are:

papá's zapatos (= los zapatos de papá/Papas Schuhe)
('Daddy's shoes'): German genitive form used in Spanish
die Ohrens (= die Ohren/ears): English or Spanish plural form
used in German

The following contain lexical or phrasal mixes:
Tee schon gepourt (= Tee [ist] schon eingegossen) 'Tea has
been poured': English lexical item adapted into German morphology
play mit water (= play with water): use of German preposition
male con lápiz (= malen mit dem Bleistift) ('draw with the pencil'): use of Spanish noun phrase with German verb
                    (examples from my children, at ages between 2:6 and 3:8)
And the froggie's getting nass ('wet')
Das ist ein Knochen pour chien ('that is a bone for dog')
Le cheval ist zu müde ('the horse is too tired')
                    (examples from Redlinger and Park 1980: 340)

The following instance is from an English-Arabic child (aged 6:2).
It contains an English lexical part which has been morphologically
adapted to Arabic (example provided by my colleague Stephen Thomas):
          huwa believe fii ilghaabi
          he 'lives' in the jungle

The four children in Redlinger and Park's study, and the three in
Suzanne Schlyter's, were all in their second year, and their language
development ranged from one-word utterances (Brown's Stage I) to the
more advanced phase of grammatical complexity involving subordinate
clauses (Stage V). The elements most often replaced by the children
were nouns and frequently used expressions (e.g. guckmal!, 'look!'),
followed by verbs, which were usually conjugated correctly and in
some cases adjusted morphologically. This pattern confirms other data
about bilingual language acquisition (e.g. Taeschner 1983; Fantini
1985; Hoffmann 1985). With regard to function words, there seems to
be a wide range of possibilities: articles, prepositions, conjunctions and
adverbs were all observed to have been mixed in various ways.
    In this connection Vihman (1985) makes the interesting point that
the proportion of mixed functors (or function/grammatical words) increases drastically if one puts all types of such items into one category

and then compares them with the frequency of content (or lexical) words. In the study of her bilingual Estonian–English son, Marilyn Vihman found that in the early stages of language production he relied heavily on English functors (25 per cent of the time) when speaking Estonian, although 61 per cent of these were matched by an Estonian equivalent which he had already learnt or was on the brink of acquiring. The author gives phonological and morphological reasons for the occurrences, pointing to the greater complexity of the Estonian items in comparison the English equivalents.

Mixing may occur for a number of reasons, the most important of which can be summarized as follows.

(1) If an item has been acquired in one language but not yet in the other, the child may use the one device (s)he has available to express a certain lexical or grammatical meaning.
(2) If an item is temporarily unavailable, the subject is likely to resort to an equivalent form in the other language (or what (s)he thinks is one).
(3) If an item is more complex, or less salient, in one language, the young bilingual may make use of the corresponding one from the other.
(4) If the child is exposed to mixed input (s)he will often respond with mixed production.

With respect to this last point, Genesee found that many of the studies he re-examined contained scant reference to adult input. More often than not, researchers would accept their own general impressions, or reports from parents, that the languages were used separately, when in fact they were not. And he adds: 'Evidence that mixing by bilingual children can be traced in part to mixed input would weaken arguments that mixing during early bilingual development *necessarily* reflects an underlying undifferentiated language system' (Genesee 1989).

Observers of bilingual language development agree in their reports that mixing diminishes as the child gets older, but they differ in the explanations that they offer, again reflecting the divergent theoretical stances that they have adopted. By some of them, a decrease in mixing is seen as evidence of the gradual separation of the child's initially mixed language system. But one can also argue that, as the child's languages develop, her vocabularies become more extensive and her other linguistic resources reach a higher degree of sophistication, so there is less need for her to borrow. A drop in the frequency of mixing

can also be explained in terms of the young bilingual's growing awareness of sociolinguistic norms and her greater susceptibility to linguistic
clues in her environment.

Some studies have tried to find out why some children mix more
than others and why there is a difference in the pattern of their language separation. A number of inter-connected factors are seen to be
operating, which can be classified as relating to:

(1)   the language input
(2)   the linguistic development
(3)   the general cognitive development.

(1) A number of linguists stress the importance of consistent and well-
balanced (both quantitatively and qualitatively) *language input*. There
seems to be general agreement that children raised on the one-parent-
one-language rule mix less than those who acquire their languages in
fused contexts. Arnberg and Arnberg (1984) remind us that it is also
important to expose young bilinguals to monolingual speakers of both
languages. The monolingual interlocutor, they argue, is less likely to
understand a child's mixed language output, thus forcing him to look
for the 'correct' item or try to paraphrase what he wants to say.

Schlyter's (1988) study shows that mixing, in the German–French
children she considered, was affected by such factors as visits to
France or from French-speaking relatives. Increased exposure to the
language resulted in less mixing of German elements in their French.

(2) The linguistic factors influencing differentiation are those relating
to certain aspects of *language development*. The longer and more complex the child's utterances become, the better he will be able to
distinguish his two codes, as he becomes more familiar with them.
Schlyter suggests in her study that for the children she observed this
language separation took place somewhere along Stages II or III, i.e.
the children showed a sharp decrease in their rate of mixing as they
progressed from the two- to the three-word stage.[1]

(3) Vihman (1985) discusses the importance of *cognitive development*
for language separation at some length, particularly the interplay of the
child's increasing general self-awareness and his growing perception of
the two language systems. While not denying or playing down the significance of a child's overall intellectual development for all aspects of
his maturation process, including his linguistic progress, it must be ad-
mitted that the relationship between cognitive development and

linguistic progression is a problematic area to assess, since the former is measured, at least partly, by linguistic means (for example, by looking at how and how often the child refers to himself).

We can say, then, that all children go through a stage of mixing. The linguistic items that they mix may be known to them but temporarily not available, or they may genuinely be known to the child in only one of his languages. Input and situational factors (such as one-sided exposure or distractions) can influence mixing in terms of both quality and quantity.

There are, however, many well-intentioned but uninformed people who often become alarmed when they hear a child's first mixed-language output, because they take it as a sign of the child's inability to cope with two languages and as a warning that there is some risk that (s)he may get confused or retarded in her/his linguistic or cognitive development. As a result, parents are sometimes advised against encouraging their children to use more than one language during infancy. The consequences can be that the child will then have to figure out why the parents and family have suddenly changed their linguistic behaviour. They may also be deprived of the possibility of benefiting from the intimacy that a shared language provides, and from the wider social and cultural contacts with other speakers of the parents' language(s). Bilingual children are always likely to be viewed differently from monolinguals by society at large (if they live in a mainly monolingual society), because of their parents' different background. If this disadvantage is going to be there anyway, they might as well be allowed to get the full benefit of being familiar with two cultures and languages.

5.5   Code-switching

It might be argued that code-switching is potentially the most creative aspect of bilingual speech. It has, however, also been considered as a sign of linguistic decay, i.e. evidence that bilinguals are not capable of acquiring two languages properly or keeping them apart. The topic has certainly aroused the curiosity of many researchers, and a host of different aspects of it have been studied. Sociolinguists have looked into speech communities, both monolingual and bilingual, trying to establish reasons for, and patterns of, changes of style and language switching. The bilinguals who have received their attention often include immigrant groups like Hispanic speakers in the USA (e.g.

Gumperz and Hernández-Chávez 1972 and 1975; Valdés Fallis 1976; Silva-Corvalán 1983), Estonians in Sweden and the United States (Oksaar 1974) and both minority and majority speakers in minority areas, such as Catalan and Spanish speakers in Catalonia (e.g. Calsamiglia and Tusón 1984) or Alsatian speakers in Alsace (Gardner-Chloros 1985). Linguists have been more concerned with the question of the linguistic status to be assigned to code-switching, whether one can establish different types of switches and what kinds of constraints can be at play, if any (see, for example, Pfaff 1979; Poplack 1980; Aguirre 1985; and, for a good summary of the issues involved, Appel and Muysken 1987).

5.5.1 What is code-switching?

The most general description of code-switching is that it involves the alternate use of two languages or linguistic varieties within the same utterance or during the same conversation. In the case of bilinguals speaking to each other, switching can consist of changing languages; in that of monolinguals, shifts of style. McLaughlin (1984) emphasizes the distinction between mixing and switching by referring to code-switches as language changes occurring across phrase or sentence boundaries, whereas code-mixes take place within sentences and usually involve single lexical items. Much of the data presented on code-switching involve cases of single-word switches/mixes, (e.g. Oksaar 1974; Mkilifi 1978; Grosjean 1982; Aguirre 1985). In Oksaar's examples switches at the word level were always morphologically adapted, as in the following:

(From an Estonian–Swedish bilingual):
    'Möödunud aastal ma sain *skátti* [skat't'i] tagasi'
    ('Last year I got some taxes back')
    ('skatt' is Swedish for 'tax')

(From an Estonian–American):
    'Nää, Sven, *hítshaíker* tahab *lifti*'
    ('Look, Sven, a hitch-hiker wants a lift')
    (here the first switch is phonologically adapted, the second also morphologically)

                                              (Oksaar 1974: 494–8)

Grosjean gives the following example to illustrate the difference he sees between code-switching (a) and borrowing (b):

(a)   'ça m' étonnerait qu'on ait *code-switched* autant que ça'
(b)   'ça m' étonnerait qu'on ait *code-switché* autant que ça'

(Grosjean 1982: 308)

Both sentences mean the same ('I can't believe that we code-switched as often as that'). Borrowing, for Grosjean, involves morphological adoption, code-switching does not. This distinction expresses the underlying belief that code-switching is part of the bilingual's 'parole', while borrowing belongs to his 'langue'.

5.5.2 What types of code-switches are there?

The following examples show a variety of code-switch patterns:

(1)   A Spanish–English bilingual:
        'I started going like this. *Y luego decía* (and then he said), look
        at the smoke coming out of my fingers'

(Valdés Fallis 1982: 220)

(2)   A French–English bilingual:
        'Va chercher Marc (go and fetch Marc) *and bribe him* avec un
        chocolat chaud (with a hot chocolate) *with cream on top*'

(Grosjean 1982)

(3)   An English–German–Spanish trilingual:
        Mother: 'Na, wie war's beim Fußball?' ('How was the foot-
        ball?')
        Pascual (9:3): 'Wir haben gewonnen. Unsere Seite war ganz
        toll. Ich war der ('We won. Our team was brilliant. I was . . .')
        goalie. I stopped eight goals. They were real hard ones. (And
        turning towards the pan on the cooker he continued) 'Was gibt's
        zu essen?' ('What are we eating today?')

(4)   A Catalan–Spanish bilingual, in reponse to a Spanish speaker
        who had said 'Y se van a molestar, ¿no? No tienen por qué'
        ('They are going to be annoyed, aren't they? [But] there is no
        reason why they should'):
        'Bueno! Sí que tienen por qué. ('Well! They do have a reason')
        'O sigui, o l'encenen amb nosaltres o . . .' ('I mean, either
        they have the bonfire with us or. . . ')

(Calsamiglia and Tusón 1984: 114)

(5)   A Spanish-Catalan bilingual:
       'Hay cuatro sillas rotas y' ('There are four broken chairs and')
       prou!' ('that's enough!')

                                                                    (Ibid.: 115)

   Code-switching can also occur at the phonological level i.e. when
the speaker changes the pronunciation patterns, as in:

(6)   Cristina (4:0): (introducing her younger brother to a new friend
       of hers)
       'This is Pascual' [paskwál]
       Friend: 'What's his name?' (i.e. she didn't catch it)
       Cristina: '*Pascual*!' [pəskwæɬ]
       Friend: 'Oh. . . '

(The switch here consisted of changes in the vowel sounds from [a] to
'schwa' or [ə] and, in the consonants, from initial unaspirated to aspir-
ated [p'] and from non-velarized to velarized [ɬ], to follow a more
English pattern.)

(7)   An adult Spanish–Catalan bilingual:
       '. . . y si dices "perdón" en castellano, se te vuelve la mujer y
       te dice:' ('. . . and if you say "sorry" in Castilian Spanish, the
       lady turns to you and says:')
       '*En catalá*' ('In Catalan!')

                                                   (Calsamiglia and Tusón 1984: 115)

(8)   An adult Spanish–American English speaker:
       '. . . Oh! *Ay!* It was embarrassing! It was very nice, though, but
       I was embarrassed!'

                                                         (Silva-Corvalán 1989: 185)

(9)   An adult Spanish–English bilingual:
       'Tenía zapatos blancos, un poco, *they were off-white, you know.*'
                                                         (Silva-Corvalán 1989: 181)

   These examples illustrate the fact that there are many types of code-
switches. Examples (1) and (2) contain switches within a sentence
('intra-sentential switches'), while in (3), (7) and (9) the switch occurs
between sentences ('inter-sentential'); number (3) also involves a word
within a sentence, 'goalie'. In (4) Spanish is used so as to establish
continuity with the previous speaker (who spoke in Spanish); once this
was done, the Catalan speaker continued in Catalan. (5) and (8) illus-

trate what Poplack (1980) calls 'emblematic switching', items such as tags (*'prou'*) or exclamations (*'¡ay!'*) serving as an emblem of the bilingual character. In (6) the switch involves a change of pronunciation features.

5.5.3 Who code-switches?

Code-switching has been observed to occur in the speech of children as well as adults, for instance by Cornejo (1973); Padilla and Liebman (1975); and Lindholm and Padilla (1978 a + b), who point out that it begins to happen after the bilingual has become aware of speaking different languages, i.e. it is not seen as part of early language mixing. McClure (1977) reports that children tend to use various kinds of code-switches, depending on their age: whereas the younger children she observed employed, for the most part, just English nouns in their Spanish, the older ones would switch over phrases and sentences, and would also use mixes at the word level. This suggests that a certain level of linguistic proficiency has to be reached before bilinguals are able to switch in the middle of an utterance. Poplack (1980) confirms that only the fully bilingual Puerto Ricans she studied were able to code-switch.

Bilinguals, particularly older ones, are normally able to control the amount of code-switching they do. Many contextual, situational and personal factors influence the speaker. In an informal conversation between people who are familiar with each other and have a shared educational, ethnic and socio-economic background, code-switching can occur quite frequently. On the other hand, in a formal speech situation between persons who have little in common code-switches may be avoided because factors relating to prestige, language loyalty and formality influence the language behaviour in such a way as to concentrate the mind of the speaker on trying to approximate or keep to monolingual standards. Bilinguals also differ among themselves in their attitude to code-switching, both their own and other people's. Some have a relaxed disposition towards it, others consider that to code-switch is a linguistic impurity or a sign of laziness and therefore try to avoid it or correct themselves when they realize they have code-switched; the latter group are also likely to signal intolerance towards their bilingual interlocutor's code-switching.

5.5.4 Can code-switching occur anywhere?

The two basic types of code-switches are those found across sentence
boundaries (inter-sentential) and those occurring inside sentences
(intra-sentential), as we have seen. Some efforts have been made to
find out whether there are likely to be universal constraints, or language-specific ones, on where switching can occur, and several
possible lines of exploration have been singled out. But there are certain methodological problems that make it inadvisable, at the moment,
to try to make valid general statements on these issues. One area of
difficulty refers to the fact that the pattern of language switching may
well be determined by the specific pair of languages involved. Another
stumbling block lies in the nature of the research techniques employed:
in order to find out where in sentences switches are acceptable, recorded material is analysed and bilinguals are asked to pass judgement
about possible switches; but sometimes these opinions have been found
to be in contrast with the comparable findings of other studies.

Some constraints on code-switching that have been proposed
(mainly in studies involving Spanish–English bilinguals in the USA)
are:

(1) a switch can occur within a noun phrase but only after the deter-
     miner, e.g. 'se lo di a mi *grandfather*', but not 'se lo di a *my
     Grandfather*' ('I gave it to my grandfather');
(2) adverbial constructions may be switched, as in 'Vamos *next
     week*' ('We'll go next week'), but not as interrogatives: 'When
     vamos' does not appear to be acceptable;
(3) an adjective may be switched after an adverb: 'es muy *friendly*',
     but it is not acceptable to switch the adverb in front of the adjec-
     tive ('Es *very* amistoso').

                                    (All three examples are from Aguirre 1985.)

Timm (1975) proposes that an auxiliary and a main verb, or a main
verb and an infinitive, must be in the same language. On the other
hand, switches are possible between the antecedent and the relative
clause: '. . . those friends from Mexico *que tienen chamaquitos*'
('who have little children') and also between the subject and the predicate in a copular construction: '. . . and my uncle Sam *es el más
agabachado*' ('is the most Americanized'). (Both examples are from
Gumperz and Hernández-Chávez 1975.)

Poplack (1982) suggests that a switch such as: 'Mi hermano está *watching the game'* is possible, and also one that involves phonological adaptation of the main verb, e.g. 'Mi hermano está *huachando the game.'* But a switch is not permissible between dependent morphemes, so that something like 'Mi hermano está *watch*ando *the game'* could not occur (examples from Silva-Corvalán 1989: 181).

There is, however, ample evidence that bilinguals do engage in this last type of code-switching as well:

> '*Taip*eo las cartas' ('I type the letters')
> '*Puch*amos el carro' ('We pushed the car')

> 'Va a *mist*ir el tren' ('He is going to miss the train', where an epenthetic 't' appears).

(Reyes 1982: 154)

These occurrences can be explained in terms of borrowing. As has already been stated (in section 5.2), there is no clear dividing line between borrowing and switching.

A third area of methodological issues involved in the analysis of code-mixing concerns the notion of 'host' (or 'base') language: the language into which the switches are made. Appel and Muysken (1987: 121) remind us, however, that there are different ways of thinking of a base language. Psycholinguistically, it is the speaker's dominant language, i.e. the one which determines his overall speech behaviour; sociolinguistically, the base language should be defined as that of the speech situation, that is, the unmarked linguistic form into which the switch is made. In the above examples of Chicano code-switching, Spanish would be the base language if psycholinguistic considerations are given priority, but English is the sociolinguistic base language. From a purely grammatical point of view, the base language may be the one determining particular restrictions to specific switches.

5.5.5 Why do bilinguals code-switch?

The reasons for code-switching are manifold. Many of them (as illustrated in section 5.5.2) are of a contextual, situational and personal kind. Talking about a particular topic may cause a switch, either because of lack of facility in the relevant register or because certain items trigger off various connotations which are linked to experiences in a particular language. Example (2) (page 111) shows this last point, whereas (3) has a switch to 'goalie' possibly because the German item was not known – and this switch then caused the rest of the utterance to be in English as well.

Switching typically occurs when the subject is quoting somebody else, as in example (7) (page 112), or being emphatic about something, e.g. in (4) and (5). This kind of switch often takes the form of an interjection, as in (8), or a repetition used for clarification, as in (9); in both these cases the switches underline, in addition, the speaker's personal involvement and desire to be well understood. Contributions by Oksaar (1974), Poplack (1980) and Calsamiglia and Tusón (1984) suggest that code-switching is also used to express group identity, i.e. belonging to a bilingual community, like Estonians in Sweden or Puerto Ricans in the USA, and solidarity with such a group. Code-switching seems to be quite frequent among teenagers in immigrant communities. This has been shown in studies carried out, for instance, among guest worker communities in Germany (see Auer and Di Luzio 1984). Hewitt (1982) indicates that even members of majority groups (in this case, young whites in London) may switch (into Jamaican Creole) in order to be accepted by a particular group.

Oksaar (1974) gives linguistic reasons for the code-switching she observed. When asked why they had code-switched certain items for which there existed acceptable Estonian equivalents known to them, her informants gave her to understand that the Swedish or English they used carried certain desirable connotations and reflected shared experiences, which was not the case in the other language. McClure (1977) points out that children's code-switches are often used with the intention of clarifying the speech content for the interlocutor (example (6) above shows this, too); only at a later age, perhaps eight or nine, does the child begin to code-switch for emphasis or in order to focus on a particular topic.

Code-switching, then, constitutes a habitual and often necessary part of social interaction among bilinguals. Whereas monolinguals have only one linguistic code at their disposal, bilinguals can rely on a four-way choice (the two languages and various forms of mixed and switched codes, since they are able to code-switch in both their languages). We can therefore represent the choices involved in the bilingual's speech behaviour schematically as follows:

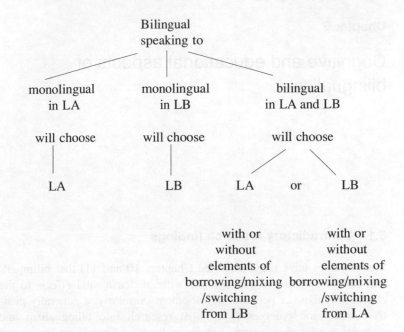

Notes

1.   Stage II is defined as mainly two-word utterances, no auxiliaries
     or modals and hardly any grammatical morphemes. Stage III
     consists mostly of three-word utterances, S/V/O or S/V/Adv
     structures, auxiliaries, modals, verb flexions, prepositions and
     personal pronouns (Brown 1973). Schlyter (1988) suggests that
     language-specific word order begins to emerge during Stage III,
     although the children she studied showed slightly different mix-
     ing patterns. It is also during this developmental stage that the
     input factors mentioned under (1) above play an important role.

Chapter 6

Cognitive and educational aspects of bilingualism

6.1 Contradictory research findings

Many studies have suggested (see Chapters 10 and 11) that bilingualism can be established successfully without detrimental effects to the child's linguistic or personal development. Similarly, a generally positive impression emerges from most research into bilingualism and immersion education, carried out for instance in Canada, in Wales and more recently in Catalonia. In immersion programmes involving initial instruction (usually of majority children) in the L2, high levels of achievement after some years, at no cost to the L1, have been reported (e.g. Lambert and Tucker 1972). There is even some evidence that L1 skills may become enhanced by the experience (see below).

However, correspondingly positive results were not observed in many minority children who underwent schooling in the majority language. According to Cummins (1976; 1978a; 1978b; 1978c; 1978d; 1979a; 1979b; 1981; 1984b; 1984c) and Skutnabb-Kangas (1976; 1977; 1979; 1984b), who spearheaded research into this issue in North America and Scandinavia, children who had to use different languages at home and at school (either because they were members of a linguistic minority or because they belonged to an immigrant family) often showed an inadequate command of both the L1 and the L2, and they performed poorly in academic work.

Similar observations have been reported (Pfaff 1980; 1981) from West Germany. The education of the children of migrant workers is not necessarily more successful, nor is bilingualism established, by making what is called 'Vorbereitungsklassen' available. These classes offering immersion teaching of German are preparatory ones, and they are attended before the children join mainstream education.

How can this apparent contradiction be accounted for? It was noted that Lambert's (1974) distinction between additive and subtractive bilingualism helped to explain why studies of certain groups of children (the first three of Skutnabb-Kangas's four types – see section 2.3) produced mainly positive results, whereas those in which negative conclusions were obtained involved children in settings of subtractive bilingualism. It has now become generally acknowledged that minority children require the sort of educational provision that takes note of both their social and their linguistic situation. Bilingual education programmes – whether of the immersion or submersion (= 'sink or swim') types, mother tongue or vernacular instruction – must consider a variety of social and attitudinal factors such as community support for the programmes, relative prestige of the L1 and the L2, parental and teacher expectations, and the relationship of minority and majority language teaching. Bilingual education programmes in Sweden and, more recently, also in Germany have shown considerably improved results when certain pedagogic conditions were met, such as (1) the integration of mother-tongue teaching and immersion teaching in the child's normal curriculum, (2) the presence of a mother-tongue teacher during the immersion class, and (3) the teaching of the immersion course by a bilingual teacher. Cummins (1978d) argued that the outcome of bilingual education (of whatever kind) appeared more or less successful depending on

> the developmental interrelations between a bilingual child's proficiency in his two languages, his cognitive development and his academic progress. In other words, in addition to specifying the regularities between societal inputs and academic outcomes, it is necessary to pursue the connecting links in the causal chain.
>
> (Cummins 1978d: 396)

With the aim of establishing a theoretical framework for investigating the ways in which the bilingual child interacts with his educational environment, a central role was assigned to the developmental interrelations between the L1 and L2, and to the level of competence in both languages. James Cummins has made a considerable contribution in this area, putting forward a number of theoretical models. Some of these are discussed below.

6.1.1 Bilingualism and cognitive functioning

The debate about the relationship between bilingualism on one hand and intelligence and various cognitive processes on the other has a long history. Sometimes prejudice and passion were allowed to enter into the discussion, particularly in the more distant past. Also, some of the early views (pre-1920s or thereabouts) presenting a negative picture of bilingualism were based on flimsy evidence and can be discarded as unsubstantiated claims. Present-day research on the subject can be grouped into three overlapping periods that Baker (1988) terms:

(1)   the period of detrimental effects
(2)   the period of neutral effects
(3)   the period of additive effects.

The question most commonly asked was: what effect does bilingualism have on intelligence? The assumption was that the causal chain of events works in this particular sequence. It would of course be perfectly justified to ask the question the other way around, but the fact is that this has not been done. Intelligence was seen as central to a child's cognitive development and school success. It was thus considered essential for parents to know about the nature of this relationship when they took the decision as to whether or not to raise their children bilingually. For teachers and people involved in education the issue was of even greater importance since, so long as the view that bilingualism had negative effects on intelligence prevailed, there could be no support for any kind of bilingual programmes. The justification of establishing bilingualism must rest, at least in part, on the conviction that the child will benefit cognitively from being bilingual.

Some aspects of explorations of bilingualism and intelligence are controversial. De Avila (1987), for instance, mentions the confusion of issues which has ensued in some American research projects into minority children's poor academic performance. He points out that low school achievement is often explained by saying that these children are at an academic disadvantage, as shown in intellectual, verbal, motivational and cognitive style-differences – all of which have been equated with bilingualism: 'Unfortunately, studies offered in support of this contention have tended to confound both poverty and ethnolinguistic group membership with linguistic proficiency.' (De Avila 1987: 150.)

Baker (1988) suggests that most research into the relationship between bilingualism and intelligence fails to acknowledge that the nature of the latter is a controversial issue in psychology, sociology, genetics and semantics. He calls our attention to the difficulty of observing and specifying intelligence in a totally satisfactory way, its variably defined structure and the unresolved question of the extent to which it derives from hereditary influences. Furthermore, he raises the problems inherent in IQ tests, pointing out that they tend to be used not only as tests measuring intelligence, but as predictors of future academic achievement, thus changing their intended function. Consequently, they may be less fair to minority than to majority children: 'IQ tests have tended to reflect and reinforce mainstream culture, the educational *status quo* and a curriculum where convergent thinking skills are highly valued. . . Given a more multicultural, creative and progressive curriculum, IQ tests may have a much lower predictive power'[1] (Baker 1988: 7).

6.1.2 Overview of research on bilingualism and cognitive functioning

(1) *Period of 'detrimental effects'* Nineteenth- and early twentieth-century philosophers, educators and philologists have repeatedly expressed the belief that bilingualism has an adverse effect on the cognitive development of the child (see also section 7.1). This conviction was not, however, based on empirical research. More influential on educational thinking (and also, probably, on political decision-making) were the results of a number of IQ tests carried out in English-speaking countries where bilingualism was seen to cause problems, e.g. in the USA, Britain (Wales and Gaelic-speaking Scotland) and Ireland. Specifically, the difficulties encountered related to the education of minority or immigrant children who, quite consistently, achieved lower IQ scores than did monoglot ones.

Nowadays these tests are considered invalid. Contemporary standard testing takes into account a number of additional factors, such as socio-economic background, school conditions and emotional aspects, which have a bearing on marginality and low status. In the former tests in question these variables were not controlled, and in most cases the language of the tests was the one common to both monolinguals and bilinguals, which usually meant that the latter were tested in their weaker language. The tests themselves were also criticized for containing, as they did in some instances, verbal items which would run counter to a valid assessment of the members of the bilingual group. A further controversial point is the inclusion of questions which might be seen as biased towards a certain class-culture.

From the 1920s onwards research was undertaken in Wales, often by people who, according to Baker's (1988) review, were in favour of the use of Welsh as a second language. Nevertheless, they obtained results which appeared to lend support to the view that bilingualism can have a negative effect on intelligence. The studies by Saer (1922; 1923) were carried out, in rural areas and small urban districts in South Wales, on a large number of children and (another set of tests) on college students. Both English and Welsh were used as test languages. Few differences were found between the scores of urban bilinguals and urban and rural monoglots, but rural bilinguals had lower scores, and they were found to be two years behind peer monoglots. Saer concluded from his investigations that not only were rural bilinguals disadvantaged *vis-à-vis* English monolinguals, but in addition they were mentally confused, a negative consequence of their bilingualism which was likely to stay with them for the rest of their lives. These findings were taken very seriously by the school authorities. They proved an obstacle for Welsh mother-tongue teaching and bilingual education, but they also became the subject of intense scrutiny. The upshot was that a number of methodological errors were detected, thus questioning the validity of the conclusions (for a detailed discussion, see Baker 1988).

(2) *Period of 'neutral effects'* This stage overlaps both with the above-mentioned one and with the period of 'additive effects'. Its main contribution was the various reviews of investigations on the subject that it produced. For instance, the articles by Arsenian (1937) and Darcy (1953) reported on certain inadequacies in the methods previously employed. But, whereas their general conclusion was that bilingualism itself does not affect intelligence, they, too, reported on the imperfect knowledge of the L2 possessed by many bilinguals, which was apparent in tests requiring the use of verbal skills.

Studies carried out in the 1950s by W. R. Jones in Wales (e.g. Jones 1953; 1955; 1959) were concerned with measuring the intelligence levels of a large number of bilingual children. At first they appeared to show a correlation between monolingualism and higher intelligence scores. However, after re-analysing the data and re-categorizing several variables (too high a proportion of his bilinguals had a manual-group background, so they had been over-represented, whereas most monoglots belonged to the non-manual group) he came to the conclusion that there were no significant differences between the two as far as non-verbal IQ tests were concerned. His final results, published in 1959, therefore point towards no effect of bilingualism on intelligence. Jones concluded that bilingualism was not necessarily a source of intellectual disadvantage, and that there were no significant differences in IQ scores between bilinguals and monolinguals if the variable 'parental occupation' was taken into account – which presumably means that the differences between the two groups were attributable to factors arising out of socio-economic dissimilarity.

(3) *Period of 'additive effects'* A turning point in the debate was reached with Elizabeth Peal's and Wallace Lambert's investigations in a Canadian setting (1962). Starting against the background of the mainly negative nature of previous research, they expected to find a bilingual deficit in their subjects. Their aim was 'to pinpoint what the intellectual components of that deficit might be in order to develop compensatory strategies' (Lambert 1977: 16).

Peal and Lambert were aware of the shortcomings of previous research, and they took care to control the important variables. Their test groups (all children came from middle-class French schools in Montreal) were matched for socio-economic class, gender, age, school grades and language proficiency, and only balanced bilinguals and monoglots were included, thus reducing their original sample of 364 to 110. Their findings were surprising. In Baker's words, they ' . . . provided an appetizer, stimulant and menu for future research' (Baker 1988: 17).

They found that bilinguals scored more highly than monolinguals in both verbal and non-verbal measurements of intelligence. The authors argued that the former had a more diversified structure of intelligence and greater mental flexibility, and that therefore the cognitive functioning of bilinguals benefited from their bicultural experience and from positive transfer between languages.

These conclusions have, in turn, been critically examined and found to contain a number of weaknesses. The facts that the children tested came from middle-class homes and that only balanced bilinguals were selected made it doubtful whether the subjects could be seen as representative of bilinguals in general. MacNab (1979), and others after him, noted that choosing children according to parental occupation or socio-economic background might well mean that factors such as cultural milieu and social environment were not adequately accounted for, although they could be of crucial significance for a child's language experience. Another problem area concerned researchers' ways of argumentation. If test results show that there is a correlation between bilingualism and intelligence, this does not necessarily imply a causal link in either one direction or the other. Baker (1988) suggests that there may even be a third dimension to the 'chicken and egg game', namely that one (IQ) is simultaneously the cause and effect of the other (bilingualism); in his words, there is ' . . . mutual interaction and stimulation between dual language and cognitive abilities' (Baker 1988: 19).

However, Peal and Lambert's research had a profound impact on studies in this field. The techniques that they used were sophisticated and their tests well constructed. Their findings became widely known and led other people to look for positive effects of bilingualism on various other aspects of cognitive functioning. Some of these findings are outlined below.

In the context of research on cognitive development, an observation by Leopold (1949a), which is found in his case study of child bilingualism, appears to be relevant. He states that his daughter was not in the habit of clinging to particular words in songs, rhymes and stories, as is normal in young children; instead, she would readily accept new names for objects, and she did not repeat her favourite stories with stereotyped wording. Leopold attributed this looseness of the link between words (i.e. their phonetic shape) and their meaning to her bilingualism. A special sensitivity to language, manifested in the form of remarks on different forms of conveying meaning (including the use of other codes), was also noted by Imedadze (1967) and Fantini (1985), while Vygotsky (1962) had already argued that the positive side of bilingualism was that it led to greater awareness of linguistic operations.

In the 1970s a number of studies tried to establish the extent to which bilinguals were superior to monoglots in certain aspects of cognitive functioning, such as divergent and creative thinking and analytical orientation towards language. Anita Ianco-Worrall's (1972) study was carried out in South Africa with English–Afrikaans bilinguals whom she tested for metalinguistic ability. Only in the tests where the children had to make choices according to semantic or phonetic criteria did she find a significant difference between monolinguals and bilinguals. For example, in a test in which they were asked 'I have three words, CAP, CAN and HAT – which is more like CAP, CAN or HAT?', the bilinguals tended to select the semantically related word, but virtually all the monolinguals chose according to sound. Among the older children, both bilinguals and monolinguals tended towards a choice according to meaning. It could therefore be concluded, she claimed, that the bilingual children were at a more advanced stage of metalinguistic awareness, i.e. they had a greater ability in their consciousness of language forms and properties. Cummins (1978a) extended Ianco-Worrall's tests to Irish–English and Ukranian–English bilinguals and found similar results.

Sandra Ben-Zeev's experiments (1976) were carried out with Hebrew–English children (from Israel and the USA) and with Spanish–English bilinguals in the United States. Her tests involved word associations and word substitutions. One item, for instance, was in the form of a 'game' in which it was decided to call an airplane a 'turtle', and the question to be answered was 'Can the turtle fly?' (correct answer: yes). A more complex version entailed sentence production with a substituted word that resulted in a violation of conventional rules of grammatical agreement, e.g. in the game the word 'macaroni' had to be used for the first person pronoun 'I', so that the question 'How do you say "I am warm"?' was supposed to be answered 'Macaroni am warm'. In her various tests she found that bilinguals obtained better scores in word substitution exercises and also when they had to disregard grammatical rules of sentence construction (e.g. they avoided incorrect – in the game – replies such as '*I am warm*' or '*Macaroni is warm*'). Ben-Zeev inferred that bilinguals showed greater cognitive flexibility and were capable of more complex analytical strategies in their approach to language operations.

Sheridan Scott's (1973) study in Montreal aimed at finding a link between bilingualism and divergent thinking. Her study differed from others in that the children she considered were in the process of becoming bilingual (i.e. they were not bilingual already, before the testing began), and her approach was thus geared towards finding out whether their becoming bilingual would have any impact on their cognitive development. She compared two groups of children: one was given the opportunity of becoming bilingual in English and French during the seven-year period of the testing, by means of an immersion programme; the other group followed a conventional English-language curriculum. The two groups had been matched for IQ levels and social class. Again, her results point towards positive effects, because the bilinguals were the higher scorers in tests which required the subjects to focus their attention on something, e.g. a paper clip ('think of a paper clip'), and then asked them to list all the things that one could do with it which came to their minds.

Both Ianco-Worrall (1972) and Ben-Zeev (1976) suggest that bilinguals may possess greater sensitivity towards verbal and non-verbal feedback cues than monolinguals. This point has been taken up by other researchers (e.g. Bain 1976), and it finds expression in some of the ideas put forward by Cummins (1976). The argument is that bilinguals have a wider and more varied range of experience than monolinguals, as they have access to two cultures and operate in two different systems. Even if this does not result in doubling the total range of social and cultural experience, there may be a potential gain for bilinguals. Their need to switch from one code to another has also been seen as beneficial to flexible thinking, as each language may provide the speaker with distinct perspectives. Although neither of these ideas can yet be supported by conclusive research evidence, they do suggest an interesting panorama.

A substantial amount of 'positive effect' research is going on at the moment. However, as in the case of the less optimistic findings, close inspection of aims and procedures can disclose shortcomings – often concerning, once more, methodological issues. Many research schemes are set in contexts of additive bilingualism where children receive encouragement about their use of two languages, and also about learning in general. The problems of sampling and matching that seem to be inherent in all testing involving bilinguals have already been mentioned, as has the question of a possible causal relationship between bilingualism and cognitive processes. Baker (1988) comes to the conclusion that the trend of research appears to point towards positive effects rather than negative ones, but he is prudent enough to add that further advances in the field are needed before we can confidently answer the questions of whether the extent of the advantages is significant and whether bilingualism actually fosters educational progress. We shall have no real reason to be optimistic until such day as bilingual children receive, as a matter of course, widespread encouragement and some form of bilingual education, so that they can achieve their fullest possible potential in each of their languages.

6.2 Linguistic competence, cognitive functioning and the education of minority children

6.2.1 Semilingualism – 'BICS' and 'CALP'

The debate on semilingualism[2] that started in Scandinavia in the early 1970s (see section 1.3) led to further discussion of what precisely constitutes competence in a given language. It was found that the children of Finnish immigrants in Sweden frequently had poorly developed language skills in their home language when they started school, and that their levels of proficiency in Swedish (then the only school language) were also below those of comparable monolingual children in spite of their average intellectual ability. Skutnabb-Kangas and Toukomaa (1976) point to the social origin of the phenomenon: the children they had observed tended to come from socially deprived families with an unstimulating home-language environment, and they found themselves compelled to acquire the L2. These researchers argue that semilingualism should not be seen as a purely linguistic concept, but as one that includes cognitive aspects as well. Thus, they use the term for children who did not show 'full command of Swedish' (p. 28) in the measurements taken in vocabulary tests, taking also into account their understanding of abstract concepts and synonyms (p. 21). These authors remark on the discrepancy between the children's apparent linguistic competence (the impression of fluency they gave) and the lack of conceptual linguistic knowledge that became clear only when they had to perform in tests which required more complex cognitive operations.

In his earlier work Cummins (1978c; 1979a; 1979b) had referred to these two aspects of linguistic competence as 'surface competence' and 'cognitive linguistic competence'. By the former he meant 'those "visible" features of language which are relatively easy to measure, e.g. pronunciation, vocabulary, grammar, fluency, etc.', whereas the latter denoted 'the ability to make effective use of the cognitive functions of the language, i.e. to use language effectively as an instrument of thought and represent cognitive operations by means of language'. When considering the relationship of the bilingual child's L1 and L2, Cummins' notion of language competence referred to the latter type.

In later publications Cummins distances himself, just as others have done, from the notion of semilingualism, because of the ambiguous and even pejorative associations the term came to acquire. But he maintains his basic idea of language competence as consisting of two different components. He distinguishes 'BICS' ('basic interpersonal communication skills', which are those aspects of linguistic skills that are necessary for functioning in everyday contexts) from 'CALP' ('cognitive academic language proficiency', that is, the skills which are required outside immediate everyday communication situations). 'BICS' are sufficient for cognitively less demanding situations, and they can be measured by pronunciation and fluency tests. 'CALP' skills, on the other hand, are said to show high correlation with verbal sections of intelligence tests (Skutnabb-Kangas 1984a). Cummins (1981, 1984b) developed his ideas further by incorporating into linguistic competence the notions of context and cognitive complexity. Thus, he sees some communicative tasks as being cognitively undemanding, particularly when they are accompanied by paralinguistic features and if situational clues can provide feedback. On the other hand, certain activities (for instance, in the classroom) involve decontextualized language and are therefore of a more cognitively demanding type.

Cummins argues that surface fluency, or 'BICS', can develop fairly easily in minority children if they attend a classroom where a good deal of contextual support for language learning is provided. Furthermore, surface fluency in each language, L1 and L2, can develop with relative independence from the other. By comparison, context-reduced and cognitively demanding communication develop interdependently. This means that the kind of cognitive skills required for success in the more intellectually demanding tasks must be dependent on the relationship between the L1 and the L2, and that unhindered learning can take place only if both languages are sufficiently well established. Cummins' *Developmental Interdependence Hypothesis* suggests that the level of second language competence a child acquires depends to some extent on the stage of development that has been reached in her first. This theory provides the rationale for the kind of bilingual education that advocates the use of the child's mother tongue during the early stages of education, adding the second language only when she has developed higher-order cognitive and linguistic skills in the first. The assumption is that the ability to handle cognitively demanding tasks can be transferred to the L2 successfully.

6.2.2 The Balance and the Think Tank models

Speculation about the nature of the relationship between the bilingual's two languages has produced many hypotheses. With respect to the question of cognitive functioning and its educational implications, two models have been particularly influential.

(1) *The Balance theory* This model makes two basic assumptions. One is that the brain has only a limited capacity and therefore the addition of a second language automatically leads to a decrease of proficiency in the L1. When commenting upon it, Cummins (1981) uses the analogy of balloons: the bilingual has two half-full spaces, depicted as balloons, in his head, representing his L1 and L2 language proficiencies, while the monolingual has only one, better-filled balloon. The other assumption concerns the storage of language ability: the L1 and the L2 are seen as separately stored systems, and it is considered that they function independently of one another. Cummins refers to this as 'separate underlying proficiency' (or 'SUP').

This theory encourages the belief that bilingualism may result in some form of linguistic deficit, and that cognitive and educational development may become impaired by the bilingual experience. It is unable to account for code-switching and other features of bilingual speech in any terms except as interference. In view of the substantial amount of research which suggests probable positive effects of bilingualism on cognitive functioning, this theory has few advocates today, although it may still be adhered to by some lay persons who view bilingualism with suspicion.

(2) *The Think Tank model* Cummins (1981) made this proposal in response to the Balance theory. In place of the two balloons, he suggests the metaphor of a Think Tank containing the bilingual's L1 and L2 proficiency. Each maintains its separate linguistic characteristics, which are dependent on input and feedback received from output, yet the same mental expertise underlies reception and production of both languages. The notion of 'common underlying proficiency' (or 'CUP') is crucial to this model, expressing as it does cognitive activity as being centralized and independent from a particular language. Employing both languages will foster the bilinguals' think tank. However, if forced to make use of the weaker one only, for instance in the classroom, the bilingual child may encounter problems in understanding whatever is being taught, and this may in turn hold back the develop-

ment of the think tank and, consequently, lead to poor performance in tasks involving skills in both the home and the school language.

This theory can explain the successful acquisition of bi- or multilingualism, and it has no problems accounting for phenomena of bilingual speech. It is also congruent with other theories about the relationship of language and educational attainment. Like the previous model, however, it has certain limitations (see section 6.2.3 below).

6.2.3 The Threshold Theory

The Threshold Theory was developed in the attempt to deal with the inconsistency in findings regarding bilingual children's cognitive ability. It was proposed by Skutnabb-Kangas and Toukomaa (1977) and by Cummins (1976; 1978d), and based on their examination of issues relating to the education of minority children. It was concerned, especially, with establishing at what point bilingualism can be seen to lead to positive cognitive consequences.

Two thresholds are proposed in the levels of the bilinguals' linguistic competence. The lower threshold must be attained if negative cognitive effects are to be avoided, as limited linguistic skills will

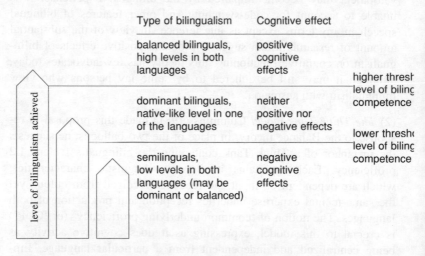

Source: Toukomaa and Skutnabb-Kangas (1977: 29)

FIGURE 6.1 Diagrammatic representation of the Threshold Hypothesis, showing cognitive effects of different types of bilingualism

hinder academic progress and cognitive growth. If the child achieves a level of bilingualism somewhere between the lower and the higher threshold (i.e. if she can function effectively in at least one of her languages), there are likely to be neither positive nor negative effects on cognitive abilities. High attainment in both languages occurs beyond the upper threshold. Such linguistic competence may entail positive cognitive effects.

6.3 Summary of the issues

Cummins' hypotheses concerning language proficiency and educational success of bilinguals take into account the various types of competence and skills required of pupils for performing different learning tasks. Together with the Developmental Interdependence Theory, the Threshold Theory is able to provide an explanation for the fact that migrant children who become bilingual in subtractive contexts, and who are taught through the medium of their weaker language, fail to develop sufficient competence in their second language and are underachievers in school tests. These models underline the requirement that transitional education programmes (where the child is taught in her L1 before she joins mainstream education in the L2) must be sufficiently long to permit the development of cognitive processes, which is necessary for coping with school tasks. Equally, the theories may explain why initial reception classes (for instance the 'Aufnahmeklassen' or reception classes in Germany, where Turkish children are taught German before joining monolingual peer groups) may not provide the hoped-for basis for migrant children to succeed in majority education. Similarly, the models offer an explanation as to why immersion programmes (such as the ones offered, on a voluntary basis, to majority children in Canada) can be successful. Although there may be temporary lags in achievement once the second language (French) is developed to a level that enables the children to cope with concepts through this medium, educational schemes that include immersion programmes (in Canada) have not been reported as having had detrimental effects on the children's progress. Naturally, in other parts of the world, where social and cultural conditions may be different (e.g. the Netherlands, Germany, Wales, Catalonia or the Basque Country), immersion programmes offered to minority children may produce quite different results.

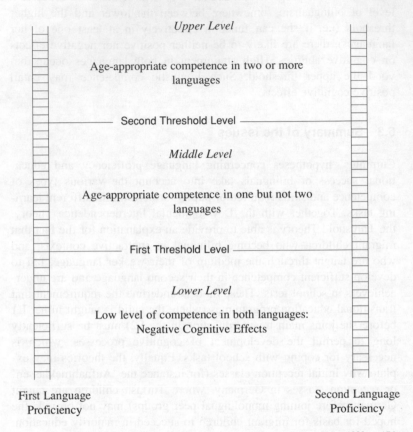

FIGURE 6.2 Bilingualism, Cognitive Functioning and the Threshold Theory

For the linguist these theories are less satisfactory than for the educationalist. They provide a neat representation of bilingualism and cognitive functioning, but although they use the notions of 'levels of bilingual attainment' and 'bilingual competence' there are no concrete examples of what these should be – for either 'BICS', 'CALP' or the thresholds levels. Baker's (1988) representation of the Threshold Theory provides us with a little more information than the original models. He shows language competence separately for each language, and he specifies the threshold levels by reference to an assumed 'age-appropriate' norm. So within each of the three levels one could represent an individual's bilingualism by indicating his or her language proficiency in L1 and L2 on the 'rungs'.

In an article in which they review some of the research into semilingualism with a view to reassessing this notion, Marilyn Martin-Jones and Suzanne Romaine (1986) point out that in his definition of language competence Cummins appears to be equating semantic with cognitive development. They argue that the relationship between language and thought processes may in fact be a great deal more complex than Cummins seems to suggest, and that it is oversimplistic to claim that the various language skills can be compartmentalized and tested separately in the way that he proposes.

Another criticism relates to the vague and rather narrowly defined concept of 'school success'. The idea of what constitutes success appears to be applied in the same way to all children, majority and minority, yet it tends to be defined in terms of traditional, middle-class values deduced from measured school tests, and thus reflecting majority-group standards. The minority child's perceived need and motivation to learn the second language and her expectation of education are likely to affect the outcome of the whole range of school activities.

Terms such as semilingualism[3] and notions like 'BICS' and 'CALP' will remain vague as long as there are no reliable means of testing the bilingual child's whole bilingual competence. At the moment it is not clear whether a supposed deficiency, as measured in formal tests and shown, for instance, as simplified language using fewer morphological devices, word-order irregularities or limited vocabulary, actually affects communication. Some linguists (e.g. Stölting 1980; Grosjean 1985a; Martin-Jones and Romaine 1986) have warned against proposing theories that may be misused as deficit interpretations outside the original remit within which they were conceived. It should be remembered that the above-mentioned models take a narrow view of cognitive functioning and bilingualism, as they do not allow for a wide range of cultural, social and political factors that can also influence the school achievement of minority children. Such aspects as the child's motivation towards learning in general, attitudes towards the L2, its speakers and school, parental support and attitudes, and the expectations and disposition of teachers regarding minority children may in fact be just as influential in determining attainment as linguistic and cognitive factors. They must be taken into account in interpreting the often observed phenomenon that, within certain multicultural settings, children belonging to some minorities have a higher success rate in educational achievement than those from other minority groups.

Lastly, we must remind ourselves that research findings present average scorings, i.e. they level out individual scores which may show considerable variation in relation to each other. Human beings experience language, culture and education in various differing ways, and whereas some may be more affected by cognitive or linguistic determinants, for others bilingualism and educational performance can be influenced largely by factors of a motivational or attitudinal kind.

An attempt has been made in the last two chapters to show that one cannot assume an *a priori* relationship between bilingualism on the one hand and personality development and cognitive functioning or educational achievement on the other. If the human mind can cope with a multitude of different functions and operations without suffering any detriment, why should bilingualism represent an exception? Whatever link between language and mind we want to postulate, it must be of such an abstract nature that it is able to accommodate any number of natural languages in this binomial relationship. There is no evidence that bilinguals suffer any negative effects in their development on account of their bilingualism, nor do they acquire a split view of the world. The once-famous Whorf-Sapir Hypothesis, which claimed that speaking a given language inevitably leads to holding certain cultural values (in other words, that the language one speaks determines one's world view), has remained a hypothesis. It would certainly be difficult to support it with regard to a bilingual – for which of his two languages would determine his experience of the world? Or does the bilingual have some kind of fluid values that can be adhered to or abandoned according to the language used at particular times? This, however, is not to say that bilinguals do not adjust their cultural behaviour as they switch from one language to another, so as to comply with the norms of communication and social conduct peculiar to each speech community. But their view of the world remains unaffected by this.

Naturally, the bilingual's cognitive and educational development is likely to be affected by social and psychological factors, but so is the monolingual's, even if the process is manifested differently. Like all children, bilinguals need parental support and favourable social attitudes around them to maintain their motivation for learning. They have special needs in so far as attention has to be paid to both their languages, at least until the two systems have become firmly established. There are a number of bilingual education programmes that provide support for the non-majority language, but only for a relatively short period of time, which means that afterwards the maintenance of the L2 comes to depend on the home or community efforts. It is frequently the case that the child remains bilingual but becomes dominant in the language of the majority and therefore establishes stronger (although not necessarily exclusive) links with the culture of the latter. Older immigrants or socially stigmatized migrant groups are more likely to suffer from psychological problems, brought about by home-sickness, feelings of guilt at abandoning previous cultural values, low self-esteem, social isolation, unemployment, poor housing and health-care – the list is long. However, these are not problems resulting from bilingualism, but rather the consequences of migration or minority status.

Notes

1. Traditional IQ tests require a correct reply for each question. This focus on one single acceptable answer has been termed 'convergent thinking'. 'Divergent thinking' represents a more open-ended skill which allows the use of imagination and creativity. Measurement of divergent thinking may be in terms of absolute numbers of sensible answers, but other ways of assessing can include scores for fluency, originality, flexibility (i.e. a number of different categories into which replies could be fitted) and elaboration of responses.

2. In a number of studies the expression 'foreign children' was used, which perhaps reflects the attitudes felt towards the children of immigrants; the term was dropped later, presumably as a result of changing attitudes.

3. Or, rather, 'double semilingualism', because the notion refers to the bilingual's two languages, both of them known only partially.

Chapter 7

Sociocultural aspects of bilingualism

7.1 Issues raised in the discussion of bilingualism

The controversy between proponents and opponents of bilingualism is an old one. We can find statements on the effects of bilingualism made as long ago as the beginning of the nineteenth century, and even earlier (the distinction between bilingual education and bilingual upbringing was not made at the time). The debate was often fuelled by people who seem to us today to have been unqualified to pass judgement because of their apparent lack of first-hand experience of bilingualism and bilinguals. Yet the views of philosophers such as Fichte (1762–1814) and Herder (1744–1803), educationalists like Jahn (1778–1852) and Laurie (who published a series of famous lectures in 1890), philologists such as Wilhelm von Humboldt (1767–1835) and, earlier this century, Schmidt-Rohr (1932; 1936) and Weisgerber (1933), and perhaps even some psychologists and paediatricians (e.g. Sander 1930; 1934; Pichon 1936), have done much to discredit bilingualism.[1] The present century has seen a good deal of polemical writing on the issue, especially in the wake of extreme nationalism and fascism in various parts of Europe and beyond. During the last thirty years, however, an increasing amount of detailed investigation has led to a re-assessment of some of the issues raised previously; with the application of more modern methodologies based on empirical research, new insights have been gained and a more balanced picture has emerged.

If we consider some of the views on bilingualism advanced over the last 150 years or so it is possible to discern the main issues that have attracted the attention of scholars. It will also become apparent that opinion has swung full circle, at least among those who may be regarded as experts in the field. Nowadays bilingualism is no longer considered to impair the intelligence of the individual (or the whole ethnic group) or to be the cause of emotional problems. Some even say that, on the contrary, it can contribute to enhanced intellectual abilities (see Chapter 6). Bilingual education, for so long scorned and neglected, is now seen by many as an attractive proposition. What has caused this dramatic change?

The main point of departure in the debate on bilingualism has usually been the assumption that it has some kind of influence on the bilingual individual. Numerous studies have defended the theories of either positive or negative effects of bilingualism on, for instance, cognitive development or character formation. In fact, it is not easy to find anyone today, whether specialist, teacher or lay person, who does not hold an opinion, often a strongly felt one, on the subject. But why should bilingualism have a particular effect on the individual? No one ever asks whether *mono*lingualism exerts a specific influence on the speaker – and in view of the fact that well over half the world's population is bilingual this does not seem to be an unreasonable question to ask. Why should bilingualism, any more than any other concrete skill or ability (e.g. musical), carry any consequence for a person's development and character? It is rarely bilingualism itself (on its own) that has been proved to have had any measurable impact. More often than not, it is the socio-psychological context of the bilingual individual that can be shown to have a bearing on his or her evolution as an individual and a member of society.

Bilinguals differ from monolinguals only in that they use two different linguistic codes (which in the case of child bilinguals have been acquired largely in the same way as monolinguals acquired theirs), and in that they may have access to two different cultures. Just like monoglots, they use language in order to communicate and socialize, i.e. in order to function as members of a social group. Whether their tool is one language or two, or a sign language, does not *by itself* make any difference.

7.2 Views of bilingualism

The idea of a close link between language, nationality and nation which arose out of the Romantic movement, in the late eighteenth and early nineteenth centuries, was to have far-reaching consequences for bilingualism, as well as in other respects. It was seized upon by some writers and politicians during the next few decades, who used it to support their arguments in favour of the supremacy of the nation state. A national language was seen as a sign of the nation's unity and a symbol of its identity. This kind of ideology paid scant attention to the needs of linguistic minorities. The influential German educationalist Friedrich Ludwig Jahn, best known today for his efforts to introduce physical training as part of the curriculum, spoke out strongly against bilingual education, claiming that it would retard the linguistic and cognitive development of children. He, and others after him, argued that a child can cope with only one mother tongue. The first language was also said to impart a particular view of the world, so if the young learner was confronted with two different visions or perspectives he was likely to be torn between divergent *Weltanschauungen* and loyalties (Jahn 1808). At the end of the nineteenth century this view was still widespread; for instance, the English educationalist Laurie said:

> If it were possible for a child to live in two languages at once equally well, so much the worse. His intellectual and spiritual growth would not thereby be doubled, but halved. Unity of mind and character would have great difficulty in asserting itself in such circumstances.
>
> (Laurie 1890: 15; quoted in Baker 1988: 10)

The claim that bilingualism causes intellectual retardation, linguistic chaos and conflicting or split identity was still being made by various writers in the first third of the twentieth century. Some, such as Weisgerber and Schmidt-Rohr for example, were directly influenced in their thinking by the prevailing German nationalist ideology. But there were others – linguists, doctors and sociologists from many different backgrounds – who, on the basis of bona fide research and without any apparent ideological bias, wrote that bilingualism had a negative effect on the development of the individual: left-handedness and stuttering, or even, in certain cases, intellectual or moral inferiority and social marginality were, in their view, possible consequences.

In his book *Languages in Contact* (1953) Weinreich included an appendix entitled 'Effects of bilingualism on the individual', in which he surveyed the writings of some fifty authors on the subject. In the majority of cases negative views had been expressed. This is not surprising, because it was clear (from Weinreich's survey and from later work by other linguists) that people's feelings about bilingualism were shaped by their opinions at the time on matters as diverse as intelligence, language learning, education, the position of minorities, and the status of one's mother tongue as a world language.

For a long time many European states pursued centralist policies which allowed for little expression of cultural or linguistic diversity. This meant that members of linguistic minorities were obliged to learn the language of the dominant majority in order to survive and to partake in public life. The majority's views on bilingualism were (and still often are) influenced by their associations with, and prejudices about, the minority or minorities existing in their midst. If the minority group is suppressed, placed in a position of social and economic disadvantage and made to feel culturally insecure, and if their language receives no support, that society's negative attitudes towards the members of the minority group(s) extend to their behaviour, including their linguistic behaviour – and from that point on to bilingualism itself. If this is the case, it is easier to blame bilingualism for unsatisfactory school achievement or low social status than to attribute shortcomings of this kind to inequality of treatment for which the nation as a whole could be held responsible. Eventually, some minority members end up having a low opinion of themselves and, as a consequence, their bilingualism may help to reinforce the idea that using two languages creates problems for the individual. This is why bilingualism has been considered by many immigrants as a sort of halfway house between monolingualism in the 'home' language and monolingualism in the language of the new country, and as a sign that total integration and acculturation have not yet been achieved.

Bilingualism is sometimes regarded by minorities as a necessary evil, representing a compromise between the need, on the one hand, to hang on to their own language and identity and, on the other, to maintain political and economic links with the majority. This may well involve a conflict of interests – the desire for independence clashing with economic and political improbabilities – and bilingualism might then be seen as a symbol of such conflict. The fact is that, in some parts of the world bilingualism has been (or is still) viewed with suspicion by members of both majorities and minorities. For the former it may mean the threat of possible conspiracy, a code in which the minority communicate in ways not understood by the majority. For the latter, the minority aware of the unstable nature of their bilingualism, it may represent the last stage before linguistic capitulation, i.e. shifting towards monolingualism brought about by the decline of the minority language and all it stands for.[2]

Attitudes towards minorities are slowly changing. The people of many states are finding it increasingly easier to take a certain pride and interest in their indigenous minorities. On the other hand, their attitudes towards some of their new minorities tend to be guarded, even hostile at times. It is true that most European minorities today enjoy more freedom and support for their language than fifty years ago, and many bilingual services are available where previously there was none. The reason for this is that no European country has failed to feel the impact of the wave of post-war migration, greater social mobility, and phenomena such as temporary work abroad and intermarriage, as well as new initiatives in political, military and economic cooperation. All of these have brought together, to a greater extent than in the past, many different individuals, including members of minorities. As a response to social reality, views on bilingualism were bound to change. The large number of publications, often using more reliable methods of investigation than the old ones, that have challenged the negative sentiments expressed by earlier writers have also done their share in bringing about a better climate of opinion.

To a large extent, therefore, the discussion of bilingualism has centred around social issues raised by the coexistence of majority and minority groups. In this section, we shall look at three areas of research which have received special attention, all three connected with the debate about the possible effects of bilingualism (as Grosjean 1985a: 469 put its, 'the "effects" literature'): the psychological, the linguistic and the cognitive consequences of being bilingual. They bear strongly on questions of pedagogy and school curriculum; this literature deals, then, with matters relating to the education of bilinguals as well.

Much has been written about bilingual education; so much, indeed, that this area of study has developed into a subject in its own right. In 1953 UNESCO published an historic document in which it declared that every child had the right to receive primary education through the medium of the vernacular. Discussion of the education of the children of minorities, both indigenous and new ones, has been continuous ever since. Unfortunately, the amount of knowledge gained has not (in Europe especially) been matched by state provision in this field. The subject of bilingual education is covered in detail, for instance, in Swain and Lapkin (1982) and Genesee (1987) which deal with immersion programmes in Canada; Spolsky (1986), on multicultural and multilingual educational issues in various parts of the world; and

Husén and Opper (1983), Shapston and D'Oyley (1984), Cummins (1984a), Churchill (1986), Byram (1986b), Boos–Nünning *et al.* (1986), the OECD CERI Report (1987), Baker (1988), Skutnabb-Kangas and Cummins (1988) and Byram and Leman (1989), which look into a variety of aspects of the education of minorities, mainly within the European context.

7.3 Psychological aspects

In this section we consider two areas. The first is of a psychosomatic type, and it will be only touched upon so as to concentrate more on the question of whether bilingualism can be said to have any detrimental effect on the bilingual's personality development.

7.3.1 Stuttering

It has been claimed that bilingual children are more likely to stutter than monolingual ones. This claim was based on reports on the observation and treatment of several instances of language disorder in which bilingualism was deemed to have been a contributing cause. For instance, in 1937 the French doctors Pichon and Borel-Maisonny published a book on stuttering (it was reprinted in 1964); 14 per cent of the children in their study who stuttered used more than one language. Pichon (1936) had previously argued that bilingualism had detrimental effects on children's cognitive development, which perhaps helps to explain the background to the later work. Investigations carried out later by Lebrun and Paradis in east Chicago indicate that the symptoms described in the Pichon and Borel-Maisonny case histories are also found in monolingual stutterers (Paradis and Lebrun 1984: 12 ff.). Another study undertaken in the 1930s (Travis et al. 1937) also came to the conclusion that the incidence of stuttering was higher among bilinguals (2.8 per cent) than for monolinguals (1.8 per cent). Paradis and Lebrun deal with this claim, too: in their reassessment the subjects are listed according to race and linguistic origin, and they find that, if this is done, black English-speaking monolinguals and children who could not speak English well are much more likely to have higher scores for stuttering than the rest. They show, therefore, that any correlation between bilingualism and stuttering must be unreliable. They suggest that stuttering is a neurotic symptom for which there may be any number of psychosomatic or socially induced reasons; bilingual-

ism, however, has not been shown to be one of them, although stam-
mering may of course be brought about in a bilingual child whose
social and educational experience is so devastating as to disturb his/her
psychological well-being.

7.3.2 Personality development

Much of nineteenth- and early twentieth-century thinking on education
was influenced by the conviction that the development of the personality of the child is shaped by the language and culture in which the
individual grows up. For some authors, e.g. Weisgerber (1929) and
Schmidt-Rohr (1932), this meant positing a close connection between a
particular language (say, German or English) and the development of a
German or English child. Naturally, such theoretical standpoints came
up against the problem of how to accommodate two languages and
cultures, in the case of the bilingual child, and the view that bilingualism would bring about 'marginal men' suffering from split identities
was voiced fairly frequently (see Goldberg 1941). But long before a
series of German authors had condemned bilingualism in the 1920s
and 1930s, writers in other parts of the world had been warning about
emotional problems caused by bilingualism (see Weinreich 1968: 117
ff. for a survey and some striking quotations).

The basis for many of these claims was anecdotal evidence in the
form of informal observations and comments by individuals; later more
systematic work was undertaken into phenomena of social alienation
and the possible detrimental effects of bilingualism on personality development among members of minorities and immigrant communities.
In 1943 Child carried out a study of second-generation Italian Americans, looking into their attitudes towards their dual heritage. He
concluded that his subjects had reached varying degrees of acculturation. He identified three different groups:

(1)   those who identified strongly with American social and cultural
      values;
(2)   those who orientated themselves more strongly towards their Ita-
      lian background, rejecting everything American;
(3)   those who refused to think in terms of these parameters.

As part of a wider study of Italian immigrants in Bedford, Great
Britain, Arturo Tosi (1983) also describes three distinct sets of attitudes

he observed among second-generation Italian Britons, classifying them according to their reactions to social forces and to the pressures exerted by their rather conservative Italian home background,

(1) People who displayed 'apathetic' reactions were in the majority. They were those who could not cope with the pressures resulting from the two cultural contexts in which they found themselves and therefore yielded to the greater influence – that of the wider social environment – trying to conform to British values while trying to suppress their Italian background (but of course not being able to do so totally): 'Here the passive attitude that has made him [the individual second-generation immigrant] unable to sort out his own personal conflict also prevents him from understanding the functions and roles of the two opposing sets of values and behaviour' (Tosi 1983: 116).

(2) The 'in-group reaction' is the name given by Tosi to the attitudes displayed by those who identify strongly with the values of the Italian community. He argues that the very limited facilities available to the immigrant group he studied, and the lack of opportunity for more varied social interaction, were largely to blame for the youngsters' apathetic and in-group attitudes towards the 'host' society.

(3) Only a small group of young people showed what he calls 'rebel reaction', i.e. rebellion against the previous two extremes. In a conscious effort to become bilingual and bicultural, they have refused to retreat into the old culture (Italian) or to 'sell out' to the new one (British). Again, Tosi emphasizes here the importance of wider social opportunities, educational help and communication outside the host community (i.e., contacts with Italy and Italian culture).

A series of studies on young people's attitudes towards their mixed parental background was carried out by Lambert and his associates in the 1960s and 1970s. Their subjects were American and Canadian English–French bilinguals, both children and adolescents. None of these investigations, which were carefully matched with monolingual control groups and controlled for factors such as socio-economic status and linguistic standards, found any correlation between bilingualism and adversely affected personality. Different patterns of attitudes could be discerned, in line with the ones described by Child (1943) and later by Tosi (1983): some people oriented themselves towards the English or towards the French backgrounds, others did neither, and a third group was successful in adapting to a mixed French and English sociocultural environment (Aellen and Lambert 1969; Gardner and Lambert 1972).

The largest groups in Child (1943) and Tosi (1983) were undergoing a shift from bilingualism towards monolingualism. But the assumption that shedding a language speeds up acculturation or helps avoid culture conflict is probably an erroneous one. For the individual who finds himself/herself cut off from his/her first language it may be necessary, or practical, to concentrate on his/her new language and culture. But for a minority group a shift away from bilingualism may not solve the social or psychological problems its members experience – on the contrary, they may become aggravated. A Turkish community in, say, the Federal Republic of Germany is likely to be considered foreign whether they have lost their mother tongue or not. Therefore, to abandon the home language in the hope of ridding oneself of the stigma of being a member of an 'immigrant group' may be too high a price to pay – and pointless, anyway.

The incidence of psychosomatic illness among migrant workers and refugees in western Europe seems to be disproportionately high (Appel and Muysken 1987). Their children are reported as showing a comparatively frequent occurrence of behavioural disturbances, and they are said to underachieve consistently at school. But there is no indication that these problems are caused by these people's bilingualism. There are, on the other hand, plenty of reasons to think that they may be the result of the diverse pressures they are exposed to, as a consequence of being the most stigmatized and underprivileged members of society: the subjects are more likely to suffer from poor housing, unemployment and social marginalization than any other section of their communities. It has been shown that many problems can be eased when subtractive bilingualism is turned into additive bilingualism. This is the case when the majority begins to show some appreciation of the minority group's culture and language, for instance by allocating radio and television time to it and including its study in the school curriculum. Appel and Muysken (1987) report on research carried out in the Netherlands on the social and emotional development of Turkish and Moroccan children; those who took part in a transitional bilingual programme showed fewer problems than a comparable group of children who had attended monolingual Dutch schools.

The two studies by Lambert and others mentioned earlier (Aellen and Lambert 1969; Gardner and Lambert 1972), as well as the one undertaken in cooperation with Tucker (Lambert and Tucker 1972), involved settings of additive bilingualism. Subjects were all reported to be happily settled in their English–French backgrounds in Canada and the USA; many of them came from middle-class families which provided strong support for bilingualism. Lambert was also closely involved in a Montreal pilot project (known as the 'St Lambert Experiment'), which aimed at making monolingual majority (English-speaking) children bilingual in French and English. For this purpose, a group of children who were monolingual in English were given their initial schooling entirely in French. Their progress was carefully monitored and compared with that of a monolingual control group taught in English (reported in Lambert and Tucker 1972). Although the medium of instruction was French and the teachers tended to use only French when speaking to the pupils, the latter could use their common L1 in the classroom and in the playground. This was in significant contrast with the situation of the minority child who enters mainstream education in the L2. The children's acquisition of French was very successful, and the positive results led to the launch of national immersion programmes all over Canada. The main benefits (for the state) of these programmes can be seen in the part they play in lessening linguistic prejudice towards the French-Canadian minority. In their 1972 publication Lambert and Tucker reported that a change in attitudes could be observed in children who, after grades five and six, had become functionally bilingual: these children were beginning to identify with Canadian and European French culture, as well as with English Canadian; they felt at ease in French social settings and expressed positive feelings towards French-speaking people. The authors' researchers therefore felt confident enough to voice their conviction that biculturalism had been achieved with no loss of English identity. Up to now these immersion programmes have involved only French for English-speaking majority children. One must hope that eventually the several other linguistic minorities of Canada (for example the speakers of Inuktitut, an Eskimo language spoken in northern Canada by the Inuit people) will also be able to benefit from the additive bilingualism afforded to its linguistic majority by means of bilingual education programmes.

The vast majority of bilinguals in the world never have a choice between staying monolingual or learning two languages. With the exception of élite bilinguals and children from majorities undergoing immersion programmes, bilingualism is usually a social or economic necessity. It is with respect to these people that the phenomenon of *anomie* has been discussed. The term was originally introduced by the French sociologist Dürkheim (1858–1917), to describe the feelings of rootlessness, social isolation and personal disorientation experienced by those who were in the process of moving from one social class to another. Applied to the bilingual (and also to people who, through intense motivation, become proficient in a foreign language), *anomie* may denote 'feelings of chagrin or regret as he loses ties in one group, mixed with fearful anticipation of entering a relatively new group' (Lambert, Just and Segalowitz 1970: 274).

Anomie may also result from pressures brought about by conflicting cultural norms and loyalties felt by second-generation immigrants. Both Child (1943) and Tosi (1983) mention the inability of many young immigrants to make positive choices and to resolve the discordant demands made on them by the home and the wider communities – what usually happens in practice is that they are not at all free to choose. Baetens Beardsmore (1982) sees *anomie* as one of the more important problems implicit in becoming bilingual. The person 'who tries to reconcile two widely divergent linguistic and cultural patterns may find the inaccessible goals [of achieving balanced ambilingualism] presented to him by his two environments leading to feelings of frustration' (Baetens Beardsmore 1982: 127).

He argues both that *anomie* is more likely to result when the cultural norms of the two communities are highly differentiated, that it affects adults and adolescents more deeply than children, and that it is more often found among individuals of low socio-economic status.

It appears that *anomie* is primarily a psychological phenomenon brought about by certain sociocultural and socio-economic constellations. Whilst there is no necessary correlation between features of bilingualism and factors of personal development (i.e. a bilingual's personality cannot be said to be pre-determined to evolve in any particular direction), it does seem that at certain times particular bilingual groups or individuals may be especially vulnerable to some kind of psychological instability. As a result of a feeling of being pulled in different directions and being unable to resolve the ensuing problems by turning to either one language or culture, *anomie* may, in extreme cases, occur. The question of 'Who am I?' is of course asked by monolinguals and bilinguals alike, but in an attempt to find an answer the latter has the additional dimension of his/her biculturalism to contend with. There is now a growing number of immigrant writers who have expressed their search for identity in literary form. Some are intrigued by the pluralist nature of migration, a consequence of the fact that this century has experienced migration – and loss of self – on an unprecedented scale. An atmosphere of linguistic and cultural equilibrium, brought about by parental and social support of both languages and cultures, can serve as counterbalance, as it will facilitate a sound development of the psychological make-up of the bilingual child. The most effective way in which a state can contribute to the bicultural person's well-being is by providing a variety of types of educational and cultural facilities, so as to suit the different needs of bilingual citizens.

In connection with the issue of the development of personal identity, bilinguals themselves sometimes report having experienced problems when asked by monolinguals about their national allegiance. Children, in particular, often find such questions embarrassing. They do not normally identify with large groups, and the concept of nationality is not really understood by them, apart from some perception of a link with a particular language or person. They may say that they are a little of this and a little of the other, referring to both the parents' ethnic group(s) and the country where they live, or they may insist that they are just the same as other children in their environment. What they seem to resent most is being singled out on the basis of the languages they speak. In one of the chapters (entitled 'So I think I'll stay halfway') of her book *Many Voices*, Jane Miller (1983) transcribes her interviews with some young bilingual girls in London who talked about the frustrating feeling of not being quite accepted as natives of either of the two cultures they had access to; for example, María, a girl of Spanish parents, then aged seventeen, said: 'When I go back [to Spain] they call me, "Oh look, the English girl". Oh, I get annoyed. And when I come here, "Oh look, Spanish girl". So I think I'll stay halfway. . . but you have to sort of sacrifice yourself' (Miller 1983: 24).

Similarly, one of my children was quite indignant (at the age of 9:5) when he found that, while staying with friends in Germany, some children at the school he was attending noticed at once from his spoken German that he was not from the region. They asked him where he came from, and from that moment they called him 'der Engländer'. He seemed frustrated that, in spite of his trilingual upbringing (which led him to believe that he was German, Spanish and English), he was nevertheless considered a foreigner. Such incidents bring home the message that raising children bilingually requires also that parents point out to them the various ways in which they are perceived to be different from monolinguals, so as to help them define and sort out their identities.

Bilingualism does not predispose the subject towards psychological problems, but for the individual bilingual it may require a more conscious effort to establish his/her identity. The socialization process of children entails modelling their identity on that of the community. In the case of the bilingual child two models present themselves, thus making socialization more complex.

7.4 Linguistic aspects

Before the spate of research carried out in the 1960s into various aspects of bilingualism, minorities and education, one view that was commonly held among lay people was that bilingualism had a detrimental effect on the child's linguistic skills. The idea that a second language is acquired at the cost of the first, and that therefore neither can ever be mastered fully, was widespread. The observed markers of bilingual speech were regarded negatively, and they offended monolingual speakers' ideals of purity of language. Little thought, if indeed any at all, was given to the notion of bilingual language competence as being different from the monolingual's; nor was it ever suggested, at that time, that mixed language could be anything but a sign of imperfect linguistic knowledge.

7.4.1 Assessing bilinguals

The early literature on bilinguals (reports on both individuals and groups) varies greatly in methodology and therefore in reliability. It was often the case that the bilinguals who were the object of attention were compared with monolinguals without any attempt being made at controlling the variables that today are known to play an important part, such as the children's socio-economic and educational backgrounds, and their levels of intelligence and motivation. Also, the research tools available for measuring and comparing linguistic ability and performance were sometimes crude, consisting for instance of simple language tests administered to both bilingual and monolingual groups in the common tongue, without paying any heed to such issues as which was the weaker/stronger language in the case of the bilingual speakers. But considerable progress has been made in the last few years in the areas of assessing bilinguals and measuring their language skills by making reference to (1) those features which are evident in monolinguals and (2) those which are characteristic of bilinguals only.

7.4.2 Linguistic competence as the object of assessment

Bilingualism is an unstable phenomenon and, as we know, bilinguals differ a great deal from one another in the degree of proficiency they achieve and the extent to which they maintain their languages. Bilingual children usually gain full communicative competence in at least one of their languages; this competence includes both the internalized knowledge of a particular linguistic code and the ability to use it (more or less) effectively in acts of communication. Carolyn Kessler (1984) establishes a theoretical framework for communicative competence in which she identifies four areas of knowledge and skill. Taken together, they provide a breakdown of what is involved in the process of language acquisition.

(1) *Grammatical* (or linguistic) competence refers to the mastery of the linguistic code.

(2) *Sociolinguistic* competence applies to the acquisition of the sociocultural rules that define the appropriate use of language in different social contexts, e.g. children have to learn where, when and to whom they can(not) use informal speech/styles.

(3) *Discourse* competence is concerned with learning to combine utterances into meaningful entities; it entails, for instance, the knowledge of how to introduce or close a topic, and turn-taking conventions.

(4) *Strategic* competence refers to the pragmatic strategies a native speaker resorts to when communication breaks down and (s)he needs to compensate for a failure in language performance: paraphrase, circumlocution, repetition and avoidance are examples of such strategies, which may be used for 'survival' or for rhetorical purposes.

Developing certain aspects of communicative competence can be a long process for monolingual children. There are bound to be at least some similarities between the acquisition of competence in Language A and Language B, in the case of those acquiring skills in two or more languages, particularly if the cultures involved are not too diverse. But there may be wide variation in the extent to which these different aspects of competence are developed. Also, as Kessler (1984: 30) points out, there is a linguistic dimension to consider: 'the acquisition of communicative competence in two languages must further take into account the interaction between two language systems'.

A number of interrelated factors will impinge upon the simultaneous or sequential acquisition of communicative competence in two languages.

(1) The *linguistic environment* will determine the nature and degree of language input. For instance, language used in the home and among friends tends to be highly context-bound, and speakers can depend on paralinguistic features such as mimicry, gestures and non-linguistic sounds. Language at school, on the other hand, differs increasingly from the ordinary use outside as the child progresses through the educational system: the content is constantly being renewed, and the language is often (whenever issues unrelated to the immediate classroom environment are discussed) highly decontextualized. In addition, language is employed frequently for developing new skills, such as reading and writing, and cognitive processes – for example, calculation or multiplication.

(2) The *relationships* between the child and, on one hand, the home and, on the other, the teachers, school friends and members of the peer group, will influence the kind of social interaction and communication situations experienced by the child.

(3) *Affective variables*, such as the child's emotional bonds with various speakers of her two languages, or the perception of prevailing attitudes towards both her languages and cultures, may also be of crucial importance, as will a large number of personal characteristics.

(4) *The need to use the L1 and the L2* will result from a combination of factors (1), (2) and (3), to name just some.

Any change in the environment can affect a bilingual person's communicative needs. Contact with one of the languages may be interrupted, or increased, and as a result the pattern of her bilingualism will be altered: passive may turn into active bilingualism, or vice versa. There are only a few studies that deal with recessive bilingualism, and it is not yet clear to what extent a language can be fully forgotten, or retrieved, once left behind. Burling (1959) and Murrell (1966) report on the rapid loss of a second language in early childhood, once all association with it had ceased. In the case described by Søndergaard (1981), language loss or, as he puts it, the 'decline of bilingualism' was probably due to a combination of lack of continuity of contact and emotional factors. Berman (1979) writes on her young daughter's temporary loss and subsequent recovery of Hebrew, while maintaining English, the language of the parents. Older bilinguals are less likely to descend into total unavailability of one of their languages, as in most cases they will retain at least some rudimentary form of passive bilingualism on which they can rebuild or 'restructure' (Grosjean 1985a) their language competence. So, the detailed configuration of a bilingual's language is quite likely to vary over the period of his/her life. Competence in either language may change and shift in order to adapt to new situations, new environments, new communication needs; but, of course, one's general communicative competence is not radically altered by this.

As far as communicative competence and language learning and forgetting are concerned, Grosjean challenges bilingual research to explore new avenues: rather than trying to measure levels of attained grammatical competence in each language taken individually and out of context, one should endeavour to find out, he believes, 'how the human communicator adjusts and uses one, two or more languages – separately or together – to maintain a necessary level of communicative competence' (Grosjean 1985a: 473).

When investigating bilingualism, then, care should be taken to choose sample groups who are matched according to the kind of bilingualism they possess (whether active or passive, for instance), in relation to the learning situation under which they became bilingual, e.g. whether theirs was subtractive or additive bilingualism, and also with respect to their bilingual competence.

7.4.3 Measuring bilingual language skills

The traditional method of gauging bilingualism was to assess individual language skills and proficiency in each language by, for instance, testing bilinguals' understanding and production of certain lexical or grammatical items, in either spoken or written form, or by measuring their reaction to various linguistic clues (in terms of speed, or correctness), or by asking them to carry out linguistic operations (such as filling in blanks, retelling a story, completing sentences etc.). A number of different techniques have been devised for appraising bilinguals, with a view to arriving at valid ways of comparing them with monolinguals. For example, records of spontaneous speech can be analysed for a number of variables, such as sentence length and complexity or richness of vocabulary; the recordings are often played back to monoglots, who pass judgement on the language (without necessarily knowing that the speakers are bilingual); a wide range of language tests can be used to assess mastery of syntax and lexis. There are also procedures for finding out which of the bilingual person's languages is the dominant one. They include word-association tests, true/false statements and presenting lists with cognate pairs (e.g. French 'plume', Spanish 'pluma') or words with identical form and meaning in the two languages (e.g. German 'real', English 'real') but of course different pronunciation, to be read out (the language to which the pronunciation chosen most often belongs is considered to be the stronger one). Other ways of assessing relative proficiency involve various translation exercises, responses to spoken/written stimuli, or verbal/pictorial instructions. Many of these tests are carried out under laboratory conditions, and the response time is recorded; the higher speed of reaction is then attributed to the dominant language.

7.4.4 The problems of assessing bilingual proficiency

Measuring bilingualism remains notoriously difficult, and so far none of the methods and techniques used has been found to be generally satisfactory. It is not easy to construct tests that are entirely valid if the appropriateness of the setting within which they are administered is taken into account. Any sampling and matching procedures with control groups raise the question of comparability. Another problem area concerns the nature of the linguistic means employed. For instance, the language used for a given test may be related to a topic, or couched in a style, unknown to the bilingual person being assessed; it may not accurately reflect his/her social or cultural experience; or it may require the use of skills (e.g. reading or writing) not normally used by the subject in the language being evaluated. Another danger is the failure to take account of the fact that a bilingual's language competence (which draws on the knowledge of two languages) is different from that of a monolingual. If the test battery is designed in such a way that it is to be used with monolinguals as well as bilinguals, then it is unlikely to contain the kind of language many bilinguals are most familiar with, namely language incorporating speech markers (such as mixes and switches) that are frequently present in bilingual talk. Also, it may provide few opportunities to use such bilingual language as the subject would normally employ.

More generally, with reference to the interpretation of bilingual data it is imperative to approach the task from different angles (see Hoffmann forthcoming for examples). Grosjean (1985a) highlights the importance of recording also the bilingual speech modes. These vary according to the situation in which the speaker/hearer finds himself, ranging from interaction with monolinguals in either of the two languages to talking with bilinguals who share his/her two codes. What might look like interference from one language on the other may well be intentional borrowing or code-switching in the bilingual mode. As Grosjean laments: 'Rare are the bilingual corpora that clearly indicate the speech mode the bilinguals were in when their speech was recorded; as a consequence, many unfounded claims are made about the bilingual's knowledge of his or her languages' (Grosjean 1985a: 474).

Formal tests tend to stress linguistic form, as in order to answer any given item it is necessary to produce or recognize specific linguistic units. However, such responses may not reveal the bilingual's ability to communicate. Thus, in many cases, the results obtained can only allow the formulation of tentative statements about the bilinguals' partial proficiency in each language, but not about his or her full bilingual communicative competence.

Notes

1. The case of Humboldt is remarkable. At least two of his children grew up bilingually while they were staying with their father in Italy; in letters to his wife (see some extracts in Porsché 1983: 68 ff.) he comments on their language use, in which Italian was becoming increasingly dominant, and it seems that he saw nothing unusual in bilingual acquisition. It is curious that Humboldt's theories on the structure and meaning of language were later used for the idealization of monolingualism.

2. Several instances from various chapters of European history could be quoted. One clear example is provided in the 1847 'Report of the Royal Commission of Inquiry into the State of Education in Wales'. The three Commissioners, all Englishmen, found that schools in Wales were inadequate (which is not surprising, as many were so in most of Britain at the time). However, they blamed the Welsh language for the failures of education in the Principality, calling it 'a manifold barrier to the moral progress and commercial prosperity of the people' (cited

in Baker 1985: 42). As far as the administration of justice was
concerned, their judgement was even harsher, as they contended
that the 'evil' of the Welsh language was obviously great, since
it distorted the truth, favoured feud and abetted perjury. In a different century and another part of Europe, the careful avoidance
of any reference to bilingualism in the wording of Catalonia's
many official pronouncements on language use in the region can
be taken as evidence of many Spaniards' suspicion of the subject. Castilian Spanish is the national language, and therefore
every citizen (according to the 1978 Spanish Constitution) has
the duty to learn it. Catalonia promotes Catalan as its own language – so bilingualism is the result. But no mention is ever
made of the word: Catalan, not bilingualism, is officially promoted (see section 13.2 for a fuller discussion).

SOCIOLINGUISTIC ASPECTS OF BILINGUALISM

PART II

SOCIOLINGUISTIC ASPECTS OF
BILINGUALISM

Chapter 8

Societal multilingualism

8.1 Multilingualism in society

There is no reason to believe that monolingualism is the normal state of affairs in human society. In fact, bilingualism is more widespread, since more than half the world's population can claim to be bilingual. At the societal level multilingualism is quite common, particularly in the continents of Africa and Asia. Bilingualism in the individual results from a person's contact with two (or more) languages. Multilingualism comes about when speakers of different languages are brought together within the same political entity. In the history of the world, the organization of human society into states has rarely followed ethnic or linguistic groupings.

Most countries display considerable linguistic diversity. Political frontiers have proved to be much less stable than linguistic ones, and each border change was likely to bring with it a change in linguistic patterns. Many governments, particularly those of western Europe, have chosen to ignore the language diversity within their frontiers, or they have promoted the interests of the mother tongue of the dominant élite. The philosophical underpinning for this attitude was the ideal of 'one nation–one language', which became fashionable in Europe well over a hundred years ago. There is a history of suppression of minority languages, for instance in Britain, France and Spain, which goes back several centuries. However, neither indifference nor negative attitudes towards non-dominant languages have resulted in general societal monolingualism, although there is a threat to the survival of some lesser-used languages. In what follows, the main focus will be on the factors that have contributed to the emergence of multilingualism in society.

8.2   Factors contributing towards societal multilingualism

The quest for political power and economic influence invariably in-
duces language contact. By adopting first a diachronic and then a
synchronic stance, it is possible to see how a variety of factors all lead
to the same phenomenon, language contact, which often takes the form
of the spread of one tongue and its eventual dominance over another,
or several others.

8.2.1   Historical factors

(1) *Military conquests, occupation, secession and annexation* These are
some of the oldest ways of spreading language. Greek, Latin and
Arabic reached many parts of the world by these means in earlier
times, and in some territories they were the instrument of radical political and administrative changes; but once the political dominance
waned, the influence of the languages diminished as well, although in
varying degrees and at different speeds in the various parts of the
world where they left a mark. The Roman occupation left few direct
traces on the older languages of Britain (although Latin of course made
considerable impact on English later), but it contributed quite extensively to the lexicon of German, and it exercised a profound influence
on the development of French, Spanish, Portuguese, Catalan and
others.

(2) *Political marriages and succession arrangements* often brought
about changes in the linguistic make-up of particular areas. The marriage in 1469 of Isabel of Castile and Ferdinand of Aragon marked the
beginning of the downfall of Catalan and the dominance of Castilian
Spanish in Catalonia. Another marriage, that of Mary of Burgundy to
Maximilian of Austria in 1477, eventually brought the Low Countries
under Spanish rule (Charles V inherited the Burgundian territories
from his paternal grandmother, as well as the kingdom of Spain from
his mother, the daughter of Isabel and Ferdinand), as a result of which
Dutch and Flemish speakers found themselves governed, from 1519 to
1648, by a Spanish-speaking administration. And when the German-
speaking House of Glücksburg acceded in 1733 to the Danish throne,
German became the language of the Danish nobility and higher echelons of society. However, neither Spanish in the Low Countries nor
German in Denmark became permanently established, and such bilingualism as had existed soon reverted to monolingualism.

Border changes often came about as a result of treaties following large-scale armed conflict. Such arrangements sometimes resulted in longer-lasting multilingualism. Examples are Italian-speaking South Tyrol (the districts of Bolzano and Trento), on the border between Italy and Austria, or the German-speaking parts of Belgium (Eupen and Malmédy). Both of these present-day linguistic minorities were the outcome of territorial changes stemming from the Treaty of Versailles in 1919, after the First World War.

(3) *Colonization*, mainly from the sixteenth century onwards, often on a large scale, of vast areas in the Americas, Africa and Asia, was fuelled by the political and economic ambitions of the colonial powers. Because of its forceful nature, it can also (and perhaps more appropriately) be called imperialism, although, as Fasold (1984: 10) points out, this is a 'loaded word'. Colonization involved a relatively small number of people taking control of territories inhabited by other peoples, exerting political power and controlling economic development. The colonial (or imperialist) groups, mainly the British, French, Spanish, Portuguese and Dutch, adopted different policies with respect to the administration of their colonies; but all of them introduced their own languages in the areas under their influence. Some powers were more concerned than others about spreading their languages. The British and the Dutch took an essentially pragmatic position, one of their prime objectives being the smooth running of the colonies; their languages were used for purposes of administration and higher-level economic transactions. English also became the language of education, usually at the secondary level and beyond. For the Spanish and Portuguese, colonization also meant the spread of the Christian faith, so territorial conquests were followed (and in some cases preceded) by missionary efforts – and it was part of the missionaries' duties to teach the languages alongside the Gospel. French colonialism, too, was accompanied by a sense of mission, although one of a more cultural than religious nature: it was part of the 'mission civilisatrice' to disseminate a knowledge of French and of the ideas of metropolitan France, and therefore in the French colonies most aspects of public life were organized according to French models. The French language, consequently, was promoted in order to achieve 'civilizing' goals.

(4) *Migration and immigration* have taken place throughout the history of mankind. Migrant groups have often become assimilated into main-

stream society after some generations, as has usually been the case in countries of immigration such as the USA, Canada and Australia (it is not the case, however, that every single immigrant group or individual has become assimilated in these countries). The type of large-scale migration that assumes the form of colonization has often resulted in a noticeable spread of the language of the settlers. For instance, the colonization of eastern Europe by German speakers in the thirteenth and fourteenth centuries contributed considerably towards the geographical expansion of this language. But whereas at the beginning of the twentieth century German was still widespread in eastern Europe, changes in the political fortunes of Germany since then have led to a much-reduced presence of the language in that part of the world today. On the other hand, migration by a sizeable group of Germans, united by religious belief and the fear of persecution, to Pennsylvania brought a particular variety of an eighteenth century south-west German dialect to the United States, where it is still used by some of the descendants of the original immigrants to this area. The language of these people, the Amish, is sometimes referred to as 'Pennsylvania Dutch'. It is marked by heavy influence of English on all linguistic levels.

(5) *Federation*, whether of a voluntary or forced nature, has also contributed towards societal multilingualism. Switzerland and Belgium have constituted themselves into federations of their own free will, and in both countries the language groups that came together have achieved official status for their languages, although it took a long struggle for Flemish to achieve equal status with French in Belgium and, in the case of Switzerland, the smallest community, the Romansch speakers, were not successful until 1938. Forced federation often came about when European colonial territories in Asia or Africa were brought together under a single administration. After independence some federations remained united, but in other cases some of the federated groups concerned tried to secede from the larger body: Bangladesh is a country that attained secession (from Pakistan), whereas Biafra (from Nigeria) represents an unsuccessful attempt.

8.2.2 Contemporary factors

(1) *Neocolonialism* Most former colonies are independent states today; but imperialism has left many legacies in the linguistic field. Neocolonialism is characterized by economic (often coupled with political) dependency and by the maintenance of the old colonial language. Lin-

guistic imperialism can therefore be seen as a consequence of economic domination. For reasons of simple convenience, or on account of financial stringencies, and in some cases because of the lack of a commonly agreed alternative, many states have kept the old colonial language as either the sole or joint official language. Many states nowadays find themselves increasingly dependent, economically as well as for purposes of obtaining the military equipment that they want, upon larger countries – notably the USSR, the USA, Australia, China and France – which also contributes to spreading the currency and use of the respective languages. Tanzania was able to install Swahili as its national language, but neighbouring Kenya was not – instead, it kept English. India's 1947 Constitution selected Hindi as the national language, and the intention was that it would gradually replace English; however, the opposition of many Indians, particularly those in the southern regions, forced an amendment to the Constitution in 1965 which allowed the continued use of English, alongside Hindi, for all official purposes.

(2) *Present-day immigration and migration of labour* are continuing to disseminate many languages across the world, thus contributing to creative language contact, even in areas whose inhabitants have for a long time considered themselves monolingual. The inhabitants of Central and South America and the Caribbean have migrated to North America in considerable numbers, especially in the latter half of the twentieth century, and they have not been assimilated into the host society as quickly as were earlier waves of immigrants. The new immigrants took their own languages (mostly Spanish) with them; they have often become bilingual, and they show no sign of giving up their mother tongue. Britain, France, Belgium and the Netherlands have seen a steady influx of people from their former colonies who, in many instances, have formed their own communities and have been successful in maintaining their languages. The post-war economic boom in many European countries attracted a large labour force from Mediterranean countries. Some Scandinavian and certain EC countries have also experienced the arrival of many political refugees from the Middle East and Far East. It is too early to be able to say to what extent these various groups of people will acquire the language of their new host country and for how long bilingualism will remain a predominant feature among them. At the present time, however, bilingualism is certainly experienced as both an individual and a group phenomenon

among immigrant groups of various kinds, each language fulfilling specific functions.

(3) *Language promotion* refers to government decisions reflected in (more or less) well-defined language policies. This factor can contribute to the spread of multilingualism quite considerably. The bluntest kind of language policy is the imposition of one official language in a particular area by suppressing the local one. This has occurred frequently in Europe, for example in the cases of the Basques, along with the Gallegos and the Catalans in Spain, the Corsicans and the Bretons in France, and the Gaelic and Welsh in the British Isles. Policies of promoting Castilian Spanish, French and English, against the wishes of local people in the respective areas, as the sole codes to be used in administration and education have in the past proved very effective.

Language policies can also be of a more acceptable character, as the promotion of modern Hebrew in Israel has shown. In some countries where there is rich linguistic diversity and the continued use of the colonial language is no longer desired, governments have actively encouraged the development and use of certain pidgins, creoles and local languages by declaring them official, or even national, languages. This was the case with Bahasa Indonesia and Bahasa Malaysia in the respective areas. Language promotion sometimes takes the form of language recovery or language replacement programmes: a language whose use has diminished is promoted with the aim of halting its decline or enabling speakers to use it as an expression of their national identity. The gradual reintroduction of Catalan as the official language used in all walks of public life in Catalonia can serve as an example, as can the efforts of the Greenlandic government, after independence from Denmark in 1979, to establish their own autochthonous language in administration and education. Whatever form language promotion takes, it can be successful (that is, bring multilingualism in its wake) only if it receives widespread popular support. It is heavily dependent on positive attitudes, as otherwide it is unlikely to be allocated sufficient funding or receive public response.

(4) *Internationalization* The conditions of life in today's world, including the mobility of labour across linguistic frontiers, require many of us to deal with people from different language backgrounds. International cooperation and communication needs have brought about the advancement of certain languages, especially English. In many coun-

tries, foreign-language teaching in schools and in higher education has contributed to producing many people with some kind of bilingual skills. In some instances, whole communities and international organizations (such as the agencies of the European Community) are actively promoting language learning. Such endeavours tend to lead to individual rather than societal bilingualism, but they can also give rise to a sort of temporarily bilingual group, as happens, for example, when scientists from different countries come together for an international meeting and agree on the use of a common conference language.

Multilingualism, then, is the result of a variety of factors, only *some* of which have been indicated above. Language contact can take different forms and follow diverse routes, leading to multilingualism of a more transient or more permanent nature. The factors that have initially caused language contact are not necessarily those which maintain multilingualism.

8.3   Patterns of societal multilingualism

The pattern of language use that emerges in a particular multilingual community depends, in part, on (1) the factors which contributed towards language contact in the first place; (2) the forces that determine the extent to which the languages involved are now used; and (3) the functions that each language has been allocated, whether by central governments, local authorities or individuals.

8.3.1   Determinants of multilingual patterns

(1) The types of *pressure* under which language groups find themselves are often reflected in the speech behaviour of their speakers. A linguistic minority group can find itself politically suppressed by a dominant élite group which may (but need not) be in a numerical majority. In present-day Europe economic pressure is a more subtle form (than political coercion) of ensuring one group's dependence upon another. If a community that constitutes a linguistic minority wishes to share in a country's economic progress, its members will have to adjust linguistically, i.e. adopt the language of the group that holds the political and economic reins. The need which they perceive to learn the language of the dominant group, both for reasons of educational and social advancement and in order to share fully in the country's public life, can be considered a form of cultural pressure. Whatever kind of

pressure is involved, the group which is affected by it is more likely to become bilingual than the one which exerts it.

(2) The *distribution* of speakers of different languages within the same country produces varying patterns of multilingualism. In terms of geographical distribution, there are few isolated communities that have avoided the need to become bilingual. For a linguistic minority to remain monolingual, the people concerned have to be cut off from the mainstream communication network of the country in which they live. Conversely, if speakers of minority languages are in close contact with those of another language, as happens in the case of many migrants in Europe's larger towns and urban areas, the need to become bilingual becomes paramount. But when the numbers of migrants are so large, and their settlement so concentrated, that it amounts to ghettoization, some of the minority members can remain monolingual and rely on others of their group to act as intermediaries. In some minority areas, such as the present-day Catalan-speaking one (which extends to both sides of the eastern French-Spanish border), we find both a geographical and a demographic concentration of local-language speakers in one part (in this case Catalonia itself), whereas in another (on the French side) speakers are more dispersed and societal multilingualism is less widespread.

As far as social distribution is concerned, there are bilingual groups who belong to the social élite of a country and those who do not. 'Élite bilingualism' was common, for instance, within the Russian and German aristocracies in days gone by, when French was used in their social and political dealings. This kind of bilingualism was also widespread in colonial territories throughout the world at one time. 'Popular bilingualism', on the other hand, is associated with linguistic minorities for whom acquiring the language of the dominant group has become a question of survival. Most linguistic minorities in Europe today fall into this category.

8.3.2 Basic types of societal multilingualism

No two countries display identical patterns of multilingualism. Language groups differ from one another, firstly, because different sets of factors are brought to bear on each community and, secondly, because the reaction of each individual member of society to those factors will be unique. Yet it is possible to discern some basic types of multilingualism.

The term *horizontal bilingualism* (Pohl 1965) describes the situation in countries where different languages enjoy equal status. It is not easy to find examples that exactly fit this category, because the requirement of 'equal status' is seldom met. Italian, Romansch, French and German have equal official status in Switzerland, but Italian and Romansch are less widely, and less frequently, used than the other two, and therefore they can be said to have been attributed lower social prestige. Flemish in Belgium, and French in Canada, are in a similar position. Unless, therefore, 'equal status' is defined broadly as meaning 'enjoying official or co-official status', the concept is not useful.

It is probably better to distinguish between multilingual countries in which the principle of *territorial monolingualism* applies and those which have opted for *territorial multilingualism*. The former means that, in each language area of a state, linguistic provision is offered in only one language. Thus most inhabitants of French-, German- and Italian-speaking Switzerland can, if they so wish, remain monolingual, just as the Walloons in French-speaking Belgium often do and the Flemish could (though many do not). In border areas it is more common to find widespread bilingualism, i.e. territorial multilingualism, as for instance in the Swiss towns of Biel/Bienne or Freiburg/Fribourg and in many towns and villages near the frontier in French- and German-speaking Belgium. In countries with official territorial multilingualism one finds that both languages are used side by side. In western Europe this occurs only in minority areas where the minority language is officially recognized, such as Finland and Catalonia, some parts of Wales, and Friesland in the Netherlands; it is also the reality of the officially Romansch-speaking Swiss canton of Graubünden, where German and Italian are widely used. In other parts of the world this kind of language organization is more common, e.g. in India, South Africa, Singapore and Hong Kong.

The type of multilingualism most frequently found in western Europe is characterized by the social inequality of the languages concerned. The states of western Europe tend to contain large monolingual groups presiding over linguistic minorities lacking both official recognition and language rights. Bilingualism is widespread among the members of these minorities but rarely encountered among the majority group, who are less likely to feel the need to learn the minority language.

8.3.3 Diglossia

In all speech communities it is common to find different social and regional dialects being used in ways that reflect a formal as well as a functional separation of language varieties. In western Europe the standard variety tends to be preferred for use in the media, on formal public occasions and for wider communication beyond the region. It is usually one of the objectives of the education system to impart familiarity with the standard form of the language to children who may or may not have already had access to it in the home environment. A person who habitually uses a speech variety which closely resembles the standard form does not need to know any other dialect, but clearly this does not hold for the dialect speaker.

There are, however, speech communities where *all* speakers need to know at least two varieties because each language form is associated with a specific set of social functions. This language situation has become known as *diglossia*. Pohl (1965) calls it *vertical bilingualism*, since the two varieties exist within the same speaker. Ferguson's (1959) article, entitled 'Diglossia', has become a classic study of the phenomenon. The definition that he gives is:

> Diglossia is a relatively stable language situation in which in addition to the primary dialect of the language, which may include a standard or regional standard, there is a very divergent, highly codified, often grammatically more complex, super-posed variety, the vehicle of a large and respected body of literature, heir of an earlier period or another speech community, which is learned largely by formal education and is used for most written purposes, but is not used in any sector of the community for ordinary conversation.
>
> (Ferguson 1959: 336).

The most important feature of diglossia is the functional specialization of two varieties of the *same* language. The High variety (H), Ferguson suggests, is typically used for sermons (in church or mosque), formal speeches and public lectures, news broadcasts, in official documents and written communication, most books and newspapers, and in poetry. The Low variety (L), on the other hand, is the usual medium for less formal situations, for purposes such as conversation with family, friends and colleagues, instructions to waiters, servants and workmen, informal radio and television programmes (e.g. 'soaps'), captions in political cartoons, and in personal letters and folk literature. Both the H and the L varieties are used for oral and written purposes.

Ferguson discusses diglossia under nine rubrics, which include both linguistic (e.g. grammar, lexicon, phonology) and sociolinguistic (e.g. prestige, function, stability) entries, and he uses examples from four speech communities and their respective languages: Arabic (H = classical Arabic, L = local varieties of individual Arab countries), Modern Greek (H = katharévusa or katharevousa, a kind of puristic variety containing linguistic features of classical Greek, L = dhimotiki), Swiss German (H = Standard or High German, L = the various dialects of Swiss German) and Haitian Creole (H = French, L = the local French-based Creole). According to Ferguson, in diglossic societies speakers have a clear notion of the appropriate use of each variety. To use the L in situations where the H is required constitutes, therefore, a serious social blunder, while the opposite mistake would be an object of ridicule.

This study was based on the linguistic situation found in countries where, as pointed out, the two varieties, H and L, belong to the same language. The notion of diglossia was later revised and expanded by Fishman (1967), who proposed terms of reference which would allow the linguist to account for bilingualism and diglossia, and the relationship between the two, within one conceptual framework. Fishman maintains that the two phenomena are quite distinct: diglossia is a feature of society, to be studied by sociologists (and, presumably, sociolinguists); bilingualism, in contrast, concerns the individual's ability to use different language varieties (or separate languages) and therefore belongs to the realm of psychological (and psycholinguistic) investigation. Fishman extends Ferguson's notion of diglossia by broadening it to include different dialects, vernaculars or classical varieties, as well as distinct languages – so long as they are functionally differentiated. He proposes to accept more than just two varieties (whereas Ferguson mentioned only the High or super-posed and the Low or 'primary dialect' forms of the language). Fishman represents the relationship of diglossia in a quadrant diagram, and he then discusses each possible construct in some detail.

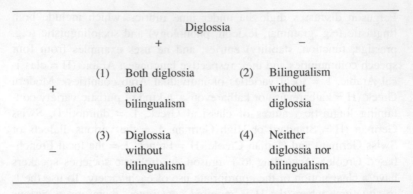

Source: (Fishman 1967: 30)

FIGURE 8.1 The relationship between bilingualism and diglossia

In a speech community where both diglossia and bilingualism are present, almost all speakers will know both the H and the L varieties. Fishman cites as examples language situations involving Swiss German and Arabic, and also Guaraní (an American Indian language) and Spanish in Paraguay, where Spanish, as the official language, is used in higher-level education, the media and for formal communication, whereas Guaraní is spoken by nearly all Paraguayans in informal situations. Bilingualism without diglossia is found in areas where there are large numbers of bilinguals who use either language for almost any purpose. Fishman considers that this situation pertains only to 'circumstances of rapid social change, of great social unrest, of widespread abandonment of prior norms before the consolidation of new ones' (1967: 35). Clearly, when bilingualism is widespread in a community it is more usual to find social consensus as to the functional and situational distribution of languages (i.e. type 1 Figure 8.1). Fasold (1984), quoting Verdoodt (1972), gives as an example of this type the German-speaking area of Belgium, where a shift from German to French is under way but there are still many speakers who use either language for most purposes.

The third type of relationship, diglossia without bilingualism, exists only when two or more quite different groups come together within the same political, economic or religious organization (Fishman uses the word 'unity') but do not have much contact with each other. The ruling group uses the H variety, to which the other group(s) may have only restricted access. Fishman points out that there are many examples of ruling élites who use a different language from those whom they rule – in economically undeveloped and socially immobilized societies 'locked into opposite extremes of the social spectrum' (1967: 34), e.g. in India, where the caste system contributes to a strict separation of social groups. In pre-First World War Europe such a linguistic situation could be found in czarist Russia, where the nobility spoke French and the rest of the people spoke Russian and other languages. These examples, and Fishman's conception of diglossia without bilingualism, show that in a type 3 situation there is a fairly rigid separation of the two (or more) speech communities and in the absence of interaction between the groups communication is possible only through interpreters or by using another language altogether, e.g. a *lingua franca* which may be a pidgin.

The fourth quadrant in Fishman's construct tends, in his own words, to be 'self-liquidating', as it is virtually impossible to find speech communities where only one linguistic variety exists, that is, with no stylistic variation (which he includes in his concept of diglossia).

Fishman and Ferguson differ in their approach to, and interpretation of, the notion of diglossia, but they agree on the functional distribution of language varieties in society. This is the crucial point if we wish to make use of the concept in order to classify the various patterns that are found in the study of societal multilingualism. Fasold (1984) describes other forms of diglossia that involve one H and several L varieties, and he mentions also the possibility of having different 'layers' of varieties where the High and the Low forms overlap. His examples are taken from Tanzania and India, and they emphasize the role of diglossia in creating bilingual and multilingual language situations in those contexts.

8.3.4 Examples of multilingual patterns in contemporary Europe

This section contains an outline of some types of multilingual patterns found in western Europe. It is important to bear in mind that individual countries usually include a number of different language varieties (belonging to the same or to distinct languages) within their borders, and that therefore a multiplicity of language patterns can be found almost everywhere. On the other hand, language behaviour varies from group to group, as does the way in which languages are officially recognized and used for communication and/or education purposes.

(1) *Switzerland* Switzerland (or the Swiss Confederation – of twenty-three cantons and three demi-cantons) is a small country of some six million people which has four 'national' languages: German, French, Italian and Rhaeto-Romansch. Only the first three, however, are mentioned in the Swiss Constitution, which means that Romansch does not enjoy the same rights in the federal parliament and in administration as the other three. Since Switzerland follows the principle of territorial monolingualism, the individual cantons are linguistically autonomous. Most cantons are monolingual, a few are bilingual (e.g. Jura and Freiburg/Fribourg) and the Graubünden canton is trilingual. In the sixteen German-speaking cantons a range of regional and local dialects (collectively referred to as Swiss German or Schwyzertütsch – also spelled Schwyzerdütsch) is used; some of them have become widely accepted beyond their original regions, e.g. Zürichdeutsch (Ris 1979 refers to these as *Großraumdialekte*). In addition to dialect varieties there is diglossia, the Swiss-German dialects being the L form, used for everyday (mainly spoken) communication, and standard German serving as the H variety, reserved for formal uses, both oral and written. German or a German-based dialect can be said to be the first language of more than two-thirds of Swiss people.

French is dominant in six cantons, three of which are bilingual. Although High German is taught in schools, few French-speaking Swiss people learn any Swiss-German dialects, and their representatives in parliament insist on the use of the H variety (standard German), rather than Schwyzertütsch, for parliamentary business. French is spoken by at least 20 per cent of the Swiss population. Italian dialects are spoken by 10 per cent, principally in the Ticino canton. Standard Italian is used mainly for written purposes. Ticino has experienced a large influx of non-Italian (mainly German) speakers who have been reluctant to adopt the Italian language and have set up their own German-medium schools, societies and associations.

Rhaeto-Romansch is the mother tongue of only about 1 per cent of the country's population, perhaps even less. There are five main dialects spoken, but no standard language. Owing to Graubünden's difficult accessibility, its long history of migration and lack of social unity, and also because of the recent permeation of the area by German and Italian speakers, the Grisson (as the region is also called) is today a trilingual canton where the number of Romansch speakers is steadily diminishing.

One further point is that Switzerland has the highest proportion of foreign residents of any country in Europe, perhaps over one million people, many of whom speak English at least as a business language. Furthermore, in the last thirty years or so Switzerland has attracted large numbers of foreign workers who have settled in the country. (They are, of course, also 'resident' but tend to be referred to separately, usually as 'migrant workers'.) Migration has brought yet another form of language contact, often encompassing both multilingualism and diglossia.

The language situation in Switzerland is marked by polydialectalism in all cantons, by monolingualism in most German- and French-speaking areas, and also by bilingualism and trilingualism in some parts. Besides all this, there is diglossia in the German-speaking cantons.

(2) *Luxembourg* The Grand Duchy of Luxembourg is one of Europe's smallest nations (population 350,000 approximately) and also one of the most interesting linguistically. It has been referred to as triglossic, since three languages figure prominently in the country: German, French and Lëtzebuergesch (or Letzeburgisch, or Luxembourgish), an Alemannic variety related to Alsatian and the Swiss dialects. All three varieties have remained a stable part of Luxembourg's language pattern, and each is used for specific purposes in certain well-defined situations. German is used as the written norm; for oral communication it is used only at school, as a language of instruction. Lëtzebuergesch is perceived to be a separate language, and it is used by every Luxembourger for virtually all spoken purposes except official speeches in parliament and in court, where French is used. French is also employed as a medium of education at secondary level, and it serves as the language of all official written communication. There exists a certain diglossic relationship between French and Lëtzebuergesch, and also with German, but the main feature of Luxembourg's language situation is that adults use all three varieties, and that this accords with the country's constitutional provision.

(3) *Spain* The Spanish (1978) Constitution divides the country administratively into seventeen 'autonomous [or self-governing] communities', and it allows for those which have their own language to use it as an 'official' language in the respective areas alongside Castilian Spanish (the Constitution mentions 'the languages of Spain'). While extensive parts of Spain are polydialectal but monolingual, bilingualism is found in three *comunidades autónomas*: Catalonia,

Galicia and the Basque Country or Euskadi. In these regions language choice follows individual rather than societal criteria. For instance, whether a Basque will use Spanish or Euskera (the Basque language) depends on aspects such as topic of conversation, interlocutor and situation, rather than on commonly agreed social norms. The autonomous government of Catalonia, the Generalitat, has pursued a linguistic policy which aims at furthering the establishment of such norms, as Catalans tend to put their language on a stronger footing than anyone else in Spain (see further details in Chapter 13). The significant change that has taken place since the middle 1970s is that there is now, everywhere in the country, active encouragement of local languages, dialects and accents (in education and the media for example), whereas formerly Castilian Spanish was singled out and officially promoted, although only about one Spaniard in four speaks Spanish with the accent of this prestige variety. "

(4) *Denmark* The Danish sociolinguist Normann Jørgensen describes (1984) four kinds of bilingualism found in some industrialized societies, such as Denmark and other Scandinavian countries. His first type relates to the use in the home of a minority language which is also a 'world language', whereas the national language (Danish) is used outside the family circles; the example he gives is the German-speaking minority group living near the southern (Danish–German) border. The second type of bilingualism found in Denmark concerns speakers of the national language who have achieved a high degree of competence in a foreign language (in most cases English) learnt at school and beyond; he says that many Danes, in addition to their mother tongue, also master English, which is taught from the fifth grade and is seen as a highly prestigious language that can be heard on radio and TV, the cinema, popular music, etc., and which most people consider to be essential for international business, travel and study purposes. Jørgensen's third type involves the use of a classical dialect (of Danish) as the home language and the national majority language elsewhere; he points out that there are still in Denmark peripheral areas where a dialect is spoken among members of the community, although standard Danish is the only variety people employ in schools and for all official communications. This sort of bilingualism could perhaps better be termed *bidialectalism* (Jørgensen does not do so; he takes the view that the use of two differentiated varieties of the same language is another form of bilingualism). Jørgensen's fourth and last type refers to

the linguistic situation found among migrant workers and refugee groups in Denmark, whose minority home language is not a world language and who also speak the national language of the host country. He cites the children of Turkish workers who speak both Turkish and Danish.

The kind of bilingualism exemplified by Jørgensen's types 3 and 4 is sometimes referred to as *popular bilingualism* (see section 8.1.2). His type 2, which is the result of schooling rather than natural acquisition, has been called *cultural bilingualism* by Skutnabb-Kangas (1984a).

A fifth type can be added: *élite bilingualism*. In Europe (and also elsewhere) we find many bilinguals who are members of international communities, mainly in metropolitan areas, i.e. people who work for multinational firms and organizations or world agencies using an international language, and whose children are brought up bilingually.

Denmark provides a good example of present-day linguistic patterns in western Europe. Many countries nowadays have new linguistic minorities created by migration or immigration, alongside their one or more old-established linguistic group(s), a situation which results in different kinds of élite, cultural and popular bilingualism, in addition to the previously existing bi- or polydialectalism. Education, mobility and internationalization have all contributed to the emergence of a changing linguistic situation, such as seems to be prominent today in some parts of Scandinavia, the Benelux countries and Switzerland.

8.4 The unstable nature of multilingual situations

A country's linguistic situation is never static. Changes in its political and economic fortunes may bring about an alteration of its language pattern, just as changes in the social conditions under which its inhabitants live may cause them to modify their linguistic behaviour (e.g. as a result of migration into or out of a minority area). In multilingual countries such developments imply that the languages change also in relation to each other. In the Swiss canton of Ticino, as we saw, tourism and the arrival of non-Italian speakers have brought about a situation where the newcomers have not assimilated linguistically to Italian, the local official language, as was traditionally expected of those who move from one language area to another. As a result, the Ticinos are undergoing a remodelling of their linguistic patterns, and

Page 174

there is some fear that the position of Italian may become further weakened. Belgium's capital, Brussels, has undergone a massive language switch in recent times, as a result of urban migration, centralization of the country's administration and internationalization. Whereas 150 years ago the city was predominantly Dutch-speaking (it is, after all, situated in the Flemish-language region of Belgium), today its population is mainly French-speaking (Baetens Beardsmore 1983).

Modern western society demands a good deal of conformity from its citizens. Part of the price that is often exacted by economic progress seems to be a reduction in linguistic diversity, although there is no reason to assume an inherent causal link between monolingualism and prosperity. We can observe that polarization of language use has occurred virtually everywhere in Europe, as most linguistic minorities have seen a steady decline of their languages. At the same time, it is possible to see new linguistic situations arising from changing social and economic circumstances. Migration and immigration have created patterns of multilingualism hitherto unknown in most European countries, and a revival of regional nationalism in several areas of the old continent (both east and west) has brought a renewed interest in regional languages in their wake.

The description and analysis of multilingualism must take account of the changeable nature of language patterns. Multilingualism and monolingualism should not be regarded as discrete categories, but rather as points on a sociolinguistic language continuum. Groupings of categories along this gradient make up specific speech communities which, in turn, are composed of individuals who have different patterns of communicative competence and language behaviour. At both the individual and the social levels, bilingualism/multilingualism is a *sui generis* phenomenon, subject to its own laws.

Chapter 9

Language choice, language maintenance and language shift

9.1 Language choice

One way of looking at language use in society is to see it in terms of making choices. Human communication entails selecting from the linguistic and stylistic items available, i.e. favouring some and rejecting others. This choice can be made consciously or unconsciously. Whereas monolinguals will choose according to the conventions of the members of their speech community and their own idiosyncratic preferences, the speakers of diglossic communities will have additional choices to make, as they must also decide whether the High or the Low variety should be employed. Similarly, members of bilingual or multilingual societies are faced with wider choices in their language use. In Part I (particularly Chapters 4 and 5) the bilingual individual's language use was examined with a view to finding some answers as to when, why and how Language A, or Language B, or a mixture of both, is used.

In this chapter the focus is on language choice in bilingual/multilingual communities. It is obvious that many factors which influence language choice in the bilingual individual will also affect groups of such people. But we must distinguish between (1) those bilinguals who live in multilingual settings, i.e. in places where two or more languages are used throughout the community, and (2) bilingual persons who are members of a monolingual larger group or society, that is, people who have become bilingual as a result of migration, marriage or being the offspring of couples who use different languages in speaking to them, but who are not themselves members of a bilingual community (although they are members of a bilingual family). The language choice of these two types of speakers will be determined by different sets of social, psychological and linguistic factors.

Whether we are considering the bilingual living in a multilingual society or the bilingual individual in a monolingual setting, their language choice will always presuppose: (1) that more than one language is available to the speaker; and (2) that (s)he will be sufficiently proficient in the languages concerned for a genuine choice to present itself. These prerequisites do not imply equal competence in both languages on the part of the individual, nor that each member of the bilingual community is fully bilingual. In the studies that touch upon the subject of language choice (some of them are referred to later), the members of language groups were not tested as to their individual proficiency, because the emphasis was on the group as a whole and its use of the languages studied. The correlation between knowledge and use of the language will, however, be relevant in the context of a group's willingness to maintain or abandon one of its languages. Clearly, an individual or a group whose command of a language becomes weak will use it less often, and this may in turn accelerate language loss. This is true in general, but we shall see that there are few predictable factors in the process of language maintenance or loss.

There is available a good amount of research which, explicitly or implicitly, examines the pattern of language use in bilingual communities. Much of it focuses also on questions of language maintenance and shift. In some cases the groups studied are of considerable size, e.g. Rubin's (1968; 1970) work on bilingualism in Paraguay, Fishman's (1964; 1968) studies of Jewish and Puerto Rican immigrants to the United States, and Greenfield's (1972) enquiry into Puerto Rican bilingualism in New York. In other instances the communities were smaller, or they were settled in remote or isolated parts of the world, or a combination of both; for example, Sankoff (1972) studied the Buang in New Guinea, Gumperz (1978) the Slovenes in Austria, Gal (1978a and b and 1979) the Hungarians also in Austria, and Dorian (1981) the Scottish Gaelic community in east Sutherland. In most of the studies in this latter group the information was gathered in small rural communities – which are, naturally, more easily accessible to researchers working on their own. Sociolinguistic research in urban areas is more complex, in the sense that many different socio-economic and socio- cultural variables converge. At least two bilingual cities have been considered: Baetens Beardsmore (1983) studied language shift in Brussels, and Lieberson (1972) examined language maintenance in Montreal.

Fasold (1984), in his excellent textbook on sociolinguistics, takes particular care to explain the methodological approaches adopted by various researchers into language choice. In his chapter on the topic he discusses in some detail the contributions of three disciplines, sociology, social psychology and anthropology, which he illustrates by reference to studies undertaken in the last twenty-five years. These three approaches will now be considered in turn, in the hope of bringing out some of the interesting issues involved in the question of language choice.

9.1.1 Domain analysis: person, place and topic

The contribution made by sociologists towards an understanding of multilingualism is reflected both in the research methods that have been established and in much of the terminology adopted. The starting point for any study of language choice in multilingual communities is the recognition that, as this choice does not constitute random decisions on the part of the speaker, there must be a certain pattern.

A good part of Joshua Fishman's work in the 1960s was concerned with analysing and describing patterns of communication within multilingual groups, and also between them. In one oft-quoted article, 'Who speaks what language to whom and when' (1965a, revised 1972), Fishman says that '*Proper* usage dictates that one of the theoretically co-available languages or varieties will be chosen by particular classes of interlocutors on particular kinds of occasions to discuss particular kinds of topics' (Fishman 1972: 19). The aim of the study was to find out the descriptive and analytical variables that determine language choice. Perhaps the most important part of the discussion is the section concerning the 'particular kinds of occasions', which Fishman describes as 'domains' of language behaviour and defines in terms of '. . . institutional contexts or socio-ecological co-occurrences. They attempt to designate the major clusters of interaction situations that occur in particular multilingual settings' (1972: 19).

The type and number of domains which have been established by sociolinguists and used in their research vary somewhat. The designation of the relevant domains obviously requires a good deal of inside knowledge of the communicative behaviour and the sociocultural features of particular speech communities. Fishman mentions the domains described in an older piece of research, which was carried out by Schmidt-Rohr (1932) among 'Auslandsdeutsche' (i.e. émigré Germans who, in this particular study, were affected by language shift). The nine domains outlined by Schmidt-Rohr were: the family; the playground and the street; the school (language of instruction, subject of instruction, language of recreation and entertainment); the church; literature; the press; the military; the courts; and government administration.

Incidentally, it is curious that Schmidt-Rohr overlooked the work sphere as a domain. Other studies (e.g. Greenfield 1972 and Parasher 1980, both discussed in Fasold 1984: 183 ff.) limit their enquiries to fewer domains. Greenfield refers to locations such as home, beach, church, school, and workplace; and Parasher works with the following seven domains: family, friendship, neighbourhood, transactions, education, government, employment.

Looking at these lists it should be clear that a 'domain' can be seen as the configuration of at least three component factors:

(1)   the participants in a conversation;
(2)   the place where it occurs;
(3)   the subject under discussion.

The participants or interlocutors will be characterized by such features as age, sex, social status and socio-economic background, and also by the kind of relationship existing between them, which will determine the degree of intimacy or formality that they display in relation to each other.

There is, of course, a multitude of places or locations where conversations may take place. Many of them will not have any particular bearing on bilingual speakers' language choice, but there are certain areas where a particular language is more likely to be used than another, e.g. the home, government offices, etc. It is interesting to see that an item such as 'school', as listed in Schmidt-Rohr's early study, already shows that subcategorizations are often necessary.

Topic has long been recognized as an important factor governing language choice. Individual speakers will usually have preferences for using a particular language when speaking about a certain subject. This preference can become particularly clear when the discussion of a topic leads the speaker(s) to switch from one language to another. There are many possible reasons for such switches: the speaker may feel more competent in handling a topic in a particular language, perhaps because (s)he has learnt the appropriate terminology only in the context of one language; or (s)he may feel that the other language does not possess the required terms; or (s)he will somehow consider one language to be better than another for speaking about a particular subject. It is not the topic *per se* which requires the choice of one language rather than another, but the personal experience and perception the speaker has of a particular topic. Thus when a student from Wales who was educated bilingually tells me that 'you cannot talk about maths or chemistry in Welsh, but it is all right for music, history or literature', he is saying that he has not learnt maths or chemistry through the medium of Welsh, and that therefore he has no experience of talking about chemistry-related topics in this language, for it is indisputable that Welsh has the necessary linguistic tools for dealing with these subjects.

So instead of looking individually at topic, place and person, it may be more interesting to bundle them into situations such as 'conversing with friends and acquaintances', 'talking to people at social gatherings' or 'arguing with friends/colleagues in a heated discussion' (Parasher 1980). Such situations can then be arranged into the more and the less formal ones, which may be useful when looking at language choice in diglossic communities. The typical situations outlined by Ferguson (1959), where the two varieties, High and Low, are distinguished, are separated into more formal/less formal ones (see section 8.3.3). In these situations one can also distinguish the medium employed, i.e. whether spoken or written language would be used.

Another approach to language choice, similar to domain analysis, has been adopted by Joan Rubin in her study of bilingualism in Paraguay. (Paraguay is a bilingual country; Spanish and Guaraní are used in a diglossic relationship, with Spanish as the High and Guaraní as the Low variety.) She set up a number of categories, indicating both positive and negative values. These categories correspond broadly to place, topic and person.

Rubin found that, broadly speaking, it could be said that a Paraguayan's decision to use Guaraní or Spanish was based on a series of considerations which could be ordered in a specific hierarchical way. This kind of representation of ordered language choice is called a 'decision tree'. It shows the sequence of choices a Paraguayan bilingual will go through when deciding whether to use Guaraní or Spanish. First (s)he will consider whether or not (s)he is in a rural location: if (s)he is, Guaraní is the likely choice; if (s)he is not, then the formality of the situation may decide; if it is formal, Spanish will be appropriate;

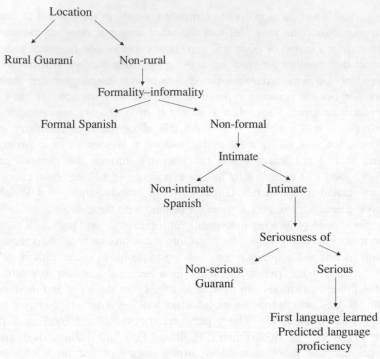

Source: Joan Rubin, 1970; in Fishman, *Readings in the Sociology of Language*, 1970: 526

FIGURE 9.1 National bilingualism in Paraguay: ordered dimensions in the choice of language in a diglossic society

if it is not, the additional consideration of a relationship between the speakers may bring about a decision – if there is no intimacy, Spanish is the likely language to be chosen, but if there is a degree of intimacy other factors must be taken into account. Such a decision tree, if based on accurate observation and statistical data, can then be used also to predict language choice, not only to explain it. However, not all decisions on language use can be attributed to factors determined by social structure.

9.1.2 The socio-psychological approach: linguistic accommodation

The social psychologist approaches the study of human communication from a different angle. (S)he claims that not only social considerations, but also factors relating to the psychological forces which influence the individual's actions, need to be taken into account. For instance, the individual's desire to identify with, or dissociate from, a particular language group can be a determining factor in language choice. Howard Giles and his associates (Giles, Bourhis and Taylor 1977) looked at language choice in terms of the individual's desire to emphasize or weaken her/his ties with the respective language groups. The basic idea of their *accommodation theory* is that normally a speaker will 'converge' and choose the language which suits the needs of the interlocutor. The opposite decision, 'divergence', would represent a conscious decision not to adjust one's speech to the person one is talking to. Linguistic adjustment can take various forms. It may be a total switch from one language to another (one of which the interlocutor has a better command), or it may involve speaking more slowly, pronouncing the words more emphatically; speakers may also choose to use more elements such as pronunciation features, or words and expressions from the other language, or short-passage translations. The main emphasis is on the speakers/listeners as members of groups, and the terms used for the languages involved are 'ingroup language' and 'outgroup language'. The factors that influence convergence or divergence depend on whether or not:

(1) the interlocutors see themselves as members of the same group;
(2) they would like to be considered as members of the other's group;
(3) conflict exists between the groups;
(4) the two groups are equally aware of a conflict, if it exists.

Multilingual communities more often than not consist of one dominant group and one or more subordinate groups, the former being characterized by being in possession of the economic and political power of the country and (particularly in highly centralized states) being in a position to impose their language upon the subgroup. The subgroup's language behaviour will typically include linguistic accommodation (convergence) in ingroup–outgroup contact situations. The pattern of convergence will usually involve movement in one direction only, namely speakers of the subgroup converging towards the language of the dominant group; e.g. members of the Italian community in Britain will use their 'best' English when communicating with their Bank managers (or similar formal situations). However, any attempt on the latter's part to converge by, for example, adjusting their pronunciation to Italian or using Italian words would probably be construed as mockery.

Linguistic accommodation by subordinate groups is very common, but it is not an inevitable occurrence. Some linguistic minorities in Europe are gaining more self-confidence, which is coupled in some instances with the attainment of greater recognition or even a degree of self-government. It has been observed (for example in Wales, South Tyrol and Catalonia) that speakers of the minority language show less willingness to switch automatically to the majority language when speaking to a member of that speech community. Thus, a change in accommodation patterns may indicate that a social change is under way. When more and more Catalans use their language in situations where Castilian Spanish was formerly the norm (e.g. in public administration), and when they begin to demand convergence from the former dominant group (now that Catalonia has achieved autonomy within the Spanish state, the aim is to make Catalan the language of the school, which means that the children of non-Catalan homes have to learn it), then this is evidence of a social change; that is to say, the former status as subordinate group changes to that of equal-status group.

9.1.3 Anthropological methods of observing language choice

The anthropologist's contribution towards the study of language choice can be seen in terms of orientation and methodology. Language choice, in the anthropologist's opinion, should reveal something about the attitudes and the cultural values held by speakers in multilingual communities. Linguistic behaviour and the demonstration of cultural values (explicitly or implicitly) can be ascertained only by observation. Therefore, sociologists and psychologists use data collected from censuses, interviews and questionnaires, or look at people's behaviour under controlled experiments. The information obtained is then usually presented in numerical form and statistically analysed, in the hope that the results will indicate significant trends. The anthropologist, on the other hand, needs to observe her/his informants in as many normally occurring situations as possible, as the aim is to gain insights from uncontrolled behaviour. The methodology that has been adopted in many cases is called *participant observation*, which requires the researcher to live among the members of the community under investigation and to take part in their daily lives. Joan Rubin (1968),

Susan Gal (1978a and b; 1979) and Gillian Sankoff (1980) all spent
long periods of time living among the speakers whose language behaviour they studied, and Nancy Dorian (1981) spent over a decade
working on language shift in northern Scotland. It is understandable
that research which combines data collected through interviews, questionnaires and records of actual observation should prove particularly
attractive. If the results achieved by each method are kept separate
until the end of the study, then compared with each other and found to
be consistent and mutually corroborating, such research can be said to
have high validity. But statistical analysis is not usually employed in
this kind of anthropological research, and the main emphasis remains
on the observers' intensive involvement with the communities they are
studying; any statistical data that are collected may be used only as
supplementary material.

Fasold (1984: 193) makes the point that anthropological work on
language choice has thrown considerable light on community structure.
He develops a model of basically two types of structure that can be
found in certain bilingual communities.

The first type would be one in which the two communities (one the
ruling élite and the other the governed group) exist side by side without much contact, except the minimum necessary, perhaps by means of
a pidgin. The members of each group do not need to be bilingual, and
both groups perceive themselves as separate from each other. This kind
of structure is not frequently found in the world, although some societies do approach this model to some degree; but it is useful to bear
it in mind for contrasting purposes.

The second type of community structure can be seen, for instance,
in a minority language community such as the Frisians in the Netherlands or the Slovenes in Austria. This structure represents a social
arrangement that is different from the previous one. As in the first case,
one group is the dominant one, with more power and prestige, using
the majority language, and the other is the low-status one, which habitually uses the minority language. However, this group does see itself
as part of the other, i.e. as included in the high-status group. Membership of this 'dual group' can have important linguistic consequences.
For example, members of the low-status group will tend to be monolingual in the minority variety at the beginning of their life; but, as
they grow older, their contact with the majority variety may increase
(e.g. through formal education), and they may become bilingual. At the
same time they may develop allegiances towards both their original

group and the other social group, which is perceived as including their own. The language choices of the members of these bilingual groups may show the kind of allegiance the speakers feel towards each group. But the dual loyalties can also cause some degree of conflict. Attempts at solving the problems arising can take various forms and may have interesting linguistic consequences.

An instance of such a linguistic strategy, attempting to resolve conflict between two varieties, is the gradual change from one variety to another within the same interaction (see an example in Blom and Gumperz 1972). Another example could be the sudden switch from the minority language to the majority upon demand from, or in the presence of, monolingual members of the majority variety (as reported by Gal 1979: 166). Gal's work shows several types of language choices which reflect the group dynamics of the community she was studying in Oberwart, Austria, near the Hungarian border, where a Hungarian-speaking population has existed for many years. Until the last century this area was rural and isolated, and the Hungarian speakers had little contact with the German-speaking Austrians. Political and social changes which have taken place in the present century have led to a situation where German speakers have become the majority and, because of the high status of German as the official language and the medium of education in Austria, Hungarian has come to be regarded as the low prestige variety, spoken by the members of the community who see themselves as Hungarian Austrians and who are bilingual. Gal found that age was an important indicator of whether or not a member of the Oberwart community would speak Hungarian. The general pattern was that the older members of the bilingual group spoke more Hungarian than the younger ones, and also that the latter spoke German more fluently than their elders. An even more important finding was that language choice seemed determined by the interlocutor, rather than by any other factor. Even the younger members whose parents did not speak Hungarian to them reported that they used this language in hymns and prayers addressed to God (Gal did classify God as an interlocutor); many also used Hungarian to their grandparents and members of the older generation. The use of Hungarian for religious purposes can be explained in terms of situation as well, because in Oberwart almost all the members of the Hungarian-speaking community are Calvinists, and Hungarian is the language in their churches. The use of Hungarian in other situations, on the other hand, depended, according to Gal's observations, on the participants involved and, to some extent, on whether monolingual members of the community were present.

We can therefore say that language choice is determined by linguistic considerations as well as by external and internal factors. Among the linguistic determinants we can include the codes available to a bilingual community and the degree of fluency the speakers have in each of them. *Location* (place and setting are other terms used), *community structure*, *situation* (or degree of formality), *topic* and *participants* (or interlocutors) are the variables which have been most frequently discussed by researchers, who often approach the subject of language choice from different angles (corresponding to their academic leanings), emphasize diverse aspects and use distinct methodologies.

9.2 Language maintenance

We have seen how the observation and analysis of linguistic choices within a multilingual community can provide us with insights into the social structure of the group and into the dynamic forces that regulate their speech behaviour at a given time. We now come to consider the study of language maintenance and language shift, which can, in addition, point to social changes that have taken place, over a period of time, in the community under observation. Language maintenance and language shift should not be seen as complete opposites: when one focuses on one the other may still be present, albeit less prominently.

The expression *language maintenance* refers to a situation where members of a community try to keep the language(s) they have always used, i.e. to retain the same patterns of language choice. Language maintenance can thus be said to reflect collective volition. In a multilingual community this may find expression in a group's conscious efforts to protect its language and ensure its continued use. Such measures reflect the group's self-consciousness and also some degree of political independence, which allows it to determine its own language policies. When language maintenance efforts result in the use of the minority language in the realms of administration, education *and* industry and business (on the basis of a largely monolingual infrastructure), then such efforts can be maximally effective. This type of policy (which Nelde, 1984, calls the 'Belgian cure') has been practised in French-speaking Canada and in Catalonia with a good measure of success. In multilingual countries language maintenance over long periods of time can be a strong indicator that each of the groups involved considers its language to be an important feature of its ethnic or national identity. Unless the groups are very isolated from each other, it will usually be a sign, also, of a stable social arrangement whereby the component groups enjoy equal status or some degree of self-determination. Switzerland is a good example of such a multilingual country, since each of the four language groups has maintained its language over a long period of time. However, close inspection of the two smaller groups, the Italian- and the Romansch-speaking communities, shows that some degree of language shift has taken place in spite of the collective decision of the respective peoples concerned to retain their language.

9.3   Language shift and its causes

When a community does not maintain its language, but gradually adopts another one, we talk about *language shift*. The shift can be complete, involving a change from one kind of monolingualism to another, with only the transitional period marked by group bilingualism. The change from Cornish to English in Cornwall can serve as an illustration. The shift can also be incomplete, as for instance in those cases where a section of a speech community retains the old language in addition to acquiring the new one; this is the case in Wales, where everybody speaks English but about one-fifth of the population can also speak Welsh. Another form of incomplete shift can be that all (or a large majority of) the members of the community maintain some degree of proficiency in the language, because they continue to use it for certain functions; we saw in the previous section the example of the bilingual community in Oberwart, where Hungarian continues to be used as the language of religious worship.

The distinction between language shift and *language change* is one of viewpoint rather than substance. The latter is a phenomenon of particular interest to linguists who look at the small phonetic, lexical, syntactic and stylistic changes continuously taking place within one language system. The study of language shift in a community always entails examining language use in two (or more) languages. The subject offers two broad areas of interest, the linguistic and the sociolinguistic. The codes involved in language shift often experience changes, such as loss of inflections, borrowing, and appearance of new pronunciation features, which can be the object of the attention of the linguist. The sociolinguist is more interested in finding out why and how communities undergoing language shift change the pattern of their language use.

Language shift is sometimes also called *language decline* and *language death*. Both terms seem to imply a considerable degree of personalization. Typically, they would be applied to situations where the language is spoken by fewer and fewer people until it is no longer spoken by any member of that community, nor by any other group outside it; the language disappears with its last speaker. Perhaps the terms imply also that those who use them regret the passing of the language(s) in question into oblivion, as the use of the word 'death' suggests that there was a previous state of 'living'. But languages in themselves are not living things, and they are not 'brought to life' by their users, either. They are inherited from previous speakers. Edwards (1985: 49) expresses this idea succinctly when he says: 'Languages do not possess "an inner principle of life", nor do they have intrinsic qualities which bear upon any sort of linguistic survival of the fittest.' Languages are tools for human communication, and under certain cultural, social and political conditions a community may opt to change one set of linguistic tools for another. The change may be accompanied, or accelerated, by sheer external pressure, but it may also be the effect of more subtle causes.

Language shift has always been a common occurrence all over the world. In Africa, America and Asia the process was speeded up by colonization and, more recently, state-building; both created favourable conditions for the spread of the 'big' colonial languages (e.g. English or Spanish). Many American Indian languages disappeared within a period of 200–250 years without any trace being left as no written records of note existed.

In western Europe relatively few languages have become totally extinct, but there are quite a few 'endangered species', i.e. languages that are in the process of being abandoned in favour of another. Examples are Frisian, Romansch and the Celtic languages (Scottish Gaelic, Irish Gaelic, Welsh and Breton – Manx and Cornish no longer have any native speakers). Many studies of linguistic minorities consider questions such as whether a minority language is 'at risk', that is, whether it is being maintained adequately (e.g. in Belgium) alongside the language of the majority and whether efforts are being made to recover (as in Catalonia) or even revive (as in the Irish Republic) the language.

Many cases of language shift that have been studied involve communities that constitute a minority within the state and consider themselves part of that state, but whose language is seen as the low-prestige variety. In the European context this generally means that the language of the majority is also the national language. However, there are exceptions; for instance, in Finland both Finnish and Swedish (which is spoken by fewer people there than Finnish) are national languages; and in some countries the minority language has official status in the minority area, as German in east Belgium, Catalan in Catalonia and Welsh in Wales.

Bilingualism does not inevitably lead to shift. There are many bi-lingual/multilingual communities that have had perfectly stable language situations for a long time. In fact, this century has seen a considerable increase in bilingualism and multilingualism, as more and more countries have adopted English, and to a lesser extent French (e.g. in Cameroon) and Russian (e.g. in the USSR) as a second language. At the moment it looks quite unlikely that such countries (in eastern Europe and Asia, and particularly in Africa) will ever want to give up either their first or the new second language.

The process of changing from one language to another does not often occur within the life span of one person; it is usually a matter of several generations. But it *can* happen within one's lifetime, as in the occasional cases of abrupt shift caused by military conquest leading to extermination of a group along with its language. One does also come across some cases of people who, in the course of their lives, have given up the language of their childhood, never used it later in life and eventually lost the ability to speak it. Among immigrant groups who were anxious to assimilate quickly to their host country and/or who (for whatever reason) took the decision to speak the 'new' language to their children, the languages from their countries of origin survived in some form for at least two generations. Since it is a gradual process, language shift has to be studied over a long period of time. Data from the past, such as censuses or other official records, need to be consulted, and observation (if that method is adopted) has to span years rather than months. Only with the appropriate perspective is it possible to see unequivocal signs that change is under way; normally, the first symptoms are that the new language acquires functions and uses that were formerly the attributes of the old.

But why do some communities become involved in language shift, whereas others maintain stable bilingualism? There is general agreement in the literature on the subject as to the conditions that may bring about language shift. Not all of them may cause change in all communities, as the prevailing circumstances are never identical. This is also the reason why one can only speculate about the imminent onset of shift, but never reliably predict it. The most frequently mentioned causes of language shift are the following.

9.3.1 Migration

The members of language groups leave the area where their language is spoken by the majority of the population (or at least by a sizeable minority). Usually they move to a part of the world where their language does not serve them any longer, and they adopt the language of the new area. European immigrants (from both majority and minority language groups) to the United States are a valid example. Conversely, the area may attract large numbers of migrants, who bring their language with them and spread it among the local population. This happened, for instance, when many English speakers moved into south Wales in the wake of the Industrial Revolution. In Catalonia immigration is considered the biggest stumbling block in the present efforts to recover Catalan, as the influx of non-Catalan speakers into the area earlier this century is proving a considerable obstacle in the attempt. A mixture of in- and out-migration has contributed to weaken the Romansch-speaking community. Many Romansch speakers have to migrate in search of employment, while at the same time the tourist industry is being developed in their homeland (the canton of Graubünden in Switzerland) by entrepreneurs who bring their capital and their language from the German-speaking part of the country. During the tourist season large numbers of non-Romansch speakers fill the resorts of Graubünden, requiring services from the local bilingual population in German or Italian, not in Romansch.

9.3.2 Industrialization

Industrialization has always triggered off migratory movements, and this can adversely affect the linguistic stability of an area, in the same way as other major economic changes. Nancy Dorian's study (1981) of the disappearance of the Gaelic dialects spoken in east Sutherland, in Scotland, shows the relationship between the decline of the local fishing industry and the language of the fishermen (Gaelic). Similarly, industrialization brought large numbers of speakers of Castilian Spanish to the Basque Country (Carr 1973), just as it brought French speakers to Brittany (Timm 1980). The vulnerability of minorities to sudden economic changes was demonstrated again recently in Scandinavia. The Same (often called Lapps by outsiders) have traditionally been a nomadic people who made a living from breeding reindeer which they moved around various parts of northern Sweden, Finland and Norway. After the Chernobyl disaster in May 1986, the grazing grounds of their herds became seriously contaminated by radioactivity and are likely to remain unsuitable as pastures for at least a generation. Thus the whole life style of these people was affected in such a way that many had to give up reindeer herding, disperse through other parts of the nordic countries and settle among speakers of Finnish, Swedish and Norwegian. It is at the very least questionable whether the Same language will survive as the living idiom of a community much beyond the year 2000.

9.3.3 Urbanization

Urbanization is a phenomenon related to both migration and industrialization. The movement of sections of the rural population into towns and cities, linked with the improvement in transport and communication systems, contributes to the dispersal of linguistic communities and brings them into increased contact with the high-prestige language or other linguistic groups. The lack of a linguistic heartland greatly weakens the survival of a low-status language in a bilingual community, as life in modern urban societies favours monolingualism, i.e. the use of the high-status language only. The effects of industrialization and urbanization upon the use of Alsatian in cities such as Strasbourg and of Catalan in the Barcelona conurbation are discussed in Chapters 12 and 13.

9.3.4 Prestige

Another factor which often (but not always) comes into play is the small size (in relation to the larger group) of a speech community that is in the process of changing its language for that of the majority, with the consequent higher prestige of the new language. Studies by Gal 1979 (of Hungarian in Austria), Dorian 1981 (of Gaelic in Scotland), Gumperz 1977 (of Slovene in Austria), Walker 1987 (of Frisian in Schleswig-Holstein, Germany), and Greene 1981 (of Faroese and Celtic languages) all describe instances of language shifts concerning small, low-status groups who are in the process of adopting the high-prestige variety. In many bilingual communities personal wealth, professional standing and general technological advance are seen as attributes of the high-status group, so that if members of the minority language group wish for upward mobility, improved living standards and/or a share of power, they relate these feelings to the need – which may be real or simply perceived – to change one's language. For the use of the native language makes people instantly recognizable as members of communities which may be regarded as rural and backward, suspicious of modernization and political power.

9.3.5 Use as school language

One of the most powerful causes of language shift can be seen in those areas where the school language is that of the high-status group and no provision is made for the children of the low-status group to learn to read and write the language of their ancestors. Unless they receive good-quality bilingual education, the survival of their first language will be in question. Monolingual schools (where only the low-status language is used) have little attraction for a population that is well aware of the need to be able to master the language of the dominant group.

As was pointed out earlier, language shift can be brought about as a result of pressure being applied to a community by the dominant group, but this is not the only way in which a shift may take place. Sociolinguists have pondered the question of whether languages are 'murdered' or 'commit suicide' (for a discussion with reference to language shift in the Irish Republic, see Edwards 1985). European history, is full of examples of state suppression of its linguistic minorities. In actual fact, there is hardly a European state not guilty of having indulged in attempts of this kind at some point in its past. But the survival of so many languages in spite of prolonged suppression shows that it may not be possible to eradicate a language if its speakers are determined to keep it alive, and if they see its continued use as an effective means of defying the oppressor. Nationalism and separatism may resist 'language murder' attempts in some cases. But in many others it is not so much a question of open hostility on the part of the dominant group, but rather one of ignorance and neglect on everybody's part. People who describe themselves as liberal-minded members of the majority may express their tolerance for the use of the minority language, even their admiration of it. But they frequently see no need to go any further. The survival of a minority language depends on a great deal more than kind words. Similarly, ignorance on the part of the minority group can speed up language shift. Admiration for the dominant group and the adoption of their values, mixed with a degree of pragmatism, can be equated by the cynic with 'language suicide'. Minority members may feel a strong attachment to the language of their forefathers and still not pass it on to their children. If the sentiment is not matched by actual language use, the consequences are clear: once a language ceases to be the language spoken at home, its continued existence will be seriously threatened.

Chapter 10

Language and national indentity

The topics to be examined in this chapter relate to multilingualism in that they touch on issues of central importance to the language groups that make up multilingual societies. The relationship between language and group identity has long been deemed to be of considerable significance in the context of the emergence of modern states, both in Europe and in post-colonial America, Africa and Asia. When language comes to be considered an essential component of national or regional identity, either by individual language groups or by a state comprising two or more such groups, then certain consequences flow from this situation – for instance, language planning policies have to be formulated, accepted and carried out so that national harmony can be maintained and the smooth running of the affairs of the state ensured. The study of the relationship between language and nationalism has, however, proved to be difficult, as the issues involved, particularly those relating to ethnic or national identity, are complex, and, quite often, intangible. On the other hand, the subject of language planning is more accessible, since planning strategies normally become evident in government action.

10.1 Language and nationalism

Edwards (1985: 1–2) mentions that the relationship between language and identity has been touched upon within a number of disciplines (history, sociology, psychology, linguistics, education and others). While acknowledging that the various perspectives help to see the findings presented in different lights, he criticizes the fact that many researchers have not taken into consideration the work done in neighbouring fields. Thus the study of political, economic and social history has rarely included the treatment of linguistic issues. Perhaps the reason for this was that, for many years, language was thought to belong to the realm of philology, where it was largely viewed in terms of the linguistic changes that have taken place over the centuries. Another difficulty that Edwards highlights is the nature of the subject. He makes the point that to talk about identity often raises emotional issues; while there is nothing wrong with a polemical treatment of the subject, he argues that this is sometimes done under the guise of objective social analysis.

There exist a number of markers of group identity, such as age, sex, social group, religion, geography, cultural traditions and race. Language is only one of them. Many people (particularly if they are interested parties, e.g. linguists, or speakers of the languages concerned) claim that language is the most important marker, for they see the continued use of their linguistic code as an essential condition for maintaining their group identity. As will become apparent later, this may be an extreme view. But language may be a significant indicator of the vitality of a group where it is part of the core system of values of that community.

10.1.1 Basic concepts

In what follows *ethnicity* and *ethnic identity* are treated as essentially the same construct. *Ethnic group* is used to refer to a group of people who share a feeling of ethnic identity. The three notions have been the object of attention in many studies, often in relation to nationalism, and sometimes in connection with minorities. But definitions are seldom offered. Isajiw (1980) examined sixty-five studies of ethnicity and found that only thirteen of them gave an explicit definition. As will be seen from the attempts at defining the concepts, there is something elusive about the phenomenon of ethnicity or ethnic identity – and, by extension, also about ethnic group – which explains the reluctance of some writers to commit themselves to a statement of meaning.

Edwards (1985) mentions some definitions which see nationalism as an extension of ethnicity, e.g. Francis (1947; 1976), who refers to ethnicity as nationalism which is not completely self-aware, and Weber (1968), who notes that the presence of ethnic solidarity does not in itself constitute a nation. In other words, ethnicity is seen as an ingredient of nationalism, a prerequisite or a preliminary stage. Likewise, several ethnic groups (as in many countries in Africa) can make up what we call a 'nation'; this is the nation tied to the state (see later). In an earlier treatment of the subject, Edwards (1977: 254) suggested that 'at a very simple level, ethnicity can be thought of as a sense of group identity deriving from real or perceived common bonds such as language, race or religion.' He concedes, however, that such a general definition invites more questions than it answers – questions relating, for instance, to the nature and relative significance of these common bonds. The definition that he puts forward in his later treatment of the subject (quoted below) is considerably longer, and it takes into account many of the factors which emerge in the majority of discussions on the subject. The first point to note is that ethnicity should not be taken to imply minority group identity or the identity of a social sub-group. In the immigrant context, particularly the North American one, this equation has often been made, perhaps because a majority group does not usually define itself in terms of ethnicity, but rather by reference to some aspect of its superior status (often its political power *vis-à-vis* another group). But there is no intrinsic link between ethnicity and minority.

It is also important to emphasize that there are two different sides to the subject of ethnic groups: (1) the particular features that they may show; and (2) the boundaries that set them off from other ethnic groups. In considering these two aspects, we will find that, even though cultural or other ethnic features may change over generations, the ethnic groups tend to remain intact as long as the perceived group boundaries stay. A group can, for instance, change its language, i.e. lose its original language and, for whatever reason, adopt another one. But the lost language may still retain symbolic value for that group and therefore contribute to the maintenance of boundaries. A case in point here is the Republic of Ireland where, over the centuries, English has become more and more the language of daily communication, but Irish Gaelic, although used in very few situations (mainly for ceremonial functions), is retained as the country's national language because of its symbolic value.

The next factor that must be considered relates to the necessity of incorporating both objective and subjective approaches into the discussion of ethnic identity. The objective approach looks at certain observable features (linguistic, religious, racial, etc.) and defines ethnicity in terms of a 'given' historical fact, as something into which group members are born. Edwards (1985: 8) argues that it is useful to do this 'as a quick means of categorisation'. But it falls short of explaining the persistence of ethnicity across generations. In order to answer the question as to the nature of the basis on which ethnicity is maintained, a subjective viewpoint should be adopted. Such an approach recognizes the significance of perceived features (as different from objectively observed ones). A number of definitions reflecting this kind of perspective stress that ethnicity is a matter of belief in common descent and presumed identity (e.g. Shibutani and Kwan 1965: 40–1; Weber 1968: 389; Fishman 1972b). We can readily accept that all feelings of allegiance and loyalty are highly subjective.

Here, then, is the definition of ethnic identity put forward by Edwards (1985: 10):

> Ethnic identity is allegiance to a group – large or small, socially dominant or subordinate – with which one has ancestral links. There is no necessity for a continuation, over generations, of the same socialisation or cultural patterns, but some sense of a group boundary must persist. This can be sustained by shared objective characteristics (language, religion etc.) or by more subjective contributions to the sense of 'groupness', or by some combination of both. Symbolic or subjective attachments must relate, at however distant a remove, to an observably real past.

As *ethnic groups* we can consider those which are bound together by feelings of shared ethnic identity. Smith (1982: 147) proposes a definition of an ethnic community as:

> . . . a group of people who possess a myth of common ancestry, a shared history, one or more elements of common culture and a sense of solidarity.

In all parts of the world we find both ethnic groups whose geographical origins lie within the country in which they reside, i.e. indigenous ethnic groups, and those who originated from a region which lies beyond the frontiers of their present abode. In the British context, examples of the former would be the English, Gaels and Welsh, and of the latter the Chinese, Afro-Caribbeans and Asians who now live in the British Isles. Many other examples could be given from other parts of Europe.

The close relationship between ethnicity and nationalism has already been mentioned. Ethnic groups are seen as preliminary stages of nationalities, i.e. groups which are 'simpler, smaller, more particularistic, more localistic' (Fishman 1972b: 3). *Nationalism* is,

correspondingly, an expanded version of ethnicity. The similarities between the two are of substance, whereas the main difference is one of
scale. In ordinary usage, a *nationality* is a body of people who share
common features like language, history and cultural tradition. Fishman
sees nationalities as 'sociocultural units that have developed beyond
primarily local self-concepts, concerns and integrative bonds' (Fishman
1972b: 3).

In his consideration, the concept of nationality does not imply the
possession of autonomous territory. It is true, however, that many
others who discuss nationalism as the basic notion that sustains nationalities include the idea that nationalities are linked to a particular
territory and that they have a claim to, or at least a desire for, self-
determination or some form of autonomous government. For instance,
Kedourie (1961: 9) includes the feeling that 'the only legitimate type
of government is national self-government' in his description of nationalism, and Edwards (1985: 13) sees the existence of 'an idea, the
conscious wish for self-control' as the essential difference between ethnic and national groups. The characteristic features of nationalism,
then, must comprise a sense of community, and they may also include
the desire for at least some degree of self-determination and the wish
to strengthen and preserve the group ties in relation to other groups.
Objective features such as religion or language are considered secondary to the sense of a group's own perceived self-consciousness and
uniqueness.

The term *state* is slightly more specific than 'country', as it refers
to a political and territorial unit which is defined on the basis of its
geographical frontiers and administrative autonomy. The use of the
word 'state' implies nothing about the ethnic composition of the unit.
It may be ethnically homogeneous (as is, for instance, the Irish Republic) or ethnically diverse (as is Yugoslavia).

The meaning of *nation* is less concrete, in that both subjective and
objective considerations come into play. A nation can be characterized
with respect to the psychological ties and the nationalistic sentiments
that keep its members together. It can, however, be difficult to identify
its component features: we would be hard-pressed to describe the difference between, say, the Icelandic and the Portuguese nations, unless
we resorted to looking at their individual ethnic traits, in so far as they
are discernible.

Care should be taken not to confuse 'state' and 'nation'. The term
'state' is used in political science to refer to a politically organized

body which is defined with respect to its sovereign status, its territory and its people. A state may contain more than one nationality (which, in turn, may consist of several ethnic groups). The concept of 'nation-state' (a political unit comprising one homogeneous national group) refers to an ideal that was promoted by some philosophers from the seventeeth century on. In the nineteenth century it was used as an excuse for the suppression of smaller nations within a state. But a nation-state is seldom a naturally occurring phenomenon, as many states contain within their boundaries more than one nation. Thus the expression 'United Nations' is really a misnomer, as it is an organization that includes, as its members, states, not nations. On the other hand, the body representing those European nationalities which do not enjoy some degree of autonomy bears its name, 'Bureau for Unrepresented Nations', correctly.

Keeping the distinction between state and nation in mind, and turning back for a moment to the subject of *nationalism*, it should now be clear that it is nations, not states, that are usually the object of nationalist sentiments. (However, nationalists also typically aspire to having a state through which to exercise self-determination.) Only in nation-states would the citizens' loyalties towards the nation coincide with allegiance to the state. It follows, then, that (for instance) a Welsh person's feelings of loyalty towards the British state are not the same as her or his nationalistic feelings towards Wales; indeed, that person's feelings may, in some way, be in conflict. Another example is Catalonia, where nowadays many Catalans claim to be Catalan rather than declare themselves Spanish (which often causes annoyance to other Spaniards). The fact that the feelings towards the state and the nation may be conflicting is one of the reasons for the frequent tension between the two; and it can help explain (but not justify) the eagerness of states to suppress the expression of nationalist feelings, including language.

It is important to be aware of the way in which the term *nationalism* is used in sociolinguistics, because in its general use in other contexts it has, in modern times, acquired negative connotations precisely because of its association with states rather than nations and with political right-wing extremism. This became particularly clear in the case of facist Germany, Italy and Spain.

The main difference, therefore, between an ethnic group and a nation is that nations are bigger, more self-aware groups who share a desire to determine their own political destiny; this may not be the case with ethnic groups. It is precisely because a political element is involved that multinational states tend to be politically less stable than multiethnic nations. It is difficult to say when exactly an ethnic group ceases to be one and starts becoming a nationality. In sociolinguistics, contrasting concepts often allow themselves to be seen as points on a continuum, rather than discrete entities. Norway and Austria are examples of states clearly consisting of one nationality each but containing several ethnic groups. States such as Spain, France and Britain are more difficult to classify, as they are comprised of more than one nationality (the Welsh, the Catalans, the Bretons, possibly the Scots, claim to constitute separate nationalities) and also various ethnic groups (e.g. Moroccans, Pakistanis, Latin Americans – with their subdivisions – living in these countries, etc.). India and the USSR could serve as examples of multinational states that also contain different ethnic groups.

10.1.2 Language and nationalism

In facing the question of whether one is dealing with a nationality or an ethnic group, language can be a useful indicator. In themselves, the two concepts do not require language as a component. But the extent to which a group is prepared to defend and maintain the use of its language, or the ease with which it will acquiesce to abandon it, may be significant.

The connection between language and nationalism has often been noted. Language is a tangible, immediately noticeable indicator of group identity. In the history of nations, especially in Europe, the survival of a nation's language has frequently been equated with the continued existence of the nation itself. The belief in this equation is often shared by both the nations which constitute the majority within a state and those which form a minority. Since majority nations are usually in a politically superior position, they can afford to be more aggressive in the expression of their convictions, thus posing a threat to the survival of the minority language(s).

Nineteenth-century Europe was full of cases of larger nations imposing their language on smaller ones, irrespective of whether or not the latter were prepared to change their feelings of national loyalties. The systematic suppression of Welsh in Wales, for example, led not only to a decline of the language, but also to the weakening of national sentiments. When Prussia became the leader of the new Germany in

1871, its centralization policies meant the suppression of the rights of minorities such as the Poles in East Prussia and Poznan and the Danes in Schleswig-Holstein, which had until then enjoyed cultural autonomy. In Alsace, which had been taken from the French in 1871 after the Franco-Prussian War, German efforts were geared towards trying to turn Alsatians into convinced Germans. Many Germans thought that this was a perfectly legitimate undertaking, since Alsatians, after all, spoke a variety of German. The fact that, for historical reasons, Alsatians felt more akin to French people was not accepted – not in 1871, nor again in 1940, when Alsace-Lorrraine was, once more, annexed by German forces. The famous German sociologist Max Weber recalled a visit to Colmar in Alsace which prompted him to reflect on the interplay between national identity and history:

'The reason for the Alsatians not feeling themselves as belonging to the German nation has to be sought in their memories. Their political destiny has taken its course outside the German sphere for too long; for their heroes are the heroes of French history. If the custodian of the Colmar Museum wants to show you which among his treasures he cherishes most, he takes you away from Grünewald's altar to a room filled with tricolours, pompier and other helmets and souvenirs of a seemingly most insignificant nature; they are of a time that to him is a heroic age.'

(Quoted in Gerth and Mills 1948: 176)

Another example of linguistic nationalism, mentioned by Stephens (1976), is Hungary's change of language policy in the last century. Before 1840 the Hungarian state encompassed Hungarians, Slovaks, Germans, Romanians, Croats, Ruthenians and Slovenes. For nearly a hundred years they had coexisted in the kingdom and, one must assume, found some common identity in its traditions. Latin was the official language of government, but the vehicle for trade, education and science was German. In 1844 Hungarian replaced Latin and the way was prepared for a monolingual Magyar state. However, the policy of magyarization at all levels infringed the linguistic rights of those citizens who spoke languages other than Hungarian (although German fared better than others). The concept of a multilingual and multinational state had clearly been abandoned, presumably for the sake of creating a more powerful nation-state (and perhaps also in order to secure the dominance of the Magyars).

The twentieth century, too, has seen many instances of language, politics and nationalism intermingling in the affairs of countries. The

First World War was fought, among other things, for the rights of small nations, and it was the intention of the Treaty of Versailles (1919) to solve many of the problems that smaller nations had experienced by implementing the principle of self-determination. Thus a number of nations, e.g. Poland, Finland, Estonia, Latvia, Lithuania and Czechoslovakia, gained independent status. The Turkish and Austro-Hungarian empires were dissolved, and autonomous status was granted to some of their component nationalities. Language played a prominent part in arriving at these decisions, because many of the nations in question defined themselves in terms of their languages. However, it proved impossible to satisfy the aspirations of all the nationalities involved, and several of the newly created states were themselves ethnically and linguistically diverse.

Also today we find plenty of examples in the world where language assumes a political role. The 1960s saw considerable civil unrest and militant activity in Canada, where members of the French-speaking province of Québec demanded separation from the rest of the state. In Belgium many governments have been brought down because of their inability to satisfy the demands of the two main national groups, the Flemings and the Walloons. Although further major linguistic confrontations have probably been averted by the substantial constitutional changes that have now been made, Belgium was in the news again in 1986 when the inhabitants of a little-known area called Les Fourrons voiced their grievances about linguistic borders. In Wales, too, nationalists have frequently been prepared to resort to such acts as daubing or taking down road signs, or even burning holidays homes owned by English people. Their fight for a separate television channel in Welsh (which they saw as beneficial for the language) was won from the British Government only after the leader of the Welsh party, Plaid Cymru, who was a well-known pacifist, had vowed to fast to death if the demand was not granted.

Of course, it must be recognized that many of the problems mentioned above can be attributed to sociocultural and socio-economic causes, i.e. that such questions are not purely linguistic in nature or in their origins. But language issues seem to be highly sensitive, and the way people talk about their language does show that they attach a great deal of importance to it. People do not normally think or talk much about language, as it is something one takes for granted. But when we feel threatened or provoked in our language use we may express our feelings towards our own tongue in highly emotional terms. On such occasions language is identified as an important element of one's nationality, as a common heritage that provides the link, not only with one's own forefathers, but also with the group's history. Fishman (1972b) points out that language serves as a link with 'the glorious past' and with the authenticity of the group. Others have referred to their language as the living memory of their history.

Within the context of nationalism, we can discern two different functions of language: (1) it provides for its speakers a link with their past and with their fellow-speakers, and therefore it helps to maintain the group's feeling of unity; and (2) it helps to set the group apart from others. These are actually the two sides of the same coin. Fishman (1972b) refers to them as 'contrastive self-identification.' Garvin and Mathiot (1970: 369), in their more general discussion of the roles of standard languages, talk about 'the unifying and separatist functions'.

The existence of a national language may provide a nation with welcome ammunition in its fight for independence or at least some form of autonomy. The Catalans, for example, have taken this last route (autonomy) and been successful, on the basis that a majority of people in the area speak Catalan. In Wales, by contrast, less than one-fifth of the population speak Welsh, and among them only the Welsh nationalists would advocate full autonomous status for the region. As mentioned earlier, we cannot automatically equate language with nation. There are many nations that share the same language, e.g. the Canadians, Americans, Australians and British (among many others), but could not be said to have the same nationalist feelings. Similarly, Spanish and Mexican, or French and French-Canadian, nationalisms are of a totally different nature. It is equally inappropriate to define nationalism purely in terms of language. In Alsace and Luxembourg it is the regional spoken varieties of German, Alsatian and Lëtzebuergesch, that form part of the national identity, not Standard German, although the latter is used as the written medium.

A language may contribute, then, to shape and maintain feelings of national identity and solidarity. But in the origin and preservation of such feelings there are other aspects that are just as important: shared ethnicity and history, religion and colour-consciousness, too, to name but a few. Language may also play a central role in separatist movements, as in the emergence of new states, and in the maintenance of power in multilingual nation-states.

10.1.3 The political dimension of language

The idea that there is a strong link between language and nationalism
and, consequently, that language should be the basis for political decisions (in the wider, programmatic sense), is a thoroughly European
one, even though it has subsequently spread outside this continent. It
emerged after the Reformation, when Latin ceased to be used as a
lingua franca and most countries saw the standardization of the language of the dominant national group.[1] The foundation of bodies
concerned with the preservation and purity of linguistic standards need
not be seen, in itself, as an act of linguistic nationalism, but as reflecting a preoccupation with matters of language and, perhaps, also pride
in one's national language.

Language became an important political issue later in the eighteenth
century. In Spain the centralist policies of the new Bourbon dynasty
resulted in the systematic suppression of the indigenous minority languages (Basque, Galician and Catalan). In France the supremacy of
French over the other regional languages was already advocated under
the *ancien régime*. But the Jacobins (radical revolutionaries), at the
time of the French Revolution (1789–99), were far more rigorous in
their approach to fostering linguistic uniformity. By proclaiming the
ideal of 'une langue, une nation' they openly linked language and politics, claiming that national unity under a new democratic system could
be achieved only by abandoning the regional languages of France.

In Germany the rationale for the link between language and politics
was provided by philosophers such as Herder (1744–1803), Fichte
(1762–1814) and Wilhelm von Humboldt (1767–1835). Herder's ideas
about language and nationalism developed from his philosophical work
on the origins of language, contained in his essay 'Über den Ursprung
der Sprache' ('On the origin of language'), for which he received a
valued prize from the German Academy of Arts and Sciences in 1770
and which was published in its final version in 1789. The political role
of language was implicit in Herder's argument that language is an im-
manent part of the development of individuals and groups that speak it
and, as such, it expresses the consciousness of groups and therefore
constitutes the most important and precious possession of its speakers.
More simply, language is the mirror of a nation. The relationship between language and national identity was thus established. Fichte took
Herder's general (and neutral) ideas about the nature of language further, pronouncing value-laden judgements on specific languages in a
nationalistic manner which would be unacceptable today. For Wilhelm

von Humboldt, the spirit of a nation was best expressed by its language (indeed, 'its spirit is its language'); the possession of a language with a long history is, consequently, the most valuable asset that a nation can have.

Nowadays language can still be a powerful factor in nationalism, both at the level of theoretical discussion and when ideas are translated into political action. The language policies adopted in Hungary, France and Spain have served as historical illustrations. Events in eastern Europe, where an increasing number of nationalities (Latvians, Ukrainians, Moldavians, Slovaks, etc.) demand greater political and linguistic independence, provide vivid examples of the late 1980s. The history of the world is full of instances of nationalism (turned into imperialism) leading to human misery and cultural destruction, as people have frequently trespassed on the linguistic and geographical territory of others in the name of national unity. Yet nationalist feelings have also proved to be a positive force in cases where they have kept together groups of people which have felt threatened by other groups. At times, they have helped to ensure the survival of a national language (e.g. in Catalonia, which constitutes one of the most impressive examples in present-day Europe – see Chapter 13). Whether one sees nationalism as good or evil, rational or irrational, there is no doubt that in the past it has proved to be a powerful force in the world, as is still the case today. Chapters 11–14, which deal with linguistic minorities in general and specific multilingual settings, further illustrate the importance of these issues.

10.2 Language planning

One of the most important decisions an emerging new nation (or newly autonomous region) has to make is the selection of its national language (or its official regional one). Choosing a flag and a national anthem usually presents relatively few problems. The making of a constitution may be a more difficult undertaking. But the choice of a language that is to have symbolic function and practical application for a nation can be a complex issue with far-reaching consequences. Ideally, the chosen language should also serve as official language, i.e. be used as the medium of internal communication. We shall look now at the role language plays in nation building and in the development of a nation, and will conclude the chapter by dealing with some practical considerations raised by language policies.

Nowadays very few nations actually find themselves in the position of having to select a national language. But there are many countries attempting to change from one particular strain of language to another, or trying to change the assignment of particular functions from one language or variety to another. Some countries are reconsidering their language policies with a view to establishing more than one national language or more than one official language, while others find themselves forced to provide administrative or educational services for one or several of their linguistic minorities. These decisions require, in some instances, the linguistic systems themselves to be the subject of close scrutiny. When this happens, the language(s) may be found not to be adequate for particular communicative purposes, or to be in need of elaboration or standardization. Language planning is concerned both with the symbolic function of language within a society and with the instrumental use that its speakers make of their language.

In the following section two main areas of language planning will be discussed: (1) language development, which centres on the language itself; and (2) language determination and allocation of language use, which deals with language selection and the attribution of status to particular languages.

10.2.1 Language development

Kloss (1968) differentiates two basic aspects of language planning by distinguishing between *corpus planning* and *status planning*. The former refers to changes made in morphological or syntactic structure, vocabulary or spelling (the 'corpus'); it may even include the adoption of a new script. The purpose of 'status planning' is to develop a language or a variety of a language, with a view to making it a useful instrument for communication, i.e. one that can fulfil all functions within society. Ferguson (1968) speaks of *language development* rather than corpus planning, and he describes its three basic stages as graphization, standardization and modernization.

Graphization involves taking decisions such as what kind of alphabet is to be adopted for a language that has not yet been reduced to writing, and what the conventions should be for spelling (including accentuation if appropriate), punctuation and capitalization. In established nations the development of a particular writing system usually spans a long period of time, and it can involve changes which, at the time when they are made, may be quite small.[2]

Standardization refers to the selection of one variety which is considered to be 'the best' and is to serve as the norm for the speech community. Ferguson refers to standardization as a process of becoming more and more widely accepted throughout a given society, thus emphasizing the fact that, usually, a standard variety emerges gradually. The absence of a standard, however, often appears to be an obstacle for the survival of a language, at any rate in twentieth century Europe. This is certainly the case in the Romansch-speaking areas of Switzerland. Some attempts are being made at standardization with regard to Romansch, but they may have been started too late (Schläpfer 1982).

Modernization means the development of a variety so that it will be suitable as a vehicle for communication able to fulfil all functions. A process of modernization is one during which the linguistic resources of the language are increased, so as to make it a more useful tool for its users. This may imply extending the lexicon, either by coinage or by borrowing, and introducing new expressions. Vocabulary expansion normally suffices for the introduction of new ideas, products, technical terms, etc. Sometimes it is also undertaken in the hope of ridding the language of foreign influences.[3]

Modernization can also be applied to a spelling system, either partly or totally. For example, in the 1920s when Atatürk set about establishing a modern Turkish state, he changed the writing system from the Arabic script to the Roman. Similarly, the USSR had to take a decision on writing conventions within its vast multilingual and multigraphic state. Modernization there involved, among other things, the extension of the Cyrillic script to nearly all the languages of the Soviet Union. In China language development has taken the form of trying to make Chinese easier to write – the aim being to simplify about half of the estimated 7000–8000 characters. Although the simplified characters should, one would think, really benefit everyone, an important obstacle is that they are employed only for materials printed in China itself – in Hong Kong, Taiwan and other Chinese-speaking communities the traditional characters continue to be used. Simplification in one area, then, may lead to splitting up the language into divergent forms, perhaps reflecting political divisions. In general, language planners may make recommendations, but ultimately language use is subject to uncontrollable and even, at times, irrational forces.

10.2.2 Language determination and allocation of language use

Language development (or 'corpus planning') and *language determination* (or 'status planning') can be treated as theoretically separate notions, but in practice they are interlinked. The involvement of the Welsh Language Society or the Catalan autonomous government in language development, for instance by expanding the lexicon, is also a reflection of the fact that certain decisions have been taken at a political level – namely, to use Welsh, or Catalan, in schools, as a medium of instruction, or in local administration. But what prompted these decisions? How were they reached, and what is their ultimate aim? The section of the discipline of language planning that attempts to address such questions has received a good deal of attention in the last twenty years or so, as it concerns decision-making processes regarding the status and function of particular languages or varieties, as well as the allocation of state resources. Various labels have been proposed for this area of study. Neustupny (1970: 4) speaks of a 'policy approach', whereas Jernudd (1973: 16–17) discusses 'language determination'. Kloss's (1968) concept of 'status planning' has already been mentioned. Rubin (1983: 341) suggests that the term 'allocation of language use' would be more useful, as does Cobarrubias (1983: 42), who refers to 'allocation of language functions' for a language in a given speech community. The areas dealt with do not correspond exactly with each other in coverage or in approach, but they may be loosely grouped together for convenience.

In his 1968 study Kloss uses the term 'status planning' to refer to those planning decisions intended to enhance or diminish the status of a language. He establishes four categories that relate to language status.

(1) The *origin* of the language used officially. It may be an indigenous language, i.e. one spoken by a large part of the population, in which case the state is called an *endoglossic state*. Most European countries are examples of endoglossic states. If, on the other hand, the national/official language is an imported one, we speak of an *exoglossic state*. Many of the states that used to be colonies, which may be linguistically heterogeneous, have chosen the former colonial language as their national one, usually for purely practical reasons; examples are Ghana, Nigeria, the Cameroons and some of the smaller South East Asian countries, e.g. Malaysia, East and West Samoa, and the Philippines. In order to accommodate those states which are neither

endoglossic nor exoglossic but show features of both, the term *mixed states* is used. They include, for instance, states that are in the process of shedding the colonial language in favour of an indigenous one, like Papua New Guinea (which has three official languages: Hiri Motu, Neo Melanesian or Tok Pisin, both pidgins, and English), or Tunisia (which also has three languages: Arabic, Tunisian and French).

(2) The *developmental status* of a language is the second criterion for Kloss. According to the degree of elaboration, i.e. as a result of language development, a language may achieve one of six types of status:

(a)   a fully modernized standard language that fulfils all needs of modern society, e.g. French;
(b)   a standard language spoken by a relatively small group only which, because it is not used by many speakers, has limited scope, e.g. Welsh;
(c)   an archaic language, which once flourished but is not now equipped for coping with modern science and technology, e.g. Latin;
(d)   a young standard language, recently codified and standardized for some specific purpose (e.g. for education), as for instance Luganda in Uganda;
(e)   an unstandardized language for which alphabetization has only recently been carried out, as has happened with Somali in Somalia;
(f)   a preliterate language, i.e. one which has not yet undergone graphization, e.g. Gallah in Ethiopia.

(3) The third category of language status considers languages with regard to their *legal position*. As a result of language-planning decisions, a language may be recognized as:

(a)   the sole national official language, such as French in France or German in Germany or Austria;
(b)   a joint official language, i.e. co-equal in terms of use for government functions, as happens with French and Flemish in Belgium, English and Afrikaans in South Africa, or French, German and Italian in Switzerland;
(c)   a regional official language, i.e. one which enjoys official status on a regional basis, like Catalan in Catalonia, German in eastern Belgium, or Ukrainian, Georgian and Armenian (among others in the Soviet Union);

(d)   a promoted language, which is one that is used by various auth-
      orities for specific purposes, as is the case with Spanish in some
      parts of the United States or with West African Pidgin English in
      Cameroon;
(e)   a tolerated language, i.e. one that is neither officially supported
      by public agencies nor proscribed; there are many languages in
      western Europe which are more or less left to their own devices,
      e.g. Basque and Catalan in France, the Asian languages of immi-
      grants in the UK, or Turkish, Greek, Italian, Spanish and other
      migrants' languages in western European countries;
(f)   a proscribed language, i.e. one against which there exist govern-
      ment restrictions and sanctions; this was the position of Catalan,
      Basque and Galician in Franco's Spain, of Welsh and Irish
      Gaelic until the 1920s in the United Kingdom, or of Scots Gaelic
      after the uprising of 1745.

(4) The *ratio* of users of a language to the total population is Kloss's
last factor among those that can affect language status. He does not try
to establish any kind of quantification-based criteria. The question of
ratio alone does not actually say much about the status of a language;
for this reason, he suggests, this factor should always be considered in
conjunction with others.

These categories, however, do not take into account the area of *language function*, i.e. the uses to which it is put (for instance, in
education, or in religious worship), which is today considered to be
highly relevant in determining language status. Experience has shown
that the prestige of a language is enhanced significantly, for example,
once it becomes accepted as the medium of education. The adoption of
Swahili in Tanzania as a language of instruction up to secondary level,
or that of Quechua in Peru or Welsh in Wales, contributed to making
these languages more acceptable, apart from gaining more speakers for
them. The decision by the Catholic Church in favour of the use of
vernacular languages instead of Latin provided a substantial boost for
minority languages (e.g. in American Indian communities in Central
and South America) and also for Creole varieties, which began then to
be used in religious services in place of the standard forms.

Kloss, then, sees status planning primarily as resulting from a series
of planning decisions and in terms of official attitudes towards a
country's language or languages. But language status can be viewed
from a different perspective. Mackey makes the point that the status of

a language depends on the individual and ethnic circumstances of the people and the languages that they use:

> The status of a language depends on the number of people using it, their relative wealth, the importance of what they produce, their social cohesiveness and the acceptance by others of their right to be different. In other words, the faces of language status are demografic, economic, cultural, social, political and juridical
>
> (Mackey 1983: 174).

10.2.3 Language-planning policies – some examples

North America Mackey, when he wrote the above, was comparing Canadian language policies with those of the United States. He makes the point that a number of notable differences exist between the French-speaking population in Canada and the Spanish-speaking groups in the neighbouring country, which would make the adoption of the Canadian language planning policies unworkable in the United States. The main differences can be seen in the fields of education and the law. In the United States various types of bilingual education programmes involving Spanish and English have been adopted over the past twenty years or more. For a number of reasons, these programmes have not been very successful, in particular at the higher levels of education, where there is no provision for Spanish at all. In Canada bilingual education has also encountered problems, mainly outside the French-speaking province of Québec. In Québec French-language education has been available for a long time and at all levels, and this has promoted the teaching of French to children of French-speaking minorities outside Québec. There are now also bilingual education programmes providing for the teaching of French to the English-speaking majority. These are measures that have no counterpart anywhere else in America.

The legal status of a language will, of course, to some extent determine what kind of education programmes a state may embark upon. The status of Spanish in the United Sates is based on two pieces of legislation, the Voting Rights Act of 1965 and the Bilingual Education Act of 1968, but neither of them officially accords Spanish 'official status' – they just pave the way for Spanish to be used, or officially supported, for specific purposes such as in education, for voting, in the courtroom and in the media.

In contrast, after two centuries of struggle and as a result of active participation in the political decision-making process of Canada, the French-speaking population has achieved official status for its language (Languages Act of 1969). There followed a series of major legislative reforms that first changed Canada from an officially monolingual to an officially bilingual state, and subsequently Québec from a bilingual area to a monolingual one with French as the official language. In language-planning terms, these reforms represented a reallocation of language functions. But the repercussions of these language policies go beyond linguistic matters, as they affect social planning as well. The Act to Promote the French language in Québec (Bill 63 of 1969) affirms the rights of parents to choose either French or English as the language of education for their children; and it provides for children from non-French backgrounds to acquire a working knowledge of French. The Official Language Act (Bill 22 of 1974) establishes French as the official language of Québec; it declares that the French text of Québec's statutes must prevail over the English version in cases of disagreement, thus defining the official character of French. It allows for bilingualism but specifically states that professional bodies and public agencies must provide their services in French, just as all official texts must be printed in this language. The Charter of the French Language (Bill 101 of 1977) enacts the shift from bilingualism to monolingualism, by declaring that only the French texts of all state publications are official, and it requires every public utility and business firm to use French in their publications (brochures, catalogues, order forms, job application forms, etc.) and to obtain a 'francization certificate' which attests that the firm is applying a 'francization programme'. All public education at primary and secondary level is to be in French. A number of supervisory bodies are set up to monitor the implementation of the Charter. It is easy to see in this case how a language-planning decision can directly affect people's lives. There is no doubt that the Charter represents a major piece of planning designed to enhance the status of French in Canada.

Spain The Spanish Constitution of 1978 is also interesting in this context, as not only does it make provision for the official language, but it refers also to the status of the other languages of Spain which, for much of Spain's history, were not officially recognized. Thus Article 3 of the Spanish Constitution states that 'Castilian Spanish is the official language of the Spanish state' and that 'all Spaniards have the duty to know and the right to use it'. As regards Catalan, Basque and Galician, it acknowledges in the next paragraph that 'the other languages of Spain will have co-official status in their respective autonomous communities as laid down in their Statutes' (of Autonomy), affirming that 'the richness of the different linguistic varieties of Spain is a cultural heritage that must be the object of special respect and protection'. When the *Generalitat* drew up its own Statute of Autonomy for Catalonia it gave the language question considerable weight, stating in its Article 3 that:

> Catalonia's own language is Catalan;

> The Catalan language is the official one in Catalonia, together with Castilian Spanish, which is official throughout the Spanish state;

> The Generalitat will guarantee the normal and official use of both languages, will take the necessary measures to ensure the knowledge of them and will create conditions which will allow them to attain full equality with respect to the rights and duties of the citizens of Catalonia.

The first sentence reflects the link between nation and language, which has always been perceived by Catalans. It also seems to confirm an underlying territorial principle which implies that Catalan is to be used 'in Catalonia', not just 'by the Catalans'; and it paves the way for subsequent legislation (the Law of Linguistic Normalization of 1983) to aim at making Catalan the language normally used in all walks of life, particularly in the fields which can be more directly influenced by the regional government, namely education and administration. The second statement declares the official status of Catalan. The third part of the Article is a guarantee of bilingualism, while at the same time it provides for the promotion of Catalan (since it can be taken for granted that everyone knows Castilian Spanish already).

The Catalans were well prepared for language planning when they finally found themselves in a position to do something about Catalan. They had taken on board some of the experiences of other countries (in particular Wales and Canada), and they understood the limitations of officially sponsored bilingualism: only a considerable reallocation of language functions from Castilian Spanish to Catalan would, in their view, ensure a degree of success in their efforts to halt the decline of Catalan (see Chapter 13).

United Kingdom Language policies are seldom formulated and carried out in one fell swoop. Quite often they are not officially stated at all, and language is allowed to develop without any kind of planning, car-

ried along by social and political forces. The development of English
as the *de facto* national (and official) language of England took over
200 years; for decades after the Norman Conquest most political decisions were taken by men who spoke Norman French and used it in
administration. Individuals, rather than governments or institutions,
were responsible for enhancing the status of English, thus contributing
to its eventual adoption as the language of the government and of English society (for an account see Heath and Mandabach 1983). Any
form of legal regulation or official involvement with language has been
singularly absent in British history. In the United Kingdom there is no
law proclaiming that English is the national language, as there is no
written constitution, and no official body, such as an 'Academy', entrusted with looking after the language. There have been, however,
instances of negative language policies, such as the suppression of
Scottish Gaelic, Irish and Welsh, or the imposition of English, to the
exclusion of the official use of the vernacular, in the colonies. Perhaps
one of the most extreme statements of linguistic chauvinism is Thomas
Macaulay's 'Minute on Education' of 1835. Macaulay was a member
of the Supreme Council of India and he became involved in the debate
over the medium of instruction in Indian schools. It was his idea that a
class of Indians should be educated to acquire English moral and intellectual values, so that they could act as interpreters between English
rulers and those ruled by them. On the question of which language
should be used he wrote:

> The claims of our language it is hardly necessary to recapitulate. It stands
> preeminent even among the languages of the West. . . It may safely be
> said that the literature now extant in that language is of greater value than
> all the literature which three hundred years ago was extant in all the lan-
> guages of the world together. . . The question now before us is simply
> whether, when it is in our power to teach this language, we shall teach lan-
> guages in which, by universal confession, there are no books on any
> subject which deserve to be compared with our own.
>
> (Quoted in Edwards 1985: 31)

In the 1920s important steps were taken in Wales and Ireland:
Welsh became an officially accepted (but not promoted) language and
Irish was chosen as the national language of the new Republic of Ireland. The latter was a particularly significant choice, as only a fraction
of the population spoke Irish – yet a majority of the people, for reasons
of nationalism, felt that Irish Gaelic was a better symbol of their ident-

ity than English; also, demands to preserve, and if possible revive, the Irish language had come from respected quarters. But the Irish Constitution spells out that English is the second official language, and today virtually everyone in Ireland uses English for most functions.

More recently, language policies have been initiated at a local level with a view to making some educational provision for Britain's new linguistic minorities. This has primarily involved teaching English as a second language to children who started school with little or no knowledge of it. Some local education authorities now also provide mother-tongue classes to non-native English speakers, although often in a rather informal, unsystematic manner. The initial impetus, incidentally, was due to EC legislation (see Appendix A).

10.2.4 Practical considerations

Language policy decisions can be put into practice in a variety of ways. A government may formulate laws which specify the use of a particular language, for instance in government administration; or it may encourage the world of business and commerce to adopt certain linguistic practices by offering subsidies or threatening sanctions; and publishing may be sponsored in one particular language and/or restricted in another. The education system is by far the most important tool for implementing a government's language planning policy.

Government policies can also be carried out indirectly, in the sense that they may not be deliberately set out by the government but nevertheless reflect official attitudes. For instance, in the last 200 years or so the attitudes of the state towards minority languages often came to the fore in the armed forces. In countries with military conscription the rule was usually to insist on the use of the national language within all sections of the services. Consequently, speakers of regional languages or varieties, for example in France and Spain, had to learn to use the official language or at any rate to improve their knowledge of it; in Italy and Germany dialect speakers had to conform to the standard variety. The armed forces (through the system of compulsory military service) thus played a part in promoting the official language and in suppressing regional variations.

At a non-government level, political parties and other organizations interested in promoting a language, such as the Welsh Language Society, can put pressure on governments to take actions that favour their language, and they can organize language classes or engage in cultural activities in the languages concerned, as does the Cèrcle René Schickele in Alsace.

There are many different reasons why deliberate language planning is undertaken. Political, educational and practical considerations may lead planners to formulate policies that have the effect of changing the status of a particular language or variety. Cobarrubias (1983) argues that certain planning tasks are not 'philosophically neutral' and that moral issues are often involved in planning. One such issue concerns the question of language rights: do immigrants give up their right to use their language and keep their cultural identity when they choose to migrate, or is it the right of people to retain and maintain their language wherever they are? The United Nations and UNESCO have declared that ethnic groups do have the right to maintain their language(s), but few countries have incorporated this principle into their legislation. Directive 486/EEC (see Appendix A), issued by the European Community in 1977, confirmed the right of migrants' children to receive mother-tongue teaching. This directive goes some way towards recognizing certain language rights. It has not, however, been a very effective measure, as its application was left to the discretion of each individual country.

Cobarrubias (1983: 63) suggests four typical ideologies that may motivate language planning:

(1)   linguistic assimilation;
(2)   linguistic pluralism;
(3)   vernacularization;
(4)   internationalism.

Linguistic assimilation is the name given to the notion that all inhabitants of a country should speak the dominant language, regardless of their origin. There are numerous examples of states which have adhered, consciously or unconsciously, to this belief. A corollary of this position is that linguistic superiority is attached to the dominant language, and that minority languages are not, *per se*, granted equal rights. The United States has practised linguistic assimilation widely (and still does) in areas which it has annexed, colonized or acquired, such as Hawaii, New Mexico, the Philippines and Alaska.The case of the hellenization of Macedonia in 1912–13 can be seen as a European example of a country that has indulged in the same kind of policy.

Linguistic pluralism, roughly speaking, recognizes the coexistence of different language groups, which are granted the right to maintain their languages. There are various forms of pluralism, depending on the status of, and the official support given to, the individual languages. South Africa, Singapore, Belgium, Switzerland and Finland are examples of countries where two or more languages are officially recognized.

Vernacularization concerns the restoration or development of an indigenous language or variety, and its adoption as an official language. The promotion of Quechua in Peru and of Tagalog in the Philippines are examples of this.

Internationalism involves a country choosing a language of wider communication (rather than an indigenous one) as an official language, or as one to be used for education purposes. The choice of English in Kenya, India, Singapore and Papua New Guinea illustrates this type of ideology.

The underlying ideology and a country's interpretation of language rights will therefore shape its language policies. Planning decisions, in turn, will often determine the fate of minority languages, thus reflecting official attitudes towards minorities. Cobarrubias (1983: 71 ff) discusses a number of these attitudes (but it is worth remembering that he was not trying to present a complete taxonomy):

(1)   attempting to kill a language;
(2)   letting a language die;
(3)   unsupported coexistence;
(4)   partial support of specific language functions;
(5)   adoption as an official language.

Of course it does happen that official attitudes change over the years. For instance, in Spain government policy towards Basque has shifted from total suppression ('attempting to kill') in the years after the Spanish Civil War, through 'unsupported coexistence' in the last years of Franco's dictatorship, to official recognition and regional support in present-day democratic Spain.

Language planning is also an ongoing process in older nations in Europe, where the question of language status seems to have been decided long ago. But changes need to be made from time to time as linguistic minorities, both the indigenous and the non-indigenous ones, become more articulate in formulating their demands. States that used to see themselves as monolingual now find themselves compelled to address the question of language allocation anew. Finland, Sweden and Norway, for example, have already made some changes with respect to the status of Same (or Sami), and the Netherlands have allowed Frisian to be used as the medium for instruction in schools in Friesland; Germany and the Scandinavian countries are making special provisions for the education of the children of migrants. In Canada, as we have seen, the emphasis is not only on supporting bilingual education, but on reallocating a language (French) in the domain of business and commerce, where it played little part before.

The United States, too, provide an interesting example of language planning measures being taken in response to a changing linguistic situation – and also of public reaction to them. By far the biggest wave of immigrants in recent times (particularly from the 1960s onwards) consisted of Spanish-speaking people, followed by speakers of Asian languages. By 1984 an estimated 17.5 million (Wardhaugh 1987) Hispanic people had settled in the country and, contrary to what happened with previous immigrants, had shown little sign of being in the process of assimilating linguistically to American English. The 1968 Bilingual Education Act and subsequent legislation had been passed to promote bilingual and mother-tongue provision in various fields of public life. At the beginning of the 1980s, however, public opinion had turned against bilingualism, and demands for curbing bilingual education programmes and other facilities were being frequently voiced. The peak of reaction was reached in 1981 (and again in 1983) when proposals were put before Congress for an amendment to the Constitution so as to declare English the official language of the United States. The moves did not succeed. If such proposals had been accepted, the federal governments would have been prevented from maintaining, as a general entitlement, such pluralist policies as were reflected in the bilingual education schemes and the decision to publish official documents (e.g. voting papers) in several languages. The debate about language rights in the United States has not subsided, and some individual federal states have actually proceeded to declare English the official local language (for a detailed discussion, see Wardhaugh 1987; Marshall 1986).

Notes

1. Before the end of the eighteenth century most of the major European countries had produced authoritative grammars, including spelling rules, and famous writers, philosophers and scientists, by using the national languages, were enhancing their prestige. In many countries national academies were established and charged with the task of maintaining linguistic standards. The Accademia della Crusca in Florence was founded in 1582, the Académie Française in 1635, the Deutsche Akademie der Wissenschaften (Berlin) in 1700, the Real Academia Española de la Lengua in 1713 and the Russian Academy in 1724, to name some of the major ones.

2. One example would be the dropping of the final 'me' in words like 'programme' in some forms of contemporary English, another the decision to remove the written accent from monosyllabic words such as 'fue', 'fui', 'vio', 'dio' in Spanish, taken by the Royal Academy in the 1950s. The German Federal Republic decided, after the Second World War, to use the Roman alphabet and to give up printing and writing in the Gothic script. In other cases, as for instance in Indonesia, the decisions to adopt the widely-used pidgin (Bahasa Indonesia) as official language meant that graphization covering a whole language had to be carried out within a short period of time.

3. There have been many such attempts – and almost as many failures, e.g. the 'Sprachgesellschaften' (learned societies concerned with the protection and furtherance of the German language) in eighteenth- and nineteenth-century Germany, trying to fend off French influences, Atatürk's efforts to rid Turkish of Arabic and Persian loanwords, Israel's desire to expand modern Hebrew by means of new coinages rather than borrowing words from European languages, and the exertions in present-day France to resist the increasing use of English words in ordinary people's use of French; one typical example was the short-lived attempt, in the early days of Franco's rule in Spain, when football was becoming a popular spectator sport, to coin the word 'balompié', which was considered to be authentically Spanish, for people to use instead of the loanword 'fútbol', which is now firmly established in the language.

Chapter 11

Linguistic minorities

The basic concepts introduced in Chapters 8, 9 and 10 are exemplified in the rest of the book. The discussion in this chapter deals, in the main, with general aspects of the subject of linguistic minorities and issues that are relevant to language use and language maintenance within these groups, as well as the factors which bear upon their continued existence as separate communities. The focus of attention is the linguistic minorities of western Europe (the analysis of the rich linguistic diversity and complex patterns of language use in central and eastern Europe falls outside the scope of these chapters). The case studies that follow later (Chapters 12 to 14) present a more detailed consideration of three very different sets of situations in which linguistic minorities in western Europe today find themselves. It is therefore hoped that the present chapter illustrates the theoretical points made previously and that the case studies will draw together the various strands of political, socio-economic, cultural and educational issues that have been analysed in preceding chapters.

A look at a map of western Europe (including the north and the south) reveals an astonishingly diverse picture: of the eighteen countries included in it (Greenland, Iceland, Finland, Norway, Sweden, Denmark, Germany, Austria, Switzerland, Belgium, Netherlands, Luxembourg, France, Spain, Portugal, Italy, the UK and the Republic of Ireland, leaving aside the very small communities of Andorra, Monaco, San Marino, Lichtenstein and Vatican City), only two, Portugal and Iceland, have no indigenous linguistic minorities. In some of the bigger countries such as France, Britain, Spain and Italy, there are several linguistic minorities, yet these countries are often thought of as monolingual. One is used to thinking that in Britain people speak English, in

11.1   Indigenous linguistic minorities in western Europe

France French, in Spain Spanish, and so on. This happens, not so much because the minorities are small in terms of numbers of speakers (indeed, some of them have millions of them), but rather because some of these minority languages are not perceived by the population as a whole as having equivalent status to the national language, and therefore there may be insufficient social support for them. On the other hand, smaller countries such as Switzerland, Belgium and Luxembourg, which officially recognize the existence of other languages within their borders, are considered multilingual, although the numbers involved are relatively small.

11.1 Indigenous minorities in western Europe

An *indigenous linguistic minority* is a community of people who share a number of common characteristics, among them the fact that they speak their own language, and who perceive themselves as different from the groups of speakers of the majority language. They are settled in a given area, *the minority area*, where they have lived for a considerable length of time, usually for centuries. In that area the language in question, which is not that of the majority of that state's citizens, is spoken by all, or at any rate a sizeable proportion, of the members of the linguistic community. The following list (based on Stephens 1976) mentions some of the more important linguistic minorities of western Europe.

TABLE 11.1 Linguistic minorities of western Europe

State	Minority	Name of minority language
Finland	The Swedish Finlanders	Swedish
	The Same	Same (or Sami)
Sweden	The Finnish Swedes	Finnish
	The Same	Same
Norway	The Same	Same
Denmark	The Germans of North Schleswig	German
	The Faroese Islanders	Faroese[b]

State	Minority	Name of minority language
West Germany	The Danes of North Schleswig	Danish
	The North Frisians	Frisian
Netherlands	The West Frisians	Frisian
Belgium[a]	The Flemings	Flemish
	The Walloons	French
	The Germans of Old Belgium	German
Luxembourg	The Letzeburgers	Lëtzebuergesch[c]
France	The Bretons	Breton
	The Flemings of Westhoek	Flemish
	The Occitans	Occitan
	The Catalans of Roussillon	Catalan
	The Northern Basques	Basque
	The Alsatians	Alsatian[d]
	The Corsicans	Corsican
Spain	The Basques	Basque
	The Catalans	Catalan
	The Galicians	Galician (or Gallego)
Italy	The Piedmontese	Piedmontese[g]
	The Occitans of Piedmont	Occitan
	The Aostans /Valdotains	Provençal
	The South Tyroleans	German
	The Romagnols	Romagnol[g]
	The Friulans	Friulian
	The Ladins	Ladin
	The Slovenes of Trieste	Slovene
	The Sards	Sardinian
	The Catalans of Alghero	Catalan
	The Greeks, Albanians and Croats of the Mezzogiorno	Greek, Albanian and Croatian
Austria	The Slovenes of Corinthia	Slovene
	The Magyars and the Croats of Burgenland	Hungarian and Croatian

State	Minority	Name of minority language
Switzerland	The Ticinese	Italian
	The Jurassians	French
	The Rhaetians	Romansch
UK	The Gaels of Scotland	Scots Gaelic
	The Lowland Scots	Scots
	The Gaels of the Isle of Man	Manx[e]
	The Gaels of Northern Ireland	Irish Gaelic
	The Welsh	Welsh
	The Channel Islanders	French
Irish Republic (Eire)	The Gaels	Irish Gaelic[f]

Notes

a. The case of Belgium is somewhat special, since its entire population can be said to consist of minorities. The German-speaking minority is small (1 per cent), but the French- and Flemish-speaking minorities number 32 per cent and 56 per cent respectively.

b. Faroese is not recognised by the Danes as a language in its own right, but as a dialect of Danish. The Faroese people use standard Danish for written purposes.

c. The vast majority of Luxemburgers use Lëtzebuergesh, which is another Allemanic dialect, alongside French. Lëtzebuergesh shares many of the features of other minority languages, e.g. until not so long ago it was common only in its spoken form, as High German was used for written communication. Today High German continues to be used as a written medium, but Lëtzebuergesch has been standardized and is also used for certain written purposes.

d. Alsatian is an Allemanic dialect. It is more similar to the German dialect forms spoken in Luxembourg and Switzerland than to High German. Traditionally, High German was used for written purposes, but more recently Alsatian is also used in writing. (See Chapter 12 for more details.)

LINGUISTIC MINORITIES

e. Manx is more or less extinct now as a spoken language. It is included here because it is still considered to be a part of the islanders' cultural identity. The same, although to a lesser degree, could be said of Cornish. This language is said to have become extinct by the end of the eighteenth century.

f. Irish Gaelic is the national language of the Republic of Ireland, but only a small proportion of Irish people use it as a language for daily communication.

g. Piedmontese and Romagnol belong to the Gallo-Italic group of dialects, the largest of the northern dialects in Italy.

h. Friulian and Ladin both belong to the Rhaeto-Romance language family.

The names of the minorities refer to the language with which they are associated, not to their citizenship. Thus, for example, the Danes of North Schleswig hold German or dual nationality, while they see themselves as belonging to the Danish-speaking community.

Those minorities whose language (e.g. French or German) is also that of another independent state, usually speak a regional variety (which may be quite different from the standard variety), while using the standard form for written purposes.

In Europe historical boundaries between languages spoken natively in each country do not, in most cases, coincide with present-day frontiers. Minorities have been the result of political decisions that have seldom been taken on the basis of cultural, ethnic or linguistic considerations. Chapter 9 included a discussion of historical and contemporary factors that have led to the emergence of multilingualism, i.e. new language groups were formed from the subdivision of existing ones.

11.2 Two main types of indigenous linguistic minorities

The above-mentioned European minorities can be divided into two broad categories:

(1) The first type of linguistic minorities are those whose *language is not the official language of any state*. These minorities are ethnic groups, mostly nations in their own right, whose ethnic homeland is in

the territories where they live. The French ethnologist Guy Héraud (1963) calls this type 'les ethnies sans état'. Examples of such self-contained groups would be the Occitans and the Bretons in France, the Basques and Catalans in Spain, the Welsh and Gaels in Britain, the Frisians in the Netherlands, and the Same in north Scandinavia.

Whether or not they are recognized as nations and their languages as national ones depends on the extent to which their speakers have demonstrated a nationality consciousness and on the status that the majority of the inhabitants or the host nation as a whole has afforded to them.

(2) The second type comprises those linguistic minorities whose *languages are official ones elsewhere*, i.e. communities who are in the minority in the state of which they are citizens, but who look to their ethnic homeland outside the state where they live. Such minorities are usually younger than those of the first type in that they owe their existence to comparatively recent alterations in state frontiers: for example, the Alsatians in France, the Danes in North Schleswig and the Germans in Denmark, the Tyroleans in Italy and the Swedes in Finland. These minorities are free of the onus of having to prove that they are nations in their own right. Instead, they may have the advantage that their languages enjoy a cultural prestige out of proportion to their numerical strength. Their speakers are also able to benefit from recorded and written material produced in the ethnic homeland, such as television and radio programmes as well as all forms of printed (including educational) material. This is a very important factor for the maintenance of their language, both at a private level and in the field of education. It is also a facility that the minorities of type (1) lack; it is therefore much more difficult and costly for the latter to keep up their languages.

In the case of the second type of minorities, their languages are officially recognized. This recognition may take different forms as far as the use of the language in public life and administration is concerned, and some form of educational provision may be made for it. For example, German-speaking children in Tyrol are catered for in Italy's education system, and the same happens in Sweden in relation to its Finnish minority (in both countries this is only a recent development). The interests of the Danish and German minorities in North and South Schleswig are attended to, both educationally and in the field of administration, with the support of the two host countries. But France does not take Dutch into account in education or public life for its Flemish minority.

The broad definition of 'linguistic minority' given at the beginning of the chapter has been the basis of the two types just described. It should be pointed out, though, that the term is useful only as long as one uses it in a general way. In fact, minorities differ greatly, and in many respects, from one case to another. They differ, above all, in the way they see themselves and in the ways they are seen by others, and in the kind of pattern of language use found among their members. The Corsicans, for instance, consider themselves to be a separate national group, but the majority of mainland French people do not recognize their claim. The Germans in Denmark seem to share the national identity of those of the Federal Republic of Germany, as well as that of the Danes among whom they live, but, in contrast, the Alsatians (who speak a Germanic dialect) do not share any feelings of belonging to the same ethnic group with the Germans across the border, even though they consider themselves to be ethnically different from the French.

11.3 Ethnic, regional, national and minority languages

The terms 'ethnic language', 'regional language', 'national language' and 'minority language' are all equally vague, as their connotations depend on the political persuasion and national feelings of their users. In addition, 'minority language' is unsatisfactory because it seems to suggest that only a small number of people speak it. Yet as far as linguistic minorities are concerned, size is very relative indeed. In Schleswig-Holstein (north Germany) the number of Frisians who speak Frisian is actually smaller than the section of this group of people who do not (the same applies to the Welsh in Wales). But in South Tyrol the group of German speakers is larger than the number of speakers of Italian, i.e. the linguistic minority is the majority in that particular area; the same is true for the Catalans in Catalonia, but not for Catalan speakers in the País Valencià next door, where they are in a minority, the majority being native speakers of Spanish.

As we shall see later, the Catalans are unusual in many ways: there are about six million of them who speak Catalan, which makes them the biggest linguistic minority in western Europe and a community larger than those of many European states, living in an area which is more extensive than Belgium, the Netherlands or Switzerland. Catalonia was mentioned earlier (p. 225) as a linguistic minority of type (1), yet there is an independent state where Catalan is spoken as the official language, the Principality of Andorra – which, at least theoretically, makes it eligible for type (2) membership. Andorra may be an extremely small country, but the fact that Catalan is spoken there means that the Spanish government in Madrid supports interpretation into and out of Catalan in some official transactions between the two states, a facility which it does not grant to other languages spoken within Spain.

The case of Belgium is another one that shows up the inadequacies of the term 'linguistic minority'. Leaving aside Brussels, which is officially bilingual and accounts for 11 per cent of the population, the country is divided into two almost equal territories, Flanders and Wallonia, but some 56 per cent of Belgians are Flemish speakers, 32 per cent are French speakers and only 1 per cent speak German. Of course there is no problem in referring to the Germans of the eastern region (Altbelgien) as a linguistic minority, but it is more often the Flemish rather than the French-speaking Walloons who are held to be the linguistic minority. Belgium also has over 10 per cent foreign residents, many of whom are migrant workers and their families. On the other hand, the Gaels in Ireland, who make up about 3 per cent of speakers, are very much in a numerical minority; yet their language enjoys a social prestige among the population which is out of all proportion to the actual number of native speakers, as it is the national language of the whole of the state of Eire. Clearly, then, size is not particularly important in the discussion. The expression and perception of national or ethnic identity, the status and prestige of the minority language and its speakers within the state, and linguistic factors such as whether or not the language has undergone standardization or is backed by a literary tradition, as well as social aspects like the purposes for which the language is used, appear to be more relevant.

11.4 A historical perspective

The concept of nation and its relation to language has a complicated history in Europe, as the brief discussion at the beginning of this chapter (section 10.1) has shown. Within the scope of this study it is possible only to suggest some of the themes that have emerged in what one could call linguistic nationalism.

Broadly speaking, modern nationalism is a phenomenon predominantly of the nineteenth century. Before that time there existed a variety of competing loyalties ranging from feudal allegiance, membership of an estate, clan or guild, loyalty to village or town versus country, faith or region. Some of these might be expressed in particular linguistic ways, such as the widespread use of dialectal forms or the use of a certain language (e.g. French) among members of other groups (e.g. the Polish, German or Russian nobility) or for specific purposes (e.g. Latin in the liturgy of the Catholic Church). It was seldom the case, however, that the preference for some linguistic forms stood in the way of wider loyalties.

The idea of nation and the nation state became a central force only after the French Revolution (see section 10.1.3). However, whilst language assumed a new importance in the identification with the state and as a symbol of nationality, nationalism created a range of points of linguistic tension. For example, nineteenth-century France was a highly centralized state, and the only language which it was possible to speak in the transaction of public affairs was French; this meant that the other languages of France were excluded from the education system (successive French governments to the present day have defended and maintained this decision). Such problems were even more acute in larger territorial units such as the Habsburg Empire, where language policy became a means of suppressing particular ethnic groupings. At the same time, broader language-related trends (e.g. the Pan-Slav and Pan-Nordic movements) were used to weld common linguistic groups together beyond national and imperial boundaries.

In all these cases (and in smaller countries, too) a new sense of linguistic identity was asserted and, to some extent, created anew. Nationalist movements sprang up in many places, with sentiments that were expressed in a variety of ways: in the use of dialect for literary and other written purposes, in renewed interest in national myths, traditions, legends and folklore, in efforts to standardize minority languages, or in attempts to nurture a particular language variety. Feelings of nationalism were also expressed by more militant, even violent, attitudes with which the more active members of minorities confronted the majority, who more often than not sought to suppress them. In effect, then, the linking of nationality with language found acceptance in many parts of Europe, both at the higher ideological level and on more practical and political grounds.

While language (or, more precisely, certain national languages) assumed a new importance, nationalism itself was a source of conflict.

Many countries experienced a number of developments (industrialization, urbanization and, above all, centralization of the administration) that invariably brought suppression of regional differences. There were also problems arising out of the changes in the political map of Europe which were the consequence of the emergence of new nation states after the dissolution of the Ottoman Empire: some nations became independent, others were reduced to the status of a minority within a state or remained as they were before, a minority within another nation. By the end of the nineteenth century some forty-five million people were members of linguistic minorities in various parts of Europe (Stephens 1976).

The origins of the First World War were manifold, but nationalism at both state and minority levels was a contributory cause. One of the slogans of the day that appealed most to the inhabitants of many parts of Europe was 'For the rights of small nations'. The post-war settlement in Europe can be seen as an example of the problems that can result from the attempt to reconcile linguistically-based national feelings with economic and territorial realities. The point of departure was the principle of self-determination contained in President Wilson's famous Fourteen Points for Peace, proclaimed in 1918 before the American Congress just prior to the official end of the war. At the same time, the dissolution of the Russian Empire resulted in the setting up of the new independent states of Estonia, Latvia, Lithuania and Finland. Poland, Europe's whipping boy, who in her long history had endured so many changes to her borders, on this occasion regained some territory and with the establishment of the Polish Corridor obtained access to the Baltic Sea. Most of the states that emerged after the demise of the Austrio-Hungarian and Ottoman Empires were faced with intractable problems from the outset, either because sizeable minorities were included within them (for instance, up to 40 per cent of the populations of Poland and Czechoslovakia consisted of minorities that had little in common with each other) or because their minorities made territorial claims against each other.

The emergence of fascism in Spain, Italy and Germany was to have a profound effect on linguistic minorities. Language was considered an essential part of nationality and a symbol of national identity and allegiance. At the end of the 1930s the Basques and the Catalans, in Spain, faced another kind of difficulty. During the Spanish Civil War they had fought 'on the wrong side', that of the losing Second Republic, which had given them a considerable degree of autonomy during its short existence, and therefore they found themselves in 1939 at the mercy of the victorious fascists. Franco's dictatorship retaliated with a most severe repression of the so-called 'traitor provinces', which was to have serious consequences for the survival of the Catalan and Basque languages.

The Nazis showed total disregard for the rights of non-German minorities in Germany and they considered all German-speaking minorities outside the national territory as belonging, or wanting to belong, to the Reich. Their justification of expansionist policies was that they were efforts to bring again all Germans to where they belonged: *heim ins Reich*, 'home to the Reich', was the slogan used. The annexation of Austria and the Sudetenland (the German-speaking part of Czechoslovakia), as well as the invasion of Poland, France, Luxembourg and Belgium, were presented in this light. Not surprisingly, many minorities did not want to be identified with Nazi Germany, just as many had failed to see themselves as having much in common with the Kaiser's First Reich. Alsace, Luxembourg and Altbelgien had, in the years since the end of the First World War, developed their own sense of national identity, in which dialect, cultural heritage and shared history were the most important ingredients. While they used standard German as the preferred form for written communication, their allegiance was towards the French, Luxembourgish and Belgian states. An event from the Second World War serves to illustrate this. In 1940 the Germans invaded Luxembourg; in order to demonstrate to the world that they were really just enabling the local inhabitants to return to the Reich, they held a referendum in which they asked them whether their native language was German or French: over 90 per cent of those questioned answered neither the one nor the other, but wrote 'Lëtzebuerguesch' on the ballot papers. The cases of Alsace, Belgium and Luxembourg show that linguistic minorities can achieve a sense of identity within some countries and that problems need not be insoluble.

At the end of the Second World War Europe's minorities had been reduced considerably: in 1945 their number was estimated to be about ten million, one-third of what it had been before the war (Stephens 1976). The excesses of fascist regimes, deportation, resettlement, immigration and the ravages of war had all contributed to this decline. Neither the Allied powers nor the United Nations had anything constructive to offer to the European minorities, as there were no provisions in international law that could be called upon in cases of conflicts breaking out over disputed areas involving linguistic minorities. The Turkish invasion of Cyprus in 1974 was a vivid reminder of this.

11.5 The contemporary situation in western Europe

The survival and protection of the culture and language of linguistic minorities therefore depend largely on their own efforts and on the policies of the host governments towards them. There is only one international body which campaigns on behalf of minorities in Europe, the Federal Union of European Nationalities (FUEN). In its statutes a nationality is defined as 'a national group which manifests itself by criteria such as its own language, culture or traditions and which constitutes in its native soil no proper State or is domiciled outside the State of its nationality'. Although the FUEN is an independent body, it does act as a pressure group as well as a centre of information, supporting and advising institutions such as the Council of Europe and the United Nations on matters concerning minorities. For instance, for years it has been campaigning for international legislation to cover the rights of minorities. Its aim is to introduce into international legislation the principle that a member of a linguistic minority has the right to use his/her own language in education, administration, court cases, etc.

A step forward was taken by the European Community in its 1977 Directive, which set out to establish the principle that all children should receive teaching in their mother tongue (see Appendix A). Although it was aimed at the children of migrant workers in particular, it was thought that educational provision for minorities in general would benefit. However, progress on the whole has been very slow. In general, it can be said that those minorities who find themselves members of a federal state or of one that grants some degree of autonomy to its regions fare better than those who have to live in a centrally administered system. In countries such as Britain and France the conflict between central government and linguistic minorities has traditionally been bitter. Centralist policies aimed at suppressing expressions of the minority's national identity, such as their language and culture, have brought about a serious threat to their very survival. In the course of its short existence Belgium has been torn by many conflicts which have caused the downfall of many governments. The causes are generally perceived as being linguistic, although (as is usually the case in disputes involving minorities) a host of other factors are also involved. Until 1960 Belgium was a highly centralized state, but since then the Belgian Constitution has been changed several times to allow for a greater degree of federalism. Decentralization was seen as the only answer to solving the country's problems brought about by the mutual antagonism of the Flemings and the Walloons. Switzerland has assumed the role of Europe's most successful multilingual state. There is no doubt that relative linguistic harmony has been achieved in the Swiss Federation because the four major language areas enjoy virtually full political and cultural autonomy.

Other countries in western Europe have also seen a conversion to federalism or regional autonomy. In Italy the process of devolution of central power was set in motion in 1947, and it has taken over forty years to be finalized. But Italy is not a fully federal state. Although the regions have wide-ranging powers in some areas, the central government in Rome retains considerable power in matters of finance. Also, Italy's regions differ greatly from each other in terms of politics, culture and economic prosperity; so long as this imbalance persists, regional and minority problems are bound to remain. Thus unrest in South Tyrol has flared up periodically ever since it became part of Italy under the Treaty of Versailles – there was a spate of bombings and angry demonstrations as recently as 1986.

Spain is Europe's latest convert to something approaching federalism. Franco's death in 1975 and the country's return to democracy put an end to over forty years of centralist government. The new 1978 Constitution established principles under which a number of regions achieved a considerable degree of autonomy in the years to follow, among them the linguistic minority areas of Galicia, Catalonia and the Basque Country. In all three measures have been initiated to strengthen the local language – a daunting task in view of the problems posed by large numbers of native speakers of Castilian Spanish who have settled in the regions concerned and the fact that the autonomous local governments receive no funds from the central administration specifically allocated for their endeavours of language recovery (although the regions can decide how they spend their own funds).

The best guarantee, or at least chance, for the protection of minorities, then, seems to lie in some form of federalism, at both national and international levels. Ever since the idea of European integration was first discussed, federalists, such as the Breton leader Yann Four with his notion of the 'Europe of a hundred flags' and the former German Chancellor Helmut Schmidt with his demand for a polycentric

Europe, a 'Europe of the regions', have played an important role in the promotion of European unity. However, such suggestions have been vigorously opposed by supporters of other ideas, e.g. functionalism. France, one of the largest and most centrally situated states of the European Community, is also its most centrally administered member country. Successive French governments have insisted that a united Europe should be a 'Europe of the States', and this view has found favour with Britain, where federalism has never been seriously considered.

Where does this leave Europe's minorities? Those who enjoy some form of autonomous or federal status obviously have greater possibilities to preserve and to foster their national identity, culture and language than those who receive no support from a centralized government. The only agency through which the latter can work towards an improvement in their situation is the Bureau for Unrepresented Nations in Brussels. Indirect help and encouragement (for example, in the form of study scholarships and grants for research into matters of interest to minorities) is provided by such institutions as the Council of Europe and the European Commission. But of course such measures are a far cry from anything that might enable any minority the form of self-determination that it might seek.

11.6 Use and maintenance of minority languages

The extent to which a minority is able to use and maintain its language depends on the inter-relationship of a large number of political, economic and social factors. In no two minorities is this interplay of forces identical. Minorities vary in size, geographical situation, social composition and economic strength, and the political status that they enjoy may range from almost full autonomy to total suppression. Yet there are also some features which many of them share and which (either alone or in combination with other factors) have posed a threat to the survival of the minority's language. For centuries minorities have suffered various forms of political persecution. Imposing restrictions on their rights (e.g. to own land or to vote), banning the use of the minority language in schools, courts and local administration and generally neglecting local cultural traditions are all negative measures that have been taken by centralist governments. In eastern Europe many minorities have even, in the course of history, become virtually extinct as a result of such policies coupled with large-scale expulsions or extermination and subsequent repopulation with peoples of different ethnic stock; and their languages (for instance, Yiddish, Latvian, Lithuanian and Estonian, and German in the USSR) have suffered with them. Another, perhaps less violent form of political suppression, is total denial of the existence of a minority. This is, for example, what the Turkish government does with respect to the Kurds who live in the south-eastern corner of Turkey. The Kurds have their own language, culture and religion, and many of them do not speak Turkish, which means that government officials and members of the armed forces who are sent to the region to fight Kurdish separatist guerrillas have to learn their language – yet Ankara refuses to allow them minority status.

Most minorities have suffered from a common economic fate, namely rural decline and depopulation. This has happened in Wales, Scotland and Ireland, in Galicia and in practically all the minority areas in France, in Friesland as well as in the Romansch-speaking part of Switzerland, in both Corsica and Sardinia. Sometimes the rural exodus was speeded up by industrial exploitation in other parts of the minority area, as happened with coalmining in Wales, Wallonia, Alsace-Lorraine and Sweden. Then, after a period of over-production, the coal-mining industry all over Europe slumped into recession, and these areas became subject to further decline and emigration. More prosperous regions, such as the Basque Country, Catalonia and some parts of northern Italy, experienced large-scale immigration as their industries expanded, and with the influx of native speakers of the majority language the homogeneity of the region and communication in the minority language became diluted. As regards the development of tourism, in many minority areas it has brought mixed blessings. It can boost the local economy and provide jobs for the population, but it also means that for at least part of the year large numbers of non-minority language speakers stay in the area, and so communication in the majority language becomes a necessity, thus putting further pressure on the minority population, as happens in many areas along the Mediterranean coast of Europe and in the Alps.

There are also social factors that may affect language maintenance negatively among some minorities. One of these is conscription. There is evidence of this, for example, in Lepschy and Lepschy (1977), who discuss the development of standard Italian and the decline of regional languages and dialects in Italy. These authors point out the levelling effect that conscription has had, and is still having, in this country. The same is true in France, Spain and a number of other European nations with a tradition of conscription. For a period of time, young men from different parts of the country have to communicate using the majority language, and this interrupts or brings to an end their use of the mother tongue and weakens its position.

11.7 Assimilation of minorities and cultural pluralism

So far we have discussed some of the political, economic and social factors that in the course of their history have threatened the survival of minorities. Ultimately, whether a minority is able to maintain its cultural and linguistic identity will depend on the policies of the state of which it forms part.There are two opposing stances that a state can decide to take *vis-à-vis* its minorities: either it adopts a policy of *cultural pluralism* (which will normally go hand in hand with some form of federal organization) or it insists on the *assimilation* of the minorities.

Edwards (1985) notes that assimilation has many connotations, two of which he describes as conformity and complete homogenization. The former implies that groups adapt themselves to the dominant mainstream culture which itself remains stable. Within the English-speaking world this kind of assimilation has also been termed 'Anglo-conformity', a reflection of the preferred policies in the English and American colonizing contexts. The idea of the 'melting pot', although used mainly in relation to the United States, more properly reflects the idea of complete homogenization, where all elements of society, indigenous as well as immigrant, minorities as much as the majority group, intermingle to produce a new identity for all. The development of post-colonial societies in many central and south American countries probably corresponds more closely to the 'melting pot' image than the case of their northern neighbours. Both types of assimilation have been criticized as 'a surrender of identities before some New-World juggernaut' (Edwards 1985: 104).

In some national contexts the assimilation of minorities has proceeded along more moderate lines and in different ways, resulting in the partial retention of some ethnic characteristics (e.g. religion or language) while assimilating along other cultural lines, such as giving up certain customs, dress or language(s).

There are many features that make up the ethnic and cultural distinctiveness of a linguistic minority, such as social institutions (e.g. family structure and common law), religion, social customs and cultural traditions (e.g. food, dress, feast days, marriage, birth and death rituals, etc.). A comparison of minorities which have been partially assimilated into a majority society is fascinating as it shows that certain ethnic features are given up more readily by some than by others. It would be difficult to prove that any one characteristic is more important than others for the survival of the minority, but religion and language are frequently found among the central features. Thus for the large number of Jews who left their native Russia, where they had lived for a long time in Yiddish-speaking communities, at the beginning of the century to settle in Britain or the United States, the maintenance of religion (which, it is true, embraces many social and cultural aspects of Jewish life) took precedence over everything else, including the language. The same can be said of many second- and third-generation immigrants in Britain, who may have succeeded in preserving their religion but perhaps not their language, e.g. the Greek and Turkish Cypriots, the Armenians and the Italians.

Those states which have pursued policies geared towards pluralism have provided their minorities with much better opportunities to develop. In present-day Europe there are not many nations that can claim to be genuinely pluralistic (Switzerland, which has a long polyethnic and pluralist tradition, comes close to one, at least with regard to its indigenous minorities). Integration results, in such states, when positive relations with the mainstream society are encouraged by members of both the minority and the majority groups. Edwards (1985) refers to this as *voluntary pluralism*. If, on the other hand, this does not happen, segregation (either self-imposed or forced) is the result. Clearly, some form of pluralism or modified assimilation is preferable as an approach towards minorities, as either makes it possible for them to maintain part of their identity and at the same time allows for a normal working relationship between the groups and with the institutions of the state. Nevertheless, there are reports from all parts of the world about ethnic conflicts – the ideal of harmonious diversity, even in apparently pluralistic societies, remains in most cases unattainable. A quite considerable degree of consensus is necessary to keep ethnic harmony, but this consensus can be achieved only if all sides are prepared to give up certain demands.

11.8 Separatism and separate identity

While many young states in Africa and Asia are still in the process of nation-building, which requires a great deal of effort in order to overcome the problems of ethnic diversity, the old world (including the United States) is experiencing a trend which has been termed *the ethnic revival*. Whether we are faced with a genuine revival (in the sense of renewed interest in, and resurgence of, things ethnic) and whether or not ethnic minorities are now in a better position to express their identity and pursue their claims are questions that fall beyond our remit. It is clear that ethnicity is in people's minds in many European countries in one form or another. It is also a fact that certain well-organized separatist movements have attracted widespread support for a range of activities (both legal, militant and of an extreme kind) from members of minorities and even some others: lobbying members of parliament, putting up candidates for local government elections, taking part in demonstrations in the regions and in the capital, pursuing legal cases to the highest level when minority issues were involved (perhaps under the protection of European legislation where neglect by a national government was involved) – as well as the more fanatical actions resorted to by separatists, such as daubing road-signs, putting up signs in the regional language and, more exceptionally, going on hunger strike and carrying out bomb and arson attacks or kidnappings. Wales, the Basque Country, Brittany, Corsica, the Jurassim and South Tyrol are all places where separatist movements have been active in trying to achieve their aims of gaining independence or some form of autonomy from the majority government, in some cases more successfully than in others. Their common belief is that if their activities and demands are adequately reflected in the media, the attention of the public will be drawn to the various issues relating to minorities. Providing that activities are kept within the bounds of legality, this kind of publicity can have a positive effect on general attitudes and foster greater ethnic and linguistic tolerance and, in turn, benefit mutual relations. Several minority groups have gained a larger degree of independence and recognition in the past decade or two in this way, and there can be little doubt that this has come about as a result of, among other things, pressure exerted by separatists.

In discussing the basis of separatism, Williams (1984) points out that the belief of nationalist leaders in their nations' uniqueness is invariably followed by a claim for independence. Sooner or later,

minority leaders come to see that their nation or ethnic group will not
be able to realize its full potential so long as it remains a constituent
part of a state. Smith (1982: 22) presents this idea quite clearly when
he says: 'The watchwords of ethnic separatism are identity, authenticity
and diversity. . . It seeks through separation the restoration of a de-
graded community to its rightful status and dignity, yet it also sees in
the status of a separate political existence the goal of that restoration
and the social embodiment of that dignity'. For a group of people to be
able to claim a separate identity it must show that it is different from
the majority in what Williams (1984) calls *cultural infrastructure*. It is
not enough for a group to identify with a particular territory where it is
concentrated. Through its shared history and sociocultural heritage the
group must have retained distinctive ethnic features which set it apart
from the mainstream society of a particular country. In Europe religion
and, particularly, language have always been the most powerful indica-
tors of ethnic identity. Language is a real and demonstrable expression
of separateness, whereas ethnicity, strong sentiment though it may be,
is somewhat vaguer. Following Williams, we can argue that ethnic separatism incorporates descent as the basis of individual and group status,
it provides spiritual confirmation, and it explains its uniqueness by a
shared history of suffering and isolation. Williams argues that ethnic
separateness sustains the myths of origin, development and uniqueness.

11.9 Language and separateness

Language is the most powerful means of expressing separateness. On
an immediate functional level, as a means of communication, it serves
to include group members and to exclude those who are not, i.e. it acts
as a group barrier. On a broader cultural plane it provides a link with
the past, as well as continuity and prestige, particularly if the minority
has a rich literary tradition, as is the case with most minorities in
Europe. It is also able to unite different sections of the group (e.g.
different social classes), just as it can be instrumental in cultural division. It is undoubtedly the strongest barrier to assimilation and, not
surprisingly, it has played a key role in separatist movements. These
have always been most successful when they have been able to appeal
to a wider group by combining ethnic and regional-based grievances
with a claim for the preservation of religion or language – in other
words, when a coherent political organization has enabled them to rely

on the minority's widely held sense of separateness and find appropriate expression for their perceived inequality *vis-à-vis* the state's distribution of economic resources. In their campaigns language has always been used both as a means of communication and as a symbol of group identity.

In an earlier study, Williams (1982) covers ethnic separatism in four different geographical areas: Wales, Brittany, the Basque Country and Québec. He argues that in all cases language has been accorded group-defining significance and that the conflicts experienced by these minorities (as well as others) can be described as language conflicts. The primary concerns of these minorities may not be genuinely of a linguistic nature, but since language is such a powerful divider of groups and can be a barrier to communication, it also makes compromise difficult. Williams (1982: 186) claims that '. . . in multilingual societies differentiation according to language is unavoidable. . . Since coalitions rarely form across communication barriers, this pattern reinforces the language divide, predisposing both parties to conflict rather than co-operation'. This view appears to offer little hope for the peaceful coexistence of minorities and majorities, but it does explain why separatism in our modern times is still an issue. It may also serve to remind us that in order to ease what is termed *language conflict* we have to find solutions that take into consideration both the importance of language maintenance for minorities and the socio-economic and political grievances that minorities feel that they have.

11.10 Attributes of minority languages

So far the discussion has tried to bring together some of the sociocultural factors that affect all minorities and the features that form part of their identity. But probably the most fascinating aspect of the study of minorities is the linguistic one. There is an extraordinarily varied pattern of language use to be detected: no two minorities will turn out to have followed the same linguistic route or be going towards exactly the same linguistic future. It is true for all minorities that language maintenance is by no means guaranteed, but there are many forms of (language) life before (language) death.

In a state where minority languages are not proscribed, linguistic pluralism can take a variety of forms. A minority language can enjoy the legal status of a national language, such as Irish Gaelic in Ireland,

or that of the official language of a particular region, as happens with
Flemish in Flanders and Catalan in Catalonia. It may be considered a
region's language by the majority of its inhabitants without having any
particular legal status, as Ukrainian or Alsatian, or it may be one of
two officially recognized languages in a given area, e.g. Welsh in
Wales. It can also lack any kind of official status and still be employed
by a state's authorities for specific purposes, as is the case with Spanish in New Mexico (USA) or Urdu as used by some institutions in
Britain.

In the European context (perhaps more than elsewhere) the presence
or absence of official legal status can usually be taken as a good indicator of the state of the language, the prestige it and its speakers enjoy,
and its active use (how frequently and on what occasions they speak or
write it). As regards the linguistic state of the language, it is easier and
less controversial for the authorities to afford legal status to a minority
language (e.g. Catalan, Welsh, French in Canada) that has been standardized and can be related to a body of written documents and books,
both of a literary and non-literary kind, than to a minority language
(such as an emerging Creole) that has no literary tradition or a language which has not been standardized (e.g. Romansch), or is
considered by the authorities to be a dialect (e.g. Alsatian see Chapter
12).

The prestige a language has depends on a number of factors relating
to the language itself, its users and the attitudes of the majority. If a
language has a standard and a literary tradition, and it is used by most
minority members, representing all sections of society, and for all
forms of daily communication, then it is likely to enjoy more prestige
both within the community and outside it than if it is only used for
certain purposes by some sections of the group. As so many minority
areas have suffered economic depression and loss of investment in new
technologies, their inhabitants have become associated with rural backwardness and their language may have been tainted with the same kind
of stigma. It is this factor that provides the most challenging task for
language planners to overcome. For it is generally accepted that in
order to secure the survival of a minority language as a living entity it
is necessary not only to gain legal recognition for it, but also to prove
that it has at its disposal all the linguistic resources needed for successful communication in a modern, industrially advanced world.
Minorities which use a language that is official elsewhere (e.g. French,
German, Italian) clearly have an advantage over those who speak lan-

guages that for centuries have been labelled dialects or vernaculars by the majority in an attempt to devalue them and their speakers.

Linguistic pluralism in a minority area can be territorially based or individually based, or we may find some combination of the two. Multilingualism in Switzerland and Belgium is based on the principle of territorial monolingualism, which means (as we saw in Chapter 8) that only one language is the official one in a particular area; bilingualism will be a feature of individuals rather than the community as a whole. However, in the Swiss Canton of Graubünden virtually all inhabitants who speak Romansch are equally proficient in Swiss German, i.e. the whole community is bilingual. In many of the Soviet republics the local language (or one of several regional languages) is used by the majority of the population for most of the time; yet Russian, as well as being used by some members of the population all the time, is the norm for certain functions such as higher education or administration. It is a common pattern in large, linguistically diverse states, that the language of the ruling élite is employed for certain high-ranking functions, whereas the regional language is used for all other purposes by the majority of the population. But everybody is supposed to know the language of the rulers, and since it is usually favoured in and for education, the long-term aim appears to be to reduce the use of the local language.

In the case of most of Europe's minorities the number of monolinguals (in the minority language) is diminishing quickly, so that one can probably say that all the members of the younger generations are either bilingual or monolingual in the majority language. Whether the state institutions (administrative, educational, welfare, etc.) in these minority areas are (wholly or partly) bilingual depends on the legal status of the minority language – in Wales some are, at least in certain areas, in Brittany and the French Pyrenees they are not. Thus in any minority area we find three types of speakers:

(1) Monolinguals in the ethnic minority language (usually the very young and the older generations);
(2) Monolinguals in the national language of the state (numbers may range from a minority of the population to the vast majority);
(3) Bilinguals.

11.11 Non-indigenous minorities in Europe

Non-indigenous minorities are those ethnic groups who are not long-established members of a state. They comprise those people who have moved to their current place of residence, or whose parents or grandparents did so. These 'new' minorities (Churchill 1986) are the protagonists of one of the most profound changes in the social structure of many European countries in post-war years. The phenomenon as such is not an entirely new one, as there have been many instances in the history of the world of groups of people who changed their domicile because they were forced to leave their native countries for political or religious reasons (e.g. the Huguenots who in the sixteenth and seventeenth centuries settled in Prussia, England and Denmark, or the Hutterites who in 1874 emigrated to America) or because they were encouraged by particular rulers to settle in their territories for specific reasons (e.g. the Dutch who were invited to cultivate the marshes in Lincolnshire, England, in the seventeeth century). In most cases these minorities eventually became assimilated to their new societies. What is new about the present-day non-indigenous minorities is simply the sheer numbers which are involved, both in terms of ethnic groups and in terms of individuals.

Immigration (change of permanent residence to another country) and migration (temporary residence away from home) are the two phenomena that have created new minorities in Australia, the United States, Canada and Europe. As immigration countries, the former three encouraged large-scale immigration for nearly two centuries, and this entailed a formal change of nationality and national allegiance on the part of those involved. In Europe, France and Britain were the favoured places of destination for a long time, but up until the outbreak of the Second World War immigration took place on a comparatively modest scale and involved, in the main, people from other European countries. Britain, for example, saw different waves of immigrants: Germans who after the abortive 1848 Revolution had to flee their country; Jews from Eastern Europe who fled from Tsarist and later Bolshevik pogroms; Ukrainians who left their country after it attempted unsuccessfully to become independent in 1920; Poles in the 1920s and 1930s; and Jews from Germany and other European countries who escaped Nazi persecution. The situation changed quite dramatically after 1945 when France, Belgium, the Netherlands and Britain received large numbers of immigrants from their former colonies. Most of them came for economic reasons, and many (at least initially) may have considered their stay as temporary. They tended to settle in areas of industrial concentration and, in view of the numbers involved, they were able to form their own communities. Until the European countries involved changed their nationality laws in an attempt to curb the rise of immigration, those who came usually shared the nationality of their former colonial masters, although they did not have a common ethnic identity or (in many cases) even speak the same home language. But the authorities somehow assumed that immigrants would be able to communicate in the language of their new country, and it was only with the realization that the children of these new residents did not know the school language that a language problem became acknowledged. It took some European countries a long time to realize that the new immigrants would not assimilate quickly or easily. The acceptance that the countries involved have become multi-ethnic and multicultural, as well as multilingual, started only in the late 1970s – the Netherlands proved more progressive in this respect, Britain and France less so.

Migration of workers and their families started in the 1950s with the expansion of the economies of western Europe. For three decades migration moved in a south-to-north direction, involving millions of people (in terms of numbers, it has been surpassed only by European immigration to the United States). Most migrant workers came from Turkey, Yugoslavia, Greece, Italy, Spain, Portugal and Morocco to work in France, the Federal Republic of Germany, Switzerland, Denmark, Sweden, Belgium, the Netherlands and, to a lesser extent, Britain. At the beginning of the 1980s nearly twelve million people were involved. Although most migrants settle in their new country of residence on an ostensibly temporary basis, many of them become *de facto* permanent residents, staying far beyond the initially intended four or five years. In the case of, for example, the Turks in the German Federal Republic, or Moroccans in the Netherlands and France, their numbers are so large that they constitute sizeable communities, often closely knit, with little need for outside contacts – for which the only help needed is the services of interpreters, i.e. bilingual minority members. This, together with the intended temporary nature of their stay, the work and legal restrictions imposed on them, and a generally negative attitude on the part of mainstream society (both at an individual and institutional level) can make their integration more difficult than that of immigrant communities.

A number of reasons can be suggested to explain the fact that these minorities pose particularly complex problems with regard to the linguistic situation and the host country's appreciation of the issues involved. One is that the majority of migrant workers come from the most underprivileged sections of their home society, which means that their standard of formal education can be quite low, often involving illiteracy or a lack of familiarity with the standard language used in their country of origin. A further reason is that, since communication between them and the representatives of their countries (e.g. teachers and interpreters) can be difficult, mother-tongue educational provision for their children is often rendered ineffective. A third reason is that, with so many different groups involved, making special educational provision for them is a complex task – and this complexity is frequently considered a convenient excuse for not tackling the problem at all. It is the children of migrant workers who are likely to experience the most profound cultural, linguistic and psychological problems, and we are only just beginning to realize what is really involved in these issues. So long as small numbers of migrant workers stay temporarily in another country, they can be disregarded, or simply considered as a special feature of a particular area. But when they stay in large numbers and subsequent generations maintain their cultural distance, we can talk of a genuine minority. At the present time, many second-generation migrants are experiencing marginality, a feeling of not really belonging either in the native country of their parents or in their own country of birth and residence. It remains to be seen how, and to what extent, they eventually establish their own identity as 'German Turks' or 'French Moroccans' or 'Swiss Spaniards' (see Chapter 14).

11.12 The study of linguistic minorities

Linguistic minorities constitute a relatively new subject of investigation. Whereas older studies showed a preference for the description of the history, the language and the sociocultural heritage (particularly the literary tradition) of individual minorities, the emphasis has now shifted towards a sociolinguistic and comparative approach. This can be seen as a reflection of widespread interest in ethnic revival and ethnic identity. There is also a growing awareness of the sociocultural problems faced by minority members which, in some cases, has led to a demand for language rights, notably bilingual education. In 1986 the

Commission of the European Communities published a Report on Linguistic Minorities, which is an indication that in political circles, too, minorities are being taken into consideration more and more. This Report contains little that, at the level of proposals for political action, could actually help to preserve linguistic minorities, but it does provide a systematic collection of data.[1]

The investigation of multilingualism is necessarily interdisciplinary, i.e. two or more social sciences must contribute towards the elucidation of particular issues from various angles. Sociology and education are the two disciplines which have made the greatest advances in the field of minority studies, both driven on by immediate social and political concerns. But interdisciplinary investigation further requires the establishment of a theoretical framework within which research can be carried out. It also necessitates the use of different techniques, and it ultimately demands some form of synthesis. For research to be interdisciplinary (not just multidisciplinary) there must also be integration of concepts. In the context of linguistic minorities this integration can become particularly problematic, as there are many variables at work relating to the languages under investigation, the social groups who speak them and their historical background. It is a challenging task to have to take note of all the relevant factors. While, for example, it may be relatively straightforward to describe and compare language use among two given minorities, it may prove impossible to account for the fact that one has largely lost its native tongue although the other has not. One of the reasons for this difficulty is that no long-term studies have ever been carried out in this area, since it is impossible to undertake academic projects that span several generations. Other studies (e.g. Edwards 1984; 1985; and Williams 1984) have pointed towards the researchers' tendency to project their own biases when discussing minority issues. Linguistic minorities – whether indigenous, immigrant or migrant – present western European societies with challenges and questions that they have never before had to face, and it is virtually impossible to remain dispassionately objective. Also, the sociolinguist's and psycholinguist's old problem of the 'intimate relationship between the observer and the observed' (Gardner 1965) may stand in the way of objective investigation. Not all researchers appear to be aware of the fact that they view reality from their own moral or ideological standpoint, and that this may influence their results. It is therefore necessary for those interested in such research to be wary of possible bias.

Another problem that the researcher of linguistic minorities faces is concerned with access to reliable material. Short of carrying out one's own fieldwork, one has to rely on what other investigators have found out from official data. With regard to the latter, national and federal government agencies often have surprisingly few (if any) reliable figures about speakers or users of languages other than the national one. There are many possible reasons for this. Apart from the inherent difficulties involved in large-scale data collection, there is the additional problem posed by the fact that many countries have in the past seldom carried out reliable censuses – even today they still engage in this activity only every five to ten years. In any case, censuses rarely incorporate questions relating to language use, although they may include items about nationality – by which more often than not what is meant is state (rather than ethnic) nationality, i.e. 'British' rather than 'Welsh', for example. In addition, a question about mother tongue can be quite inconsequential if it is not backed up by further requests for information about the frequency and function of language use. One notable exception to this situation is Catalonia, which, after achieving autonomy and adopting a policy of promoting Catalan with a view to making it the real language of the region, included in its 1986 census, for the first time, several quite detailed questions about people's use of, and proficiency in, Catalan and Castilian Spanish. In this instance, the information obtained will probably enable Catalonia's language planners to carry out their policies more efficiently. But census results can also prove problematic, as has been demonstrated by the case of Belgium. Until 1962 the census questions on language (asked every ten years) decided whether or not the boundaries of minority areas had to be adjusted and whether provision for language services would be maintained or withdrawn. But it became clear that the answers were not always a truthful reflection of the prevailing linguistic situation, so the aims of the census (i.e. to provide a sound basis for a fair distribution of territory and facilities for the minorities involved) could not be achieved. In the context of major linguistic reforms in Belgium in the 1960s, the linguistic borders were made definitive and the language questions were withdrawn from subsequent censuses.

A further problem area is raised by the large number of illegal immigrants and migrants who, not being entitled to live in the country, do not figure in the official data. In western Europe their number is estimated (Power 1984) to be millions rather than thousands. Because of their status, they do not enjoy any form of protection or special provision. They, and especially their children, represent a particularly problematic section of the new minorities.

Notes
1. Studies on the subject of linguistic minorities have been undertaken, for instance, by Stephens (1976); Allardt (1979); Foster (1980); Edwards (1985); Churchill (1986); and Hinderling (1986).

Chapter 12

Case study I: The Alsatians

12.1 The language

'Of all the regions within the borders of the French state, Alsace has one of the most clearly defined personalities' (Stephens 1976: 341). This statement may sound surprising in view of the extraordinarily complex history of the region, which has been profoundly influenced by two major nations (France and Germany). The Alsatians have gone through many periods of conflicting loyalties, which have caused some writers on the subject to talk about a 'crisis of identity' (e.g. Haug 1984) or 'le particularism alsacien' (Philipps 1975).

Apart from the approximately 200,000 speakers of Flemish in French Flanders (which has a population of four million), the Alsatians are the only long-established minority in France whose language is closely related to the official language of a neighbouring state. They also constitute the only minority in France whose speakers, some 1.3 million, are demographically concentrated: some three-quarters of the region's population are speakers of Alsatian.

Alsatian is a variety of German. It is similar to the Swabian and Swiss dialects spoken to the east and south of Alsace, and to the Rhenish dialects of the north. Although it is sometimes used in a written form (e.g. in folk literature, songs, poems, advertisements, captions in newspapers), the written standard has traditionally been 'Hochdeutsch' (Standard German). Alsatian is thus basically a spoken language. Its special features are particularly noticeable in the lexis, where a large number of words and expressions are borrowed from French. Similarly, the Alsatian variety of French (i.e. the French spoken by many Alsatians) is marked by German influence (e.g. intonation that shows the transposition of the German tonic accent on the first syllable as opposed to the last syllable in each group as in Standard French) and by 'Alsatianisms' in lexis and expressions.

LORRAINE
ALSACE

FRANCE

Thionville
Diedenhofen

Boulay
Bolchen

Forbach

Saareguemines
Saargemund

M O S E L L E

METZ

Faulquemont
Falkenberg

Bitche
Bitsch

Wissembourg
Weissenburg

Saare-Union
Saar-Buckenheim

Chateau
Salins

Fenetrange   Finstingen

Haguehau
Haugenau

Dieuze
Duss

Saverne
Zabern

Saarbourg
Saarburg

B A S - R H I N

STRASBOURG
Strassburg

Molsheim

FEDERAL REPUBLIC OF GERMANY

Ville
Weiler

Selestat
Schlettstadt

Sᵗᵉ.-Marie-Aux-mines
Markirch

Ribeauville
Rappoltsweiler

COLMAR

Munster

H A U T - R H I N

Guebwiller
Gebweiler

Thann

MULHOUSE
Mulhausen

Altkirch

BASEL

Cordier

SWITZERLAND

Lucelle
Lutzel

MOSELLE   - LORRAINE

BAS-RHIN }
HAUT-RHIN } ALSACE

━ ━ Present linguistic frontier
        French–Alsatian

---- Border of département

Alsace Lorraine

Alsatian in fact consists of different dialect varieties. The four principal ones are:

(1) 'francique mosellan' (*Moselfränkisch*), spoken around the frontier with Luxembourg, e.g. Thionville;
(2) 'francique rhénan' (*Rheinfränkisch*), spoken in Lorraine, Alsace Bossue, Wissembourg;
(3) 'bas alémanique' (*Niederallemannisch*), spoken in the greater part of Alsace;
(4) 'haut alémanique' (*Hochallemannisch*), spoken near the frontier with Switzerland.

The Alsatian dialects thus range from Franconian, a central German one, to Alemannic, which belongs to the Upper German dialect group.

These dialects are spoken as their mother tongues by the majority of speakers throughout the region, although in the north this is true to a lesser extent than elsewhere: in northern Alsace, as in the neighbouring but quite separate region of Lorraine, the language most widely spoken is a local variety of French. The absence of one single 'standard' variety of Alsatian is sometimes mentioned as a reason why it would be difficult to teach Alsatian in schools. Lack of an agreed standard is not an unknown problem in minority areas: for instance, in the Romansch-speaking areas of Switzerland, or in the Gaeltacht in the Irish Republic, speakers see this as a drawback, too. Gardner-Chloros (1983: 35) makes the point that, unlike German dialect speakers, 'Alsatians cannot, or do not wish to, approximate more or less to Standard German'. One could add that, if this is so, this feature would distinguish them from speakers of the various Swiss German dialects, who will switch relatively easily from dialect to Standard German. In contrast, the Alsatians will usually switch to the standard variety of an entirely different language, namely French (for instance, when talking to a foreigner).

12.2 Historical overview

Geographically, Alsace (the 'départments' of Haut-Rhin and Bas-Rhin) is shaped like a corridor in the Rhine Valley between north and south. It is separated from Germany by the River Rhine and from the west of France by the Vosges mountains. It therefore forms a distinct, self-contained area. As we know, political frontiers rarely coincide with linguistic ones, but the latter are found more often along mountain ranges than alongside rivers. This may explain, at least in part, the survival and widespread use of a distinct German dialect within the French state. It has been observed that in this region more similarities are found between the dialects spoken along a given horizontal line on the French-German border (i.e. across the river) than between the varieties of Alsatian used in the north, near the frontier with Luxembourg, on the one hand, and those spoken in the south, near the Swiss border, on the other.

Given its geographical situation and topography, Alsace has been exposed to innumerable invasions from the times of the Franks and Alemans onwards. And ever since Charlemagne's empire was divided among his successors it has been claimed by the powers on either side of the Rhine. However, because of its geographical situation, religion, art, economy, language and culture, Alsace was always part of the Rhine area (*Rheingebiet*), and it was therefore intimately linked with the German world. Alsace's more recent history can be divided into six periods:

(1) Until 1648 Alsace was part of the (German) Holy Roman Empire. In the Middle Ages, towns such as Strasbourg and Colmar were great centres of literary and other cultural activities. Later they played an important role in spreading the use of German as an official language (when Latin was abandoned) and as a language used in church. The first bible translated into German was published in Strasbourg in 1466, well before Luther published his translation (1521).

(2) *1648-1870* Under the Treaty of Westphalia, at the end of the Thirty Years War, Alsace was annexed to France. The rich economic and intellectual life of the region was disturbed both as a consequence of the war and as a result of Louis XIV's policies. But Alsace's language (initially, at least) was respected. Indeed, the region retained more independence than other minority areas in France: for example, its schools were not subject to interference, and Alsatians were exempt from military service – two factors which contributed to the survival of Alsatian as a language. The process of assimilation to France began as soon as the aristocracy, the upper classes and the intellectuals were forced to use French in their contacts with the new administration. But in most areas of life in local society Alsatian remained the language used for daily interaction, while documents and official papers were written in German.

Stephens (1976: 343) quotes the Alsatian André Ulrich, who in 1789, just before the French Revolution, was able to declare: 'There are three hundred inhabitants of Alsace who do not know French for every one who does'. Alsace's identity as a region was dealt a heavy blow by the French Revolution, which proclaimed the principle of 'une nation, une langue' and set about enforcing linguistic uniformity, often by strong-arm methods such as threatening to execute or deport those unable to speak French. Apart from brute force, other factors contributed towards the spread of French during the nineteenth century, reaching, as usual, the upper and middle classes first: French became the language of secondary and higher education, and in 1853 it was officially introduced as the language of primary schooling, although at least one lesson of German was taught each day. The growing industrialization of the region, the development of transport and the consequent increase of bureaucracy also favoured the spread of French. But the Church remained a staunch supporter of Alsatian identity and the German language. And although most educated people acquired a knowledge of French, their native tongue remained Alsatian.

(3) *1870–1918* After the Franco-Prussian war Alsace changed hands again. The process of germanization that was instigated by its new masters was only made more palatable by the promise of greater regional autonomy. The late nineteenth century saw Alsace's economy flourish, and at the same time nationalist movements, both literary and political, began to emerge. Many writers argued that the only solution to the Alsatian predicament of being French in sentiment and German in speech consisted in political autonomy for the entire region (that is to say, in the institutionalization of Alsatian identity). This expression of 'national' identity should be viewed in the wider European context, in which an interest in philology, nationalism (originally of a non-political nature), folklore and history during the nineteenth century led to the development of many a national movement. Alsace's dilemma, her split national loyalties, came vividly to the fore when the Great War broke out in 1914: 250,000 men from Alsace were conscripted into the Kaiser's army, while 20,000 volunteered to fight on the French side.

(4) *1919-40* Following the Treaty of Versailles, Alsace was returned to France. As part of the highly centralized French state, it no longer enjoyed any administrative autonomy, and Alsatian as a language was firmly suppressed in all areas of public use. The late 1920s and 1930s saw the emergence of political parties which, to varying degrees, campaigned for more administrative and cultural independence from Paris and demanded the introduction of official bilingualism. With the rise of Hitler in Germany, however, the Alsatian movement lost much of its momentum. Nazism had the effect of furthering the French cause in

Alsace, in the same way as it fostered distinctly anti-German sentiments in neighbouring Luxembourg and Switzerland. In these two
countries this was to the benefit of the regional dialect (Letzeburgish
and Swiss German), which became upgraded in perceived prestige;
since the 1930s Standard German has been losing ground as a spoken
variety.

(5) *1940–45* During the Second World War Alsace was occupied by
German forces, who immediately proclaimed that Alsatians were German by origin (including those who spoke French!) and that German
was the language to be used. It was now the turn of French to be
banned from public life, and an intensive programme of germanization
was set in motion.

(6) At the end of the Second World War Alsace was once again returned to France, and again it became part of that country's centralized
system of government, but this time no linguistic concessions were
made. German was dropped completely from public use, and it ceased
to be a language of instruction in schools. In fact, it was relegated to
the status of a 'foreign language'. The justification given for these
measures was that they would enable French to 'regagner le terrain
perdu' (i.e. regain lost ground). The intention was to ensure, of course,
much more: that the region really became French, and this time for
good. And it *has* become French, to a large extent. Since 1945 French
has gained ground at every level of public life. Among members of the
older generations there are still those who have changed their nationality and official language two or three times in the course of their
lives, but everyone born after the war has been educated entirely in
French. For the new generations, French is the language of all levels of
education, of administration, the courts of justice, the police, the media
– in short, all areas of public and intellectual life. Certain legal
measures have been taken, aimed at the preservation (but not active
encouragement) of regional languages in France. The passing of the
Loi Deixonne in 1951 represented a turning point in France's linguistic
policy: it decreed that certain regional languages (Alsatian was not included) could be taught in their respective areas if a set of given
conditions were met. The Act was extended in 1961 to include Alsatian, but its provisions remained ineffective because of a long delay in
the publication of the necessary 'décrets d'application'. A more successful reform came about in 1971 with the 'Méthode Holderith',
which has resulted in more widespread teaching of German in secondary schools, sometimes from the age of nine, usually for half an hour a

day, and in the encouragement of the use of dialect and the teaching of dialect literature. Cellard (1976: 18) explains the measures as 'pour l'essentiel la méthode Holderith consiste à mener parallèlement, dès l'école primaire, l'apprentissage de l'allemand à partir du dialecte, et celui du français a partir d'une "potentialité bilingue" du petit dialectophone'. Research on language use among young Alsatians indicates that the bilingual potential remains dormant or, as the pessimists would have it, is non-existent. Alsatian is not used at school, and Standard German is taught as an optional subject, available in secondary schools only, for a few hours a week. These factors, together with the ignorance of parents and school staff on matters of bilingualism (which often leads to the view that the acquisition of the dominant language might be affected negatively) all contribute to the limited impact of the Holderith reforms.

French is used throughout Alsace in public administration, the media and education. All public notices, advertisements, road signs and street names are in French. There are publications in Standard German (Alsatian is not used for written purposes); but if newspapers are involved they have, by law, to appear under a French title with the subheading 'édition bilingue' and a quarter of the material must be in French. It can be taken as a subtle form of linguistic manipulation that articles addressed to young people and on sport must appear in French; they are allowed to be followed by a summary in German, but that seems a rather meaningless concession (Gardner-Chloros 1983).

The Church is the only influential body that still uses Alsatian. The Catholic Church celebrates Mass in both French and German (or Alsatian), but the Protestant Churches use Standard German in their various liturgies. As in other minority areas, the Church, particularly at the lower levels of the hierarchy, is playing a significant role in maintaining the minority language.

12.3 The use of Alsatian

Sociolinguistically, the language situation in Alsace has been described as diglossic, not in the 'classical' sense of Ferguson (1959), because the two varieties involved are not forms of the same language, but in Fishman's (1967) extended version, which includes varieties of different languages in addition to the criterion of separation of function. However, there are two factors that make Alsace's diglossia more complex. One is the presence of High German as the written standard and the variety taught in schools (the use of a standard variety for

written purposes and a dialect one for oral communication is a common enough phenomenon in dialect areas). The other factor relates to
the question of separation of function. One can say that, in general,
Alsatian is the language of the home, the family, interaction with close
friends and neighbours and small-scale commercial transactions, and
French is the language of public life and education. But this separation
of languages is not completely clear-cut. At one end of the scale there
are those Alsatians who are monolingual French speakers, and at the
other end there are those who use Alsatian in many kinds of communicative situations. For, whereas French can be used at all times and in
all situations (virtually all Alsatians can speak French), the use of Alsatian is determined by factors relating to the speaker, the listener, the
setting and the topic under discussion.

It is not unusual to encounter difficulties when trying to find reliable data about language use among linguistic minorities. Most
authors on the use of Alsatian, for instance, quote data published by
the *Institut national de la statistique et des études économiques*
(INSEE). The latest census figures for language use were published as
long ago as 1962. According to them, 85 per cent of the population
spoke Alsatian and 80.7 per cent French. This represented an increase
of 14 per cent of French speakers since 1946. In 1980 the INSEE carried out a survey based on ten questions on the use of dialect in
Alsace, and the figures were published in 1981. They revealed that in
the region of Haut-Rhin 73 per cent of the population spoke dialect
and in Bas-Rhin 77 per cent. Ladin (1983) criticizes this survey for not
seeking information on such aspects as frequency of use of Alsatian,
the exact functions for which it is used, competence in the dialect and
young people's expressed language loyalties. However, despite its
shortcomings (the most fundamental being that it was a survey and not
a census covering the whole population), the INSEE report does contain data that points towards specific factors which appear to determine
the amount of Alsatian spoken by a given individual. Age is probably
the most significant of these. Among the population at large the distribution by age shows that, whereas 88 per cent of those over
sixty-five years of age claimed to speak Alsatian, the figure falls to 65
per cent for those between sixteen and thirty-four. Ladin (1983) carried
out a detailed study of the language use of Alsatian-speaking young
people (fourteen to sixteen years old). His questionnaire covered
seventy-eight items which were grouped into bundles and aimed at eli-
citing information of the following kind:

(1)   a sociolinguistic profile of the informants;
(2)   language use in a number of communicative situations (fam-
       ily/friends; inner monologue/dreams/thoughts; religion; public
       life; cultural activities);
(3)   the image of the three languages used in Alsace;
(4)   linguistic self-evaluation;
(5)   linguistic competence (consisting of a translation from French
       into Alsatian and a task of labelling certain items in Alsatian).

Of the young people who took part, 77 per cent stated that they had
acquired Alsatian as their first language; for 23 per cent of them the
first language they had acquired was French. Only 4 per cent claimed
to have acquired the two languages simultaneously. When classified
according to parental background, the figures for use of dialect varied
considerably: whereas 97 per cent of children of farmers spoke Alsatian, only 64 per cent of those whose parents were clerical or
white-collar workers ('Beamte und Angestellte') did so. An even lower
proportion (44 per cent) of the children whose parents worked in the
professions or were top executives or high-ranking civil servants were
said to be speakers of Alsatian.

Another significant factor in the use of language is the distribution
by setting, i.e. urban versus rural.The French sociolinguist Andrée Tabouret-Keller carried out a survey between 1957 and 1962 that showed
a strong correlation between the use of Alsatian and the percentage of
the population working in agriculture, and she found farmers to be
extremely conservative in their linguistic habits. Gardner-Chloros
(1983) points out, however, that 'rural' is not synonymous with 'farm-
ing population'; the latter now makes up only 4.7 per cent of the total
population of Alsace. But generally speaking it is true that more Alsatian is spoken in rural areas than in towns. The INSEE study covered
3000 households and found that 88 per cent of the inhabitants of rural
communities claimed to speak Alsatian, whereas in towns of between
10,000 and 15,000 people the figure was 69 per cent. We have already
seen that in the last century French was more widely used in urban
areas and Alsatian in the countryside, where the inhabitants' contact
with French was much more limited than in the case of the *bourgeois*.
So there was then a clear correlation between setting and language use.
In modern times new factors have come into play which have been
highlighted by research. For example, Neville (1986) mentions the split
urban/rural as important, and she adds a new dimension, that of em-
ployer/employee, quoting Gauthier (1982: 80): 'Si, dans l'enterprise,
on parle encore en dialecte, c'est en français cependant qu'on s'adresse

au patron (en Alsace).' (The use of 'encore en dialecte' is interesting as
it indirectly seems to point to the speaker's perception of the future
demise of Alsatian.)

Naturally, the communicative situation is also relevant. Another section of the INSEE report, mentioned earlier, shows that of the families
questioned, 60 per cent said that they used Alsatian at home, 52 per
cent used it in the shops and 30 per cent for social security transactions. When asked whether they spoke Alsatian at work, 71 per cent
answered that they used it 'a lot' or 'quite a lot', which seems to tie in
with Gauthier's observations about language use among employers and
employees.

All these findings indicate that level of formality, rather than do-
main/setting, is important: the more formal the situation the more
likely it is that French will be used. It should be remembered that in
minority areas such as Alsace switching between majority and minority
languages is the commonest phenomenon. In her study of code-
switching among Strasbourg shoppers, Gardner-Chloros (1985) considered four variables which she thought were influential in language
behaviour: (1) the type of shop/department store; (2) the sort of goods
purchased; (3) the age of both customers and salespersons; and (4)
whether they were involved in in-group or out-group conversations, i.e.
speaking among themselves or not. The pattern of switching altered
according to the different variables involved, but in most cases the researcher found that the switch was from French to Alsatian rather than
from Alsatian to French. The reason for this was difficult to establish,
but Gardner-Chloros speculates that the speakers' uneasiness about
using French (because they were unaccustomed to it, or had difficulties
in talking in French over a sustained period of time) may have had
something to do with it. The study confirmed the impression of other
observers that French was generally perceived as being the prestige
form, required for use in more formal contexts, and that its use was
more frequent among younger than among older speakers. On the other
hand, the use of Alsatian was more prevalent in the downmarket stores,
in shops selling necessities rather than luxury goods, and in conversation among older customers and staff; and it was also more frequent in
in-group conversations than in out-group ones.

It is also interesting to note that women claim to use all three languages more often than men, whereas men tend to restrict themselves
to using just one or two languages. Women also said that they used
more French than men, particularly with their children once they had
started school (Tabouret-Keller 1981). In the course of the research that
he carried out into attitudes towards the Alsatian dialect, Cole (1975)

found that when he asked Alsatians of various ages whether it was important for them to speak Alsatian, between 83 per cent and 92 per cent replied affirmatively; an even more significant finding was that, of the 10–15 per cent who were just as happy to identify with 'French' as with 'French and Alsatian', two-thirds were women. Ladin (1983), too, found what he called a greater 'Dialektfaulheit' (i.e. reluctance to use Alsatian) among mothers: 49 per cent of them used the dialect with their children, as opposed to 57 per cent of fathers. In all the communicative situations that he studied, girls were found to use French more consistently than boys. Why this should be so the researcher felt unable to explain, but he pointed towards a possible connection between women and, on the one hand, the jobs they often do, as many tend to work in the service industries where French is required and, on the other, their role as mothers, which entails contact with schools, teachers and administrative authorities. We know from classical sociolinguistic studies, such as those by Labov in Martha's Vineyard (Labov 1963) and Trudgill in Norwich (Trudgill 1972) that women tend to be more conscious of, and interested in, the language forms that carry overt prestige than men. The Alsatian data, although it is sketchy, seems to confirm these findings.

Alsatian, therefore, should not generally be considered the language of the home. The 1981 INSEE survey, which covered 1000 schoolchildren living in different parts of the region, showed that all spoke French at home, albeit in varying proportions. In the centre of Strasbourg only 8 per cent never or rarely spoke French at home, but in the surrounding area the figure rose to 29 per cent, and in the countryside 72 per cent said that they never or seldom spoke French at home. Comparing these figures with the ones about distribution by setting (urban/rural), it seems clear that young people use more French than their elders. This is confirmed by Ladin's research (Ladin 1983), which showed that, within the same family, the prime factor in the decision to use French or Alsatian is age:

Language use within the family

parents to parents:	88 per cent Alsatian
parents to children:	53 per cent Alsatian
children to parents:	63 per cent Alsatian
children to siblings:	34 per cent Alsatian
	42 per cent French
	24 per cent Alsatian and French

12.4 The future of Alsatian

The last set of figures given above is perhaps the clearest indication of the decline of Alsatian. If the preferred language among the young generation is French, and parents, especially mothers, use French rather than Alsatian for their communication needs, and if, in addition, schools do not encourage the teaching of Alsatian – how will the dialect be passed down to younger generations once the present-day youngsters are older? From the most optimistic angle, renewed interest in regional languages and dialects (which has manifested itself in France as well as in many other parts of Europe) may become more than just a quest for individual identity in an increasingly impersonal and internationalized world, and it might result in more institutional support for the Alsatian language and thereby enhance its prestige. But so far there are no signs that this may happen. The Alsatians have been profoundly affected by historical events and the resulting conflicts of loyalties. More recently, Alsace has experienced economic recession leading to a rapid decline in the area's coal, steel, agricultural and textile industries, as well as a reduction in investment by central government. Unless Alsace is officially proclaimed bilingual and bilingualism is fostered by the state and local authorities, and unless the area is able to determine its own economic and social destiny, there is likely to be little improvement in the present situation of language decline. At the moment there is no strong nationalist movement demanding autonomy and promoting the use of Alsatian, so the driving force that could ensure the survival of Alsatian is missing. Indeed, all the accounts of the present plight of Alsatian appear to indicate that, in so far as Alsatians as a whole are aware that their language is in danger, they feel no great sense of loss or urge to protect it: fewer than half of those questioned by Ladin (1983) saw the use of Alsatian as an essential ingredient in being Alsatian. Such attitudes may alleviate the Alsatians' dilemma of being torn between cultural and political loyalties towards France or Germany, and of being regarded as German by their fellow Frenchmen while at the same time not wanting to give up their allegiance to Alsace. As a linguist one cannot help feeling uneasy about their lack of any sense of urgency to safeguard their language. But, as has been argued before, language is only *one* of several group markers. The demise of Alsatian does not necessarily imply that loss of Alsatian identity will follow.

Chapter 13

Case Sudy II: The Catalans

13.1 Introduction: Catalonia and the Catalans

Catalonia is an area of special interest to the sociolinguist these days. Although politically a part of Spain, it is a region that manifests its cultural separateness clearly to the foreign visitor familiar with other

13.1 Linguistic minority areas in Spain

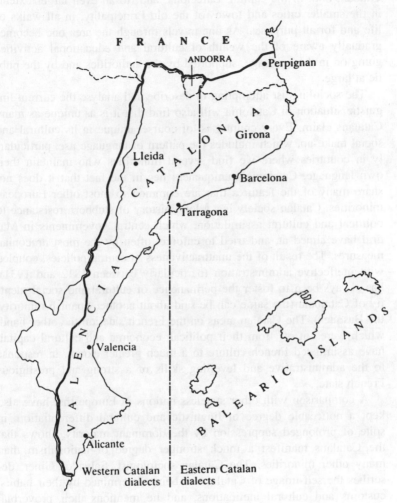

F R A N C E

ANDORRA

Perpignan

C A T A L O N I A

Girona

Lleida

Barcelona

Tarragona

V A L E N C I A

B A L E A R I C   I S L A N D S

Valencia

Alicante

Western Catalan
dialects

Eastern Catalan
dialects

—— Linguistic frontier

—·— Main dialect division

---- National frontier

—— Regional frontier

13.2 The spread of Catalan dialects

parts of Spain. The most striking feature is the use of its own language, Catalan, both in the capital, Barcelona, and (to an even larger extent) in the smaller cities and towns of the old Principality, in all walks of life and for all purposes. As one travels through the area one becomes gradually aware of the wealth of cultural and educational activities going on in the language, supported by the authorities and by the public at large.

The sociolinguist attempting to describe and analyse the current linguistic situation in Catalonia will also find that it is as unique as many Catalans claim. Every country is, of course, unique in its cultural and social make-up, which includes the pattern of language use, particularly in countries where we find several minorities who maintain their own language. Catalonia's uniqueness lies in the fact that it does not share many of the features that are common to most other European minorities. Catalan society has a long history of stubborn resistance to political and cultural assimilation, which central governments in Madrid have aimed at, and tried to enforce, often by the most draconian measures. The result of the unattractiveness of central policies, coupled with ineffective administration (particularly between 1812 and 1931), has always been to foster the permanence of cultural and social identity of Catalonia (the same can be said about another Spanish minority, the Basques). The Catalan areas on the French side, on the other hand, which were cut off from their political, economic and cultural capital, have assimilated French culture to a much greater extent, in response to the administrative and levelling skills of a strong and prestigious French state.

A comparison with other stateless nations in Europe that have also kept a noticeable degree of linguistic and cultural differentiation, in spite of prolonged suppression by the dominant majority, shows that the Catalans manifest a much stronger degree of nationalism than many other minorities. The Catalan sociologist, Salvador Giner, describes the self-image of Catalans as being determined by their habits, customs and cultural inclinations, and he mentions their proverbial fondness for hard work, careful spending and profitable investment: 'Taken together, their collective virtues are neither very heroic nor dramatic. . . . They are precisely the virtues which have largely made Western societies what they are today' (Giner 1984). The Catalans' open identification with these national traits is strong, and so is their linguistic attachment. To be a Catalan means that you speak Catalan. This prerequisite of language as an inseparable part of national identity

does not always pertain among other minority nations in Europe, as we
have seen in the previous chapter. The combination of language and
perceived national character constitutes the 'fet diferencial' (differential
factor) or uniqueness of Catalonia. Allardt (1984) considers self-ascrip-
tion to a minority group by its members as the basic criterion for the
existence of minorities. In the case of the Catalans, this self-categoriza-
tion (as opposed to being categorized by others) has survived for
centuries, and it finds its expression today in the Statute of Autonomy
(1979), which declares that Catalan is Catalonia's 'own language' (la
llengua propia) and in the Catalan government's proclamation that it is
its 'unquestionable right and duty' to restore Catalan to 'her rightful
place'. The tenet is that it is the right of every Catalan to speak Catalan. New residents, i.e. immigrants from other parts of Spain and their
descendants, must be enabled to learn it, just as those of Catalan origin
who have not learnt it yet, or not learnt to read and write in their native
tongue, have to be given a chance to recover their language.

Another aspect of Catalonia's uniqueness is more academic. It lies
in the way in which the Catalan situation seems to defy, or at least
make more difficult, traditional categories. Basic concepts and terms
that have been adopted to describe language use and language patterns
in other linguistic communities often have to be revised, because they
turn out to be inadequate politically or emotionally charged, or both.
Different philological and linguistic traditions among Iberian and
Anglo-Saxon academics, and also the inconsistent use of linguistic and
sociological terminology by Spanish politicians, past and present, have
contributed to this. For over 250 years the central governments of
Spain sought to suppress the political, cultural and linguistic characteristics of Catalans, Basques and Galicians alike, and for the same
period of time these attempts were resisted. Terms such as 'minority',
'language', 'dialect' and 'bilingualism' were used by all sides involved
in the controversies, but with different meanings and connotations (see
also section 13.3).

In terms of their size and their economy, the Catalans are a significant minority within the European context. Catalonia is, together with
the Basque Country, Spain's richest area in terms of per capita income,
and it is also the most advanced in terms of industrial and technological development; therefore it provides disproportionately high revenue
for the coffers of the Spanish state. This is not the position most other
European minorities find themselves in. Catalan history has a long and
distinguished tradition and is held in high esteem both inside and out-

side the region. It has produced many of the most outstanding Spanish artists.

It is also the only minority in Europe that has an influential government agency actively involved in extensive language planning (for which it receives no central funds) with a view to establishing Catalan as the 'normal' medium of communication within its territory (the Catalans prefer to use the term 'normal', which to the outsider may seem ambitious or ambiguous: it conveniently makes it unnecessary to use 'only language' or 'one of two languages', the former being politically explosive, the latter ideologically unacceptable; yet, at the same time, the term clearly signals the commitment to language maintenance). These features are not shared by other European minorities, but there are similarities in other areas: for example, most linguistic minorities have had to defend their language against the dominance of the majority language and have been denied political independence. Indeed, in Catalonia, the centuries of oppression have taken their toll, and the future viability of Catalan as the language of all Catalans is by no means guaranteed, in spite of the emotional, ideological and financial commitment of many people in the area.

13.2 Geographical and demographic overview

Catalonia is a politically autonomous region in the north-east of the Iberian Peninsula. It comprises the four provinces of Barcelona, Tarragona, Lleida and Girona. Of the six million inhabitants (1989: 5,978,638, approximately 15.5 per cent of the total Spanish population), over half live in the metropolitan area of Barcelona which, together with Tarragona, is the most industrialized part of the Principality. Both provinces, but particularly Barcelona, have seen a very heavy influx of immigrants from other parts of Spain, both before the Spanish Civil War (1936–39) and, especially, during the period of industrial recovery (the 1950s to the 1970s). Catalonia is surrounded by other areas where Catalan is spoken: French Catalonia (the Roussillon region) to the north of the border, Andorra, Valencia to the south, and the Balearic Islands. In none of these does Catalan enjoy the same political status or social prestige as in Catalonia itself, with the exception of the tiny state of Andorra, where it is the official language. Linguistic unity in 'els Països Catalans' has a long history and seems to provide Catalonia with the justification to take on a leading role in fostering and strengthening linguistic and cultural links. Within Catalonia the majority of the population speak Catalan, although this demographic concentration is distributed unevenly between urban and rural areas. Outside the old Principality the speakers of Catalan are geographically much more dispersed and socially more homogeneous – both factors which tend weaken the maintenance of the language.

13.3 The Catalan language

Catalan is a Romance language. It developed in the later period of the Roman Empire upon a pre-Roman substratum from a variety of Latin spoken by soldiers, administrators, local peasants, sailors and craftsmen who lived to the north and east of the Pyrenees. It has been described as a bridge language between the Ibero-Romance and Gallo-Romance languages, sharing many of the syntactic and morphological features of the former and some of the phonetic characteristics of the latter. Despite many similarities between Castilian Spanish and Catalan, there is, as has often been pointed out, more common ground between Spanish and Portuguese than between Spanish and Catalan. The Catalans have always stressed this fact, because during their long history of suppression Catalan was not granted the status of a language in its own right. In the Spanish literature on the subject, in documents, legal papers, political speeches, and in newspapers, Catalan was often referred to as a dialect, a vernacular, a variety, ('una modalidad') – all terms that usually implied negative attitudes towards Catalan and reflected a feeling of political superiority on the part of Castilians and others. Only in times of independence was Catalan called 'la lengua catalana'. On the other hand, terms such as 'la lengua española', 'el idioma español' or even 'cristiano' (as in 'hablar en cristiano' = to speak Spanish and not some foreign lingo) were applied to Castilian Spanish only. Today, Catalan is officially one of the languages of Spain, the others being Basque, Galician and Castilian Spanish; the latter is one of several varieties of Spanish, the one chosen as the standard, and also the national language.

13.3.1 A sociolinguistic historical overview
The first documentary evidence of a language recognizable as Catalan can be traced back to the tenth century, which was the time when the Catalans gained independence from the Franks and then gradually

began to win territory from the Moors in the south. Between the twelfth and fifteenth centuries Catalonia emerged as a politically and economically influential power. Its territory extended over the whole of what is today Catalonia (on both sides of the Pyrenees, i.e. including what is sometimes called Catalunya Nord on the French side), Valencia, the Balearic Islands and other smaller adjoining areas. By the twelfth century it had formed a federation with Aragón and eventually became the Kingdom of Aragón. Catalan gradually replaced Latin as the official language, and it also became one of the great literary languages of the period, producing some of Catalonia's most famous writers and poets, thus providing later generations of Catalans with a 'great tradition' (Fishman 1971) to refer back to. Such literary development was facilitated by a fairly liberal form of government. The Catalans and Aragonese had united under the Crown of Aragón on equal terms, i.e. respecting each other's legal, cultural and linguistic habits. However, with the marriage of Isabel de Castilla to Fernando de Aragón (the successor to the Catalan throne) Catalonia, at the end of the fifteenth century, became part of the Spanish kingdom. Isabel claimed for Castile the exclusive right to conquer and colonize America, whereas Fernando was committed to expanding Catalonia's maritime power in the Mediterranean. The new transatlantic routes brought immense wealth and power to successive Spanish monarchs and meant the gradual economic and, as a consequence, political and cultural decline of Catalonia.

The 200 years of the Habsburg dynasty in Spain (the sixteenth and seventeenth centuries) presided over the castilianization of the Catalan nobility and the intellectuals, but it was the eighteenth century that brought the most repressive measures against Catalan. During the War of Spanish Succession (1702–1713), which followed the death of the last Habsburg monarch, Catalonia sided with the Austrians against the other contender to the Spanish throne, the House of Bourbon. This was to have disastrous consequences for Catalonia when the Bourbon Philip V became the next king of Spain and established absolutist and centralist rule. Catalonia suffered political and cultural repression of a severity hitherto unknown. The infamous 'Decretos de Nueva Planta' (new arrangements) of 1716 abolished all traces of Catalan self-government and the official status of the Catalan language. Francesc Ferrer i Gironés, previously one of Catalonia's senators in the Spanish Cortes, devotes a large part of his book (Ferrer i Gironés 1985) on the political persecution of the Catalan language to the discussion and analysis of eighteenth-century documents which either explicitly or by implication banned the use of Catalan, discriminated against its users or undermined its status as a language. In numerous laws, decrees and regulations, measures were laid down imposing Castilian as the only official language to be used, both in its spoken and written forms, by those involved in administration, education, the armed forces and the Church.

Cultural, linguistic and political suppression was to last for more than 200 years, during which Castilian Spanish was the only language permitted for public use, in both speaking and writing. The nobility, higher clergy, military officers and higher civil servants became completely castilianized, and monolingual in Castilian Spanish; the middle classes retained spoken Catalan for informal contact with friends and relatives, and only the illiterate rural population, with little need or opportunity for contact with the state authorities, remained monolingual in Catalan. The language therefore became mainly a spoken variety, and for many it became associated with rural backwardness. For a long time a diglossic situation existed, although the domains of the use of the low variety (Catalan) gradually became extended and those of the high variety (Castilian Spanish) also shifted. One could have expected – and this was certainly the intention of eighteenth- and nineteenth-century politicians in Madrid – that with the rise of the middle classes, urbanization, improved communication and the spread of universal education, language use would have moved inexorably towards Castilian. In the history of other minorities we often see that the language of the dominant majority sooner or later becomes adopted by the middle class, thereby ensuring a wide acceptance of its enhanced status and eventually leading to a major language shift in the area. This happened, for instance, with the spread of English in Wales and Scotland, of French in Alsace and Brittany, and also in Brussels, although the pattern there was slightly different (see Baetens Beardsmore 1983). However, no such shift occurred in Catalonia.

The nineteenth century saw two important advances in Catalonia: industrial development and the emergence of Catalanism. The industrial revolution fed on fertile ground in the region and brought with it a modern economic infrastructure, increased commercial activity, an expansion of the larger towns and considerable prosperity to the area. A strong urban middle class emerged which was markedly different from the Spanish-speaking nobility and upper bourgeoisie, who were essentially agriculture-based. This new middle class was liberal in outlook, enterprising in commerce and industry, and eager to invest and partake in cultural activities. This, and the influence of the Romantic movement, fuelled the 'Renaixença' or Catalan cultural renaissance. It originated in literary and cultural attempts to revive pride in Catalan achievements during the Middle Ages and, more particularly, in the language itself. As time went by it developed into a fully fledged cultural movement and ultimately fed into Catalanism as a political creed. The foundation of the Opera House in Barcelona and the famous architectural works of, among others, Antoni Gaudí were its physical manifestations, and literary activities which blossomed particularly in the second half of the nineteenth century found their expression in the use of the Catalan language. The use of Catalan as a written medium was extended tentatively to the field of journalism, and also to private education. The beginning of the twentieth century was marked by two milestones for the codification and standardization of the language: the approval in 1913 of the spelling rules worked out by the Institut d'Estudis Catalans (the Catalan Academy, founded in 1907 and considered to be the highest authority on matters of language); and the publication in 1918 of Pompeu Fabra's *Gramàtica Normative de la Llengua Catalana* (Normative Grammar of the Catalan Language), which was to become the standard grammar of Catalan.

Towards the end of the nineteenth century, Catalonia's bourgeoisie began to embrace Catalanism, i.e. modern Catalan nationalism, as a political stance as well as a cultural one. The movement demanding political independence for Catalonia from the Madrid government gathered momentum. This body of public opinion was now joined by the upper middle classes, although more cautiously, but as Salvador Giner points out (Giner 1984), there was never any attempt to reach the lower echelons of society. The rural areas were more traditional in outlook, and largely Catalan-speaking anyway. The working classes, on the other hand, which were now growing in numbers, owing to urbanization and immigration, became the Castilian-speaking section of Catalan society and they were more open to non-Catalan political influences. Some measure of autonomy was achieved by the creation of the *Mancomunitat* in 1914, a political body consisting of representatives from all Catalan regions. The *Mancomunitat* was especially active in promoting cultural activities and in education, encouraging the training of teachers in Catalan and developing new teaching methods and educational ideas, such as those inspired by Pestalozzi and Montessori. In 1915 there were fifteen Montessori and several Pestalozzi schools in the region, an impressive demonstration of the progressive educational thinking of Catalan parents at the time.

The use of Catalan in the public sphere received a serious blow under the dictatorship of General Primo de Rivera (1923–30), who banned the use of the language in schools and public administration. But when the Second Republic was proclaimed in 1931 Catalonia was granted autonomous status. Its moderately left-wing Catalan nationalist government, the *Generalitat* (the name was taken from the liberal and independent government Catalonia had enjoyed in medieval times) continued to promote the active use of Catalan in all spheres of life, again making cultural activities and education their priorities. Catalan was used in administration, the media, commerce and, to an increasing degree, in schools, universities and training colleges. Private and semi-private schools often spearheaded the use of Catalan, as well as the introduction of educationally progressive methods. Many Castilian-speaking immigrants proved willing to learn Catalan, seeing it as the language of upward social mobility. However, the advance of catalanization, and of Catalanism, often encountered opposition, particularly from outside Catalonia, and it was slowed down considerably by clashes between left- and right-wing political forces during the last two turbulent years of the Second Republic, before the outbreak of the Spanish Civil War (1936-39).

The fortunes of Catalan deteriorated dramatically after the Civil War. Again the language was forbidden in public life, as was any manifestation of Catalanism. The restrictive measures taken by Franco against Catalonia (dubbed one of the 'traitor provinces', the other being the Basque Country, for their support of the Republican side during the war) have been described by many sociolinguists, both Catalan and foreign. All express equal dismay at the vindictiveness of these policies (e.g. Stephens 1976; Strubell i Trueta 1985a and b; De Cicco and Maring 1983; Woolard 1989). The leading intellectual élite had been forced into exile abroad, and those who were left 'were imbued with the centralist way of thinking' (Strubell i Trueta 1985a). With regard to language, the axiomatic claim was made that Castilian Spanish was a world language, the language of true Spaniards, of economic and political power and prestige, even an 'imperial' language. Catalan was branded as a vernacular, a dialect, the mark of the backward rural peasant. To use it among educated people was tantamount to a declaration of being anti-government, even anti-Spanish. Every outward manifestation of Catalan was eliminated in the early years of the Franco era: the names of towns and villages were castilianized, streets and buildings renamed, publishing houses, bookshops, public and private libraries searched for Catalan books and those found destroyed. One of the greatest losses was the priceless collection of Pompeu Fabra. It was burned in the street. Francesc Vallverdú, one of Catalonia's most prominent sociolinguists, refers (Vallverdú 1973) to the years 1939–50 as the period of 'persecuted bilingualism', which was followed, he says, by a phase of 'tolerated bilingualism'. Permission for the publication of certain books and the staging of some plays in Catalan was granted in the late 1940s. But since censorship laws applied all over Spain and a large number of titles remained on the list of books forbidden by Franco's regime, the range of works published and plays performed in Catalan was not very wide. Nor were they the kind that would appeal to those who used Catalan in private, as most Catalans were opposed to the dictatorship. The ban on the use of Catalan in the media and in schools remained in force almost to the end of the Franco period. In general, the last few years of the dictatorship saw a good deal of tolerance in practice, although officially the restrictions still applied. In the words of John Hooper, for instance, the Institut d'Estudis Catalans led

> a curious, half-tolerated, half-clandestine existence under Franco. It held weekly meetings, held courses on the language, literature and history of Catalan in private houses, gave receptions and went so far as to publish books and pamphlets, some of which were even bought by the government for displays at international exhibitions.
>
> (Hooper 1986: 235).

The Catalans had to wait until 1978 before their language was granted official status by the new democratic Constitution of Spain, a number of royal decrees and the 1979 Statute of Autonomy. The Law of Linguistic Normalization followed, in Catalonia, in 1983 (see later). However, the restrictive measures against Catalan had lasted long enough to have a severe impact on the use of and attitudes towards Catalan. Castilian Spanish had become institutionalized, and many generations of Catalan schoolchildren had grown up with little opportunity of becoming familiar with the language of their parents. More important still was the impact of those non-Catalans who had immigrated to Catalonia and had neither opportunity nor reason to learn or use Catalan.

13.3.2 The impact of immigration

Immigrants from Murcia, Aragón and Galicia who came to Catalonia in the early part of the century were able to assimilate over the years into Catalan society, and in many cases their children learnt Catalan at school. But the new wave of immigration proved impossible to integrate, because of the sheer numbers involved and the specific cultural and social conditions under which it took place. Between 1950 and 1975 approximately two million immigrants settled in Catalonia (many of them from the south, Andalusia, and again from Galicia), which meant an increase of 37.15 per cent in the population of the area, as compared to an average rise of 12.47 per cent in the rest of Spain. Around 1975 nearly one half (49 per cent) of the people living in the Municipality of Barcelona were of non-Catalan stock; the figure for the province of Barcelona excluding the capital was 46 per cent (figures from Hooper 1986). Catalan towns and cities had considerable difficulty in coping with the sudden influx of immigrants, and they were housed in new and poorly built housing estates on the outskirts; just two of them, Santa Coloma and l'Hospitalet, on the outskirts of Barcelona, now have more than 200,000 inhabitants each, the vast majority non-Catalan in origin (Strubell i Trueta 1984b). The birth rate among immigrant families was high (by comparison with the more affluent urban Catalan society), thus aggravating their poor living conditions while also adding to the number of non-Catalan speakers. Socially and educationally, they were more often than not disadvantaged; many had not completed their primary schooling at the time of immigration, and illiteracy was widespread (Strubell i Trueta 1985b). The provision of schools, hospitals and social services was totally inadequate in the dormitory towns. The resulting social and linguistic divisions are marked today by resistance to linguistic and cultural integration, by juvenile delinquency and by other signs of social disintegration which are aggravated further by the level of unemployment (the highest in western Europe) that exists everywhere in Spain.

Contact with the Catalan-speaking population has been, and still is, very limited. It has been described as contact with people one or more rungs higher up on the social ladder, like the doctor, priest, teacher and civil servant. Some have interpreted it as a positive type of contact, since it may foster the desire on the part of immigrants to learn Catalan so as to participate more fully in society, or at least to have their children taught Catalan at school. Thus, the reason most often given by those asked why they wanted their children to learn Catalan was 'that it is necessary in order to get on in life'. Such expectations, however, indicate that parental motivation towards linguistic integration is purely instrumental (i.e. utilitarian) and extends only as far as their children. For language learning and assimilation into Catalan society to be successful, immigrants, and particularly second-generation immigrants, need to be positively motivated themselves, driven by the attractions that they themselves see in becoming fully Catalan. But just what these attractions are is not always easy to detect.

Social inequality, marginalization and, above all, a rapid increase in numbers have contributed to the fact that Catalonia's immigrant population has acquired political and social significance. They are today the strongest force that poses a threat to the *Generalitat*'s attempts at catalanization, since the Catalan government depends on the immigrant vote. The immigrants are well aware of their political importance, and they know that they can resist catalanization if it becomes too unpalatable. Just which path they will take, whether they will cooperate fully or try to develop their own social and cultural ambitions separately, is not yet clear. Much depends on the *Generalitat*'s power and skill in controlling the media and the education system, on the one hand, and in finding solutions to the real social problems and divisions on the other, while still pursuing at the same time truly democratic, tolerant and pluralist policies. It is, obviously, not an easy task.

13.3.3 The present linguistic situation

The two most influential factors bearing directly on a minority language are its political status and the socio-economic position of its speakers. As regards the latter, Catalan has traditionally enjoyed the full support of both the middle classes and the rural population; in addition, by the beginning of this century large sections of the upper class, and also of the working classes, spoke Catalan. Naturally, fewer people used Catalan during the forty years of the Franco dictatorship, but at the same time Catalan became the language associated with political resistance, and began for this reason to appeal to many people from all sections of the population. As the speakers of Catalan are nowadays regarded positively, and their socio-economic status and educational background are generally higher than those of Spanish-speaking immigrants, their language, Catalan, also enjoys considerable prestige. This has caused the language to be considered to be appropriate for communication in any situation and in connection with any topic.[1] Today the language choice of a Catalan–Castilian bilingual is based rather more on the language of her or his interlocutor, and not so much on the formality of the situation or on the medium (i.e. written or spoken language) employed. Code-switching in Catalonia does not necessarily occur in one direction, from Catalan to Castilian; it may be in either direction. The diglossic situation that was, in the past, attributed to Catalonia, has ceased to exist.

Azevedo (1984) observed that bilingual conversations seemed to have become the rule rather than the exception in Catalonia – just as passive bilingualism has, too. However, the present linguistic situation in Catalonia cannot be adequately described with a single label. Several forms of bilingualism coexist among the population of the area, ranging from active to passive, and from incipient to balanced. But officially the term 'bilingualism' does not occur anywhere. The language policy of the *Generalitat* is geared towards 'restoring' Catalan, not towards establishing bilingualism. Bilingualism is a *de facto* phenomenon among Catalan speakers, but it is not usually openly advocated. Baetens Beardsmore's (1983) term of 'bilinguisme de resignation' may not be entirely inappropriate here, although perhaps many Catalans would look at it as 'involuntary bilingualism', as they prefer to use their own language only; but if required to speak Spanish it becomes clear that they are fully bilingual.

13.4 Language planning since 1975

The legal framework for the *Generalitat*'s language policies is provided by three major pieces of legislation: the Constitution of 1978, the Statute of Autonomy of 1979 and, most extensively, the 1983 Law of Linguistic Normalization in Catalonia. In the last years of the Franco era and during the period of the transition to democracy, decrees and regulations were passed which began to show some embryonic recognition of Spain's 'regional features', including its languages (terms such as 'peculiaridades regionales', 'lengua nativa' and 'lenguas nacionales' were used); and it was recommended that these languages should, at least on a voluntary basis, be included in school curricula. Little official action was taken in some non-Castilian-speaking areas, however, because of a lack of local organization and resources. In Catalonia preparations were under way, though. The reinstatement of the *Generalitat* in September, 1977 (it remained provisional until the first general election under the new constitution was held in 1979) was

an important factor. No time was lost in forming from among its ex-
ecutive council a Council for Education and Culture which in turn set
up the Catalan Language Service ('Servei del Català'), charged with
the evaluation and coordination of all aspects of teaching of Catalan
and through Catalan. In cooperation with the Ministry of Education in
Madrid, the reorganization of the curriculum and the teaching profession was also begun, so as to include the teaching of Catalan and the
establishment of the necessary new posts.

The reason why the *Generalitat* made its language policy a priority
was the realization that Catalan was facing a crisis. The Franco legacy,
plus the influx of immigrants, presented, as we have seen, a dual threat
to the language. Before 1975 no official figures existed about the number of Catalan speakers, since the censuses did not include questions
on language. According to a report published by the Spanish Government in 1975, 71 per cent of the population in the principality could
speak Catalan, although the proportion of those who actulaly did speak
it was somewhat lower. A sharp division between the capital and the
provinces of Lleida, Tarragona and Girona became evident: in Barcelona only 39 per cent of the inhabitants were Catalan speakers, whereas
the figure for the provinces was 90 per cent. Subsequent research
showed that many speakers of Catalan could neither read nor write the
language. A further problem was highlighted when a report was published showing that Catalan tended to be used more often as the
language of social interaction, i.e. in conversation and at work, than as
the language of the home. In mixed marriages the use of Castilian
Spanish was often preferred to that of Catalan – and, as is well known
(and as the example of Alsace showed), once a minority language
ceases to be the language of the family, its continued existence is seriously threatened. Other signs indicating a weakening of Catalan
vis-à-vis Castilian Spanish were seen in the increasing number of loans
and castilianisms apparent even in the language of educated speakers
and writers, a problem largely attributed to the prolonged linguistic
accommodation Catalans had been forced to undergo.

Figures published in 1980 showing the knowledge of Catalan among
the inhabitants of the region were not very encouraging. They referred to
the population as a whole and, taken together with the figures for the
school population's home language, they confirmed the impression that
the main thrust of local government language policy had to focus on the
catalanization of the education system, if any real change in language use
was to be achieved:

TABLE 13.1 Percentage of population by knowledge of Catalan:

	Percentage
No data	2%
Castilian speakers who do not understand Catalan	18%
Castilian speakers who understand Catalan	12%
Castilian speakers who speak Catalan	10%
Perfect bilinguals	6%
Native speakers of Catalan	52%
Total	100%

Source: Subirats 1980 quoted in Sabater 1984

Unfortunately, no further elucidation is offered as to the precise meaning of the category 'perfect bilinguals'. In more recent publications the term has been dropped altogether and language knowledge is indicated in terms of reading, writing, speaking and understanding. Table 13.2 gives some information on language use.

TABLE 13.2 Language of pupils in Catalonia (percentage):

	In general basic education (compulsory schooling 6–14 years)	In higher secondary education (15–18 years)	
		Baccalaureate	*Vocational training*
Catalan in the family	33.71	47.86	33.73
Bilingual families	12.64	12.83	12.06
Castilian Spanish in the family	53.65	39.31	54.21

Source: Generalitat de Catalunya Departament d'Ensenyament 1982

The figures for the groups of youngsters who speak Catalan are particularly interesting, as they clearly show that this language is spoken most often in families who value education (as they keep their children at school beyond the age of fifteen). But they also reveal that the use of Catalan within the younger group, i.e. those who were born around the end of the Franco era, is quite low.

Article 3 of the Statute of Autonomy constitutes the basis for the *Generalitat*'s language policy. It states that Catalan is 'Catalonia's own language', it spells out its co-official status and it asserts the *Generalitat*'s determination to ensure the normal and official use of both Catalan and Castilian Spanish. It also makes the *Generalitat* responsible for language policies. The means by which Catalonia's government intended to carry out these policies were laid down in the Law of Linguistic Normalization. The term 'normalization' reflects the underlying philosophy of Catalan language planning, which is expressed thus in the preamble of that Law:

> The restoration of Catalan to its rightful place as Catalonia's own language
> is the unquestionable right and duty of the Catalan people and must be pro-
> tected and respected. In this regard, knowledge of the language must
> spread throughout the whole of Catalan society, to all citizens regardless of
> the language they normally speak, within a global framework in which
> everyone will accept the use of both languages and recognize and contrib-
> ute to the recovery of Catalan as one of the fundamental aspects of the
> reconstruction of Catalonia.

The main objective was thus to overcome what was referred to as 'a situation of linguistic inequality'. The radical nature of this aim consists of the idea that the whole of the population of Catalonia should learn Catalan, not only those who are self-professed Catalans. It is of course this aspect of Catalonia's language policy that is the most controversial and even, possibly, illusory. For, whereas it is relatively easy to place Catalans in a position to use their language in all walks of life and to have their children educated in the language of their forefathers, it is more difficult to succeed in turning almost half the population, which is mainly of non-Catalan descent, into speakers of Catalan. On the other hand, it may well be the case that only aggressively radical language policies stand any chance of arresting, or perhaps reversing, the decline of a language.

In 1980 a Directorate General of Language Policy was set up and given the task of spreading the use and knowledge of Catalan; it was also made ultimately responsible for language planning. Today a number of bodies are involved in the various activities which are being carried out under the Law of Linguistic Normalization, such as providing special-purpose Catalan classes for state employees, developing technical vocabulary for government departments and the system of administration of justice, and promoting Catalan in publishing, the media and, most importantly, in education.

The 'Campaign for Language Normalization' (under the slogan 'el català, cosa de tots' – freely translated, '[learning] Catalan concerns us all') is an ongoing concern in Catalonia. It takes the shape of, for example, slogans and short features published in the newspapers, and posters and banners displayed in public places, and radio and television broadcasts. The aim is to increase language consciousness with a view to encouraging Catalans, and all the inhabitants of Catalonia, to use Catalan more frequently and consistently, and to foster positive attitudes towards this language. The campaign extends to other activities that relate to the spreading of the use of Catalan. As stipulated in the Normalization Law, certain bodies may become eligible for tax deductions, or even total exemption, by switching to the use of Catalan (e.g. within a firm), which obviously can make support for the *Generalitat*'s language policies an attractive proposition even for the less ideologically inclined world of business and commerce.

Naturally, the efforts to re-establish Catalan in all domains of public life have met with some scepticism in certain quarters and, at times, have caused politically or ideologically inspired protests by non-Catalans both inside Catalonia and in other parts of Spain. But there is no evidence that the rights of Castilian speakers have not been respected. Azevedo (1984) points out that many Catalan linguists and educationalists were among the first to show concern for those rights; and he adds: 'Actually, official efforts to re-establish the use of Catalan have been rather tactful, judging from the general tone of the 1982 Linguistic Normalization Campaign' (Azevedo 1984: 323).

13.5 The public use of Catalan

The Law of Linguistic Normalization was passed in 1983 in order to promote the 'social presence' of Catalan. It contains provisions for the use of Catalan in administration, the media and education, and it guarantees institutional support by the *Generalitat*. A general overview of these provisions, and of the impact they have had on the use of Catalan in public life, is given in the following sections.

(1) *Administration* Catalan is the language of the *Generalitat* and of the Catalan territorial administration, of local government and of those bodies that come under the *Generalitat*. New state employees are required to demonstrate a knowledge of Catalan, and those who were in employment before the linguistic changes took place are encouraged to attend language classes in Catalan. These are state-subsidized and often held during working hours, thus complying with the pledge that linguistic normalization would be carried out without discrimination against non-Catalan speakers. While internal communication in government departments and offices tends to be in Catalan, Castilian Spanish can be used on request. The public have the right to conduct their dealings with the authorities in the language of their choice, and all official material is published in both languages. It is therefore not too optimistic to assume that, within a relatively short period of time, most of the administration business will have been catalanized. It is more difficult to predict a similar situation in the media and in education, which are less easily controlled by policies, as they are subject to the influence of market forces, social factors and psychological variables – and therefore provide an enormous challenge to language planners.

(2) *The media* The *Generalitat*'s role in catalanizing the mass media is largely restricted to subsidizing the publication of newspapers, periodicals and magazines which are partially or entirely written in Catalan, and to providing some financial aid for the production of plays and the dubbing of non-Catalan films. There is only one daily newspaper (*Avui*) published entirely in Catalan, however, and in 1986, ten years after it was first launched, it had a circulation of 40,232 copies.[2] There are also a number of local papers, ranging from those printed wholly in Catalan to some which contain only a small Catalan contribution.

There are now several officially-run radio stations covering Catalonia that are subsidized by the *Generalitat* and broadcast only in Catalan. Between them they cover all kinds of programmes, from news and sports to current affairs and music. There are, in addition, numerous private local radio stations operating partially or wholly in Catalan, frequently supported by town councils. The 17 biggest stations offered

24 per cent of air-time in Catalan, 9 per cent in both Catalan and Castillian and 67 per cent in Castillian (figures for 1986).

In 1984 a Catalan television channel, TV3, was started, and by the
following year it was broadcasting some forty-four hours per week in
Catalan, and in 1988 the figure had reached 300, with peak audience
figures being achieved in the early afternoon (i.e. Spanish lunch-time,
when normally all members of the family have a meal at home) and
late evening. It is popular also because of its extensive news, its serials
(or 'soaps')[3] and (especially) sports coverage. It receives its income in
part from the *Generalitat* and partly from TV advertising.

The increased popularity of Catalan radio and television is clearly
an encouraging sign to all those involved in the recovery of Catalan, as
the use of the language in the media increases awareness and knowledge of Catalan. The problem that arises here, as in administration, is
that of finding enough people who speak grammatically and stylisti-
cally correct Catalan, so that they can provide a good linguistic model.
Journalists and broadcasters are not necessarily as competent linguistically as professional linguists would like them to be, and their speech
has been criticized for being phonetically and lexically castilianized,
which highlights yet another area in which standardization of usage
still has to take place.

Publishing in Catalonia has a long and distinguished tradition, and
there are more than a hundred publishing houses in Barcelona, most of
them publishing in both Catalan and Castilian Spanish, often with one
part of the enterprise (the Castilian) supporting the other. During the
Franco years publication in Catalan was seriously restricted, but nevertheless kept alive by dedicated authors and publishers who often
produced books at their own expense. When, in 1977, the then prime
minister, Adolfo Suárez (a native of Castile), asked somewhat scathing-
ly in a foreign publication, 'How could we write a book on nuclear
physics in Catalan?' (Fabre 1979), the response was immediate: a
whole series of books was published, on nuclear physics and a range of
other highly technical subjects. Book publishing nowadays receives
financial help from local funds, through the 'Servei del Llibre' (Book
Office), which subsidizes the publication of some 200–300 works of
fiction and non-fiction each year. Copies of these books are then made
available to the *Generalitat* and its public libraries. The number of titles in Catalan is said (in an official publication by the *Generalitat*,
'Social Communication in Catalonia', 1988) to have increased from
2175 in 1982 to 4145 in 1987. The number of copies sold overall grew

from 3.3 million in 1980 to 5.3 million in 1984, even though the average sale per book dropped by 15 per cent. With all three levels of education heavily involved in the catalanization programme, there is still a growing demand from the educational system for books in Catalan. Nevertheless, publishing is an uncertain and expensive business everywhere. In Catalonia it remains heavily dependent on sustained government aid and private support.

(3) *Education* It has long been recognized that unless Catalan is taught in schools and eventually becomes the medium of instruction, all the other efforts towards language recovery will remain cosmetic and may be short-lived. The adoption of Catalan as a medium of instruction is a challenging task, and it offers the opportunity of undertaking both linguistic and curriculum reform. Many committed Catalan politicians and educationalists have approached the enterprise with a great deal of enthusiasm. For them, the aim of language 'normalization', 'recovery' and 'restoration' in the school context is: 'to put Catalan pupils who do not know their own language (but are familiar with another one) through an immersion programme within a linguistic framework which cannot be called that of a minority.' (Abeyà 1985).

But at the same time language policy in education is a highly sensitive issue. The Catalan Government is faced with the task of overcoming the considerable problems posed by little interest and even hostility on the part of parents and teachers – not to mention the attitude of the remaining Spanish population, the reservations of central government, and a general lack of resources, both human and material.

Section II of the Law of Linguistic Normalization (1983) includes seven Articles which deal with the question of language policy in education. The first one simply (and rather ambitiously) states: 'Catalan, as Catalonia's own language, is also the language of education at all levels'. Catalan is obligatory in schools, and all children need to attain an acceptable level of proficiency by the end of their basic education (i.e. by the time they are fourteen years old). Only if children can demonstrate adequate mastery of Catalan will they be awarded the Certificate of General Basic Education (school-leaving certificate). The principle that children are entitled to receive their early instruction in the mother tongue is, however, accepted, so that upon entering school children may be taught initially either in Catalan or in Castilian Spanish. The Act lays down that children should not be segregated into different schools purely on the basis of their first language, and it adds

that Catalan should be used progressively as the medium of instruction
as pupils' mastery of it increases.

In higher education, staff and students are free to choose which language they wish to use, but all centres at tertiary level are obliged to
offer language courses for non-Catalan speakers. As far as teacher-
training is concerned, the Act is quite specific: 'All teachers must be
proficient in both official languages'. This requirement means that the
curriculum for teacher-training courses has to be designed in such a
way as to ensure that students are trained to teach their subjects in both
languages.

It will be some time before the provisions of the law are fully implemented, particularly in the public-sector secondary schools. In the
private sector, catalanization has progressed considerably faster, but
then private Catalan schools have a long tradition of promoting Catalan
culture, including the language. Some 40 per cent of all schools in
Catalonia are private. They have to conform to the general educational
objectives outlined by the Ministry of Education in Madrid, but they
are otherwise free to follow particular religious or pedagogical principles. Although school fees are not generally as high as they can be in
other countries, private schools in Spain are normally attended only by
middle- and upper-class children, which means that, once again, it is
the upper layers of society that are spearheading catalanization – but
also contributing to linguistic, as well as social, segregation (see section 13.3.3).

The linguistic normalization programme in schools is faced with
two major problems. One consists in the uneven distribution of the
Catalan- and Castilian Spanish-speaking population. In some parts of
the Barcelona metropolitan area (i.e. the districts with the heaviest concentration of immigrants), more than 80 per cent of inhabitants only
speak Spanish; in such areas the need to learn Catalan is perceived as
being at best marginal. These are also socially deprived areas, with
high levels of unemployment. Only an improvement in the quality of
public services, coupled with a higher degree of social integration between Catalan and Castilian Spanish speakers will, one feels, ensure
the successful catalanization of schools in these areas. The other problem is caused by a scarcity of qualified staff able to use Catalan as the
medium of instruction: only about half the teachers who work in Catalonia are of Catalan origin, and the number of those who have
undergone teacher training in Catalan is smaller still. A further factor
militating against linguistic reorganization in schools is the poor

knowledge of Catalan, even among teachers (Arnau and Boada 1986).

Since 1978 the *Generalitat* has assumed most responsibilities for education in Catalonia, including the appointment of teaching staff (previously controlled centrally from Madrid) and retraining in Catalan. Another important measure was the setting up of the Education Department's Office for the Teaching of Catalan (Servei d'Ensenyament del Català SEDEC), entrusted with promoting and organizing the teaching of, and in, Catalan in schools. This body supplies specialist Catalan teachers to schools that request them, it monitors the use of Catalan in schools and holds seminars for parents' and teachers' associations. Parental support and involvement is clearly a vital aspect if linguistic recovery is to succeed. SEDEC and a number of other agencies regularly carry out surveys to collect information on the spread and use of Catalan, both in schools and in other fields. The results of a survey among the school population carried out in 1981–82 show that the implementation of any aspect of linguistic legislation has to be discretional in some areas of Catalonia, as it must take into account such factors as the linguistic background of pupils, the teachers' knowledge of Catalan and variations in the local quality of the teaching services. The survey covered a total of 3399 schools, of which 1777 were private- and 1622 public-sector ones. In all schools Catalan was taught as a subject, and in 65 per cent of them instruction was either wholly or partially in Catalan. This figure may seem high, but it must be seen in the light of what was said earlier about the prominence of Catalan in private schools.

With reference to the linguistic background of pupils, the SEDEC report showed that

> 59.52 per cent of pupils could speak Catalan;
> 24.88 per cent of pupils understood Catalan;
> 15.60 per cent of pupils did not understand Catalan.

The 60 per cent or so of children who spoke Catalan were further classified into three groups:

(1)   monolingual Catalan speakers 33.7 per cent;
(2)   bilingual Catalan/Spanish speakers 12.6 per cent;
(3)   speakers of Catalan as second language 53.7 per cent.

With regard to teachers' knowledge of Catalan, the survey indicated that the proportion of those speaking Catalan was 67.73 per cent –

slightly higher than that of the pupils. Of the 32.27 per cent of teachers who said that they did not speak Catalan, 76.94 per cent claimed to understand it, which shows that the proportion of teachers who could not understand Catalan was actually higher than the percentage of pupils in the same position (23.06 per cent as against 15.60 per cent). This discrepancy may, however, be attributed to children's and adults' different views of what 'understanding' means.

The geographical distribution of Catalan- and Castilian Spanish-speaking pupils is, not surprisingly, similar to that of the population as a whole. There is considerable variation between rural and urban districts, and between those with higher or lower concentrations of immigrants. Figures from Siguán (1980) show that, for the whole of Catalonia, some 50 to 55 per cent of pupils had Catalan as their home language. The geographical variation ranged from almost 100 per cent in rural areas to 47 per cent in Barcelona and just 27 per cent in the industrial outskirts of the capital. It is, incidentally, in these areas that some of the major school projects (immersion courses specially designed and carefully monitored) are to be found.

(4) *School programmes* Since the incorporation (1978) of Catalan in schools, either as a subject or as the language of instruction, three different models have been used:

Model A: total immersion;
Model B: teaching partially in Catalan;
Model C: teaching progressively more in Catalan
           (i.e. starting with very little instruction in Catalan and
           gradually increasing it until it outweighs Castilian Span-
           ish).

Generally it has been up to individual schools to choose the model they want to follow, on the basis of the qualifications and commitment of their staff rather than according to the linguistic background of their pupils.

Arnau and Boada (1986) looked at the development of different models in schools and at the linguistic abilities and qualifications of teachers. They found that, of the three models mentioned, A had been chosen by a small but stable number (8 per cent) of public-sector schools, which had been following the General Basic Education programme totally in Catalan. In 1982 there was a marked increase, in relation to previous years, in the number of state schools following

Model B, and the figures for 1983–84 begin to show an increase in the proportion of schools adopting Model C. Altogether, during the school year 1987–88 almost 70 per cent of schools in the public sector were using Catalan wholly, partially or progressively, and in the remaining schools Catalan was taught as a school subject. Compared to the figure of 3 per cent for 1975, when Catalan was only 'tolerated', these figures look encouraging, although it is too early to be more than cautiously optimistic about the spread of Catalan among the school population. In contrast to the Welsh and Canadian experience of immersion education the Catalans need to bear one vital difference in mind: their target groups are not children from motivated middle-class homes. They are, for the most, the children of immigrants who live in the poorer working-class districts; and when they leave the school and the immersion programme there will be little need, or motivation, for them to speak Catalan.

In their assessment of the factors believed to affect school achievement in Catalan and in Castilian Spanish, Arnau and Boada (1986) found that general learning ability was of paramount importance. But the type of school model adopted was important, too, at least for the successful establishment of Catalan. Only the total and progressive immersion models (A and C) provided the necessary linguistic orientation for children whose family and social environment was predominantly Castilian.

13.6 The extent of Catalan knowledge

A good deal of statistical data on language issues can now be obtained from the various local government agencies concerned with the promotion of Catalan, based on regular surveys in different parts of the region and on census information. The 1986 census contained several entries which, taken together, provide an indication of people's language background and use of Catalan. Also, six specific questions were asked about the passive and active use of Catalan, and its spoken and written forms. The following table gives a general overview of the extent of the knowledge of Catalan in the four provinces of Catalonia for 1986:

TABLE 13.3 Knowledge of Catalan:

	Understand (%)	Speak (%)	Read (%)	Write (%)
Total for Catalonia	90.3	64	60.5	31.5
Barcelona	89	59.8	58.2	30.1
Girona	95.1	80.1	70.7	39.3
Lleida	96.3	82.8	71.6	37.1
Tarragona	92.8	72.9	63.7	32

Source: Padrons municipals d'habitants de Catalunya, 1986: Coneixement del català, CIDC, Barcelona 1987, p.15

Note – Barcelona is by far the most significant province numerically, with over 4.5 million inhabitants. The other three together have a population of about 1.4 million people. These statistics refer to inhabitants over two years old.

There is a great deal of variation in the distribution of figures if they are broken down into smaller districts. In the Barcelona areas with a high proportion of immigrant population (Santa Coloma de Gramenet, for instance) only a few people are able to read and write Catalan:

TABLE 13.3a Knowledge of Catalan in Santa Coloma

Understand (%)	Speak (%)	Read (%)	Write (%)
76	28.6	28.1	11.8

Source: ibid. p. 26

In general terms, during the five years 1981–86, knowledge of Catalan rose in this same area (Santa Coloma) by 25 per cent. The figures showing the increase in understanding alone, for the whole of Catalonia, between 1981 and 1986 are as follows:

TABLE 13.4 Understanding of Catalan

	1986 (%)	1981 (%)	Difference (%)
Barcelona	89	79.8	+11.9
Girona	95.1	90.7	+4.4
Lleida	96.3	91.8	+4.5
Tarragona	92.8	86	+6.9
Total for Catalonia:	90.3	79.8	+10.5

Source: ibid. p. 43

An examination of the data available according to age of the population suggests that the Linguistic Normalization Campaign has been particularly successful in the field of education. Knowledge of Catalan among the school population and those who have recently left school has risen quite dramatically: 78 per cent of young people in Catalonia between ten and nineteen years old speak Catalan (as against 64 per cent for the population as a whole). The point has been made, however, that oral ability does not necessarily mean fully effective use of the language (Strubell i Trueta 1988).

13.7 The future of Catalan

It is worth reminding oneself of some of the features which distinguish the Catalan situation from that of other European minorities. The importance of the long history of involvement of the urban middle classes in the promotion of Catalan language and culture on a public and private level cannot be underestimated. The bourgeoisie was a driving force in making widespread use of Catalan socially acceptable, and it went hand-in-hand with their advancement in the fields of industry, commerce, education and culture, and later also in political affairs. Any attempts to stigmatize the language came from outside Catalan society and never really penetrated it ideologically. Castilian Spanish was imposed in such a crude way, that Catalans never ceased to feel antagonism towards Castilian administrators, members of the armed forces and the police. Castilian Spanish was associated with political oppression and, during the Franco period, with fascism, whereas Catalan was seen as representing resistance to reactionary centralist forces. Early standardization of the language and a rich literary heritage also contributed to the stabilization and prestige of the language. While Corsicans or Bretons might compensate for their linguistic inferiority complex by displaying ardent nationalism and demanding political separation, the Catalans have concentrated their efforts on pursuing cultural and linguistic ends. This is not to say that nowadays in Catalonia there are no demands for political independence from the rest of Spain. But the proverbial Catalan 'seny' (common sense) seems to have accepted the present quasi-federal solution. There are of course other likely reasons for this relative contentment. One may be that, since Catalans cannot reasonably claim to be ethnically very different from other Spaniards (as can, to some extent, the Basques), political separation does not appear to many to be a particularly desirable goal.

The financial and ideological commitment of many Catalans to recover their language is considerable. Indeed, the far-reaching measures undertaken by the *Generalitat*'s language planners are without equal anywhere in Europe. In the fields of administration and communication, the policy of conscious catalanization has already brought encouraging results. It is still too early to see what effects endeavours at school level will have. But it is clear that the burden placed on the education system in terms of expectations and demands is enormous, as it is not adequately equipped at the moment, either financially or pedagogically, to make all pupils competent in Catalan. In any case, making the whole of Catalonia Catalan-speaking cannot be entirely up to the schools: a fundamental social change is necessary as well, in the form of complete social integration and the support of the entire population of the area for the linguistic normalization programme. This can come about only as a result of changing attitudes towards each other on the part of both linguistic groups. In this field schools can play a crucial role (as the Canadian experience of bilingual education has shown), but other changes have to take place at the same time: one cannot assume that positive attitudes towards Catalan, or linguistic skills acquired at school, will last a long time if young people, once they have left school, no longer feel the need, or have the motivation, to use the language regularly, and more importantly pass it on to their children.

The Catalans have been keen to learn from language planning in other countries, notably Wales and Canada. Despite some similarities, however, their linguistic situation is not really comparable. In the context of Spain as a whole, Castilian Spanish-speakers are the majority and Catalan speakers the minority, but within Catalonia the picture is reversed, with neither group possessing all the typical traits of either a majority or a minority. Whether its language policies will make it possible for the present *comunidad autónoma* to recover Catalan's lost ground, resulting in a change in linguistic behaviour among Catalans of Castilian descent, remains to be seen. Achieving these objectives would virtually amount to a sociolinguistic miracle in modern Europe.

Notes

1. There are several problems associated with the standardized version of Catalan: as it is modelled on literary language, it is not always well equipped to be an effective and modern public medium. It has been claimed that the norms laid down by rigorous reformers are at variance with the living language. As a result, influences from contemporary Spanish are difficult to eradicate fron everyday usage. Another problem arises from the various disagreements about the use or non-use of regional variants of Catalan, particularly in education. For a general discussion and references, see Azevedo (1984).

2. This low figure is probably more a reflection of the paper's quality than the Catalan's inherent interest in a Catalan newspaper. The left-of-centre daily *El País* (53,303 copies, 1986) is published in Madrid and Barcelona. In the Barcelona edition the literary supplement and the crossword are in Catalan. Several times more copies are sold of *La Vanguardia*, a centre-right daily (194,553 copies, 1986). In its Catalan edition some material is always in Catalan.

3. One of TV3's real successes was that it acquired the screening rights for the American soap opera series 'Dallas' before the other Spanish networks could do so!

Chapter 14

Case Study III: Migrant workers in the Federal Republic of Germany*

*The data referred to in this chapter on the Federal Republic of Germany was prepared prior to German reunification in 1990.

14.1 Old and new minorities

14.1.1 Indigenous minorities

There are today only two long-established ethnic minorities in the Federal Republic of Germany, and both are to be found in the north of the country.[1]

There are some 20,000 members of the Danish minority association (*Den Sydslesvigsk Forening*) and an estimated 50,000 speakers of Danish in Schleswig-Holstein (Walker 1987). The Danish minority enjoys special legal rights accorded to it by the German state (just as the German minority does in Denmark). The minority is well-organized. It sends two representatives to the state parliament in Kiel (the capital of the Federal State of Schleswig-Holstein), and it has kindergartens and schools which receive financial aid from the Schleswig-Holstein authorities, an active Danish Church and a network of Danish health, library and youth association services. Another reason why their standing is enhanced is their proximity to the country where their language has official status.

The Frisians, on the other hand, are fewer in number, with some 8000–10,000 speakers (Walker 1987). They have no legal rights, they are geographically more dispersed, many gave up their language several generations ago, and they have an undeveloped infrastructure. They live, geographically speaking, on the fringes of Germany, along the coast of the North Sea and on the Frisian Islands, a considerable distance away from their brothers and sisters (who could offer them support) in Friesland, in the Netherlands. The German Frisians do receive some financial aid now for the teaching of their language from the regional government in Kiel, but funds do not extend to the provi-

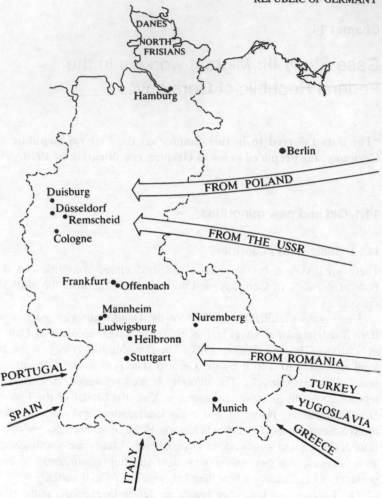

14.1 Map showing the migration and imigration to west Germany
 ← denotes countries of origin of migrants
 ⇐ denotes countries of origin of German minority members who have
     emigrated

sion of teaching materials. Walker (1987) describes the status of Frisians as 'symbolically high' but 'practically low', which can be
explained, at least partly, by its strong resemblance to *Plattdeutsch*
(Low German), the varieties of German spoken throughout North
Schleswig and other parts of northern Germany.

14.1.2 Refugees and returning German minorities

The small number of indigenous minorities in the Federal Republic is a consequence of the fact that this state is of recent creation (1949). The reorganization of Germany into two separate states and the alteration of virtually all its previous borders meant that those minorities which had been, at one time, part of the German Empire remained outside the territory of west Germany. As a result of the Second World War and political changes in its aftermath, particularly in eastern Europe, large numbers of refugees came to west Germany (some 12 million before 1961; 1.7 million after 1961, the year the Berlin Wall went up). The majority of them were German-speakers, but many also spoke a second language. A good proportion of the latter, particularly those who came from the Baltic republics, endeavoured to maintain their languages, and some were able to form well-organized systems of summer schools and associations. All those who went to west Germany as refugees have by now become integrated into the host society. The people who kept the Estonian, Latvian and Lithuanian languages alive in their families are now too dispersed and small in number even to be considered a minority.

A further consequence of the Second World War has led to a more recent development: the 're-emigration' into the Federal Republic of German minority members from eastern European countries, particularly Poland, Romania and the Soviet Union. Since the 1960s some 2 million people have settled in west Germany and many more continue to come. The absorption of this influx of people has not been easy as it has created a host of economic and social problems. It has also confronted the German nation with some interesting questions about what it means to be German. A large proportion of these *Aussiedler* ('returnees'), as they are called, do not speak German, and many others have maintained this language only as a spoken medium. The Federal State offers them language tuition and makes special provision for their children, who not only need to learn German for their schooling, but also find themselves having to adjust to a different education system. Some would argue that they are entitled to the opportunity to maintain their other language, a view held by the voluntary organizations which are also involved in teaching them German. But the Federal German state is reluctant to grant this request.

The situation, therefore, is one in which the indigenous population has had to learn to accept these newcomers as Germans, rather than 'Poles', 'Russians' or 'Romanians', and the *Aussiedler*, on the other hand, have been forced to undergo considerable adjustment. Their position has been compared to that of the post-war refugees, but the difference is that, whereas the refugees had at least lived among Germans, these people have not. The German minórity in Poland, for example, has had little or no contact with Germans over the previous forty or fifty years, even though the German Democratic Republic was relatively near. In the case of those emigrating from several Asian Soviet Republics, notably Uzbekistan and Kazakstan, and Romania, the separation from a German State went back several centuries, and for many years before the late 1980s there had been no exchange with, or support from, a German-speaking community. Many *Aussiedler*, coming as they frequently do from isolated rural backgrounds, find present-day West German values and life-styles difficult to understand. With respect to the language, they may be unfamiliar with the norms of usage of both Standard German as required in formal situations and the colloquial forms appropriate for everyday conversation. In their countries of origin they would have used Polish, Russian or Romanian in formal contexts, and either a local variety of these languages or their regional German dialect for more colloquial purposes.

14.1.3 New minorities

The 'new minorities' are the people who moved to west Germany from the late 1950s onwards. In numerical terms they are more significant than the old ones, and the social, educational and linguistic issues that they raise represent a real challenge to German society. As in other European countries, the term 'minorities' is employed here in a broader sense than, for instance, when we talk about 'the Frisian minority' or 'the Danish minority' in the north of Germany. In the present context the word is generally used in the plural, as it refers to groups of people from a number of different countries of origin. Individual nationalities among the new minorities are referred to as 'the Turks', 'the Yugoslavs', 'the Italians' etc., rather than Kurds, Croats, Serbs, Macedonians and so on. In other words, their ethnic identity is usually glossed over.

We can divide these new minorities into two groups:

(1) The migrant workers and their families (formerly referred to as *Gastarbeiter*, 'guestworkers') account for some four million people. They have been in the Federal Republic since the 1960s and have

become, it seems, a permanent feature of German society. Later sections of this chapter will be concerned mainly with this group.

(2) Political refugees, mainly from the southern parts of South-East Asia, who entered the Republic in large numbers in the early 1980s. Residence of these *Asylanten* ('asylum seekers') in the country is subject to certain regulations and procedures, which in practice make it difficult for them to have any form of close contact with the indigenous population. For instance, they are prevented from taking up employment during their first years of stay in the Republic, and they normally live in communal housing outside towns. They therefore have little opportunity or motivation to learn German, at least until they have been officially granted asylum, which many are not.

Government statistics used to list these two groups separately, but now they refer to both of them with the collective term *Ausländer*, 'foreigners'/'aliens'. By the end of 1986 there were just over four and half million 'foreign nationals' living in the Federal Republic, equal to 7.4 per cent of the total population of 61 million.

14.2 Migration

14.2.1 Background to migration to Germany

Germany has experienced large-scale immigration before. In fact, every time its economy expanded significantly it became necessary to recruit workers from abroad to meet new production requirements. Thus, a census carried out in 1907, for instance, showed that nearly 800,000 foreign workers were employed in German industry and agriculture; by 1914 the figure had risen to 1.2 million (Geiselberger 1972).

The latest big wave of migration this century started in 1955. By that time the west German economy had readjusted itself to post-war political conditions, had already absorbed the large number of refugees, and was still expanding. The west German Government, in common with other European states, signed agreements with a number of countries (e.g. Italy 1955, Spain and Greece 1960, Turkey 1961, Portugal 1964, Yugoslavia 1968) to organize the recruitment of unskilled labour. Private employers, too, launched recruitment drives, with the result that the number of foreign workers in the Federal Republic rose steadily: whereas in 1954 only 0.4 per cent of the total

workforce consisted of foreigners (72,096 people), by 1964 the figure
had risen to 4.4 per cent (or 985,616). It reached its peak at 10.9 per
cent (or 2,286,625 workers) in 1974. Recruitment and continued employment of foreign labour were dependent on the fluctuations of the
German economy, and the foreign workers thus served as a kind of
buffer (*Konjunkturpuffer* was the German term used). But as more and
more migrants brought their families to join them, planning a longer
stay in the Federal Republic, it became less and less possible to man-
ipulate the number of foreigners.

When the west German economy started to suffer the effects of the
1970s oil crisis, recruitment of foreign workers was officially halted.
Government figures for 1987 suggest that there are at present some
1,900,000 non-German workers in the country, accounting for approximately 9 per cent of the total workforce.

There are two significant features that distinguish the last of the
three migration periods this century from the earlier two. First, a large
number of those who went to work in the Federal Republic soon
brought their families as well, which in effect doubled the number of
foreign nationals living in the country. Nowadays the total number of
non-Germans registered is about 4.5 million (1986: 4,512,700) or some
7.4 per cent of the total population. This figure includes migrant workers and their families, as well as immigrants granted political asylum
(1987 *Datenreport*).

Secondly, a large number of the migrants who originally went for a
limited period of time have stayed on. They represent migration in one
direction only, even if the possibility of returning, either voluntarily or
as a result of a government decision, always exists. The Federal Republic already has, therefore, what amounts to a *de facto* first- and
second-generation immigrant population, which has a higher birth rate
than that of indigenous Germans. Official statistics forecast that, in
spite of a general decline in population from 61 million to 58 million
by the year 2000, the number of non-German residents is likely to
remain at its present level (4.5 million). This means that the proportion
of the total will increase to nearer 8 per cent.

14.2.2 Composition of the new minorities and geographical distribution

TABLE 14.1 Origins of West German foreign nationals

Country of origin	Number of immigrants	Percentage
Turkey	1,434,000	31.8
Yugoslavia	591,000	13.1
Italy	537,000	11.9
Greece	279,000	6.2
Spain	150,000	3.3

Source: Datenreport 1987

s compared to the 1970 figures, the total of Turkish nationals has trebled, whereas the numbers for the other four groups have fluctuated only slightly.

Foreigners have settled throughout the Federal Republic, but there are marked discrepancies in patterns of settlement. Over 80 per cent of the foreign population live in urban areas, particularly the large, heavily industrialized conurbations. 51 per cent live in cities of over 100,000 inhabitants (the proportion for the west German population as a whole, by comparison, is about 33 per cent).

The cities with the highest *numbers* of foreigners are the following:

TABLE 14.2 Cities with the highest number of foreigners

City	Number of foreigners
Berlin (West)	257,800
Munich	221,200
Hamburg	175,800
Frankfurt	148,300
Cologne	137,000
Stuttgart	102,600

The cities with the highest *proportion* of foreigners are slightly different:

TABLE 14.3 Cities with the highest proportion of foreigners

City	Proportion of foreigners (%)
Frankfurt	25.0
Offenbach	21.7
Stuttgart	18.2
Munich	17.4
Düsseldorf	16.1
Mannheim	15.5
Cologne	15.1
Ludwigshafen	14.3
Remscheid	13.9
Berlin (West)	13.8
Heilbronn	13.1
Duisburg	13.0
Nuremberg	12.8

Source: Datenreport 1987

In the earlier years of recruitment, immigrants (mainly single men or, to a lesser extent, single women) used to be housed in communal quarters. This changed as migrants were joined by their dependants or started new families in the Federal Republic. The great majority today live in rented accommodation, more often than not in ghetto-like conditions in run-down inner-city areas. Foreign nationals tend to be concentrated in specific districts. In Berlin-Kreuzberg, for instance, they form some 30 per cent of inhabitants, in München-Ludwigsvorstadt 40 per cent, and around the main railway station in Frankfurt as much as 80 per cent. Because Turkish nationals make up such a high proportion of the total foreign population, they are particularly affected by ghettoization.

Living under ghetto-like conditions breeds a host of social problems and renders integration into West German society virtually impossible. But it does foster a sense of cohesiveness among the minority, reinforcing their sense of identity and contributing to the maintenance of their languages (this point is taken up again in section 14.4).

14.2.3 Reasons for migration and problems of remigration

Some foreign workers from Spain, Greece and Turkey migrated for political reasons. For the majority, however, motivation was purely existential – they came in search of work and in the hope of being able to send money to their families back home and/or to save up to buy land/set up business/build themselves a house when they returned. Maria Borris (1973), in a case study of foreign workers in Frankfurt, found that most of those she interviewed were long-term unemployed in their country of origin: for example, 56 per cent of Spanish migrants in Europe came from Galicia and Andalusia, traditionally the areas with the highest unemployment rates in Spain. The reasons for migrating given to her were always the same: the need to earn money to survive, coupled with hopes for a better future on returning home. She found that even recent arrivals, whom she would have expected to have heard reports from others about the realities of migration, showed an almost total lack of appreciation of working life in the Federal Republic. More disturbing, she thought, was their rose-tinted view of their own future prospects, as it is still the case today that for many migrants returning to the home country becomes an economically sound proposition only when they reach retirement age.

Many thousands of migrants have returned to their own countries upon completing their contracts of employment. But a comparison of figures for those entering and those leaving the Federal Republic shows a consistent surplus of entries, even after the Federal Government stopped recruitment, tightened restrictions on both entry and residence, and launched a campaign to encourage remigration. The longer people stay, the more secure their legal status becomes (i.e. they are more likely to have their permits renewed) and the more stable their economic situation is likely to be. As a consequence, they are less motivated to return to their countries of origin.

Data from 1982 show the considerable proportion of migrants who had been resident in the Republic for over six years. The figures confirm the impression, gained in other countries as well, that these 'new minorities' are developing into a permanent feature of modern European society.

TABLE 14.4 Proportion of migrants from each country who have stayed in West
Germany for six years or longer:

Country	Length of stay	
	from six to eight years (%)	over ten years (%)
Spain	15.7	73.6
Greece	15.8	69.1
Yugoslavia	20.5	61.4
Italy	15	55.9
Turkey	27.8	36.3

Source: *Informationen zur politischen Bildung*, 201, 1984

Remigration, more often than not, is fraught with social, psychological and practical problems which become worse the longer the returning migrants have been away. Those who have not been able to save up enough to ensure a stable income upon returning, and those who face unemployment, often find themselves as much on the margins of society as they were when they left. Their plight is sometimes made worse by feelings of insecurity and a lack of identity caused by their long absence. Their children, who may never have experienced life in their parents' country, can be particularly hard hit. For instance, it has been reported that young Turkish girls find that their new society expects standards of behaviour, both at school and in general, with which they are unfamiliar (Fritsche 1984; Berber 1984). In many cases their knowledge of German will prove to be of little value to them in their new lives, and through lack of practice they will gradually lose it (Wolff 1984). In view of the serious problems that can arise, it is not surprising that relatively few families have decided to remigrate voluntarily.

14.2.4 Official policies towards migrants

For years the German Federal Republic did not have an official policy towards foreigners (*Ausländerpolitik*), apart from the recruitment of labour. Politicians and trade unionists used to insist that the Republic was not a country of immigration, thus disclaiming responsibility for the foreign population or for the lack of special provision for it. While the 'economic miracle' lasted, workers were hired on fixed-term contracts, and those who did not want to return when their contracts expired usually had little difficulty in finding new employment. When, in 1973, the oil crisis brought about a general recession, all recruitment officially ceased, and measures were taken to restrict the issuing of entry visas; more stringent conditions were set on the renewal of work and residence permits. In 1975 Child Benefit regulations were changed so as to allow payment, not according to the number of children in the family, but only for those children living with their parents in the Republic. However, migrants were still able to bring their families (including all dependent relatives), in accordance with the policy of *Familiennachzug* ('family reunification'). Large numbers of dependants were, in fact, brought to the Federal Republic in the mid- and late 1970s (which for older children and adolescents, in particular, often had a destabilizing effect). To avoid a situation in which the *Familiennachzug* policy would result in more young people on the look-out for employment being brought into west Germany, legislation was passed in 1981 barring immigrants' children of over fifteen from joining their families; another law of the same year specified that, in general, a four-year period between entry into the Federal Republic and the issue of a work permit would apply.

Today less than 40 per cent of foreigners living in west Germany form part of the working population. The rest are non-working women, children, young people and unemployed.

The measures taken after 1973 halted the entry of new workers, but they did not result in a significant reduction in the number of foreign nationals resident in the country, as few of them opted to go back. The economic crisis had hit other parts of the world as well, so there was little point in leaving one precarious existence for another. The Federal Government's attempt to reduce the number of foreigners by promoting remigration (by, in effect, buying it) was only partly successful, as the financial incentives were combined with severe conditions such as a commitment never to return to west Germany to take up employment again.

Official policies towards foreigners were designed to protect the German labour market. This they have done, but at the same time they have contributed to a rise in unemployment among migrants. Foreigners do not enjoy the same rights as German citizens living in the Republic, and their permanence in the Federal Republic is uncertain, since it is subject to residence permits being renewed or revoked at the discretion of the authorities. Yet the Government recognizes that the German economy cannot do without its foreigners, since they (as a part of the workforce, as consumers, taxpayers and ratepayers, and also as employers, mainly in the hotel, catering and food retail industries) are an integral part of West German economic life.

14.3 Sociolinguistic aspects

14.3.1 Socio-demographic composition

As mentioned before, the new minorities are composed of a variety of nationalities, each with its own set of homogeneous linguistic, cultural and religious characteristics. Germans may look upon them as one group only ('the foreigners'), but they themselves feel little sense of cohesion between nationalities. Identification occurs only among members of the same group, who tend to define themselves in ethnic terms (e.g. Kurds, Croats, Sicilians, etc.) rather than national ones. There can even be animosity between the different groups (as is the case with Turkish ones) who, depending on the region from which they originate, may speak another language, have a different religion, belong to a distinct culture, and differ in political views, and so reflect the same rivalries that exist within Turkey.

Many of those who came to the Federal Republic were among the least privileged members of their society in terms of employment opportunities, housing and education. A good number of them exchanged their previous positions for similar ones in the host country. They may be financially better off than before, but their social status, level of education and training and state of health tend to be low. As unskilled workers they are more vulnerable than others to the ups and downs of economic cycles, i.e. more likely to become unemployed than German workers. As they have to move to wherever they can find jobs, they have fewer opportunities for settling into a stable community.

Migrants not only form a 'new' minority. They are also, in a literal sense, a young one. In 1982 one-third of all foreigners were under twenty-one. The birth rate is highest among Turkish families, who account for half the total of new births among migrants. In Italian, Greek and Spanish families the birth rate is about the same as in German families.

Second-generation immigrants have added new features to characteristics of new minorities. By ethnic origin and nationality they are non-German, although they may never have been to the country whose nationals they are; they are bilingual, in many cases with German as their dominant language; they are also likely to be bicultural. They are therefore, at least potentially, intermediaries between the two cultures, but this role is seldom appreciated by either side – the Germans consider them foreigners, and their own ethnic community may resent their degree of accommodation to German customs and values. They find themselves under considerable pressure from both sides to conform. They may feel that remaining 'Turkish', for instance, will please their families and reinforce their sense of identity. It also makes remigration, which is always a possibility, less painful. Germanization, on the other hand, can cause alienation from the family group, but at the same time facilitate integration into west German society.

14.3.2 The migrants' linguistic background

The majority of migrant workers moved to Germany from regions on the fringes of their countries, in both geographical and economic terms: Galicia and Andalusia in Spain, Sicily and the Mezzogiorno in Italy, Macedonia in Yugoslavia and Greece, and Anatolia in Turkey. The linguistic varieties spoken in these areas tend to be quite different from the standard language. For this reason, and also because many migrants have undergone only a minimum of schooling, their language competence is mainly oral, and predominantly in the regional variety, with varying degrees of fluency in the standard. In the Federal Republic they find themselves in situations in which knowledge of the standard form of their own language is required of them, as the authorities tend to employ interpreters and translators who use this variety. A further, and possibly more important, problem is posed by the fact that in west Germany, as in other western societies, there is a good deal of reliance on the written mode for negotiations, agreements and official communication in general. The syntax and lexicon of the written norm tends of course to be more complex or difficult than that used in colloquial styles.

Lack of familiarity with the written form of their own language can also prove to be disadvantageous to migrants. Illiteracy rates among migrants are estimated at about 10 per cent (Auernheimer 1984), but there are indications that it may be proportionately much higher among women, since men will often have had a second chance to learn to read and write during their military service. Migrant women tend thus to become much more linguistically isolated and more dependent on their menfolk once they are separated from the wider family circle at home.

14.3.3   Problems associated with migrants' learning of German

While there is little available research on migrants' competence in, and use of, their home language, a good deal has been published about their acquisition of German and some aspects of their use of this language. Most migrants knew no German at all when they entered the country, whether as workers or as dependants. In the early days, when large numbers were contracted by particular firms, there were always middlemen who could act as interpreters; later newcomers were helped by fellow countrymen already settled in the country. The factors governing the extent to which migrants become proficient in German are numerous. In general, there is more pressure to learn German on those who go out to work than there is on people who stay at home. In fact, those who live in a ghetto-like environment have little need to learn the language of the society at large. For the formal occasions when contact with school, the authorities, health services, etc. is necessary, children or friends can help to bridge the language gap.

The opinion that ignorance of the language of the host country is a handicap, whatever the circumstances, is widespread. In most people's perceptions (Germans' as well as migrants') competence in German is a prerequisite for successful integration into German society, which is seen by many as the only satisfactory solution for the difficulties facing migrants.

From 1971 to 1981 a major project was carried out in Wuppertal, and later Hamburg and Kiel, to study the acquisition of German by Spanish, Italian and Portuguese workers (Clahsen et al. 1983). Although language difficulties were usually stated as the main problem experienced by the informants, the authors question the assumption that a better knowledge of German would by itself speed up their integration, arguing that an insufficient knowledge of the language shielded migrants, at least to some extent, from a full appreciation of negative attitudes on the part of Germans and their refusal to seek out contact with them. Others (e.g. the sociologist Nikolinakos 1973) argue that migrants are already integrated in that they have a place within German industry as a kind of 'reserve labour force', mobile and available when and where the need arises. In other words, their position within the German social system is thought by some to be determined by purely economic factors, and improved knowledge of German would not alter this. Taking this point to its logical conclusion, Nikolinakos argues that linguistic problems would disappear if the socio-economic conditions for migrants were radically improved.

The issue can be approached differently, pursuing a socio-psychological, rather than economic, line of argument. Studies of migrants' second language acquisition (some of which are listed below) consistently show that the most influential factors in successful acquisition are motivation (to learn the language) and positive attitudes (towards language learning and towards the host society). Both of these factors depend on the social environment in which the migrant finds himself/herself. The linguist Schumann (1976) uses the concept of the 'psychological and social distance' that the learner perceives between himself and the host country. He makes the point that the greater the 'distance' the more likely it is that acquisition will be hindered. By gradual integration, however, this distance can be reduced or removed, and language acquisition facilitated. In other words, integration and language proficiency are interdependent. In this view, integration is a contributory factor in the language learning process; it cannot be postponed until some future time. This goes against the attitude, often implicit in regulations or encountered among the public, to the effect that migrants ought to demonstrate their mastery of a language before integration can be contemplated. For instance, current legislation concerning foreigners in the German Federal Republic (the *Ausländergesetz*) stipulates that a foreigner can apply for removal of residence restrictions after five years' residence in the country; the precondition for obtaining it is that the applicant has become 'integrated into the economic and social life of the Federal Republic', which means that (s)he must prove that (s)he has a job, somewhere to live and oral fluency in German. In effect, a certain degree of integration is required of migrants even before they know whether they will be allowed to stay in Germany. It is of course precisely during their first years of residence in the country that they will have experienced the hardship and the problems which affect their attitudes towards Germans and West Germany negatively, thus lowering their motivation to learn the language. Integration always requires considerable effort; and it seems unrealistic to expect it from those who have not entered the country as genuine immigrants.

The problems relating to integration of migrants and their uncertain future represent two major obstacles to the acquisition of German. There are additional reasons why so many never learn to master the language of the host country, which are often of a practical nature. For instance, few foreigners attend German classes. Meisel (1975) found that only 12 per cent of the foreign workers he interviewed went to such courses. The reasons they gave were tiredness after a long day's work, shift work, looking after children or lack of confidence in their own ability to learn. Researchers claim that what German language migrants know they have learned at work (Meisel 1975; Clyne 1977; Klein and Dittmar 1979; Clahsen et al. 1983); but the amount of linguistic knowledge required there is limited, as are, in general, the opportunities for communication with Germans at the workplace.

14.3.4 Factors affecting migrants' acquisition of German

The continued presence of large numbers of foreigners with different linguistic backgrounds having to communicate in German has presented linguists with ideal conditions to undertake research into different areas of contact linguistics, contributing to the rapid growth of sociolinguistics and psycholinguistics as disciplines in west Germany.

In the 1970s a number of large-scale projects involving several different national groups of migrants were carried out in various parts of the country. These investigations were concerned with (1) the migrants' acquisition of German, in an untutored and unstructured way, as distinct from formal learning by means of tuition; and (2) the features that their German tended to show and the question of whether the so-called *Gastarbeiterdeutsch* (German used by migrants) could be described as a kind of pidgin or pidginized variety of the language.[2]

Since the end of the 1970s research interest has shifted towards the second generation of migrants. Studies have been undertaken concerning general issues related to migrants' children's acquisition of German and their maintenance or loss of the mother tongue. Other researchers have focused their attention on specific linguistic features of their first and second language, such as interference phenomena, code-switching and communication strategies. A third group is interested mainly in the education of migrant children, their integration into the German school system (or lack of it), and the provision for the teaching of both the mother tongue and German as a second language.[3]

In much of the research into (first generation) migrants' acquisition of German, the scholars concerned were keen on isolating factors that seemed to facilitate the acquisition process. Klein and Dittmar (1979) worked with a sample of forty-eight Italian and Spanish adult informants, two-thirds men and one-third women, and they used both interviewing and participant observation methods. They decided to look at nine factors which they thought were relevant, making a distinction between (a) 'bias factors', of a personal and individual type, and (b) 'environmental factors', which referred largely to the social context.

(a) Bias factors:
(1)   origin;
(2)   age (at time of migration);
(3)   attendance at school;
(4)   formal/professional qualifications;
(5)   sex.

(b) Environmental factors:
(1)   contact with Germans at the workplace (opportunities and frequency);
(2)   contact with the German language during leisure time (type and frequency);
(3)   type of accommodation;
(4)   duration of stay, i.e. how long they had been in Germany.

The informants were subdivided into three groups, according to their 'syntactic level' and the scores for the variables (the above factors) were then correlated with each informant's syntactic level. 'Contact with Germans during leisure time' turned out to be the most significant factor, followed by 'age' and 'contact at workplace'; 'accommodation' was relevant when it co-varied with 'contact with Germans', and 'duration of stay' seemed to be important only for the first two years. The authors were surprised to see the variable 'age' as having the second strongest correlation with syntactic achievement, given that only adults were interviewed. They concluded that 'age' may well co-vary with environmental factors, a young person being more willing and able to build up social contacts with Germans than an older one. Orlovič-Schwarzwald (1978) and Keim (1984), too, found 'age' to be an important factor. Keim argues that older learners can become equally proficient in two languages as younger ones, but the conditions under which successful acquisition takes place may be different – if social and psychological barriers are removed they no longer hinder language acquisition. Apart from 'contact with Germans' (in leisure time and at work), Keim (1984) also found that three other factors were beneficial to the acquisition of German by her informants, who were twelve adult Turkish migrants:

(1) the firm intention, at the time of migration, to stay in the Federal Republic for a long time;
(2) a critical and reserved attitude towards current political and religious tendencies in Turkey (which made return less attractive);
(3) an appreciation of the legal situation in Germany *vis-à-vis* their status as foreigners.

These three are called 'internal factors' by Keim, as they reflect emotional ties, experience and motivation. They are, in her view, more important to second language acquisition than 'external factors', such as age, accommodation and qualifications, the possibly negative effects of which are surmountable.

It is perhaps interesting to see the relative insignificance of the variable 'duration of stay', as many researchers (e.g. Meisel 1975; Klein and Dittmar 1979; Keim 1984) had originally thought that it was more important. In all studies, informants who had been in Germany for more than ten years varied in their 'syntactic level'. Some researchers have examined the possible reasons why the German of some migrants never progresses beyond a certain level. Klein and Dittmar suggested that:

> . . . it may well be that during the first two years a certain syntactical level is gradually acquired whose height depends on other factors such as 'contact', 'age' etc. The acquisition process then slows down, or even stops, and may well start moving again when the environmental factors change.
>
> (Klein and Dittmar 1979: 207).

Environmental as well as psychological factors, then, can be seen to have a bearing on second language acquisition. They will often co-vary and cause a chain reaction, either increasing or reducing the pressure and/or opportunity to acquire German. It is clear, however, that few of these factors come within the control of the migrants themselves, and even if societal attitudes and material conditions changed dramatically in favour of the migrants, their successful acquisition of German would not thereby be secured automatically.

14.4 The education of migrant workers' children

14.4.1 The EC Directive on the education of migrant workers' children

At an early stage of migration the Council of Europe began to show concern about the education of migrant workers' children. Several resolutions were passed demanding that migrant workers and their families should be taught the language of the host country, that mother-tongue teaching should be made available, that migrant children should be supported within the national school systems, and that provision should be made for the smooth reintegration of those children whose parents returned to their countries of origin. In the 1970s the Standing Conference of European Ministers of Education began to turn their attention to these problems, along with other international organizations, such as UNESCO, OECD and the International Labour Office. The general consensus that emerged can be summarized as follows:

(1)   migrant children should enjoy the same educational opportunities as children from the host country;

(2)   segregation should be avoided by encouraging transfer from preparatory clases to mainstream education as early as possible and by stimulating and promoting international understanding among indigenous children;

(3)   children should be able to learn, or continue to develop, their mother tongue at school.

In 1974 the EC authorities initiated a legislative process which resulted in 1977 in the adoption of Council Directive 77/486/EEC on the education of the children of migrant workers. As a directive, it is legally binding and it applies to children of migrant workers from EC member states as well as non-member ones (which is particularly important in the British context). The directive originally proposed by the Commission was more progressive in outlook and went further in its detailed provisions. Its terms, however, were toned down in certain respects by the Council, as some of its members (e.g. Britain and the Federal Republic of Germany) favoured a less binding form of words. This affected, in particular, Article 3, which deals with the provision of mother-tongue teaching. It was as a result of this EC directive that educational provision for migrants' children became part of general educational planning.

The directive requires member states to make free tuition available to the children of migrant workers in the language of the host country and also in the children's mother tongue. However, it allows member states to do so 'in accordance with their national circumstances and legal systems' (a phrase which is repeated in Articles 2, 3 and 4). This means, in effect, that member states have a great deal of freedom in deciding the amount and kind of resources they are willing to devote to such programmes. Educational provision for migrant children has not, in fact, proved to be high on the list of priorities of any member state. (See Appendix A for the full text of the directive).

14.4.2 Educational provision for migrant workers' children in the Federal Republic

According to the German Constitution, education is the responsibility of each individual Federal State or 'Land'. Thus each Land is free to decide on the detailed provision at all levels, including matters of resource allocation, types of schooling and curriculum details. An institutionalized link between the eleven Länder ministries of education is provided by the Standing Conference of Education Ministers. This body formulates general policy and issues guidelines that the individual states are free to carry out in their own way. With respect to the education of migrants' children, the Standing Conference adopted in 1976 two principles which are still considered valid today. The first is that the objective of the education of migrants' children should be:

(1)   to integrate these children into the German educational system;
(2)   to protect them from 'over-germanization' through the development of their mother tongue and native culture, so as to enable them to identify with the culture of their parents and to ease their return to their parents' homeland.

The second principle is that this double objective should be implemented in the following ways:

(1)   the same compulsory school attendance should apply to foreign children as to German ones (i.e. from seven to eighteen years of age: full-time attendance for nine years, then part-time until eighteen);
(2)   special provision should be made for German language teaching in the case of children whose command of German is insufficient for them to follow mainstream education;

(3) migrants' education should not separate them from German children, i.e. they should be taught together;
(4) provision should be made for children to be taught their parents' language.

The various *Länder* have developed different programmes with regard to the education of the children for whom they are responsible. A combination of the following types of programmes has usually been available:

(1) Preparatory classes (*Vorbereitungsklassen*) are intended to provide intensive German language teaching for groups of about fifteen children with the same or different language backgrounds. Attendance can extend for up to two years, after which the children join mainstream education. Apart from the specialist language tuition, these courses should follow the same curriculum as those for German children. If the children in the group have the same mother tongue instruction can take place, part of the time, in this language and be in the charge of teachers who speak the same native language. Transfer to mainstream education is supposed to take place as soon as the child has reached a sufficient level of knowledge of German to enable him/her to follow the normal curriculum.

(2) In bilingual classes German is taught as a foreign/second language by German teachers and other subjects – some or all of them – by foreign teachers with the same mother tongue as the pupils. Again, it is envisaged that transfer to mainstream education will take place as early as possible.

(3) Intensive courses (*Förderkurse*) are intended to offer flexible provision of German language tuition to individual pupils or small groups for varying lengths of time. These courses are offered during school hours, perhaps during the periods when lessons deemed to be of a more peripheral nature (domestic science, P.E., art or music) are taking place.

(4) Mother-tongue classes are designed to teach the language, history, geography and aspects of culture of the migrants' home country. They do not form part of the West German education system, and they are held outside school hours. Some of them provide a mixture of language tuition and background knowledge, others attempt to help children to obtain the school qualifications of the countries concerned.

They are financed by the various migrant communities themselves or by the respective national governments as in the cases of Spain and Italy. They vary considerably as to the demands they make of children – also as far as the teachers' own preparation is concerned. In the case of some countries, the respective ministries of education make resources (teachers and/or materials) available. Religious institutions can also be involved, as it is in the case of Islamic schools (*Koranschulen*). Some *Länder* support these classes financially and by cooperating in the design of teaching programmes; in return for this, they may assume overall control of the scheme – but this does not apply to Islamic schools, which concentrate on the teaching of the Muslim faith and of the Arabic required for religious purposes, rather than the teaching of Turkish.

14.4.3 Problems involved in the education of migrants' children

Because of the uneven distribution of migrants in the Federal Republic and the different measures taken by the various *Länder*, it is not possible to give a global assessment of the educational measures outlined above. Also, the instability of the immigrant population and the sharp increase in the number of migrants' children attending West German schools make it difficult to obtain a generalized picture. In some areas the proportion of foreign children has risen to 30 per cent, 40 per cent or even 50 per cent of the total school population within a decade, thus compounding the problems of provision, planning and resourcing. Among those who have reported on the education of migrants' children there is general accord about the nature of the problems; and they all agree that only massive new allocation of resources can solve them. But there are other problems (e.g. those relating to non-attendance at school and growing up against socially and culturally deprived backgrounds) which cannot be tackled simply by greater financial provision; they usually affect the children of Turkish migrants, who far outnumber those from other countries. Members of Italian, Spanish, Greek (who now enjoy EC citizenship status) and Yugoslav migrant groups tend to be more widely dispersed, and therefore proportionately fewer of their children attend the same school. In addition, the majority of them have been in the Federal Republic for a long time and have become better adjusted and more integrated.

The issues causing concern are those posed by children born outside Germany who joined their parents in the Republic after starting school in their home countries, the *Seiten-* or *Späteinsteiger* ('late joiners'). When they enter German schools they have no knowledge of the language, and even after attending preparatory or intensive classes they may never acquire enough to be able to follow mainstream education. Because of their lower achievement levels, they are not normally placed in the same classes as German children of the same age group, and they are thus even less likely to make meaningful contact with German children as, in addition to the language gap, there is an age gap as well.

Children who were born in the Federal Republic and attended kindergartens or playgroups are usually bilingual upon entering school, and they experience little, if any, language difficulty. But many of those who have had no contact with German-speaking children before starting school are disadvantaged, since they have to acquire German in preparatory classes before they are able to join regular ones.

The best results, in educational terms, seem to have been achieved when a system of bilingual education has been followed. Different models (*nationale Modelle*) have been devised. They are all still at an experimental stage. Generally, they consist of the majority of classes being taught in the children's mother tongue; only German lessons and (usually) those in art, music and P.E. are conducted in German. Children have been observed to progress well (Oomen-Welke 1985) if they do not have to compete against German children – the West German educational system is quite competitive.[4] But bilingual education means that foreign children are segregated from German ones, at least for a part of their education, and thus this type of education programme contributes relatively little to the declared aim of integration at least in the short term.

Critics have argued for some time that the various educational measures taken in the Federal Republic have not made any significant contribution to the improvement of educational progress among migrants' children. Some groups have done better than others, but overall statistics relating to foreign children in German educational institutions appear to bear out the claim. In 1985 82 per cent of migrants' children left school after the compulsory nine years, some two-thirds of them without any formal qualifications; the corresponding figures for German children were 35.5 per cent and 6.6 per cent. An equally disproportionately large section of them are sent to schools for pupils with special difficulties. It has also been suggested that an alarmingly high number of foreign children do not attend school at all: estimates

vary between 8 per cent and 25 per cent of the foreign school population (Auernheimer 1984). The employment prospects of these children
are poor, as they have to compete with German school-leavers in the
job market. It seems likely that the children will perpetuate the uncertain, low-status position their parents occupy within the economic and
social system in the host country.

Schools have been criticized for not playing a significant role in the
acquisition of German by migrant's children. Kutsch and Desgranges
(1985) report that they saw little progress made in German by the
children they observed, adding that the language is acquired more effectively outside school, as part of the general socialization process.

The schools are up against two major obstacles. The first is attributed to the migrants themselves, that is, to their special social and
legal position, and their heterogeneous cultural and linguistic backgrounds. The second is a matter of educational provision. Most West
German teachers are ill-equipped to cope with what at times can be
quite large numbers of migrants'children in their classes, children who
often have special linguistic and educational needs. Few teachers have
followed training courses in German as a second language, even fewer
know any of the languages of their pupils, and there is a scarcity of
suitable materials, which makes special courses more difficult to pre-
pare. Lessons with mother-tongue teachers can be problematic if the
latter are unfamiliar with German and the German school system. Essentially, neither German-born nor mother-tongue teachers can be
expected (without some form of retraining) to have any real understanding of bilingualism and biculturalism.

It is clearly important that everybody involved in the upbringing
and education of migrants' children recognizes that they have special
needs. They live in an environment where they are surrounded by two
languages and two cultures, and access to both should be considered to
be their right. It is only if bilingualism and biculturalism are established successfully that these children's integration into German
society, or into that of their parents' home countries should the family
remigrate, can be ensured.

Notes

1.   Because of its concern with western Europe this chapter is concerned with that part of Germany only which was West Germany
   before 3 October 1990. In the east of the new Germany there

      also exists a linguistic minority, the Sorbs, who use Sorbian, a Slavonic language.

2.   For example, the 1975 HPD Project (*Heidelberger Forschungsprojekt Pidgin Deutsch*) led to the publication of Klein and Dittmar's (1979) study of migrants' developing grammars and Klein's (1984) work on second language acquisition. Meisel (1975) and Schumann (1978) consider the question of pidginization, as did Clyne (1977) in a review article. Clahsen, Meisel and Pienemann (1983) report on the results of the ZISA Project, which looked at the acquisition of German by Italian, Spanish and Portuguese workers. Orlovic-Schwarzwald (1978), Fritsche (1982) and Keim (1984) focus on Turkish migrants, and Stölting (1975; 1980) on Yugoslav ones. Multilingualism within the family and also in the wider context of an urban area was the subject of a project carried out by the *Institut für deutsche Sprache*, reported on in Bausch (1982).

3.   Among those who have reported on more general issues of children's acquisition of German are Nelde et al. (1981), Pfaff (1981) and Rath (1983). Pfaff (1980), Pfaff and Portz (1980) and Pienemann (1980) concentrate on linguistic aspects. A major project, large-scale and long-term, dealt with various aspects of Italian migrants' children's use of both Italian (standard and dialect) and German – see Auer (1980; 1981; 1982; 1984) and Auer and di Luzio (1984). A long-term project at the University of Saarbrücken concerned itself with communication by migrants and covered also the acquisition of German by Turkish migrants' children (Kutsch and Desgranges 1985). A good number of studies of linguistic and educational issues have been carried out at the Centre for Multilingualism of the University of Hamburg, e.g. by Rehbein (1985; 1987).

4.   Failure in school achievement carries with it the threat of either having to repeat the year or, even worse, being sent to a special school for children with behavioural or educational difficulties.

Appendix

Council of the European Communities Directive of 25 July 1977 on the education of the children of migrant workers (77/486/EEC).

THE COUNCIL OF THE EUROPEAN COMMUNITIES,

Having regard to the Treaty establishing the European Economic Community, and in particular Article 49 thereof,

Having regard to the proposal from the Commission,

Having regard to the opinion of the European Parliament,

Having regard to the opinion of the Economic and Social Committee,

Whereas in its resolution of 21 January 1974 concerning a social action programme, the Council included in its priority actions those designed to improve the conditions of freedom of movement for workers, particularly with regard to the problem of the reception and education of their children;

Whereas in order to permit the integration of such children into the educational environment and the school system of the host State, they should be able to receive suitable tuition including teaching of the language of the host State;

Whereas host Member States should also take, in conjunction with the Member States of origin, appropriate measures to promote the teaching of the mother tongue and of the culture of the country of origin to the above-mentioned children, with a view principally of facilitating their possible integration into the Member State of origin,

HAS ADOPTED THIS DIRECTIVE:

Article 1
This Directive shall apply to children for whom school attendance is compulsory under the laws of the host State, who are dependants of any worker who is a national of another Member State, where such children are resident in the territory of the Member State in which that national carries on or has carried on an activity as an employed person.

Article 2
Member States shall, in accordance with their national circumstances and legal systems, take appropriate measures to ensure that free tuition to facilitate initial reception is offered in their territory to the children referred to in Article 1, including, in particular, the teaching – adapted to the specific needs of such children – of the official language or one of the official languages of the host State.

Member States shall take the measures necessary for the training and further training of the teachers who are to provide this tuition.

Article 3
Member States shall, in accordance with their national circumstances and legal systems, and in cooperation with States of origin, take appropriate measures to promote, in coordination with normal education, teaching of the mother tongue and culture of the country of origin for the children referred to in Article 1.

Article 4
The Member States shall take the necessary measures to comply with this directive within four years of its notification and shall forthwith inform the Commission thereof.

The Member States shall also inform the Commission of all laws, regulations and administrative or other provisions which they adopt in the field governed by this Directive.

Article 5
The Member States shall forward to the Commission within five years of the notification of this Directive, and subsequently at regular intervals at the request of the Commission, all relevant information to enable the Commission to report to the Council on the application of this Directive.

Article 6
This Directive is addressed to the Member States.

References

Note: This list contains the references mentioned in the individual chapters, and also the titles included among the suggestions for further reading.

ABEYÀ, M (1985) Valoraciones del programa de inmersión en Santa Coloma de Gramanet, in M Siguán, (ed): *Enseñanza en dos lenguas y resultados escolares*

ADLER, M (1977) *Collective and Individual Bilingualism: a sociolinguistic study*. Helmut Buske Verlag, Hamburg

AELLEN, C and LAMBERT W E (1969) Ethnic identification and personality adjustments of Canadian adolescents of mixed English–French parentage, *Canadian Journal of Behavioural Science* 1, 69–86

AGUIRRE, A (1985) An experimental study of code alternation, *International Journal of the Sociology of Language* 53, 59–82

ALBERT, M L and OBLER, L K (1978) *The Bilingual Brain: neuropsychological and neurolinguistic aspects of bilingualism*, Academic Press, New York

ALLARDT, E (1979) Implications of the ethnic revival in modern industrialized society: a comparative study of the linguistic minorities in western Europe, *Commentationes Scientiarum Socialum* 12, Societas Scientiarum Fennica, Helsinki

—(1984) What constitutes a language minority? *Journal for Multilingual and Multicultural Development* 5, Nos 3 & 4, 195–205

AMASTAE, J and ELÍAS-OLIVARES, L (eds) (1982) *Spanish in the United States: sociolinguistic aspects*, Cambridge University Press, Cambridge

APPEL, R and MUYSKEN, P (1987) *Language Contact and Bilingualism*, Edward Arnold, London

ARNAU, J and BOADA, H (1986) Languages and school in Catalonia, *Journal of Multilingual and Multicultural Development* 7, 2 & 3, 107–122

ARNBERG, L (1981) A longitudinal study of language development in four young children exposed to English and Swedish in the home, *Linköping Studies in Education*, Report 6, Department of Education, University of Linköping

—(1987) *Raising Children Bilingually: the pre-school years*. Multilingual Matters, Clevedon

ARNBERG, L and ARNBERG, P (1984) The relation between code differentiation and language mixing in bilingual 3- to 4-year-old children, in *Scandinavian Working Papers in Bilingualism*, 2, 43–62

ARSENIAN, S (1937) *Bilingualism and Mental development: a study of the intelligence and the social background of bilingual children in New York*, Teachers' College, Columbia University

AUER, J C P (1980, 1981, 1982) Projekt: Untersuchungen zur Muttersprache italienischer Migrantenkinder, *Papiere des Sonderforschungsbereichs*, 44, 54, 71, 79, 99, Universität Konstanz

—(1984) On the meaning of conversational code-switching, in AUER and di LUCIO (eds) *Interpretative Sociolinguistics*, Gunter Narr, Tübingen, 87–112

AUER, J C P and di LUCIO, A (1984) *Interpretative Sociolinguistics*, Gunter Narr, Tübingen

AUERNHEIMER, G (1984) *Handwörterbuch Ausländerarbeit*, Beltz, Basel

AZEVEDO, H M (1984) The reestablishment of Catalan as a language of culture, *Hispanic Linguistics*, 1, 2, 305–30

BAETENS BEARDSMORE, H (1974) Development of the compound-coordinate distinction in bilingualism, *Lingua* 33, 2, 123–27

—(1979) European Schools, in Mødet mellem sprogene i det dansk-tyske grænsområde, Åbenrå Institut for Graensregionsforskning, 38–49

—(1980) Bilingual Education in International schools, European schools and Experimental schools: A comparative analysis, in Lim Kiat Boey (ed) *Bilingual Education*, Singapore University Press, Singapore, 3–19

—(1981) Elements of bilingual theory, in H Baetens Beardsmore (ed): *1981 Study Series of the Tijdschrift van de Vrije Universiteit Brussel*

—(1982) *Bilingualism: Basic Principles*, Multilingual Matters, Clevedon

—(1983) Substratum, adstratum and residual bilingualism in Brussels, *Journal for Multilingual and Multicultural Development* 4 (1), 1–15

BAIN, B (1976) Verbal regulation of cognitive processes: a replication of Luria's procedures with bilingual and multilingual infants, *Child Development* 47, 543–46

BAKER, C (1985) *Aspects of bilingualism in Wales*, Multilingual Matters, Clevedon

—(1988) *Key Issues in Bilingualism and Bilingual Education*, Multilingual Matters, Clevedon

BAUSCH, K (1981) *Mehrsprachigkeit in der Stadtregion*. Jahrbuch 1981 des Instituts für deutsche Sprache, Pädagogischer Verlag Schwann

BEN-ZEEV, S (1976) What strategies do bilinguals use in preventing their languages from interfering with each other, and what effect does this have on non-language tasks? *Papers and Reports on Child Language Development* **12**, Department of Linguistics, Stanford University

—(1977) Mechanisms by which childhood bilingualism affects understanding of language and cognitive structures, in P Hornby, (ed) *Bilingualism*, Academic Press, London 29–55

BERBER, I (1984) Soziale und sprachliche Probleme der Remigration türkischer Jugendlicher, *Informationen Deutsch als Fremdsprache*, **3**, Jahrgang 84/85, August 1984, DAAD, 37-41

BERGMAN, C (1976) Interference vs. independent development in infant bilingualism, in G Keller, et al. (ed) *Bilingualism in the Bicentennial and Beyond*, Bilingual Press, Editorial Bilingüe, New York, 86-95

BERK-SELIGSON, S (1986) Linguistic constraints on intrasentential code-switching: a study of Spanish–Hebrew bilingualism, *Language in Society* **15**, 313–48

BERLIN, C S *et al.* (1972) Dichotic right ear advantage in males and females aged 5 to 10, *Journal of the Acoustical Society of America* **53**, 368 (Abstract)

BERMAN, R A (1979) The re-emergence of a bilingual: a case study of a Hebrew-English speaking child, *Working Papers on Bilingualism* **19**, November 1979, Ontario Institute for Studies in Education, 157–79

BERRUTO, G and BURGER, H (1987) Aspekte des Sprachkontaktes Italienisch–Deutsch im Tessin, *Linguistische Berichte III*, Westdeutscher Verlag, Opladen 367–80

BLOOMFIELD, L (1927) Literate and illiterate speech, *American Speech*, **2**, 423–39 (reprinted in Hymes 1964), *Language in Culture and Society*, Row and Harpers, New York

—(1933) *Language*, Holt Rinehart and Winston, New York (published in 1935 by George Allen and Unwin, London)

BLOM, J P and GUMPERZ, J (1972) Social meaning in linguistic structure: code-switching in Norway, in J Gumperz and P Hymes, (eds) *Directions in Sociolinguistics*, Basil Blackwell, Oxford, 407–34

BOOS-NÜNNING, K *et al.* (1986) *Towards Intercultural Education*, CILT (Alfa)

BORRIS, M (1973) *Ausländische Arbeiter in einer Großstadt, eine empirische Untersuchung am Beispiel Frankfurt,* Europäische Verlagsanstalt, Frankfurt

BRAINERD, C J and PRESSLEY, M (eds) *Progress in Cognitive Development Research: verbal processes in children*, Springer, New York

BREITENBACH, B von (1982) *Italiener und Spanier als Arbeitnehmer in der BRD, eine vergleichende Untersuchung zur europäischen Arbeitsmigration*, Kaiser Grünewald, Munich and Mainz

BROWN, R (1973) *A First Language*, George Allen and Unwin, London

BRUNER, J (1975) The ontogenesis of speech acts, *Journal of Child Language* **2**, 1–19

Bundeszentrale für Politische Bildung, Statistisches Bundesamt (Hrsg), *Datenreport 1987*, Zahlen und Fakten über die Bundesrepublik Deutschland, Band 257, Bonn

BURLING, R (1959) Language development of a Garo- and English-speaking child, *Word* 15, 48–68

BYRAM, M (1986a) Schools in ethnolinguistic minorities, *Journal for Multilingual and Multicultural Development*, 7, 2 & 3, 97–106

—(1986b) *Minority Education and Ethnic survival*, Multilingual Matters, Clevedon

—(1986c) Cultural studies in modern language teaching, *Language Teaching* 19, 322–36

—(1988) *Cultural Studies in Foreign Language Education*, Multilingual Matters, Clevedon

BYRAM, M and LEMAN, J (1989) *Bicultural and trilingual education: the Foyer Model in Brussels*, Multilingual Matters, Clevedon

CALSAMIGLIA, H and TUSÓN, A (1984) Use of languages and code-switching in groups of youth in a 'barri' of Barcelona: communicative norms in spontaneous speech, *International Journal of the Sociology of Language* 47, 105–21

CARR, R (1973) *Spain: 1808–1936*, Oxford University Press, Oxford

CARROW, E (1971) Comprehension of English and Spanish by pre-school Mexican-American children, *Modern Language Journal* 55, 299-307

CELCE-MURCIA, M (1978) The simultaneous acquisition of English and French in a two-year-old child, in E Hatch *Second Language Acquisition: a book of readings*, Newbury House, Rowley

CELLARD, J (1976) Alsacien: la langue du foyer. *Le monde de l'éducation* (Septembre), 16-18

CHILD, I L (1943) *Italian or American? The second generation in conflict*, Russell and Russell, New York

CHRISTOPHERSON, P (1948) *Bilingualism*, Methuen, London

CHURCHILL, S (1986) *The Education of Linguistic and Cultural Minorities in OECD Countries*, Multilingual Matters, Clevedon

CLAHSEN, H, MEISEL, J AND PIENEMANN, H (1983) *Deutsch als Zweitsprache: Der Spracherwerb ausländischer Arbeiter*, Gunter Narr Verlag, Tübingen

CLYNE, M (1977) The speech of foreign workers in Germany (review article), *Language in Society* 6, 268-74

—(1988) Budding linguist: some expressions of metalinguistic awareness in a bilingual child; paper presented at the 1st Hamburg symposium on Multilingualism September 1988

COBARRUBIAS, J (1983) Ethical issues in status planning, in J Cobarrubias and J Fishman (eds) *Progress in Language Planning*, Mouton, de Gruyter, Berlin, 41–86

COBARRUBIAS, J and FISHMAN, J (1983) *Progress in Language Planning: International Perspectives*, Mouton, de Gruyter, Berlin

COLE, R (1975) Divergent and convergent attitudes towards the Alsatian dialect, *Anthropological Linguistics,* 17:6

CORBELLA, J (1988) *General survey of the 1980s: Social communication in Catalonia,* Generalitat de Catalunya, Barcelona

CORNEJO, R (1973) The acquisition of lexicon in the speech of bilingual children, in P Turner (ed) *Bilingualism in the Southwest,* University of Arizona Press, Tucson (revised edn, 1982), 141–69

CRYSTAL, D (1987) *The Cambridge Encyclopedia of Language,* Cambridge University Press, Cambridge

CUMMINS, J (1976) The influence of bilingualism on cognitive growth: a synthesis of research findings and explanatory hypothesis, *Working Papers on Bilingualism,* Ontario Institute for Studies in Education **1,** 1–43

—(1978a) Metalinguistic development of children in bilingual education programs: data from Irish and Canadian Ukranian–English programs, in: M Paradis (ed) *Aspects of Bilingualism*

—(1978b) The cognitive development of children in immersion programs, *Canadian Modern Language Review* **34,** 855–83

—(1978c) Bilingualism and the development of metalinguistic awareness, *Journal of Cross-Cultural Psychology* **9,** 131–49

—(1978d) Educational implications of mother-tongue maintenance in minority-language groups, *Canadian Modern Language Review* **34** (3), 345–416

—(1979a) Cognitive/academic language proficiency and linguistic interdependence, the Optimum Age question and some other matters, *Working Papers on Bilingualism* **19,** November 1979, Ontario Institute for Studies in Education, 197–205

—(1979b) Linguistic interdependence and the educational development of bilingual children, *Review of Educational Research* **49,** 2, 222–51

—(1981) *Bilingualism and Minority Language Children,* Ontario Institute for Studies in Education, OISE Press, Toronto

—(1984a) *Bilingualism and Special Education: Issues in assessment and pedagogy,* Multilingual Matters, Clevedon

—(1984b) Bilingualism and cognitive functioning, in S Shapston and D'Oyley (eds) *Bilingual and Multicultural Education: Canadian Perspectives,* Multilingual Matters, Clevedon, 55–67

—(1984c) Linguistic minorities and multicultural policy in Canada, in J Edwards (ed) *Linguistic Minorities, Policies and Pluralism,* Academic Press, London, 81–105

CUNZE, B (1980) Lo sviluppo linguistico di una bambina bilingue italo–tedesca (PhD thesis, University of Rome)

DARCY, N T (1953) A review of the literature on the effects of bilingualism upon the measurement of intelligence, *Journal of Genetic Psychology* **82,** 21–57

DATO, D P (ed) (1975) *Georgetown University Round Table on Language and Linguistics,* Georgetown University Press, Washington DC

DE AVILA, E (1987) Bilingualism, cognitive function and language minority group membership, in P Homel, M Palij and J Aaronson, (eds) *Childhood Bilingualism*, Lawrence Erlbaum Associates, New Jersey, 149–169

DE CICCO G and MARING, J M (1983) Diglossia, regionalism and national language policy: a comparison of Spain and the Phillipines, in A Miracle, (ed): *Bilingualism*, University of Georgia Press, 38–53

DE HOUWER, A (1990) *The acquisition of two languages from birth: a case study*, Cambridge University Press, Cambridge

DE JONG, E (1986) *The Bilingual Experience*, Cambridge University Press, Cambridge

DEMONTE, V and ORTEGA, S (eds) (1982) El bilingüismo: problemática y realidad, *Revista de Occidente* **10–11**, Extraordinario II, Madrid

Departament de cultura de la Generalitat de Catalunya (1988) *The Press in Catalonia in the 1980s*, Barcelona

DE VILLIERS, A and DE VILLIERS, J G (1979) *Early Language*, Fontana, London

DIEBOLD, A R (1961) Incipient bilingualism, *Language* XXXVII, 97–112

DILLER, K C (1972) 'Compound' and 'coordinate' bilingualism: a conceptual artefact, *Word* **26**, 2, 254–61

DI LUZIO, A (1984) On the meaning of language choice for the sociocultural identity of bilingual immigrant children, in Auer and di Luzio (eds) *Interpretative Sociolinguistics*, Gunter Narr, Tübingen, 55–85

DODSON, C J (1981) A reappraisal of bilingual development and education: some theoretical and practical considerations, in H Baetens Beardsmore (ed) Elements of Bilingual Theory, Free University of Brussels, 14–27

DORIAN, N (1981) *Language Death: the Life Cycle of a Scottish Gaelic Dialect*, University of Pennsylvania Press, Philadelphia

DOYLE, A B, CHAMPAGNE, M and SEGALOWITZ, N (1978) Some issues in the assessment of the consequences of early bilingualism, in M Paradis, (ed) *Aspect of Bilingualism*, Hornbeam Press, Columbia SC, 13–20

EASTMAN, C M (1983) *Language Planning: an introduction*, Chandler and Sharp Publishers, San Francisco

EDWARDS, J (1977) ethnic identity and bilingual education, in H. Giles (ed) *Language, ethnicity and intergroup relations*, Academic Press, London

—(1984) Irish: planning and preservation, *Journal of Multilingual and Multicultural Development*, **5**, Nos 3 & 4, 267–75

—(1985) *Language, Society and Identity*, Basil Blackwell, Oxford

ELÍAS-OLIVARES, L and NASJLETI, D (eds) (1983) *Spanish in the United States: Beyond the Southwest*, NCBE, Washington

ELWERT, W T (1973) Das zweisprachige Individuum. Ein Selbstzeugnis. *Studien zu den romanischen Sprachen*, Band IV, Franz Steiner Verlag, Wiesbaden

EMRICH, L (1938) Beobachtungen über Zweisprachigkeit in ihrem Anfangsstudium, *Deutsch im Ausland* **21**, 419–24

ERVIN, S (1964) An analysis of the interaction of language, topic and listener, *American Anthropology* **66** Part 2, 86–102 (also in J Fishman (ed) *Readings in the Sociology of Language*, Mouton, The Hague, 1970, 192–211)

ERVIN, S and OSGOOD, C (1954) Second language learning and bilingualism, *Journal of Abnormal and Social Psychology Supplement*, 139–46

ERVIN-TRIPP, S (1964) Language and TAT content in bilinguals, *Journal of Abnormal and Social Psychology* **68**, 500–7

FABRE, P (1979) *Los catalanes*, Epidauro, Barcelona

FANTINI, A (1973) Social cues and language choice, in P Turner, (ed) *Bilingualism in the South West*, University of Arizona Press, Tucson, 87–111 (revised edn 1982)

—(1976) *Language Acquisition of a Bilingual Child: a sociolinguistic perspective*, The Experimental Press, Battleboro, Vermont

—(1982) *La adquisición del lenguaje en un niño bilingüe*. Editorial Herder, Barcelona

—(1985) *The Language Acquisition of a Bilingual Child*, Multilingual Matters, Clevedon

FASOLD, R (1984) *The Sociolinguistics of Society*, Basil Blackwell, Oxford

FELIX, S (ed) (1980) *Second Language Development: Trends and Issues*, Gunter Narr Verlag, Tübingen

FERGUSON, C (1959) Diglossia, *Word* **15**, 325–40

—(1968) Language development, in Fishman, J, Ferguson, C and Das Gupta (eds) *Language Problems of Developing Nations*, John Wiley, New York, 27–36

FERRER I GIRONÈS (1985) *La persecució política de la llengua catalana*, Ediciones 62, Barcelona

FISHMAN, J (1964) Language maintenance and language shift as fields of inquiry, *Linguistics* **9**, 32–70

—(1965a) Who speaks what language to whom and when? *La Linguistique*, **2**, 67–88 (revised 1971 version in Pride and Holmes (eds) *Sociolinguistics* 15–33)

—(1965b) Bilingualism, intelligence and language learning, *Modern Language Journal* **49**, 227–37

—(1966a) The implications of bilingualism for language teaching and language learning, in A Valdman (ed) *Trends in Language Teaching*, McGraw-Hill, New York, 146–58

—(1966b) *Language Loyalty in the United States*, Mouton, The Hague

—(1967) Bilingualism with and without diglossia; diglossia with and without bilingualism, *Journal of Social Issues* XXIII No 2, 29–37

—(1968) Bilingualism in the Barrio, Final Report, US Department of Health, Education and Welfare, Office of Education, Bureau of Research, vol 2 (August). Also in J Fishman (1971) *Advances in the Sociology of Language* **1**, Mouton, The Hague

—(ed) (1970) *Readings in the Sociology of Language*, Mouton, The Hague

—(1971) National languages and languages in wider communication in the developing nations, in W H Whiteley (ed) *Language Use and Social Change*, OUP London, 27–56

—(ed) (1972a) *Advances in the Sociology of Language*, 2 vols, Mouton, The Hague

—(1972b) *Language and Nationalism: Two Integrative Essays*, Newbury House, Rowley, Mass

—(1972c) Language maintenance and language shift, in *The Sociology of Language*, 76–134

FISHMAN, J, FERGUSON, C and DAS GUPTA (eds) (1968) *Language Problems of Developing Nations*, John Wiley, New York

FOSTER, C R (ed) (1980) *Nations without a State*, Praeger, New York

FRANCIS, E (1947) The nature of the ethnic group, *American Journal of Sociology* **52**, 393–400

—(1976) *Interethnic Relations*, Elsevier, New York

FRITSCHE, M (1982) Mehrsprachigkeit in Gastarbeiterfamilien, Deutsch auf der Basis türkischer Syntax, in K Bausch (ed): *Mehrsprachigkeit in der Stadtregion*, IdS Jahrbuch 1981, Pädagogischer Verlag Schwann, 160–224

—(1984) Remigration/Reintegration – ein Gegenstand der Sprachwissenschaft? *Informationen Deutsch als Fremdsprache*, **3**, Jahrgang 84/85, August 1984, DAAD, 5–8

FUNDACIÓ JAUME BOFILL (1989) *Catalunya 77–88*, Barcelona

GAL, S (1978a) Peasant men can't get wives: language change and sex roles in a bilingual community, *Language in Society*, **7**, No. 1, 1–16

—(1978b) Variation and change in patterns of speaking: language shift in Austria, in D Sankoff (ed) *Linguistic Variation: Models and Methods*, Academic Press, New York, 227–38

—(1979) *Language Shift: social determinants of linguistic change in bilingual Austria*, Academic Press, New York

GANS, H (1979) Symbolic ethnicity: the future of ethnic groups and cultures in America, *Ethnic and Racial Studies* **2**, 1–20

GARDNER, J W (1965) Foreword to: C E Osgood and T A Sebeok (eds) *Psycholinguistics: a survey of theory and research problems*, Indiana University Press, Bloomington

GARDNER, R C and LAMBERT, W E (1972) Attitudes and motivation in second-language learning, Newbury House, Rowley, Mass.

GARDNER-CHLOROS, P (1983) Hans im Schnockeloch: Language in Alsace. *Modern Languages*, **64**(1), 35–41

—(1985) Language selection and switching among Strasbourg shoppers, *International Journal of the Sociology of Language*, **54**, 117–35

GARVIN, P and MATHIOT, M (1970) The urbanization of the Guaraní language: a problem in language and culture, in J Fishman (ed) (1970) *Readings in the Sociology of Language*, Mouton, 365–74

GAUTHIER, N (1982) Alsace, in R Lafont (ed) *Langue dominante, langue dominée*, Edilig, Paris, 73–83

GEISELBERGER, S (1972) *Schwarzbuch: Ausländische Arbeiter, Herausgegeben im Auftrag des Bundesvorstandes der Jungsozialisten*, Fischer, Frankfurt

GENESEE, F (1987) *Learning through two languages*, Newbury House, Cambridge, Mass.

—(1989) Early Bilingual Language Development: One Language or Two?, *Journal of Child Language* 16, 1, 161–79

GERTH, H H and MILLS, C W (eds) (1948) *Max Weber, Essays in sociology*, Routledge & Kegan Paul, London

GIBBONS, J (1983) Attitudes towards languages and code-mixing in Hong Kong, *Journal of Multilingual and Multicultural Development* 4, Nos 2 & 3, 129–47

—(1986) *Code-mixing and Code-choice*, Multilingual Matters, Clevedon

GILES, H (ed) (1977) *Language, Ethnicity and Intergroup Relations*, Academic Press, London

GILES, H, BOURHIS, R and TAYLOR, D (1977) Towards a theory of language in ethnic group relations, in Giles, H (ed) *Language, Ethnicity and Intergroup Relations*, Academic Press, London, 307–49

GINER, S (1984) *The Social Structure of Catalonia*, The Anglo-Catalan Society, Occasional Publications No 1, London

GOLDBERG, MILTON (1941) A qualification of the Marginal Man theory, *American Sociological Review* 6, 52–8

GOLDSTEIN, J and BENVENUE, R (eds) (1980) *Ethnicity and ethnic relations in Canada*, Butterworth, Toronto

GREENE, D (1981) The Atlantic group: Neo-Celtic and Faroese, in E Haugen, J McClure and D Thomson (eds) *Minority Languages Today*, Edinburgh University Press, Edinburgh 1–9

GREENFIELD, L (1972) Situational measures of normative language views in relation to person, place and topic among Puerto Rican bilinguals, in J Fishman (ed) *Advances in the Sociology of Language*, vol II, Mouton, 17–35

GROSJEAN, F (1982) *Life with Two Languages*, Harvard University Press, Cambridge, MA

—(1985a) The bilingual as a competent but specific speaker–hearer, *Journal of Multilingual and Multicultural Development,* 6 No 6, 1985, 467–77

—(1985b) Polyglot aphasics and language mixing: a comment on Perecman 1984, *Brain and Language* 26, 349–55

GUMPERZ, J (1964) Linguistic and social interaction in two communities, *American Anthropologist* 66, No 2, 37–53

—(1977) Social network and language shift, in C Molony, H Zobl and W Stölting (eds) *Deutsch im Kontakt mit anderen Sprachen, German in Contact with other Languages*, Scriptor Verlag Kronberg/Ts

GUMPERZ, J and HERNÁNDEZ-CHÁVEZ, E (1972) Bilingualism, bidialectalism and classroom interaction, in J J Gumperz *Language in Social Groups*, Stanford University Press, 311–39

—(1975) Cognitive aspects of bilingual communication, in E Hernández-Chávez, et al. (eds) *El lenguaje de los chicanos*, Center for Applied Linguistics, Arlington, 154–63

GUMPERZ, J and HYMES, D (eds) (1986) *Directions in Sociolinguistics*, Basil Blackwell, Oxford

HALLIDAY, M A K (1975) *Learning how to Mean: explorations in the development of language*, Edward Arnold, London

HALLIDAY, M A K, MCINTOSH, A and STREVENS, P (1970) The users and uses of language, in J Fishman (ed) *Readings in the Sociology of Language*, Mouton, The Hague 137–69

HAMERS, J and BLANC, M (1989) *Bilinguality and Bilingualism*, Cambridge University Press (first published in French by Pierre Mardaga, Liège, 1983)

HANSEGÅRD, N E (1968) *Tvåspråkighet eller halvspråkighet?* Aldus series, Stockholm (3rd edn 1972)

HARDING, E and RILEY, P (1986) *The Bilingual Family*, Cambridge University Press

HARRISON, G J and PIETTE, A B (1980) Young bilingual children's language selection, *Journal for Multilingual and Multicultural Development* 1 No 3, 217–30

HARSHMAN, R and KRASHEN, S (1972) An 'unbiased' procedure for comparing degree of lateralization of dicholically presented stimuli, *Journal of the Acoustical Society of America*, 52, 174 (Abstract)

HARTMANN, C (1980) Der Sprachkonflikt in Catalunya-Nord aus der Perspektive engagierter Katalanisten, PhD thesis, University of Frankfurt

HATCH, E (ed) (1978) *Second Language Acquisition: a book of Readings*, Newbury House, Rowley

HAUG, E (1984) *Alsace und Elsass: Beiträge zur gegenwärtigen Identitätskrise einer europäischen Landschaft*, Pfaehler

HAUGEN, E (1953) *The Norwegian Language in America*, University of Pennsylvania Press, Philadelphia

—(1956) *Bilingualism in the Americas: a bibliography and research guide*, Publications of the American Dialect Society, 26, Alabama

—(1966a) Dialect, language, nation, *American Anthropologist* 68, 930–40

—(1966b) *Language Conflict and Planning: the case of modern Norway*, Harvard University Press, Cambridge, MA

—(1966c) Linguistics and language planning, in W Bright (ed) *Conference of Sociolinguistics 1964 Los Angeles*, Mouton, The Hague 50–71

—(1969) Language planning, theory and practice, in *Actes du Xe Congrès International des Linguistes, Bucharest 1967*, edited by A. Graur, Editions de L'Académie de la Republique Socialiste de Roumanie, Bucharest, 701–11

—(1983) The implementation of corpus planning: theory and practice, in J Cobarrubias and J Fishman (eds) *Progress in Language Planning*, Mouton de Gruyter, Berlin 1983, 269–90

HAUGEN, E, MCCLURE, D and THOMSON, D (eds) (1981) *Minority Languages Today*, Edinburgh University Press, Edinburgh

HEATH, S B and MANDABACH, F (1983) Language status decision and the law in the United States, in J Cobarrubias and J Fishman (eds) *Progress in Language Planning*, Mouton de Gruyter, Berlin, 87–106

HÉRAUD, G (1968) *Peuples et langues d'Europe*, Presses d'Europe, Paris

—(1974) *L'Europe des ethnies*, Presses d'Europe, Paris (first edn 1963)

—(1979–82) Le statut des langues dans les différents états et en particulier en Europe, *Annales de la Faculté de Droit de l'Université de Toulon et du Var* 5, 81–106

HERNÁNDEZ-CHÁVEZ, E, COHEN, A D and BELTRAMO, A F (eds) (1975) *El lenguaje de los chicanos*, Center for Applied Linguistics, Arlington

HERNÁNDEZ PINA, F (1984) *Teorías psico-sociolingüísticas y su aplicación a la adquisición del español como lengua materna*, Siglo Veintiuno, Madrid

HEWITT, R (1982) White adolescent Creole users and the politics of friendship, *Journal of Multilingual and Multicultural Development*, 3, No 3, 217–32

HINDERLING, R (ed) (1986) *Europäische Sprachminderheiten im Vergleich*, Franz Steiner Verlag, Stuttgart

HOFFMANN, C (1979) Bilingualism in a two-year-old child, *Polyglot* I, No. 2

—(1985) Language Acquisition in two trilingual children, *Journal of Multilingual and Multicultural Development*, 6, No 6, 479–95

—(1988) Linguistic normalization in Catalonia: Catalan for the Catalans or Catalan for Catalonia? in J N Jørgensen et al. (ed) *Bilingualism in Society and School*, Copenhagen Studies in Bilingualism, 5: 33-44, Multilingual Matters, Clevedon

—(1989) Modelos de Adquisición del bilingüismo infantil, *Actas del VI Congreso Nacional de Lingüística Aplicada*, Universidad de Santander 17–45

—(forthcoming) Problems encountered in the description of early bilingual competence

HOMEL, P, PALIJ, M and AARONSON, J (eds) (1987) *Childhood Bilingualism*, Lawrence Erlbaum Associates, New Jersey

HOOPER, J (1986) *The Spaniards*, Viking (Penguin Books), Harmondsworth

HORNBY, P (ed) (1977) *Bilingualism*, Academic Press, London

HOUSTON, S H (1972) Bilingualism: naturally acquired bilingualism, in *A Survey of Psycholinguistics*, Mouton, The Hague, 203–25

HOYER, A E and HOYER, G (1924) Über die Lallsprache eines Kindes, *Zeitschrift für angewandte Psychologie* 24, 363–84

HUSÉN, T and OPPER, S (eds) (1983) *Multicultural and Multilingual Education in Immigrant Countries*, Wenner Gren Symposium Series vol 38, Pergamon Press, Oxford

IANCO-WORRALL, A D (1972) Bilingualism and cognitive development, *Child Development* 43, 1390–400

IMEDADZE, N V (1967) On the psychological nature of child speech formation under conditions of exposure to two languages, *International Journal of Psychology*, 2, 129–32

ISAJIW, W (1980) Definitions of ethnicity, in J Goldstein and R Bienvenue (eds) Ethnicity and ethnic relations in Canada, Butterworth, Toronto

ITOH, H and HATCH, E (1978) Second language acquisition: a case study, in E Hatch (ed) *Second Language Acquisition: a book of readings*, Newbury House, Rowley

JAHN, L F (1808) Deutsches Volkstum (reprinted in *Hirt's Deutsche Sammlung,* Breslau 1930)

JAKOBOVITS, L A (1968) Dimensionality of compound-coordinate bilingualism, *Language Learning* 3, 29–56

JAKOBSON, R (1941) *Kindersprache, Aphasie und allgemeine Lautgesetze*, Almquist und Wiksell, Uppsala

JERNUDD, B (1973) Language planning as a type of language treatment, in J Rubin and R Shuy (eds) *Language Planning: current issues and research*, Georgetown University Press, Washington DC, 11–23

JONES, W R (1953) The influence of reading ability on intelligence test scores of Welsh-speaking children, *British Journal of Educational Psychology* 23, 114–20

—(1955) *Bilingualism and reading ability in English*, University of Wales Press, Cardiff

—(1959) *Bilingualism and intelligence*, University of Wales Press, Cardiff

JØRGENSEN, J N (1984) Four kinds of bilingualism in an industrialized society, *Sociolinguistic Papers, Royal Danish School of Educational Studies*, Copenhagen

KEDOURIE, E (1961) *Nationalism*, Hutchinson, London

KEIM, I (1984) *Untersuchungen zum Deutsch türkischer Arbeiter*, Gunter Narr, Tübingen

KELLER, H (ed) (1976) *Bilingualism in the Centennial and Beyond*, Bilingual Press – Prensa Bilingüe, New York

KELLY, L (ed) (1969) *The Description and Measurement of Bilingualism*, University of Toronto Press

KESSLER, C (1971) *The Acquisition of Syntax in Bilingual Children*, Georgetown University Press, Washington DC

—(1972) Syntactic contrasts in child bilingualism, *Language Learning* 22, 221–33

—(1984) Language acquisition in bilingual children, in N Miller (ed) *Bilingualism and Language Disability*, Croom Helm, London, 26–54

KIELHÖFER, B and JONEKEIT, S (1983) *Zweisprachige Kindererziehung*, Staffenburg Verlag, Tübingen

KLEIN, W and DITTMAR, N (1979) *Developing Grammars. The Acquisition of German Syntax by Foreign Workers*, Springer, Berlin

KLEIN, W (1984) *Zweitspracherwerb. Eine Einführung*, Athenäum, Königstein/Ts

—(1985) *Second Language Acquisition*, Cambridge University Press, Cambridge

KLOSS H (1967a) Types of multilingual communities: a discussion of ten variables, in S Liebersohn (ed) *Explorations in Sociolinguistics*, Mouton, The Hague, 7–17

—(1967b) Bilingualism and nationalism, *Journal of Social Issues* XXIII No 2, 39–47

—(1968) Notes concerning a language-nation typology, in J Fishman, C Ferguson and Das Gupta J (eds) *Language Problems of Developing Nations*, John Wiley, New York, 69–86

—(1984) Umriss eines Forschungprogrammes zum Thema 'Sprachentod', *International Journal of the Sociology of Language* **45**, 65–76

KRASHEN, S D (1975) The development of cerebral dominance and language learning: more new evidence, in D P Dato (ed) *Georgetown University Round Table on Language and Linguistics*, Georgetown University Press, Washington DC

KUTSCH, S and DESGRANGES, I (eds) (1985) *Zweitsprache Deutsch – ungesteuerter Erwerb Interaktionsorientierte Analysen des Projekts Gastarbeiterkommunikation*, Niemeyer, Tübingen

LABOV, W (1963) The social motivation of a sound change, *Word* **19**: 273–309 (also in Labov 1972 *Sociolinguistic Patterns*)

—(1966) *The Social Stratification of English in New York City*, Center for Applied Linguistics, Washington

—(1972) *Sociolinguistic Patterns*, University of Pennsylvania Press, Philadelphia

LADIN, W (1982) *Der elsässische Dialekt – museumsreif* SALDE (Société Alsacienne et Lorraine de Diffusion et d'Edition), Strasbourg

—(1983) Mehrsprachigkeit in Ostfrankreich, Sprachverhalten und Sprachbewußtsein der unterelsässischen dialektophonen Schuljugend, in P H Nelde (ed) *Plurilingua* IV, Ferdinand Dümmlers Verlag, Bonn

LADO, R (1957) *Linguistics across Cultures*, University of Michigan, Ann Arbor

LAMBERT, W E (1972) *Language, Psychology and Culture*, Stanford University Press, Stanford

—(1974) Culture and language as factors in learning and education, in F Aboud and R D Mead (eds) *Cultural Factors in Learning*, Washington State College, Bellingham

—(1977) The effects of bilingualism on the individual, in P Hornby (ed) *Bilingualism*, Academic Press, London 15–27

LAMBERT, W E, HAVELKA, J and GARDNER, R C (1959) Linguistic manifestations of bilingualism, *American Journal of Psychology* **72**, 77–82

LAMBERT, W E, JUST, M and SEGALOWITZ, N (1970) Some cognitive consequences of following the curricula of the early school grades in a foreign language, in J E Alatis (ed) *Georgetown University Monograph Series on Languages and Linguistics*, 23 Georgetown University Press, Washington DC 229–79

LAMBERT, W E and TUCKER, G R (1972) *Bilingual education of children: the St Lambert experiment,* Newbury House, Rowley, Mass.

LAURIE, S S (1890) *Lectures on Language and Linguistic Method in the School*, Cambridge University Press, Cambridge

LENNEBERG, E H (1967) *Biological Foundations of Language*, Wiley, New York

LEOPOLD, W F (1939, 1947, 1949a, 1949b) *Speech Development of a Bilingual Child: a linguist's record, I Vocabulary growth in the first two years; II Sound learning in the first two years, III Grammar and general problems in the first two years, IV Diary from age two.* Northwestern University Press, Evaston

LEPSCHY, A and LEPSCHY, G (1977) *The Italian Language Today*, Hutchinson University Library, London

LEWIS, G E (1972) *Multilingualism in the Soviet Union*, Mouton, The Hague

LIEBERSON, S (1972) Bilingualism in Montreal: a demographic analysis, in J Fishman (ed) *Advances in the Sociology of Language*, Mouton, The Hague, 231–54

LINDHOLM, K J and PADILLA, A M (1978a) Child bilingualism: report on language mixing, switching and translations, *Linguistics* 16, 23–44

—(1978b) Language mixing in bilingual children, *Journal of Child Language* 5, No 2, 327–35

LINGUISTIC MINORITIES IN ENGLAND, (1983) a report by the Linguistic Minorities Project for the Department of Education and Science, Institute of Education, London. Tinga Tinga, Heinmann

LIPSKI, J (1978) Code-switching and the problem of bilingual competence, in M Paradis (ed) *Aspects of Bilingualism*, Hornbeam, Columbia, 250–60

LÜDI, G and PY, BERNARD (1984) *Zweisprachig durch Migration: Einführung in die Erforschung der Mehrsprachigkeit am Beispiel zweier Zuwanderergruppen in Neuenburg*, Max Niemeyer Verlag, Tübingen

MACKEY, W F (1962) The description of bilingualism, *Journal of the Canadian Linguistic Association*, 7, 51–85

—(1970) The description of bilingualism, in J Fishman (ed) *Readings in the Sociology of Language*, Mouton, The Hague 554–84

—(1983) Language status policy and the Canadian experience, in J Cobarrubias and J Fishman (eds) *Progress in Language Planning*, Mouton de Gruyter, Berlin, 173–206

MACNAB, G L (1979) Cognition and bilingualism: a reanalysis of studies, *Linguistics* 17, 231–55

MACNAMARA, J (1967a) Bilingualism in the modern world, *Journal of Social Issues*, XXIII, 2, 1–7

—(1967b) The bilingual's linguistic performance – a psychological overview, *Journal of Social Issues* XXIII, 2, 58–77

—(1967c) The effects of instruction in a weaker language, *Journal of Social Issues* XXIII, 2, 121–35

—(1969) How can one measure the extent of a person's bilingual proficiency?, in L. Kelly (1969) *Description and Measurement of Bilingualism*, University of Toronto Press, 80–98

—(1971) Successes and failures in the movement for the restoration of Irish, in J Rubin and B Jernudd (eds) *Can Languages be Planned?* University Press of Hawaii, Honolulu

MARSHALL, D (1986) The question of an official language: language rights and the English Language Amendment, *International Journal of the Sociology of Language* **60**, 7–71

MARTIN-JONES, M and ROMAINE, S (1986) Semilingualism: a half-baked theory of communicative competence, *Applied Linguistics*, **7** 1, 26–36

MCCLURE, E (1977) Aspects of code-switching in the discourse of bilingual Mexican-American children, Technical Report No 44, Center for the Study of Reading, University of Illinois, Urbana-Champaign

MCLAUGHLIN, B (1984) *Second-Language Acquisition in Childhood, vol 1 Preschool Children* (2nd edn), Hillsdale, London (first published by Lawrence Erlbaum Associates, New Jersey, 1978)

MEISEL, J (1975) Ausländerdeutsch und Deutsch ausländischer Arbeiter. Zur möglichen Entstehung eines Pidgin in der BRD. *Zeitschrift für Literaturwissenschaft und Linguistik*, May, **18**, 7–53

—(1977) The language of foreign workers in Germany, in Molony, Zobl and Stölting (eds): *Deutsch im Kontakt mit anderen Sprachen, German in Contact with other Languages*, Kronberg/Ts, Scriptor Verlag, 184–212

—(1984) Zum Erwerb von Wortstellungsregularitäten und Kasusmarkierungen, Monograph, Universität Hamburg Romanisches Seminar

—(1986) Word order and case marking in early child language: evidence from simultaneous acquisition of two first languages (French and German), *Linguistics* **24**, 123–83

—(1987) Early differentiation of languages in bilingual children, in K Hyltenstam and L Obler (eds): *Bilingualism across the Lifespan: in health and in pathology*, Cambridge University Press, Cambridge, 13–40

MÉTRAUX, R W (1965) Study of bilingualism among children of US-French parents, *French Review* **38**, 650–65

MIKEŠ M (1967) Acquisition des catégories grammaticales dans le langage de l'enfant, *Enfance* **20**, 289–98

MILLER, J (1983) *Many Voices*, Routledge & Kegan Paul, London

MILLER, N (ed) (1984) *Bilingualism and Language Disability*, Croom Helm, London

MIRACLE, A (ed) (1983) *Bilingualism: social issues and policy implications*, University of Georgia Press

MKILIFI, M (1978) Triglossia and Swahili-English bilingualism in Tanzania, in J Fishman (ed) *Advances in the Study of Societal Multilingualism*, Mouton, The Hague

MOLONY C, ZOBL H and STÖLTING W (eds) (1977) *Deutsch im Kontakt mit anderen Sprachen, German in Contact with other Languages*, Scriptor Verlag, Kronberg/Ts

MURRELL, M (1966) Language acquisition in a trilingual environment, *Studia Linguistica* **20**, 9–35

NELDE, P (1984) Three issues in languages in contact, *Studia Anglica Posnaniensia* **17**, 147–56

NELDE, P et al. (eds) (1981) *Sprachprobleme bei Gastarbeiterkindern*, Gunter Narr, Tübingen

NELSON, K (1973) Structural and strategy in learning to talk, *Monographs of the Society for Research in Child Development* **39** (1–2 serial No 149)

NEUSTUPNÝ, J (1970) Basic types of treatment of language problems, *Linguistic Communications* **1**, 77–98

NEVILLE, G (1986) Minority languages in contemporary France, *Journal of Multilingual and Multicultural Development*, **8**, Nos 1 & 2, 147–57

NIKOLINAKOS, M (1973) *Politische Ökonomie der Gastarbeiterfrage. Migration und Kapitalismus*, Reinbeck, Rowohlt Verlag

OESTREICHER, J P (1974) The early teaching of modern language, education and culture, *Review of the Council for Cultural Cooperation of the Council of Europe* **24**, 9–16

OKSAAR, E (1970) Zum Spracherwerb des Kindes in zweisprachiger Umgebung, *Folia Linguistica* **4**, 330 58

—(1971) Språkpolitiken och minoriteterna, in D Schwarz (ed) *Identitet och minoritet, Teori och praktik i dagens Sverige*, Almquist och Wiksell, Stockholm, 164–75

—(1974) On code-switching: an analysis of bilingual norms, in J Quistgaard, H Schwarz and Spang-Hansen, H (eds) Applied Linguistics: problems and solutions, Proceedings of the Third AILA Congress, Copenhagen, Heidelberg, Vol 3, 491–500

—(1980) The multilingual language acquisition project, *International Review of Applied Psychology* **29**, 268–9

—(1983) Multilingualism and multiculturalism from the linguist's point of view, in T Husén and S Opper (eds) *Multicultural and Multilingual Education in Immigrant Countries* 17–36

—(ed) (1987) *Soziokulturelle Perspektiven von Mehrsprachigkeit und Spracherwerb – Sociocultural Perspectives of Multilingualism and Language Acquisition*, Gunter Narr, Tübingen

OOMEN-WELKE, I (1985) Erfahrungen und Reflexionen aus der Arbeit in einem 'nationalen Modell', *Deutsch Lernen Heft* **2**

ORLOVIĆ-SCHARWARZWALD, M (1978) Zum Gastarbeiterdeutsch jugoslawischer Arbeiter im Rhein-Main Gebiet. *Mainzer Studien zur Sprach- und Volksforschung,* 2, Wiesbaden

PADILLA, A M and LIEBMAN, E (1975) Language acquisition in the bilingual child, *Bilingual Review* 2, 34–55

PARADIS, M (1977a) Bilingualism and aphasia, in H A Whitaker and H Whitaker (eds) *Studies in Neurolinguistics,* 3, Academic Press, New York, 65–121

—(1977b) The stratification of bilingualism, in R J di Pietro, and E L Balnsitt (eds) *The Third Lacus Forum 1976,* Hornbeam, Columbia, 237–47

—(ed) (1978) *Aspects of Bilingualism,* Hornbeam, Columbia

PARADIS, M and LEBRUN, Y (eds) (1984) *Early Bilingualism and Child Development,* Swets & Zeitlinger, Lisse

PARASHER, S N (1980) Mother-tongue English diglossia: a case study of educated Indian bilinguals' language use, *Anthropological Linguistics* 22, 4, 151–68

PAULSTON, C B (1974) Questions concerning bilingual education, paper presented at the Interamerican Conference on Bilingual Education, 1974

PAVLOVITCH, M (1920) *Le langage enfantin: acquisition du serbe et du français par un enfant serbe,* Champion, Paris

PEAL, E and LAMBERT, W E (1962) The relationship of bilingualism to intelligence, *Psychological Monographs* 76 (27), 1–23

PENFIELD, W and ROBERTS, L (1959) *Speech and Brain Mechanisms,* Princeton University Press, Princeton

PENN, D (1990) Minority languages in Europe, *The Linguist,* Vol 29 No 2, 62–9

PETERS, A M (1977) Language-learning strategies: does the whole equal the sum of the parts? *Language* 53, 560–73

PFAFF, C (1979) Constraints on language mixing: intersentential code-switching and borrowing in Spanish/English, *Language* 55, 291–318 (also in J Amastae and L Elías-Olivares (eds) (1982) *Spanish in the United States: sociolinguistic aspects,* Cambridge University Press, Cambridge, 264–97)

—(1980) Acquisition and development of 'Gastarbeiterdeutsch' by migrant workers and their children in Germany, in E Trangott et al. (eds): Papers from the Conference on Historial Linguistics, *Amsterdam Studies in the Theory and History of Linguistic Sciences,* IV, vol 14. John Benjamin BV, Amsterdam, 381–95

—(1981) Sociolinguistic problems of immigrants: foreign workers and their children in Germany, *Language in Society,* 10, 155–88

PFAFF, C and PORTZ, R (1980) Children's acquisition of German: universals vs. interference, in *Proceedings of the Second Scandinavian-German Symposium of the language of migrant workers and their children,* West Berlin. (Also: Linguistische Arbeiten und Berichte, Heft 16, Berlin Freie Universität, 137–70)

PHILIPPS, E (1975) *Les luttes linguistique en Alsace jusqu'en 1945.* Culture Alsacienne, Grisheim-sur-Souffel

—(1978) *La crise d'identité (L'Alsace face a son destin)*. Societé d'edition de la Basse Alsace, Strasbourg

PICHON, E (1936) *Le Développement Psychique de l'Enfant et de l'Adolescent*, Masson, Paris

PIENEMANN, M (1980) The second language acquisition of immigrant children, in S Felix (ed): *Second Language Development*, Gunter Narr, Tübingen

POHL, J (1965) Bilinguismes, *Revue Roumaine de Linguistique* 10, 343–9

POPLACK, S (1980) Sometimes I'll start a sentence in English y termino en español: towards a typology of code-switching, *Linguistics* 18, 582–618 (also in J Amastae and L Elías-Olivares (eds) (1982) *Spanish in the United States*, Cambridge University Press, Cambridge, 230-63)

PORSCHE, D (1983) *Die Zweisprachigkeit während des primären Spracherwerbs* Tübinger Beiträge zur Linguistik 218, Gunter Narr, Tübingen

POWER, J (1984) *Western Europe's Migrant Workers* (in collaboration with A Hardman; revised by C Byrne-Vardin and K Stearman). Minority Rights Group Report No 28, Pergamon Press, London

RAFFLER-ENGEL, W (1965) Del bilinguismo infantile., *Arch. Glottologico Italiano* 50, 175–80

RATH, R (ed) (1983) *Sprach- und Verständnisschwierigkeit bei Ausländerkindern in Deutschland. Aufgaben und Probleme einer interaktionsorientierten Zweitspracherwerbsforschung*, M Lang,

REDLINGER, W G and PARK T (1980) Language mixing in young bilinguals, *Journal of Child Language* 7, 337–52

REHBEIN, J (1985) *Interkulturelle Kommunikation*, Gunter Narr, Tübingen.

—(1987) Sprachloyalität in der Bundesrepublik. Ausländische Kinder zwischen Sprachverlust und zweisprachiger Erziehung. *Arbeiten zur Mehrsprachigkeit* 26, Universität Hamburg

REYES, R (1982) Language mixing in Chicano Spanish, in J Amastae and G Elías-Olivares (eds) *Spanish in the United States: sociolinguistic aspects*, Cambridge University Press, Cambridge, 154–65

RITCHIE, W C (1978) *Second Language Acquisition Research*, Academic Press, New York

RIS, R (1979) Dialekte und Einheitssprache in der deutschen Schweiz, *International Journal of the Sociology of Language* 21, 41–61

ROBERTS, M (1939) The problem of the hybrid language, *Journal of English and Germanic Philology* 38, 23–41

ROMAINE, S (1984) *The Language of Children and Adolescents*, Basil Blackwell, Oxford

—(1989) *Bilingualism*, Basil Blackwell, Oxford

RONJAT, J (1913) *Le développement du langage observé chez un enfant bilingue*, Champion, Paris

RUBIN, J (1968b) *National Bilingualism in Paraguay*, Mouton, The Hague

—(1970) (ed.) Bilingual usage in Paraguay, in Fishman (1970). Readings in the Sociology of Language, Mouton, The Hague, 512--30

—(1973) Language planning: discussion of some current issues, in J Rubin and R Shuy (eds) *Language Planning: Current Issues and Research*, Georgetown University Press, Washington D C, 1–10

RŪĶE-DRAVIŅA, V (1965) The process of acquisition of apical /r/ and uvular /r/ in the speech of children, *Linguistics* **17**, 56–68

—(1967) *Mehrsprachigkeit im Vorschulalter*, Traveaux de L'Institut de Phonétique de Lund, Fasc. V, Lund Gleerup

RUSS, C and VOLKMAR, C (eds) (1987) *Sprache und Gesellschaft in deutschsprachigen Ländern*, Goethe Institut, München

SABATER, E (1984) An approach to the situation of the Catalan language: social and educational use, *International Journal of the Sociology of Language*, **47**, 29–41

SAER, D J (1922) An inquiry into the effects of bilingualism upon the intelligence of young children, *Journal of Experimental Pedagogy* **6**, 232–40, 266–74

—(1923) The effects of bilingualism on intelligence, *British Journal of Psychology* **14**, 25–38

SANDER, F (1930) Structures, Totality of Experience and Gestalt, in C Murchison, (ed) *Psychologies of the 1930s* Worcester Clark University Press

—(1934) Seelische Struktur und Sprache, Strukturpsychologisches zum Zweitsprachenproblem, *Neue Psychologische Studien* **12**, 59

SANKOFF, D (ed) (1978) *Linguistic Variation: models and methods*, Academic Press, New York

SANKOFF, G (1980) Language use in multilingual societies: some alternate approaches, in G Sankoff, *The Social Life of a Language*, University of Pennsylvania Press, 26–46 (also in Pride and Holmes *Sociolinguistics*, Penguin, Harmondsworth, 1972, 33–51)

—(1980) *The Social Life of a Language*, University of Pennsylvania Press, Philadelphia

SAUNDERS, G (1982a) *Bilingual Children: guidance for the family*, Multilingual Matters, Clevedon

—(1982b) Infant bilingualism: a look at some doubts and objections, *Journal for Multilingual and Multicultural Development* **3**, No 4, 277–92

—(1988) *Bilingual Children: from birth to teens*, Multilingual Matters, Clevedon

SCHLÄPFER, R (1982) *Die Viersprachige Schweiz*, Benziger Verlag

SCHLYTER, S (1988) Language mixing and linguistic level in three bilingual children, *Scandinavian Working Papers on Bilingualism No 1*

SCHMIDT-ROHR, G (1932) *Die Sprache als Bildnerin der Völker*, Jena Muttersprache, München

—(1936) Zur Frage der Zweitsprachigkeit, *Deutsche Arbeit* **36**, 408–11

SCHUMANN, J H (1976) Social distance as a factor in second language acquisition, *Language Learning*, **26** (1), 135–43

—(1978) *The Pidginization Process: a model for second language acquisition.* Newbury House, Rowley, Mass

SCOTT, S (1973) The relation of divergent thinking to bilingualism – cause or effect? (unpublished research report, McGill University)

SELIGER, H W (1978) Implication of a multiple critical-period hypothesis for second language learning, in W C Ritchie (ed) *Second Language Acquisition Research*, Academic Press, New York

SHAPSON, S and D'OYLEY V (eds) (1984) *Bilingual and Multilingual Education: Canadian perspectives*, Multilingual Matters, Clevedon

SHIBUTANI, T and KWAN, K (1965) *Ethnic Stratification*, Macmillan, New York

SIGUÁN, M (1980) Education and bilingualism in Catalonia, *Journal of Multilingual and Multicultural Development*, **1**, No 3, 231–42

—(1989) Escribir y pensar en dos lenguas, *Revista crítica de libros Saber Leer*, Fundación Juan March, 22 (February)

SILVA-CORVALÁN, C (1982) Subject variation in spoken Mexican–American Spanish, in J Amastae and L Elías-Olivares, (eds) *Spanish in the United States* Cambridge University Press, Cambridge 93–120

—(1983) Code-shifting patterns in Chicano Spanish, in L Elías-Olivares and D Nasjleti (eds) *Spanish in the United States: Beyond the Southwest*, NCBE, Washington, 69–87

—(1986) Bilingualism and language change: the extension of *estar* in Los Angeles Spanish, *Language* **62**, 587–608

—(1989) *Sociolingüística: teoría y análisis*, Alhambra, Madrid

SKUTNABB-KANGAS, T (1976) Bilingualism, semilingualism and school achievement, *Linguistische Berichte*, **45** October

—(ed) (1977) *Papers from the First Scandinavian Conference on Bilingualism*, Department of Nordic Languages, University of Helsinki, Series B No 2

—(1984a) *Bilingualism or Not*, Multilingual Matters, Clevedon (first edn in Swedish, 1981)

—(1984b) Children of guest workers and immigrants: linguistic and educational issues, in J Edwards (ed) *Linguistic Minorities, Policies and Pluralism*, Academic Press, London, 17–47

SKUTNABB-KANGAS, T and CUMMINS, J (1988) *Minority Education: from shame to struggle*, Multilingual Matters, Clevedon

SKUTNABB-KANGAS, T and TOUKOMAA, P (1976) *Teaching migrant children's mother tongue and learning the language of the host country in the context of the socio-cultural situation of the migrant family.* A Report prepared for UNESCO, Department of Sociology and Social Psychology, University of Tampere, Research Report 15, Tampere

—(1979) Semilingualism and middle-class bias, *Working Papers in Bilingualism*, **19**, November 1979, Ontario Institute for studies in Education, 181–96

SMITH, A (1982) Nationalism, ethnic separation and the intelligentsia, in C Williams (ed) *National Separatism*, University of Wales Press, Cardiff

SMITH, M E (1935) A study of the speech of eight bilingual children of the same family, *Child Development* **6**, 19–25

SOFFIETI, J (1955) Bilingualism and biculturalism, *Journal of Educational Psychology* **46**, 222–7

SØNDERGÅRD, B (1981) Decline and fall of an individual bilingualism, *Journal of Multilingual and Multicultural Development* **2**, No 4, 297–302

SPOLSKY, B (1986) *Language and Education in Multilingual Settings*, Multilingual Matters, Clevedon

STAVANS, A (1990) *Code-switching in children acquiring English, Spanish and Hebrew: A case study*, unpublished PhD thesis, University of Pittsburgh

STEINBERG, S (1981) *The Ethnic Myth*, Atheneum, New York

STEPHENS, M (1976) *Linguistic Minorities in Western Europe*, Gomer Press, Llandysul

STÖLTING, W (1975) Wie die Ausländer sprechen: eine jugoslawische Familie, *Zeitschrift für Literaturwissenschaft und Linguistik*, **38**, May 1975: 54–67

—(1980) *Die Zweisprachigkeit jugoslawischer Schüler in der Bundesrepublik Deutschland*, Harrassowitz, Wiesbaden

STRUBELL I TRUETA, M (1984a) *Llengua i població a Catalunya*, Ediciones de la Magrana, Barcelona

—(1984b) Language and identity in Catalonia, *International Journal of the Sociology of Language*, **47**, 91–104

—(1985a) The Catalan experience, paper presented at the Conference on Publishing in Minority Languages, Aberystwyth, July/August

—(1985b) Social psychological aspects of the language planning process, unpublished paper

—(1988) L'avui i el demà de la llengua catalana, in: *Panoràmica de la llengua catalana,* Institut d'Estudis Autonòmics, Generalitat de Catalunya, *Quaderns de Treball* **19**: 19–42

SUBIRATS, M (1980) La utilització del català entre la precarietat i la normalització, *Revista crítica de libros Saber Leer*, Fundación Juan March, 1 (February)

SWAIN, M (1972) Bilingualism as a first language, (unpublished PhD dissertation, University of California, Irvine)

SWAIN, M and LAPKIN, E (1982) *Evaluating Bilingual Education: a Canadian case study*, Multilingual Matters, Clevedon

SWAIN, M and WESCHE, M (1975) Linguistic interaction: case study of a bilingual child, *Languages Sciences* **37**, 17–22

TABOURET-KELLER, A (1962) L'acquisition du langage parlé chez un petit enfant en milieu bilingue, *Problemes de Psycholinguistique*, **8**, 205–19

—(1981) Regional languages in France, *International Journal of the Sociology of Language*, **29**

TAESCHNER, T (1983) *The Sun is Feminine: a study on language acquisition in childhood*, Springer Verlag, Berlin/Heidelberg

TIMM, L (1975) Spanish–English code-switching: el porqué and how-not-to, *Romance Philology* **28**, 473–82

—(1980) Bilingualism, diglossia and language shift in Brittany, *International Journal of the Sociology of Language*, **25**, 29–41

TOSI, A (1983) *Immigration and Bilingual Education*, Pergamon Press

TOVAR, A (1982) El bilingüismo en España, in V Demonte and S Ortega (eds) *El bilingüisimo: problemática y realidad,* Revista de Occidente 10–11, Extraordinario II, Madrid, 13–22

TRAVIS, L E, JOHNSON W and SHOVER, J (1937) The relation of bilingualism to stuttering, *Journal of Speech Disorders* **2**, 185–9

TRUDGILL, P (1972) Sex, covert prestige and linguistic change in the urban British English of Norwich, *Language in Society*, **1**, 179–95

—(ed) (1978) *Sociolinguistic Patterns in British English*, Edward Arnold, London

—(ed) (1984) *Language in the British Isles*, Cambridge University Press, Cambridge

TURNER, P (ed) (1973) *Bilingualism in the Southwest*, University of Arizona Press, Tucson

VALDÉS FALLIS, G (1976) Social interaction and code-switching patterns: a case study of Spanish/English alternation, in G D Keller et al. (eds) *Bilingualism in the Bicentennial and Beyond,* Bilingual Press/Editorial Bilingüe, New York, 53–85 (also in J Amastae and L Elías-Olivares (eds) *Spanish in the United States*, Cambridge University Press, 1982, 209–29)

VALLVERDÚ, F (1973) *El fet lingüistic com a fet social*, Ediciones 62, Barcelona

VERDOODT, A (1972) The differential impact of immigrant French speakers on indigenous German speakers: a case study in the light of two theories, in J Fishman *Advances in the Sociology of Language*, vol **2**, Mouton, The Hague

VIHMAN, M M (1982) The acquisition of morphology by a bilingual child: the whole word approach, *Applied Psycholinguistics* **3**, 141–60

—(1985) Language differentiation by the bilingual child, *Journal of Child Language* **12** (2), 297–324

VIHMAN, M M and MCLAUGHLIN, B (1982) Bilingualism and second language acquisition in preschool children, in C J Brainerd and M Pressley (eds) *Progress in Cognitive Development Reasearch: verbal processes in children* Springer, Berlin, 36–58

VILA, I (1984) La aparición y el desarrollo de términos equivalentes en el primer lenguaje del niño bilingüe familiar, *Actas del II Congreso Nacional de Lingüística Aplicada,* Universidad de Murcia, 461–76

VOLTERRA, V and TAESCHNER, T (1978) The acquisition of language by bilingual children, *Journal of Child Language* **5**, 2, 311–26

VYGOTSKY, L S (1962) *Thought and Language*, MIT Press, Cambridge, Mass

WALKER, A G H (1987) Language and society in Schleswig, in C Russ and C Volkmar (eds) *Sprache und Gesellschaft in deutschsprachingen Ländern,* Yorker Werkheft, Goethe Institut, München, 136–52

WANDRUSZKA, M (1979) *Die Mehrsprachigkeit des Menschen,* Pieper Verlag, München

WARDHAUGH, R (1986) *An Introduction to Sociolinguistics,* Basil Blackwell, Oxford

—(1987) *Languages in Competition,* Basil Blackwell, Oxford

WEBER, M (1968) *Economy and Society,* Bedminster, New York

WEINREICH, U (1968) *Languages in Contact,* Mouton, The Hague (first published in 1953)

WEISGERBER, L (1929) *Muttersprache und Geistesbildung,* Vandenhoek & Ruprecht, Göttingen

—(1933) Die Stellung der Sprache im Aufbau der Gesamtkultur, *Wörter und Sachen* **15**, 134–224; **16**, 97–236

WILLIAMS, C H (ed) (1982) *National Separatism,* University of Wales Press, Cardiff

—(1984) More than the tongue can tell: linguistic factors in ethnic separatism, in J Edwards (ed) *Linguistic Minorities, Policies and Pluralism,* Basil Blackwell, Oxford, 179–219

WÖLCK, W (1984) Komplementierung und Fusion, Prozesse natürlicher Zweisprachigkeit, in E Oksaar (ed) *Spracherwerb-Sprachkontakt-Sprachkonflikt,* De Gruyter, Berlin, 105–29

WOLFF, J (1984) Fremd im eigenen Land. Deutsch als Fremdsprache und Remigration, *Informationen Deutsch als Fremdsprache* **3**, Jahrgang 84/85, DAAD, 65–73

WOOLARD, K A (1989) *Double Talk: Bilingualism and the politics of ethnicity in Catalonia,* Stanford University Press, Stanford

Subject Index

accent, 37, 53, 58
  foreign –, 94, 96–7
Act to Promote the French Language
  in Québec, 211
age (in bilingualism), 18, 36–8
ambilingualism (equilingualism),
  21–2, 29, 35
attitudes (attitudinal factors), 25–6,
  30–1, 119–20, 134, 257–9, 270,
  281, 287–8, 302–6
  – towards bilingualism, 3–4,
    27–8, 244
  – towards code–switching, 113
  – towards languages, 201,
    215–16, 264–5
  – towards the L2, 133
(language) awareness, 68, 69, 71,
  79–86, 125

"Balance Theory", 129
BICS (Basic Interpersonal
  Communication Skills), 127–8,
  132–3
biculturalism (multiculturalism),
  28–31, 123, 312
Bilingual Education Act, 1968
  (USA), 210, 217
bilingual,
  – ability, 21–7, 28, 31

–acquisition (development,
  achievement), 21, 44–6,
  48–52, 60–5, 69–72, 75–9,
  106–9, 130, 304–6
–adults, 18, 94–5, 96–7, 102,
  103–4, 113
– bilingual children: see *children*
– bilingual or multilingual
  communities (societies,
  groups), 4–6, 43–4, 116,
  175–7, 179–80, 182–5, 189,
  191–2,
– competence, 21, 74–93, 131,
  133
– deficit, 121–3, 129, 133
élite bilinguals, 46
– environment, 38–40
– families, 44–6, 47, 175–6, 276
– individual, 24–5, 175–6
natural –, 18–19
– patterns, 24–5, 27, 40–6,
  149–51
– profile, 31–2
– speaker, 13–14, 74–5, 96–7,
  178–80
– speech, 75–6
– speech mode, 153
– upbringing (see also: *bilingual
  acquisition*), 136

Places, Languages and Peoples (including linguistic minorities and minority areas)

Author Index